RACING & FOOTBALL
Outlook
JUMPS GUIDE

2003–2004

Statistics • Results
Previews • Training centre reports

Contributors: Chris Cook, Nick Deacon, Steffan Edwards, Ken Hussey, Tony Jakobsen,Kel Mansfield, Steve Mellish, Peter Naughton, Dave Nevison, Ben Osborne, Nicholas Watts, Richard Williams.

Grateful thanks are due to Andy Scutts, Brett Campbell, Rob Winter, Rodney Pettinga and Simon Goggly.

Designed and edited by Chris Cook

Published in 2003 by Outlook Press
Raceform, Compton, Newbury, Berkshire RG20 6NL
Outlook Press is an imprint of Raceform Ltd,
a wholly-owned subsidiary of MGN Ltd

A catalogue record for this book is available from the British Library.

ISBN 1-904317-20-0

Printed by Cox & Wyman, Reading

Cover – Lord Transcend (left) and Mr Cool

RACING & FOOTBALL
Outlook

Contents

Outlook

Editor's introduction

CAN YOU have too much of a good thing? One of the talking points of the last jumps season was whether or not the Cheltenham Festival should be extended to a fourth day. The meeting as it currently stands is close to many folks' idea of perfection – all 20 races are highly competitive, but surely an extra day can only dilute the quality.

Let's hope the same principle doesn't apply to the tomb you're holding in your hot little hands. At a hefty 256 pages, this RFO annual is fatter than any of its predecessors, and a third more voluminous than last year's jumping guide.

Never mind the width, though – feel the quality. We've spent the summer months plumping up our features, so you'll have plenty to digest through the winter.

We kick off with 'Profiles For Punters', our own spin on the traditional trainer interview. The idea is to give you a gambler's insight into what kind of trainer this trainer is, what kind of horse they look for and do well with, what kind of race they're likely to do well in.

This time, we've been talking to Heather Dalton, just making a name for herself in racing after graduating from point-to-points, and Festival stalwart Nicky Henderson.

Dalton's role-model is Henrietta Knight, which will give you some idea of her ambition, but the skill she's shown in her career to date commands attention.

Henderson needs relatively little introduction. In his case, it'll be a surprise if we don't see him in the running for some big pots through the season, and he's been candid with us about his plans for the most exciting types at Seven Barrows.

Then, our News Diary gives you a reprise on what made the headlines in our narrow world over the last year.

We follow that with five-year stats on last season's top 20 jumps trainers, including some fascinating insights on how they fare with horses who haven't run for a while.

Closing our review of last season, we give you the results of last year's 150 key races, along with our interpretation of the form.

Raceform analyst Steffan Edwards is back, having generated a profit from his ante-post tips in last year's jumps annual. You can get 33-1 about each of his fancies for the Champion Hurdle and the Gold Cup, but don't delay placing your bet – Steffan's tips have a habit of shortening right up before the big day.

Dave Nevison had a fabulously profitable first day at the last Festival, and we've got no excuses for missing out, since he shared his tips with RFO readers in advance. On page 115, you can read the fruits of his research into the French imports set to make an impact in Britain this season.

Morning Mole has been digging for good prospects too, and his horses to follow are supplemented by our own list of 30 unexposed types you should be looking out for.

We've got seven regional reporters, each with their fingers on the pulse of training centres around the country. Plus, RFO's latest punting feature, By The Numbers, makes an appearance. Followers of the tips put up by this column have done well so far – here, you can get an early look at our analysis of 10 of jump racing's biggest betting races.

Throw in full course-by-course stats, with 3D maps and standard times, and you can see why we couldn't possibly have used less paper. Plus, our picture quiz gives you the chance to win a subscription to Chaseform, the official jump racing form book.

We hope and believe that this lovingly-prepared guide can help you pay for the fuel bills until spring. But, if it all goes wrong, you should get plenty of burning out of it when you throw it on the fire.

Heather Dalton

WHAT'S Heather Dalton protesting about in this picture? Maybe it's the parallel I'm about to draw between her career and that of Henrietta Knight, the trainer she most admires and would like to emulate.

It's early days, of course, but Dalton is already getting enthusiastic praise from all observers since, like Knight, she was encouraged by her success with point-to-pointers to take up a license to train. Her reputation is for placing her horses cleverly and getting the best out of her difficult charges, something else which she shares with the dual Gold Cup-winning trainer.

Knight announced last season that she'll be training for a maximum of five years more

and it's not too fanciful to see Dalton fulfilling a similar role in racing thereafter.

Now 37, she spent much of her time when younger on the point-to-point circuit, where she met her future husband, Andrew. She rode 40 winners before an especially nasty fall left her with head injuries that gave her problems for months.

Though she appeared, eventually, to overcome all symptoms, the fall had caused further damage that remained latent until she gave birth to the youngest of her two children, at which point she suddenly lost the use of her left arm.

"I feared I'd had a stroke," she says. "After various tests, it was discovered I had an identical injury to the one that ended Richard Dunwoody's career, with a nerve touching a vertebra."

"I've got the use of the arm back, but it's still not very good. I don't ride out as a general rule now."

Based in Norton House, near Shifnal in Shropshire, Dalton is very happy with her situation: "We have amazing facilities here. We've got two farms side by side, with 800 acres for riding and access to gallops, including an all-weather gallop. And the great thing is, they're all my own facilities, I'm not sharing with anyone.

"It means we can do a lot more steady work and we can keep horses sweet for longer, because they're not just going up the all-weather every day, doing the same thing. The horses last a bit longer."

That might help to explain the improvement she wrung from Quality First last season, after the gelding joined her from Ireland. Without a win over fences for more than two years, he gave Dalton her first Cheltenham success on his first start for her in a handicap chase there in January.

Similarly, Deferlant was on a long losing run when arriving from Martin Pipe's yard. For his new trainer, he reeled off a hat-trick of wins in novice chases within five months of switching yards.

But Dalton's most remarkable achievement in training remains one of her earliest. She had had a license for just 15 months when, on Easter Monday of 2001, she got four winners at three different meetings.

"We were on the computer for ages, getting everything just right," she said afterwards of the day when she sent out so many runners (ten – almost half her string at the time) that she had to enlist some of the owners to drive the horseboxes.

Unbelievably, the four-timer followed six weeks when Dalton had been prevented from using her own gallops because of foot and mouth restrictions. And there was a poignant aspect because Danzig Island, one of the fab four, had cheated death the year before; he broke his pelvis, and the vet in attendance recommended that he be put him down, but the trainer insisted he could be saved and managed to prove it.

Dalton does not bet herself but knows how the game works, and freely admits to having been involved in a couple of success-

'I would like to get more dual-purpose horses. At the moment, I've got plenty of Flat horses and chasers-in-the-making but I'd really like some hurdlers'

ful plunges on her racemare Ella Falls. But she points out that the horse was backed purely out of necessity.

She was asked by an owner to buy a horse who could win first time out but, once she'd done a deal for Ella Falls, the owner pulled out and left her holding a bill for 27,000gns. "We couldn't afford to stand that level of loss, so decided to recover at least part of the sum by backing her," she explains.

Ella Falls paid for herself with a straightforward win over hurdles at Worcester in July 2000 (7-2) and a more hard-fought Flat success at Musselburgh a year later (16-1).

Not surprisingly, Dalton would like a few more like that mare. "I would like to get more dual-purpose horses," she says. "At the moment, I've got plenty of Flat horses and chasers-in-the-making but I would really like some hurdlers."

As things stand, there are plenty of horses in the yard who will need time to be brought to their peak. "I'm worried about having a lot of babies in the yard, there's no point in rushing them to the races in order to make a target number of winners.

"It takes six years to make a jumper, and six minutes to ruin one.

"You have to find a balance, you have to bring on your young horses and try and find your star, but at the same time not run them for the sake of running them."

So where can we expect to see her horses this season? "I'd like to win any race at a Grade A track but to win a bad race with a low-grade horse takes as much training.

"I love Haydock and Bangor, which are fair, galloping tracks, also Worcester and Wetherby. I don't like Ludlow, I don't like the roads there. I've ridden there and it's horrible on soft ground, when you hit the mats [over the roads] you really know about it."

Dalton's dynamos

Ashgan
10yo brown gelding
Yashgan – Nicky's Dilemma (Kambalda)
He's a stable favourite, having won four over hurdles and three over fences for us, as well as point-to-points. He's had a wind operation and he's on holiday just now. When he comes back, he'll go point-to-pointing again, and then hunter chasing. There's a valuable handicap hunter chase at Newton Abbot in May that he might be aimed at.

Bay Island
7yo bay or brown gelding
Treasure Hunter – Wild Deer (Royal Buck)
Won his first three chases over 3m to 3m2f last term. He should be capable of winning a good £20,000 race at somewhere like Haydock or Chepstow, though the owner may also want to send him point-to-pointing, so we'll have to see.

Be My Friend
7yo chestnut gelding
Be My Native – Miss Lamb (Relkino)
Had three runs over hurdles at the end of last season, winning the last of them easi-

ly over 2m1f at Bangor. He'll be a novice chaser this season and should hopefully reward his owners for their patience. We've schooled him and he jumps well, he was pretty much always going to be a chaser. He wants good ground and, although he showed plenty of speed over hurdles, I should think 2m4f will be his best trip. He might have two more runs over hurdles just to give him experience, and then we'll start him chasing at a small track.

Bearaway
6yo bay gelding
Fourstars Allstar – Cruiseaway (Torus)
Joined us in the spring and he's had five runs so far, winning a bumper at Southwell and a novice hurdle at Worcester. He'll carry on in hurdles until May, and then he'll be a novice chaser. He should win a nice little race.

Broadbrook Lass
9yo chestnut mare
Broadsword – Netherbrook Lass (Netherkelly)
She won two out of four over fences last summer but has had niggling injury problems and has had only one run since. She's off

QUALITY FIRST (furthest left): cleared Aintree's huge fences with aplomb in the Topham

for the next six months but I hope to be able to win another race with her before she goes to stud, a handicap chase over 2m4f to 3m.

Broke Road
7yo bay gelding
Deploy – Shamaka (Kris)
Won two out of four as a novice chaser last summer but is out just now with a tendon injury and won't be back until spring.

Cassia Green
9yo grey gelding
Scallywag – Casa's Star (Top Star)
I'm looking forward to running this one, and I think he's well-handicapped. He was only having his sixth run when he got off the mark over fences in March, and he's not been out since. The owner's son, Tom Greenway, will ride; he's a good little amateur with Nigel Twiston-Davies. This horse wants 2m round a big, left-handed track like Wetherby.

Deferlant
6yo chestnut gelding
Bering – Sail Storm (Topsider)
We put him over fences not long after getting him from Martin Pipe's yard and he won three in a row as a novice chaser last summer. He's not back in yet but the plan is for him to go handicap chasing, though he's a bit harshly handicapped just now.

Frosty Run
5yo bay gelding
Commanche Run – Here To-Day (King's Equity)
A nice young horse. He's only had one run, when he was sixth in a bumper at Stratford in March and the winner, Tighten Your Belt, went on to be third in the valuable Aintree bumper. He'll run in another bumper or two and then go for novice hurdles. I like him, he's a sharp horse and quite a cheeky character. It's hard to get to the bottom of him, which is usually a good sign. But he's one for the future and this will be another easy season for him.

Mickthecutaway
11yo bay gelding
Rontino – Le-Mu-Co (Varano)
Another who's done really well for us, having won six times over fences, all at about

3m. You'll see him in handicap chases and hunter chases this year.

New Bird
8yo bay gelding
Bluebird – Nouvelle Amour (Exclavo)
He's in good form just now, and has won his last two outings, both at Newton Abbot. It was fantastic because we thought that course might be a bit tight for him. He went up 9lb for his latest win, which I thought was a lot. He'll go to Stratford or Worcester soon, or he may go to Ireland. There's a 2m open handicap chase at Cheltenham's November meeting that he might go for, and then he'll have a holiday, because he's basically a good ground horse.

News Maker
7yo bay gelding
Good Thyne – Announcement (Laurence O)
He'll be a nice staying chaser at about Class C level. He was a novice last season and won twice, at Haydock and Wetherby, over 3m both times. He ended with a disappointing run when he was pulled up at Uttoxeter, just nine days after the Wetherby win. We couldn't find any reason for that and nothing's come to light since. I think we just have to forget about that run. He's cantering now and looks well.

Premium First
4yo chestnut gelding
Naheez – Regular Rose (Regular Guy)
He's very sharp, athletic and strong. I went to a sale in Ireland to buy another horse that didn't turn up in the end, but this one was also high on my list of horses to take an interest in. I've seen the video of his point-to-point win at Summerhill in County Meath and he was impressive, he made all the running. For 30,000gns, he's a good buy. He'll start off in bumpers and hopefully progress to novice hurdles this season, but he's a chaser in the making.

Quality First
10yo bay gelding
Un Desperado — Vipsania (General Ironside)
Became our first Cheltenham winner on his first run for us last season, after joining the

Results of last season's key races – see page 71

yard from Paul Nolan in Ireland. He'd been working well before that, but he threw in a bad bit of work just before the race, so he's a bit of a character. He's in absolutely smashing form after his summer holiday – a friend of the owners, who knew him from his Ireland days, said recently that he'd never seen the horse looking so well. He may get into the Grand National this time. He missed the cut by one last year, so we ran him in the Topham instead and he jumped brilliantly, didn't touch a twig and cleared the last with a foot to spare. Like most National runners, he has to prove his stamina, but he travels well, and he was going well in Doncaster's Great Yorkshire Chase in January until he had a disagreement with Jodie Mogford and hit the fourth-last, which stopped him in his tracks. He would have been first or second but for that, and Ryalux, who was second then, went on to win the Scottish National. He's for sale to anyone who fancies having a National runner.

Sir Bob
11yo brown gelding
Aristocracy – Wilden (Will Somers)
A staying chaser, he joined us from Kim Bailey's last season. Unfortunately, he came to us a bit late and, by the time he was ready to run, there were no suitable races for him. So, although he was beaten on all three runs for us, that wasn't his fault. He'll be aimed at staying chases and, although he's getting older, he's still useful.

Terre De Java
5yo bay gelding
Cadoudal – Terre d'Argent (Count Ivor)
Raced three times in France, and was second in a big field at Auteuil on his last run, in spring 2002. The winner won again next time, beating Korelo, who has since joined Martin Pipe and won the Imperial Cup. Terre De Java is a great big horse and looks promising. He'll go for novice hurdles over the French-style brush hurdles, at Haydock, Worcester or Southwell.

SIR BOB: Dalton has high hopes of a better season than the last from this veteran chaser

Nicky Henderson

HE MAY be surprised (outraged?) at the comparison, but Nicky Henderson has something in common with our Dave Nevison, the *Outlook*'s pro punter – both had jobs in the City before deciding to do something less boring instead.

For Henderson, if not for Nevison, success has come easily in horseracing. Twice champion trainer, his haul of Cheltenham Festival winners is second only to Martin Pipe among current license-holders; it includes three Champion Hurdles, four Cathcarts, three Triumph Hurdles and three Arkles.

He has even shown a facility for getting talented runners into top handicaps on favourable ratings, making him a rewarding ally for any punter. Three wins in Newbury's Tote Gold Trophy, plus two in the Festival's County Hurdle leave no room for doubt that Henderson understands exactly how such contests work.

So, naturally, my first question was: "Do you bet?" Actually, it was the last thing I asked; you never know how much umbrage a respectable trainer may take at such impertinence, and there was a certain amount of bridling from the master of Seven Barrows, but his answer was clear.

"I do not. I don't know the first thing about betting," he says. "The one thing people know about us is that our horses always run on their merits."

At RFO, we may not bet for a living but we might fairly be said to live for betting, and the chances are, since you've paid for this book, that you've got a pretty keen interest in gambling yourself. How, then, are people like us to comprehend the motivations of a man like Henderson, so involved in the sport, yet preserving a saintly indifference to the pleasures of the punt?

Tracing his career, it becomes clear that this man has been immersed in steeplechasing from his earliest days. His father rode in point-to-points and bred jumpers, while his mother was joint-master of the Craven Hunt. Naturally, he married Diana Thorne, a world-class event rider and the first woman to ride a winner over fences in Britain.

Young Nicky rode as an amateur, benefiting from the tutelage of legendary jockey-turned-trainer Fred Winter. Famously, Winter had hated to ride at Plumpton, but that's where he sent Henderson for his first ride, in a novice chase no less. The callow youth listened earnestly as he was instructed to follow John Oaksey, and he was duly brought down when Oaksey's horse fell.

But he learned quickly and racked up 78 wins in total, including the Fox Hunters' Chase over Aintree's National fences.

Riding winners was well within the family tradition, but professionally Henderson was supposed to follow in his father's footsteps and become a stockbroker. He was soon sure, however, that it wasn't for him.

Instead, he was Winter's assistant for four seasons, when Pendil, Bula and Lanzarote were the stable stars. In 1978, Midnight Court's Gold Cup provided a high point and a natural conclusion to their partnership; by the following season, Henderson had a license of his own.

Though much in life has fallen into this lucky man's lap, he had to prove himself as a trainer. When he arrived at 30-box Windsor House stables, he brought with him two horses, one of them his wife's eventer.

Zongalero got him started. In Henderson's first season, this hefty type ran second in two valuable Cheltenham handicaps before chasing home Rubstic in the National. Next season, he was second in the Hennessy.

Thanks in large measure to Zongalero, Henderson says, "the broken promises I had received were replaced by real, live animals and I can't tell you the pleasure I get from seeing a row of nodding heads over the stable doors at feeding time."

See You Then took his trainer to the very top of his profession. Success brought the most pleasurable of problems – by 1992, even an expanded Windsor House plus a satellite yard couldn't contain his string, so Henderson moved to his current premises, the 100-box Seven Barrows.

While the flow of winners has not abated, some big targets remain. The Grand National, in particular, has not been kind ("a disaster of a race," is how Henderson describes it – he's had three other horses go close since Zongalero, as well as three consecutive first-fence fallers, but no winners).

Plainly, he would love to win a Gold Cup, but accepts that he "can't force" his best horses to be contenders at that level. Indeed, he went for 20 years without a runner in the race before the 2002 renewal, when Marlborough was fourth.

He's never managed 100 winners in a season and nominates this, unprompted, as an ambition, complaining that "we always seem to get close." But he won't be going downmarket in search of easy meat. "I like running at the Grade 1 tracks, they're the ones our owners like to go to. And, with a novice, you'd rather be jumping round there in a small field than at one of the smaller tracks against 18 or 19."

I point out what our statistics show – of the top 20 jumps trainers, he has the best strike-rate with chasers coming back from a long absence (see page 27). He professes to have no great interest in stats, but this makes sense to him: "If that was true, it wouldn't surprise me, because we do make an effort to get them fit to run."

Look out for the following horses, then, and, when they turn out, don't worry about how long it is since you last saw them.

His 25 Festival winners		
2002	Fulke Walwyn Kim Muir *(The Bushkeeper)*
2000	National Hunt H'cap Chase *(Marlborough)*, Cathcart *(Stormyfairweather)*, Stayers' Hurdle *(Bacchanal)*, Arkle *(Tiutchev)*
1999	Triumph Hurdle *(Katarino)*, Cathcart *(Stormyfairweather)*
1997	County Hurdle *(Barna Boy)*
1994	Cathcart *(Raymylette)*
1993	Arkle *(Travado)*, County Hurdle *(Thumbs Up)*
1992	Champion Chase *(Remittance Man)*, Supreme Novices' Hurdle *(Flown)*
1991	Arkle *(Remittance Man)*
1990	Kim Muir *(Master Bob)*, Cathcart *(Brown Windsor)*
1989	Stayers' Hurdle *(Rustle)*
1987	Champion Hurdle *(See You Then)*, Triumph Hurdle *(Alone Success)*
1986	Champion Hurdle *(See You Then)*, Supreme Novices' Hurdle *(River Ceiriog)*, Mildmay of Flete *(The Tsarevich)*
1985	Champion Hurdle *(See You Then)*, Triumph Hurdle *(First Bout)*, Mildmay of Flete *(The Tsarevich)*

Henderson's heroes

Back To Ben Alder
6yo bay or brown gelding
Bob Back – Winter Fox (Martinmas)
A huge horse, with a huge amount of talent and I hope he's very, very good. He won his first bumper at Kempton very easily, but had his hind legs stripped raw at Cheltenham. We've been patient with him and hopefully he's mature enough to prove himself this season. He looks like a chaser, he's got a lot of speed and he's very sharp.

Bareme
4yo bay gelding
Homme De Loi – Roxa (Kenmare)
Picked up a little injury winning his novice hurdle at Kempton in February, so unfortunately he won't be back until the second half of the season.

Calling Brave
7yo chestnut gelding
Bob Back – Queenie Kelly (The Parson)
Had a good season but wasn't quite up to it in the Royal & SunAlliance Hurdle. He's not the biggest but he's bred for fencing and he'll be novice chasing this season. I see him as a staying chaser.

Caracciola
6yo bay gelding
Lando – Capitolina (Empery)
Won a big-field novice hurdle at Newbury but then, when we jumped him up a grade, he found it a little harder. He'll go novice chas-

BACK TO BEN ALDER

ing, and wouldn't want it too soft.

Chauvinist
8yo bay gelding
Roselier – Sacajawea (Tanfirion)
Did very well last season, particularly because it hadn't gone right for him the year before. He won a valuable handicap hurdle at Ascot just before Christmas, and ended up running third in the Supreme Novices Hurdle. He's bred to be a chaser and he'll go novice chasing this season. We haven't schooled him yet, like a lot of our novice chasers, because the ground was too firm at the end of last season, but we're hopeful he'll do well. He loves to get his toe in and he'll be out when the ground's right.

Dungarvans Choice
8yo chestnut gelding
Orchestra – Marys Gift (Monksfield)
He'd been a little novicey in his schooling over fences and he completely lost the plot in his second novice chase, at Chepstow in December. I had no choice but to send him back over hurdles and he won a handicap at Newbury. But he's got no business over hurdles – he's a big horse and he'll be going back over fences.

First Love
7yo brown gelding
Bustino – First Romance (Royalty)
I'm pleased with him. He was first or second in all five starts as a novice chaser last season. We thought he wouldn't get a yard over 2m but he seems to need further over fences and even won over 3m at Perth in May. He loves soft ground.

Fondmort
7yo bay gelding
Cyborg – Hansie (Sukawa)
Won the Tripleprint on his second start last season and was second in the Mildmay Of Flete. We know about him, really, he wants 2m5f and decent ground. He'll go for those two early races at Cheltenham, the Paddy Power and the Tripleprint. He's cantering just now and looks fantastic.

Geos
8yo bay or brown gelding
Pistolet Bleu – Kaprika (Cadoudal)
Life's not very easy for him any more, it never has been, but he always finds something. He won the Grade 2 Castleford Chase at Wetherby on Boxing Day last season and was fourth in the Champion Chase. We've got nothing particular in mind but we'll be looking about for the best opportunity – it won't necessarily be over fences.

Got One Too
6yo chestnut gelding
Green Tune – Gloria Mundi (Saint Cyrien)
He's also won on the Flat this summer – we had to try that with him, because he had such a low rating. He'll go straight to fences. I thought, when he won his first chase at Leicester, he looked really, really good but it didn't quite work out like that. He wants good ground.

Iris Royal
6yo bay gelding
Garde Royale – Tchela (Le Nain Jaune)
Won a couple as a novice but was slightly disappointing at Cheltenham and Aintree. Now he's got to take on the handicappers, but he looks fantastic.

Irish Hussar
7yo bay gelding
Supreme Leader – Shuil Ard (Quayside)
He finally got to where I hoped he'd be. He just took a bit of time to get the hang of it. He won a soft race at Wincanton and even at Leicester he wasn't very impressive but I think that was the learning point because next time he was second to La Landiere in the Cathcart and then he won a Grade 2 at Aintree. He's still short on experience so I shouldn't think he'll be starting off in your Hennessys. There's a 3m race at Sandown in early December that we used for Bacchanal and I'd have thought he'd run there before we throw him in against the older boys. Hopefully, he'll keep progressing.

Isio
7yo bay gelding
Silver Rainbow – Swifty (Le Riverain)
We found a couple of soft races for him last season but I wanted to give him more of a test before the Arkle. He was down to run in a good race at Warwick, but that was lost to the weather, so we ran him at Huntingdon, which turned out to be another soft race. He ran a great race in the Arkle and really deserved to be second because we had a go at Azertyuiop. He's a very neat horse, very speedy, but I wouldn't rule out that he'll get further than 2m. We'll try him at 2m first time out. It won't be easy for him this year, because there's very few of these transition races these days, but he's looking great.

Landing Light
8yo bay gelding
In The Wings – Gay Hellene (Ela-Mana-Mou)
Was second in the Bula last season, his first run in blinkers, but he looked a bit jaded after that. Happily, running him on the Flat this summer has amused him and he's done well, and hopefully going back over hurdles will amuse him as well, though he'll probably run in the Cesarewitch first. We might send him chasing.

Lilium De Cotte
4yo bay gelding
Ragmar – Vanille De Cotte (Italic)
We got him when JP McManus bought him, after he was fourth in the Triumph Hurdle. We thought about sending him to Liverpool, but there didn't seem much point. We'll look at the Gerry Fielden at Newbury on Hennessy day, and we might go novice chasing with him – I suppose he's exposed over hurdles.

Marlborough
11yo brown gelding
Strong Gale – Wrekenogan (Tarqogan)
We thought at the start of last season that it might be his final one, but he won the Charlie Hall and was second in the King George. This isn't necessarily his final year – he's never come in looking better than he does now. We'll start him off in the Charlie Hall and take it from there. Kempton seems to suit him.

Mon Villez
4yo chestnut gelding
Villez – Europa (Legend Of France)
He's just come back in. Million In Mind have bought him from France, where he won the champion three-year-old chase last season. He can't go over fences, because of the penalties he's got, but he's a novice over hurdles. His owners always sell at the end of the season anyway, so we've got one season novice hurdling with him. We know that

Sponsored by Stan James

jumping won't be a problem with him, anyway. In terms of his trip, I would have thought 2m to 2m4f.

Nas Na Riogh
4yo bay filly
King's Theatre – Abstraite (Groom Dancer)
She needs very soft ground. I don't think I've ever seen a horse win a Grade 1 as easily as she did at Chepstow in December, but she was the only one who could go in that heavy ground. They took her off her feet early on in the Triumph but she was staying on when she fell two out. I don't know where she would have finished, she probably wouldn't have won it. She'll go chasing, almost certainly. She's big and she'll get all the allowances, for age and sex.

No Shenanigans
6yo bay gelding
King's Ride – Melarka (Dara Monarch)
Won his first bumper and was fourth in the valuable one at Liverpool in April 2002 but he's been off since. He just got a bit jarred up behind and we didn't get him back in time for last season but he's back now and I'm looking forward to running him.

Non So
5yo bay gelding
Definite Article – Irish Woman (Assert)
There were two reasons for the progress he made last year. He improved physically, and also the penny dropped with us to ride him a different way. He was showing a lot of speed at home, so, when he went to Kempton in December, I told Mick to drop him in this time, and it worked. He won the Lanzarote, was second in the Tote Gold Trophy and fourth in the County Hurdle, but the handicapper kept clobbering him. He'll go novice chasing – he wouldn't have the size or scope of Chauvinist but that doesn't mean he won't do it.

Saintsaire
4yo bay gelding
Apeldoorn – Pro Wonder (The Wonder)
I'd like to go back

and think about what he did at Newbury when he beat a big field of novices handsomely. I still think he's a very good horse and you can forget about his run in the Triumph Hurdle – he got a horrible over-reach.

Scots Grey
8yo grey gelding
Terimon – Misowni (Niniski)
He won a couple as a novice last season, and was placed in some good races. Running him in the Scottish National was a bit of a whim [he fell six out] and I'd be surprised if he stays that far. He wants a stiff 2m4f and loves good ground.

Sleep Bal
4yo bay colt
Another French import; he's won a decent race at Enghein, but unfortunately that means novice hurdling is out. He could always go novice chasing. He wants cut.

Tysou
6yo bay or brown gelding
Ajdayt – Pretty Point (Crystal Glitters)
Won three as a novice last season. He fell at Aintree but that was just a silly thing – next time, he was the only one to get round at Ayr. He loves top of the ground and I hope to get him going early on. He's a speed horse and will go for 2m handicaps. Kempton suits him well.

IRISH HUSSAR

Profiles by Chris Cook

Sponsored by Stan James

2002-2003 Review

Outlook

News diary 2002-03

September

1 Hosting an Open Day at his yard, Paul Nicholls says veteran chaser Ad Hoc will be sent novice hurdling this season. The aim is to preserve his handicap mark over fences ahead of another bid for the Grand National. Nicholls reckoned the horse was an unlucky loser at Aintree the previous season, when brought down four out. He's also looking forward to Azertyuiop going over fences, describing him as "our highest-rated hurdler to go chasing since Flagship Uberalles."

4 Winning a novice chase at Newton Abbot on Toi Express (2-5), Tony McCoy breaks his own record for the fastest 100 winners in a season, by 13 days.

5 Beau, reckoned to be unlucky in the last two Grand Nationals, has not fully recovered from an injury sustained at Sandown in April. The nine-year-old damaged a tendon and is being rested following surgery. He will to miss the whole season.

11 Sabin Du Loir, who amassed many fans during a 12-year jump racing career, dies peacefully at the age of 23, after nine years of retirement. Highlights of his career included a defeat of Dawn Run at the Cheltenham Festival and four verdicts over Desert Orchid.

13 Jockeys express renewed fears about the portable fences at Southwell after two horses are killed there in one day. Dean Gallagher says: "We've been concerned about the fences for some time and I know Richard Guest and Mick Fitzgerald are among those who have strong views. They're the only fences of their type in Britain. They haven't got much of a belly on them, so horses are inclined to get into the bottom of them. On a flat track with quick ground, that makes the situation even worse. We'd like the people at the track consult with us to see how things can be improved, because it needs to be."

19 Gunner Welburn is to join Ian and Andrew Balding with a view to being aimed at the Grand National. The ten-year-old was a prolific point-to-point winner with Caroline Bailey, for whom he has also won seven times under Rules.

22 Promising amateur rider Jamie Moore joins Martin Pipe's stable for the new season. Having ridden five winners on the Flat, he's decided his weight dictates a future over obstacles, though his brother Ryan has begun a promising career on the level.

October

3 Cheltenham are to introduce a supplementary entry stage for four of their championship races. For sums of between £7,000 and £17,500, late entries will be accepted (one week before the Festival) for the Gold Cup, the Champion Hurdle, the Champion Chase and the Stayers' Hurdle. This should ensure that the best possible field is assembled for these races, but the initiative gives food for thought to ante-post backers.

6   Panorama's investigation into racing is watched by 3.9million people, four times as many as saw the Prix de l'Arc de Triomphe earlier in the day. Without proving any particular instances of corruption within the sport, the programme attacks the Jockey Club's ability to regulate it.

Triple Champion Chase winner Badsworth Boy dies of a heart attack at the age of 27, after 15 years of retirement in South Yorkshire. He was trained for Festival glory in successive seasons by three different members of the Dickinson family.

10   The Jockey Club is described as "institutionally incompetent" by Rhydian Morgan-Jones, a BHB director and advisor to leading international owner Prince Khalid Abdullah. He calls for the Club's integrity responsibilities to be transferred to an "independent judiciary."

Barton tears a ligament in his foot. It's reported that he may be out until spring but in fact he recovers well enough to run in January.

11   Mark Johnston begins his weekly *Racing Post* column with the words: "The Jockey Club must go." At the time of going to press, we're still waiting.

13   The 112th running of the Velka Pardubicka (the Czech Republic's answer to the Grand National) goes to local runner Maksul. There were no British-trained runners after Charlie Mann withdrew Celibate due to the rain-softened going.

Gaye Brief, the Champion Hurdler of 1983, dies at the age of 25. In winning that race so emphatically, he made a mistake at the final flight, triggering a back injury that afflicted him in varying degrees for the rest of his life. Despite that, he was able to hold his own at the highest level for the next five years.

16   Alec Wildenstein is to sell off all his jumps racehorses, with the single exception of star chaser Kotkijet, winner of the 2001 Grand Steeplechase de Paris.

19   Azertyuiop makes a flawless debut over fences, albeit in a soft race at Market Rasen. Coral make him 14-1 joint-favourite with Impek for the Arkle.

21   French mare Bilboa is retired to stud in Ireland at the age of five. She had career-earnings of over £280,000 and had been third in the 2002 Champion Hurdle, but her owner decided it was time to stop after she took a heavy fall at Enghein.

As she leaves the game, jockey Timmy Murphy comes back to it. The 28-year-old is freed from Wormwood Scrubs, having served 84 days of a six-month sentence for indecently assaulting a flight attendant and being drunk on an aircraft. Shortly afterwards, he gives a frank interview with the *Racing Post* in which he admits alcoholism and talks about his struggle to give up drinking.

25   It's reported that Triumph Hurdle winner Scolardy has not yet returned to training, as he's suffering tendon trouble.

26   Henrietta Knight withdraws her three runners at Kempton, describing the grasscover at the track as "an absolute disgrace". She implies that it might even have been deliberately neglected in order to ease the way for the introduction of All-Weather racing and the abolition of jumps racing at the track. The trainer even suggests that, if the situation doesn't improve, she may not run Best Mate in Kempton's King George VI Chase on Boxing Day. Clerk of the course Brian Clifford admits mistakes had been made, though he argues the problem had been primarily caused by a lack of rainfall since summer, combined with recent frosts.

28   Entirely against his wishes, Adrian Maguire is forced to concede that his career as a jockey is over. The 31-year-old broke a vertebra in a fall at Wincanton in March and, although he'd made a partial recovery, a substantial portion of his neck is fixed rigid, leaving the remainder of his neck much more susceptible to fracture. The Jockey Club's chief medical advisor tells him that under no circumstances would he be passed fit to ride again. Despite a career plagued by injury, Maguire won a Gold Cup, a Champion Chase and two King Georges.

31   It's a bad week for jump jockeys – Champion Hurdle winner Dean Gallagher tests positive for cocaine for the second time in his career. Having suffered a six-month ban for his first offence in 2000, the 33-year-old now looks set for a much longer ban, after which he'd be highly unlikely to make a comeback.

November

1   Timmy Murphy makes his return to race-riding, partnering Fireball Macnamara into second in a novice chase at Wetherby. "You can say I'll be better for the race," he tells the *Racing Post*.

2   Marlborough wins an incident-packed Charlie Hall Chase at Wetherby. Faller What's Up Boys chips a hock and will miss the rest of the season.

5   Davy Russell, a champion point-to-point rider in Ireland, signs up as stable jockey to Ferdy Murphy, following the retirement of Adrian Maguire the week before.

9   Santenay (15-8) gives Timmy Murphy his first winner since his release from jail.

11   Polly Gundry, an accomplished and experienced amateur rider, takes the wrong course on a 3-1 joint-favourite at Fontwell and is disqualified. The much less experienced Andrew Tinkler follows her on a 20-1 shot, and suffers the same fate. Their error leaves Tullons Lane (25-1) in a clear lead over the other four runners, and he wins unchallenged.

From today, sheepskin cheekpieces must be declared by trainers at the overnight stage. They'll be marked on racecards with an 'S'.

12   Britain gets its first new jumps track since Taunton in the 1920s – it's Steepledowns, a computer-generated forum for virtual jumps racing. The result is determined in advance and there's no form – but mystifyingly some punters are still happy to bet on it. There's another one born every minute.

14   Following his positive test for cocaine (October 31), Dean Gallagher loses his jockey's licence for 18 months.

16   Though many punters like nothing better than to follow Martin Pipe, there's a sign today that the market is learning to ignore the champion trainer's bullishness about his runners. Pipe says his fancied Chicuelo should be odds-on for Cheltenham's Thomas Pink Gold Cup, and this pronouncement gets him a banner headline on the front page of the *Racing Post*, but the horse is allowed to start at 2-1 after being as short as 11-10 in the morning. He jumps poorly and gets pulled up, but Pipe is still smiling, as he wins the race with Cyfor Malta. Less happy is Tony McCoy, who wasted all week to get down to 10st1lb for the ride on the favourite; his daily diet was reduced to a piece of chicken, a jaffa cake and the odd cup of tea. Asked what went wrong, he replied: "I don't know, you'll have to ask the trainer."

17   Rhinestone Cowboy enters the Champion Hurdle betting as short as 16-1 after winning a Cheltenham bumper by a length. The race provides a first success in Britain for JP Magnier, a 19-year-old scion of the family that runs the Coolmore stud.

Richard Johnson returns to race-riding, having broken a leg in a fall at Newton Abbot 12 weeks before. Remarkably in light of his long absence, he remains second only to McCoy in terms of winners ridden this season.

19   Bruce Gibson's riding skills are tested at Kelso. Riding the Even-money favourite Silken Pearls, the jockey finds that his saddle is slipping as he takes it up three from home. Kicking his feet from the irons before the last to give himself a better chance of staying on board, he still manages to get the mare home in front.

Hughie Morrison's stable star Frenchman's Creek is out for the season after spraining a tendon.

20   The Jockey Club fines Ferdy Murphy the shamefully small sum of £4,000 for bringing racing into disrepute. A secretly-taken film of Murphy had been shown on the BBC's Kenyon Confronts, in which he appeared to be claiming that he and unspecified associates had profited from laying one of his runners, knowing it wouldn't win. In the event, it seems unlikely that the particular story Murphy told was true, and he claims afterwards that he'd been merely bragging in order to sell a horse to someone he took for a potential owner. Following the Jockey Club's ruling, he has the nerve to claim he had not expected to be fined so much.

23   Best Mate is a comfortable winner on his reappearance at Huntingdon, beating three rivals by eight lengths.

29 Graham Bradley, who won the Gold Cup as a jockey and had enjoyed early success in his new career as a bloodstock agent, is warned off for eight years (reduced to five on appeal). The ban follows the Jockey Club's decision that he was guilty of a number of breaches of the Rules of Racing while a jockey, including passing on information for reward. He plans to contest the ban in court.

Rhinestone Cowboy is an impressive winner of a novice race on his hurdling debut at Newbury. Ladbrokes go shortest about his Champion Hurdle chances, going 10-1, although 16s is available elsewhere.

30 Be My Royal wins Newbury's Hennessy Gold Cup for Willie Mullins, but it turns out to be a pyrrhic victory, as the eight-year-old finishes so badly lame that he's unlikely to race again.

December

9 Alexander Banquet, not seen in public since running third to Florida Pearl at Punchestown in April, has injured a suspensory ligament and is out for the season.

12 Jamie Osborne is fined £4,000 for bringing racing into disrepute. He was secretly filmed telling a prospective owner that he was prepared to "cheat" and knew an "in-house jockey" who could be used to that effect. The film was shown as part of the BBC's Kenyon's Confronts programme, and Osborne's fine was the same as that imposed on Ferdy Murphy, who featured in the same programme (November 20).

13 Andrew Thornton, Warren Marston and Jason Maguire are landed with ten-day bans after straying off the course during a cross-country race at Cheltenham. Thornton brands the decision "ludicrous", pointing out that the three had merely strayed onto the wrong side of some bushes, which Marston describes as "like bonsai trees."

Joining them on the sidelines will be Jim Culloty, who gets a three-day ban for dropping his hands and losing third place in a Doncaster bumper. The suspension means he'll miss the ride on Best Mate in Boxing Day's King George VI Chase.

Martin Pipe's Horus, who'd been 3-1 favourite for the weekend's big race, Cheltenham's Tripleprint Gold Cup, runs instead in a softer race the day before, to the chagrin of those who'd backed him ante-post.

15 Jonjo O'Neill is disciplined over the running of two of his horses. The Fakenham stewards hit him with a fine of £3,400 (the largest ever imposed on a trainer by racecourse officials) when 3-1 favourite Madal-yar finishes fifth in a juvenile novices hurdle, having been "never near to challenge" in the words of the Racing Post's analyst; jockey Ron Flavin is banned for 21 days and the horse for 40. Malcolm Wallace, the Jockey Club's director of regulation, describes it as being "as bad a case as we've seen for some time." At Haydock, the stewards take a dim view of the tender handling of 14-1 shot Gala Performance, also fifth, but the fine this time is just £800, while jockey Liam Cooper is suspended for five days and the horse for a month.

18 Nicky Henderson and Mick Fitzgerald score a 306-1 five-timer at Newbury.

26 Best Mate (11-8 favourite) wins the King George VI Chase and is now a best-priced 5-2 for a historic second Gold Cup win.

The race provides the middle-leg of a treble for Tony McCoy, deputising on Best Mate for the suspended Jim Culloty. He ends the day on 202 winners for the season, breaking his own record for the fastest double-century by 16 days.

At Wetherby, the shortage of jump jockeys on such a busy day is highlighted when Tom Tate withdraws his Temple Dog from the opener, for which the horse had been expected to start favourite, citing the lack of a suitable rider. Richard Guest, who'd been booked for the ride, made a last-minute switch to Wincanton.

27 Jonjo O'Neill's Mini Sensation lands the gamble in the Welsh National. Having been 25-1 a week before, the nine-year-old is sent off at 8s. On his only previous run this season, Mini Sensation had finished last of four, beaten a distance, over 2m4f.

January

2   Be My Royal is reportedly at risk of losing his Hennessy win (November 30), having tested positive for morphine after the Newbury race. He is the most high-profile of a number of cases to occur over the past two months, all of which are thought to have been caused by a contaminated feed supply. Though connections are innocent of any wrongdoing, morphine could improve a horse's performance, so all winners who test positive are almost certain to be disqualified, though the Jockey Club-managed process is still rumbling on as we go to press.

12   Clearly, Tony McCoy is dangerous if not kept busy. Bad weather has meant a shortage of jump racing in recent weeks and the champ has used some of his downtime to cut a record. Together with Adrian Maguire and Mick Fitzgerald, he's taped a version of The Fields Of Athenry, which the pitiless Cheltenham executive apparently plans to inflict on racegoers during the Festival.

14   Acquisitive jumps owner JP McManus buys Flagship Uberalles, the reigning two-mile champion chaser, for an undisclosed sum, which the vendors later claim was less than £100,000.

16   Martin Pipe runs ten of his charges in a 15-runner handicap hurdle at Taunton. Punters have trouble sorting them out and send off Nicky Henderson's Cybele Eria as 7-2 favourite, but Pipe gets the first two home with Canadiane (12-1) and Maragun (20-1). Tony McCoy is fifth on Pipe's Iorana (5-1).

19   Jumps stallion Gunner B dies of suspected heart failure, at the grand old age of 30. An Eclipse winner, his 24 crops as a sire produced Grand National winner Red Marauder and champion hurdler Royal Gait. He is thought to have been the oldest active thoroughbred stallion in Europe.

23   In a move inspired by nothing but greed, the Cheltenham executive are reportedly ready to extend their Festival to four days from 2005. Details of the added races are not yet clear, but they are reckoned to include a cross-country race and a four-year-old handicap hurdle. This is pretty uninspiring stuff, certainly by the Festival's standards, and it's obvious that such a change could only dilute the quality of the experience – but the course appear unable to focus on anything other than the increased income a fourth day would bring.

25   Bacchanal, a Festival winner and twice placed in the King George, is killed in action at Cheltenham. Having started favourite for the Pillar Chase, the horse falls heavily at the eighth fence and breaks a leg.

Willie Mullins, who had already suffered injuries to three of his best horses, now loses Davenport Milenium for the season, due to a tendon strain.

February

6   A double at Wincanton takes Paul Nicholls to 100 winners for the season, over a month faster than he'd ever managed before.

9   Novice chaser Beef Or Salmon is a convincing winner of Leopardstown's Hennessy Cognac Gold Cup and is a best-priced 9-2 to add the Cheltenham equivalent.

Len Lungo reckons his yard has a virus and the Dumfriesshire man will have only a handful of runners over the next fortnight.

15   Rhinestone Cowboy is the new Champion Hurdle favourite after an apparently effortless success in Wincanton's Kingwell Hurdle (reigning champ Hors La Loi stuffed in third). The novice hurdler is now a best-priced 11-4 for Cheltenham glory.

23   In his warm-up race for the Grand National, Davids Lad is sent out for a 2m chase at Naas. No-one imagines that this is supposed to be the horse's big day, and he duly trails around at the back of the field to finish a distant last of seven – but the stewards decide this is an example of using the track as a training ground (who

would argue?) and that jockey Timmy Murphy made insufficient effort. Accordingly, they fine trainer Tony Martin €1,000 and ban the horse for 42 days, meaning he'll miss the National, which has been his target since he fell in last year's running. Chagrined connections appeal, to no avail.

24 A week after getting his trainer's licence, Richard Guest saddles his first double, which pays 70-1.

Gold Cup-winning trainer Jimmy Fitzgerald announces his retirement.

28 Bust Out, who had been Ireland's main contender for the Festival's Arkle Chase, suffers a recurrence of the leg problem that has plagued his career. He will now be sidelined for between a year and 18 months.

March

2 Ruby Walsh's highly successful partnership with Paul Nicholls has put him in the enviable position of being able to choose between fancied mounts in more than one Festival race. He announces that he'll be on the Nicholls-trainer Azertyuiop in the Arkle, rather than Willie Mullins's Adamant Approach, but shows his diplomatic skills by also opting for Mullins's Royal Alphabet in the Bumper instead of 4-1 joint-favourite Cornish Rebel from the Nicholls yard.

10 There's some good news for bookmakers on the eve of the Cheltenham Festival, when the notorious betting shop "cheat" known as "The Pencil Man" is remanded in custody in Liverpool. But it's their last bit of good news for the week . . .

11 Favourites traditionally flop in the opening race of the Festival, the Supreme Novices Hurdle, but 3-1 jolly Back In Front laughs up by ten lengths. With the day's shortest favourite, Azertyuiop, also going in at 5-4, the second-favourite winning the Champion Hurdle, another winning fav in the last and just one winner all day at a double-figure SP, it's clear that the layers are taking a kicking.

12 Further pain for the bookies as three more market-leaders find the winners' enclosure, including Irish banker of the week Moscow Flyer. Only defeat for 7-4 Stormez in the National Hunt Chase offers some respite for the oddsmen.

13 Best Mate (13-8) becomes the first horse since L'Escargot in 1971 to win a second Gold Cup, and only the sixth dual champion in the race's 80-year history. In 16 races, he's won 11 (four of them Grade 1s) and been second in the other five. His performance triggers comparisons with Arkle, and he will bid to emulate that legend's three consecutive triumphs at the 2004 Festival.

The Gold Cup result overshadows a major achievement by Baracouda (9-4), who wins a second consecutive Stayers' Hurdle, his sixth success at Group 1 level.

Those repeat wins, together with triumphant jollies Kingscliff (11-4) and La Landiere (5-4) complete a miserable Festival for the bookies.

It's also been a tough time for Tony McCoy. The champion jockey ends the meeting with a single winner, having hit the deck four times and missed two rides on the first day through dehydration. His fourth fall resulted in a broken collar-bone, though at least that meant he missed the ride on Tarxien, who fell.

Barry Geraghty is top jock, his five wins including Moscow Flyer in the Champion Chase.

17 The Tote announce that, with effect from later in the week, they will slash their takeouts from win and place pools. The win deduction is reduced from 16 per cent to 13.5 per cent, one of the lowest in the world, while the place deduction will be down to 18 per cent from 24.

18 Papillon, winner of the 2000 Grand National, is retired after a lethargic return to action over hurdles.

22 Fancy a bet in-running? Gin Palace (returned at an SP of 4-1) gets up on the line at Newbury, having been laid at 249-1 on Betfair when he appeared to be in trouble at the top of the straight.

25 Mary Reveley, one of the winningmost

trainers of the last 20 years, announces her intention to retire before the end of 2004, at which time her son Keith will take over the yard at Saltburn, Cleveland. She hopes to achieve 2,000 winners before stopping.

31 At the age of 18, Jamie Moore (see September 22) rides his second treble in two racing days.

April

2 The Jockey Club's Appeal Board cut Graham Bradley's ban from racing to five years, from the original eight (see November 29). Bradley still feels the ban to be harsh, and will challenge it in the courts.

3 As the Grand National meeting gets under way, the 2001 hero Red Marauder is retired. Various injuries had restricted him to a single run since his day of glory, but he had been fit for the 2003 race and would have run if the ground had been softer.

5 Monty's Pass (16-1) wins the Grand National by 12 lengths for Irish trainer Jimmy Mangan. The horse's five co-owners reveal they had collectively backed him to win well over £1 million.

12 The Scottish National goes to Andy Crook's Ryalux (15-2).

19 Richard Johnson scores on Quedex (5-6), his 1,000th winner in Britain, nine years after his first. He is the eighth jump jockey to achieve this landmark; of the other seven, only Tony McCoy racked them up faster.

21 Timbera (11-1) lands the Irish National for Dessie Hughes.

23 Great news for punters, as the Levy Board decides to allow on-course bookmakers to hedge with betting exchanges and off-course layers. The newly-free market seems sure to drive down bookies' profit margins and make it easier for punters to get value prices, while making it harder for off-course bookies to influence SPs.

26 Ad Hoc (7-1) wins the Attheraces Gold Cup for the second time in three years, but the feature race is upstaged by a moderate handicap chase later on the card, which is won by Skycab (11-4), Josh Gifford's last runner as a trainer.

Summer

May

9 Royal Athlete, the Grand National winner of 1995, dies aged 20. He was the champion novice chaser of 1989/90 and ran third in the 1993 Gold Cup before giving Jenny Pitman her second National at 40-1. He died peacefully at home after seven years in retirement.

22 At Doncaster's Spring Sale, Royal Rosa becomes the most expensive jumps horse ever sold at public auction, going for 340,000gns. The four-year-old, winner of the Champion Bumper at Punchestown when trained by Nicky Henderson, will now go to Howard Johnson's yard.

June

12 Hors La Loi III is retired, due to a long-standing degenerative back condition. The champion hurdler of 2002, he planted himself at the start of the 2003 renewal and took no part.

18 Tony McCoy suffers a broken arm when his mount Kymberlya falls between hurdles at Worcester. The injury means he faces about two months on the sidelines and is a blow to his stated aim of riding 300 winners.

29 Jurancon II wins Uttoxeter's Summer National for Martin Pipe, with Rodi Greene deputising for the injured McCoy.

30 Chris and Nick Velounias, the brothers behind North London-based Burns Bookmakers, are thought to be on the run as their firm stops trading. Inevitably, their punters are owed a stack of money (initial estimates range from £500,000 to £1 million).

Allegations emerge that the firm had made unauthorised withdrawals from their clients' accounts. Scotland Yard and Interpol are quickly involved in the search for the pair but, as we go to press, no further news is available.

July

19   Ballycassidy (11-2) wins Market Rasen's Summer Plate for Peter Bowen. Chicuelo, who'd been an impressive winner the year before, trails in tenth at 10-1.

August

8   Kieran Kelly, 25-year-old jump jockey, suffers severe head injuries in a fall at Kilbeggan. Riding for Dessie Hughes, who'd given him his biggest win on Hardy Eustace at the Cheltenham Festival earlier in the year, Kelly is kicked in the head after his mount falls. He is quickly attended by paramedics and rushed to hospital but dies four days later. The tragedy is the first of its type on an Irish racecourse since amateur rider Jim Lombard was killed at Punchestown in 1986.

12   Spandau (5-1) lands what is described by Coral as "a good, old-fashioned coup" in a handicap hurdle at Newton Abbot. Though no significant bets are noted by reporters in the ring, off-course bookies estimate that the race has cost them £500,000. Those firms demand an investigation because the winner's stablemate Indian Star, ridden by Seamus Durack, led and ran wide into the final bend, carrying two other runners (including the 5-4 favourite) with him, and allowing Spandau a clear run up the inner. Both Durack and winning trainer John Tuck – who claims he doesn't bet – are exonerated by the local stewards, but a full Jockey Club investigation remains a possibility as we go to press.

Gardie Grissell, trainer of 200 winners over the previous quarter-century, announces his retirement. He hands over his East Sussex yard to his former assistant and son-in-law David Feek.

16   Blast from the past at Bangor – Michael Scudamore gets his first winner since resuming as a trainer. The 71-year-old was a successful jockey in the fifties and sixties, when he rode the winners of the Gold Cup, the Grand National and the King George VI Chase. He'd also done well as a trainer until retiring in 1996, but has been persuaded to return to boost the career of his son Peter, the former champion jockey, who will serve as his assistant. Their winner is, appropriately, ridden by Peter's son Tom.

21   It's reported that Frenchman's Creek will probably miss the forthcoming jumps season. The nine-year-old is still suffering from a leg injury that has kept him off the course since he was third in the Attheraces Gold Cup in April 2002.

22   Tony McCoy returns to action after a two-month layoff caused by a broken arm (June 18). Having led the jockeys' table at the time of his injury, he's now 18 winners behind Richard Johnson, but he immediately sets about reducing the deficit, scoring on his first ride back.

24   JP McManus is revealed to have bought Australia's top hurdler Specular, for a sum thought to be in the region of £280,000. The winner of eight of his ten starts, he was reckoned to be an unlucky loser in Flemington's Grand National Hurdle, when he was bidding to smash the weight-carrying record for the race. He joins Jonjo O'Neill and will enter full training at the beginning of October.

Quotes

"I can't wait for the new season to start because last year was a disaster. It can only get better."

Tony McCoy, who rode a pathetic 257 winners last season

"After the first race, I was almost a quarter of a million pounds up, and after the last I was about £5,000 up."

A rollercoaster ride on the middle day of the Festival for bookie Freddie Williams

"Without being dishonest, there's no way any trainer worth 30-bob is going to have his horse knocked about to pander to the betting shop punter."

Ginger McCain disapproved when action was taken against Tony Martin for using the racecourse as a training ground

Top jockeys 2002–2003

All			Chases			Hurdles			Jockey	Best Trainer	W	R	%
W	R	%	W	R	%	W	R	%					
257	841	31	88	287	31	169	554	31	Tony McCoy	Martin Pipe	150	483	31
147	725	20	64	286	22	83	439	19	Richard Johnson	Philip Hobbs	73	285	26
109	482	23	49	169	27	60	313	19	Tony Dobbin	Len Lungo	34	97	35
78	450	17	40	175	23	38	275	14	Mick Fitzgerald	Nicky Henderson	41	213	19
77	296	26	41	147	28	36	149	24	Ruby Walsh	Paul Nicholls	67	235	29
66	548	12	24	203	12	42	345	12	Graham Lee	J Howard Johnson	20	68	29
62	521	12	39	237	16	23	284	8	Andy Thornton	Robert Alner	25	150	17
61	445	14	20	146	14	41	299	14	Warren Marston	Sue Smith	29	112	26
60	359	17	30	142	21	30	217	14	Barry Fenton	Richard Rowe	15	100	15
59	494	12	26	173	15	33	321	10	Leighton Aspell	Dina Smith	6	17	35
56	388	14	35	160	22	21	228	9	Jim Culloty	Henrietta Knight	31	166	19
50	487	10	16	169	9	34	318	11	Richard Thornton	Alan King	26	180	14
48	249	19	11	58	19	37	191	19	Liam Cooper	Jonjo O'Neill	46	231	20
48	317	15	22	145	15	26	172	15	Brian Crowley	Venetia Williams	46	262	18
46	357	13	10	107	9	36	250	14	Seamus Durack	Sue Smith	8	29	28
42	407	10	23	165	14	19	242	8	Timmy Murphy	Paul Nicholls	8	34	24
41	297	14	18	99	18	23	198	12	Marcus Foley	Nicky Henderson	15	69	22
41	313	13	15	108	14	26	205	13	Paul Flynn	Philip Hobbs	24	131	18
36	313	12	14	113	12	22	200	11	David Dennis	Ian Williams	25	175	14
36	513	7	12	174	7	24	339	7	Rodi Greene	Kevin Bishop	12	65	18
35	353	10	15	135	11	20	218	9	Noel Fehily	Charlie Mann	22	184	12
33	330	10	11	100	11	22	230	10	K Wilson Renwick	Peter Monteith	16	91	18
32	292	11	9	117	8	23	175	13	Russ Garritty	George M Moore	15	89	17
32	354	9	15	119	13	17	235	7	Tom Scudamore	Martin Pipe	12	144	8
32	384	8	23	172	13	9	212	4	Mark Bradburne	Henry Daly	12	81	15
31	211	15	11	43	26	20	168	12	Wayne Hutchinson	Alison Thorpe	8	36	22
29	292	10	16	99	16	13	193	7	Paul Robson	Martin Todhunter	3	10	30
29	361	8	13	133	10	16	228	7	Carl Llewellyn	Nigel Twiston-Davies	20	208	10
28	190	15	11	47	23	17	143	12	Dominic Elsworth	Sue Smith	22	120	18
28	260	11	10	82	12	18	178	10	Jim Crowley	Alan Swinbank	9	63	14
28	329	9	10	108	9	18	221	8	Tom Doyle	Paul Webber	9	74	12
28	330	8	8	128	6	20	202	10	Richard McGrath	Chris Grant	5	58	9
27	153	18	10	50	20	17	103	17	Bobby McNally	Paul Nicholls	22	73	30
27	308	9	13	115	11	14	193	7	Pip Hide	Gary L Moore	10	68	15
26	104	25	13	49	27	13	55	24	Barry Geraghty	Jonjo O'Neill	10	33	30
24	187	13	8	42	19	16	145	11	Padge Whelan	Richard Fahey	10	45	22
24	247	10	14	96	15	10	151	7	Jason Maguire	Tom George	13	121	11
24	267	9	10	85	12	14	182	8	Ben Hitchcott	Robin Dickin	10	75	13
23	112	21	21	83	25	2	29	7	Christian Williams	Paul Nicholls	10	42	24
23	231	10	6	79	8	17	152	11	J P McNamara	Kim Bailey	7	42	17
23	260	9	8	58	14	15	202	7	Alan Dempsey	Mary Reveley	21	185	11
23	290	8	15	111	14	8	179	4	Brian Harding	Nicky Richards	9	52	17
22	235	9	8	51	16	14	184	8	Paddy Aspell	Mary Reveley	13	83	16
21	199	11	10	89	11	11	110	10	Davy Russell	Ferdy Murphy	19	164	12
20	101	20	2	38	5	18	63	29	Norman Williamson	Jonjo O'Neill	5	10	50
20	123	16	8	51	16	12	72	17	Joe Tizzard	Paul Nicholls	11	44	25
20	208	10	10	80	13	10	128	8	Brian Storey	Andrew Parker	7	32	22
19	149	13	6	44	14	13	105	12	Ron Flavin	Jonjo O'Neill	7	25	28
18	124	15	1	35	3	17	89	19	Gino Carenza	Mick Easterby	15	88	17
18	191	9	9	54	17	9	137	7	Vinnie Keane	J Malcolm Jefferson	5	18	28

Trainer statistics

On the next two pages are tables covering one year, being the 12 months before we went to press.

Following that is a 40-page section analysing the five-year record of each of the top 20 British-based trainers of last season (by prizemoney).

For each trainer, you can examine their runners over the last five complete seasons, broken down by type of race, class of race, jockeys used and time of year, as well as course-by-course (where a track doesn't appear on the page of a particular trainer, he or she has had no runners there in the past five years).

We've also had a look at how these trainers cope with getting horses fit. In our 'After a break' section, we show you their five-year records with horses running after an absence of 120 days or more. The results are reproduced below, in order of strike-rate with chasers.

The most important point for punters to realise is that 12 of the 20 have returned profits with their chasers running after a break. This indicates such horses are often underestimated by the market – most people like to back horses with a recent run, reasoning this means they'll be fit.

But Nicky Henderson wins with over a third of his chasers coming back from an absence. Nicky Richards is not far behind, and generates a massive level-stakes profit (relative to total stakes) with his chasers after a break.

By contrast, you'd want to be very wary before backing one of Alan King's unless it's had a recent run.

After a break

	Chases				Hurdles				Bumpers			
	W	R	%	£1 stake	W	R	%	£1 stake	W	R	%	£1 stake
N Henderson	42	121	34.7	+53.09	39	186	21	+15.60	1	20	5	-17.50
P Nicholls	66	229	28.8	+34.72	31	132	23.5	-10.34	7	22	31.8	+6.69
N Richards	11	39	28.2	+50.44	12	71	16.9	-13.33	0	5	0	-5.00
I Williams	17	64	26.6	+17.89	17	144	11.8	-5.78	1	15	6.7	-10.50
M Pipe	42	175	24	+18.44	62	287	21.6	-2.63	5	16	31.3	+1.79
H Knight	29	124	23.4	+1.56	11	85	12.9	-21.42	1	12	8.3	-3.50
V Williams	35	153	22.9	-2.29	22	126	17.5	-40.74	4	20	20	+6.75
P Hobbs	31	143	21.7	+4.37	41	233	17.6	-60.18	4	19	21.1	-10.75
R Alner	24	113	21.2	+30.53	9	63	14.3	+33.25	1	9	11.1	-4.00
P Webber	16	79	20.3	+31.10	8	77	10.4	-23.38	0	19	0	-19.00
N Twiston-Davies	25	127	19.7	-2.37	14	154	9.1	-87.72	4	24	16.7	-1.00
L Lungo	8	42	19	-10.31	15	150	10	-75.57	6	18	33.3	-2.51
C Mann	8	44	18.2	+23.83	12	122	9.8	+30.28	0	6	0	-6.00
J O'Neill	18	100	18	-20.16	19	155	12.3	-45.96	9	33	27.3	+12.57
S Smith	12	74	16.2	+7.60	12	107	11.2	+1.50	0	14	0	-14.00
H Daly	15	98	15.3	+15.75	10	83	12	+1.23	0	4	0	-4.00
M Reveley	12	86	14	-17.26	9	111	8.1	-55.25	6	36	16.7	-8.92
F Murphy	19	140	13.6	-61.49	13	148	8.8	-86.19	0	11	0	-11.00
R Phillips	2	22	9.1	-7.13	12	80	15	-2.88	1	8	12.5	-5.25
A King	4	47	8.5	-20.00	6	75	8	-43.26	0	2	0	-2.00

Top trainers 2002–2003, by winners

| All runs | | | | First time out | | | Horses* | | |
Won	Ran	%	Trainer	Won	Ran	%	Won	Ran	%
206	1008	20	**Martin Pipe**	48	225	21	100	225	44
174	642	27	**Paul Nicholls**	46	151	30	93	151	62
148	677	22	**Philip Hobbs**	36	150	24	84	150	56
114	567	20	**Jonjo O'Neill**	26	161	16	63	161	39
90	533	17	**Venetia Williams**	24	118	20	54	118	46
79	400	20	**Sue Smith**	15	80	19	36	80	45
74	319	23	**Len Lungo**	19	88	22	40	88	45
74	422	18	**Nicky Henderson**	22	118	19	49	118	42
68	493	14	**Mary Reveley**	13	106	12	46	106	43
57	370	15	**Ian Williams**	15	88	17	36	88	41
47	446	11	**Ferdy Murphy**	8	119	7	38	119	32
45	284	16	**Henrietta Knight**	17	83	20	29	83	35
43	299	14	**Alan King**	9	73	12	30	73	41
39	158	25	**Nicky Richards**	13	46	28	19	46	41
36	292	12	**Robert Alner**	11	77	14	24	77	31
36	345	10	**Nigel Twiston-Davies**	7	85	8	23	85	27
35	264	13	**Charlie Mann**	11	62	18	23	62	37
34	160	21	**J Howard Johnson**	3	41	7	16	41	39
34	237	14	**Tom George**	8	65	12	23	65	35
33	137	24	**Richard Phillips**	5	39	13	14	39	36
32	222	14	**Henry Daly**	12	59	20	22	59	37
27	196	14	**Gary L Moore**	8	50	16	19	50	38
25	202	12	**Heather Dalton**	7	61	11	16	61	26
25	224	11	**Kim Bailey**	8	66	12	18	66	27
24	202	12	**Mick Easterby**	6	51	12	15	51	29
24	210	11	**Paul Webber**	4	64	6	17	64	27
23	168	14	**George M Moore**	4	35	11	14	35	40
23	219	11	**J W "Seamus" Mullins**	2	51	4	16	51	31
23	240	10	**Brendan Powell**	2	59	3	15	59	25
22	136	16	**Peter Monteith**	2	31	6	11	31	35
22	151	15	**Richard Lee**	1	28	4	13	28	46
22	155	14	**Richard Rowe**	4	34	12	12	34	35
21	101	21	**Noel Chance**	5	36	14	9	36	25
20	114	18	**Peter Bowen**	1	27	4	9	27	33
20	125	16	**J Malcolm Jefferson**	4	31	13	11	31	35
20	141	14	**Richard C Guest**	9	47	19	14	47	30
20	162	12	**Tim Easterby**	1	34	3	11	34	32
19	119	16	**Martin Todhunter**	5	39	13	13	39	33
18	110	16	**Emma Lavelle**	4	34	12	11	34	32
18	170	11	**Oliver Sherwood**	4	35	11	13	35	37
18	201	9	**Robin Dickin**	4	45	9	12	45	27
17	66	26	**Richard Fahey**	3	16	19	8	16	50
16	87	18	**Charlie Egerton**	3	30	10	9	30	30
16	88	18	**Lawrence Wells**	3	22	14	11	22	50
16	120	13	**Richard Ford**	6	33	18	11	33	33
16	159	10	**Jimmy Frost**	3	49	6	12	49	24
15	94	16	**G Alan Swinbank**	5	31	16	8	31	26
15	124	12	**Dai L Williams**	4	22	18	6	22	27
15	210	7	**Norman Mason**	0	53	0	14	53	26

*Shows how many individual horses ran last season, how many won at least once, and percentage.

Top trainers 2002–2003, by prizemoney

Total prizemoney	Trainer	Win prizemoney	Wins	Class A-C Won	Ran	%	Class D-G Won	Ran	%
£2,668,397	Martin Pipe	£1,690,077	206	47	393	12	146	586	25
2,321,635	Paul Nicholls	1,659,037	174	54	261	21	101	322	31
1,564,747	Philip Hobbs	1,145,092	148	27	183	15	111	448	25
1,521,480	Jonjo O'Neill	1,186,255	114	45	185	24	57	328	17
1,079,155	Nicky Henderson	623,413	74	19	170	11	48	203	24
895,247	Henrietta Knight	610,916	45	13	98	13	29	162	18
771,057	Venetia Williams	501,934	90	19	158	12	64	339	19
668,338	Sue Smith	459,045	79	16	74	22	62	300	21
580,080	Mary Reveley	370,036	68	11	122	9	52	332	16
492,030	Ferdy Murphy	254,549	47	6	52	12	38	367	10
442,312	Henry Daly	317,115	32	9	39	23	21	167	13
438,812	Ian Williams	303,079	57	9	75	12	46	276	17
424,678	Len Lungo	348,372	74	9	52	17	56	222	25
422,061	Alan King	228,612	43	11	81	14	28	189	15
371,273	Nigel Twiston-Davies	196,398	36	4	72	6	30	242	12
364,192	Richard Phillips	286,543	33	7	23	30	24	104	23
354,098	Jessica Harrington	350,802	5	5	7	71	0	3	0
353,571	Charlie Mann	187,654	35	6	77	8	29	181	16
348,000	Jimmy Mangan	348,000	1	1	1	100	0	0	0
300,253	Robert Alner	192,588	36	6	50	12	29	217	13
268,332	Paul Webber	135,140	24	4	62	6	17	123	14
255,855	Nicky Richards	161,080	39	2	21	10	34	124	27
234,801	Tom George	157,713	34	2	31	6	30	194	15
231,649	Francois Doumen	201,112	4	4	20	20	0	6	0
211,947	Gary L Moore	127,903	27	3	33	9	24	155	15
209,221	J Howard Johnson	175,988	34	3	23	13	31	131	24
201,741	J W "Seamus" Mullins	126,247	23	4	17	24	17	171	10
184,810	Emma Lavelle	119,795	18	2	22	9	14	77	18
183,869	Heather Dalton	131,311	25	4	22	18	21	147	14
181,619	Kim Bailey	120,457	25	2	25	8	20	179	11
176,830	Pat Murphy	23,109	6	0	8	0	6	59	10
175,635	D "Ginger" McCain	51,478	12	1	18	6	11	148	7
168,827	Edward O'Grady	145,000	2	2	13	15	0	0	0
167,408	Brendan Powell	113,470	23	2	19	11	20	207	10
164,149	Tim Easterby	89,174	20	3	51	6	14	92	15
161,734	Josh Gifford	107,633	13	5	31	16	8	83	10
157,647	Peter Monteith	124,782	22	3	26	12	19	101	19
152,875	Richard Lee	98,921	22	0	16	0	19	129	15
152,842	George M Moore	92,879	23	2	16	13	21	146	14
152,632	Martin Todhunter	101,208	19	1	11	9	18	97	19
151,737	Andy Crook	98,200	9	2	8	25	7	78	9
149,373	Richard C Guest	103,096	20	3	24	13	17	102	17
149,238	Richard Rowe	118,799	22	4	18	22	18	127	14
149,169	Arthur Moore	87,000	1	1	13	8	0	0	0
144,219	Peter Bowen	108,365	20	2	13	15	18	92	20
139,480	Christy Roche	66,700	2	2	22	9	0	2	0
134,713	Noel Chance	108,871	21	3	17	18	14	57	25
132,739	Richard Fahey	102,217	17	1	12	8	14	48	29
125,085	Peter Beaumont	45,331	9	0	17	0	8	122	7
124,547	J Malcolm Jefferson	84,397	20	1	12	8	18	95	19

Race type

	Chases				Hurdles			
	W	R	%	£1 stake	W	R	%	£1 stake
Handicap	114	799	14.3	-153.11	263	1707	15.4	-367.28
Novice	167	477	35	-44.93	297	1082	27.4	-165.93
Maiden	4	17	23.5	-5.86	50	163	30.7	+48.67
Selling	1	14	7.1	-8.00	95	386	24.6	-66.28
Claiming	-	-	-	-	56	159	35.2	+9.10
Amateur	4	37	10.8	+15.00	11	56	19.6	-7.57

Class of race

	Chases				Hurdles				Bumpers			
	W	R	%	£1 stake	W	R	%	£1 stake	W	R	%	£1 stake
A	30	289	10.4	-100.76	32	365	8.8	-184.40	3	14	21.4	-0.75
B	41	228	18	-1.07	65	358	18.2	-14.92	0	3	0	-3.00
C	38	150	25.3	+1.10	51	255	20	-34.34	-	-	-	-
D	81	285	28.4	-34.00	156	611	25.5	-40.25	-	-	-	-
E	79	233	33.9	-40.50	201	791	25.4	-142.46	-	-	-	-
F	12	92	13	-39.63	100	419	23.9	-4.70	-	-	-	-
G	1	14	7.1	-8.00	103	402	25.6	-55.96	-	-	-	-
H	6	13	46.2	+10.38	-	-	-	-	35	146	24	+32.07

Winning jockeys

	Chases				Hurdles				Bumpers			
	W	R	%	£1 stake	W	R	%	£1 stake	W	R	%	£1 stake
A P McCoy	228	773	29.5	-51.69	505	1604	31.5	-49.52	24	76	31.6	-9.80
R Greene	16	149	10.7	-87.33	51	353	14.4	-114.60	4	16	25	+15.75
T Scudamore	5	83	6	-64.01	35	262	13.4	-78.53	3	9	33.3	+2.04
R Johnson	8	28	28.6	+16.46	12	44	27.3	+0.60	1	3	33.3	+7.00
G Supple	2	25	8	0.00	13	192	6.8	-82.71	5	19	26.3	+49.00
J Huet	0	7	0	-7.00	17	138	12.3	-29.02	1	4	25	+0.33
Mr A Farrant	2	9	22.2	+3.00	8	22	36.4	+4.92		0		
J E Moore	3	14	21.4	-5.26	6	38	15.8	+1.98	0	6	0	-6.00
T J Murphy	1	14	7.1	-8.00	6	34	17.6	+17.63		0		
Mr P Scouller	6	12	50	+11.38	0	1	0	-1.00		0		

By month

	Chases				Hurdles				Bumpers			
	W	R	%	£1 stake	W	R	%	£1 stake	W	R	%	£1 stake
January	32	148	21.6	-45.28	58	319	18.2	-52.84	6	19	31.6	-1.11
February	31	121	25.6	-14.03	76	337	22.6	-24.55	5	25	20	+40.75
March	16	135	11.9	-23.31	44	354	12.4	-120.22	3	21	14.3	-13.46
April	29	187	15.5	-18.57	64	341	18.8	+7.93	2	13	15.4	-5.50
May	30	120	25	-35.43	64	310	20.6	-65.69	2	17	11.8	-12.96
June	26	79	32.9	+5.21	37	158	23.4	-21.79	4	8	50	+3.08
July	21	65	32.3	-20.26	45	156	28.8	-13.36	1	3	33.3	-1.67
August	11	44	25	-14.12	71	202	35.1	-34.93	0	2	0	-2.00
September	13	36	36.1	-1.79	46	157	29.3	-23.33	1	2	50	+1.00
October	10	57	17.5	-25.49	63	228	27.6	-51.55	0	6	0	-6.00
November	37	156	23.7	-0.96	74	299	24.7	-16.06	7	24	29.2	+24.33
December	33	158	20.9	-19.82	66	341	19.4	-61.66	7	23	30.4	+1.86

Not forgetting ...

	Chases				Hurdles				Bumpers			
	W	R	%	£1 stake	W	R	%	£1 stake	W	R	%	£1 stake
Favourites	187	413	45.3	+17.49	469	1089	43.1	-90.53	24	52	46.2	+8.74
After a break	42	175	24	+18.44	62	287	21.6	-2.63	5	16	31.3	+1.79

Sponsored by Stan James

All runners

	Wins	Runs	%	2nd	3rd	rest	Win prize	Total prize	£1 Stake
Chases	289	1306	22.1	183	139	695	2,871,250.53	4,561,725.10	-213.86
Hurdles	708	3202	22.1	414	348	1731	3,550,999.03	5,489,975.00	-478.03
Bumpers	38	163	23.3	14	13	97	109,291.90	166,727.00	+28.32
Totals	1035	4671	22.1	611	500	2523	6,531,541.46	10, 218,427.10	-663.57

Martin Pipe

CHAMPION trainer for a record thirteenth time, Martin Pipe trains winners like no other British trainer has ever done.

He now holds the top thirteen records for number of winners trained in a jumps season, as well as those for most trainers' championships, and most consecutive championships. Since 1988/89, only one other trainer has had a look in (David Nicholson, twice champion in the nineties).

But, dangerously for punters, his headline-grabbing feats are largely due to the sheer number of runners he sends out. His strike-rate, while respectable, is unremarkable when compared with those of other top trainers.

Indeed, his percentage of winners to runners is poor in the very best races. Ten of the 19 other trainers in this feature have better strike-rates in Class A races, whether over fences or hurdles.

That said, he turns a good profit for followers of all his runners at Ascot, and his chasers at Cheltenham and Sandown.

Course records

	Chases				Hurdles				Bumpers			
	W	R	%	£1 stake	W	R	%	£1 stake	W	R	%	£1 stake
Newton Abbot	33	104	31.7	-18.29	70	254	27.6	-27.60	4	17	23.5	+2.88
Taunton	10	40	25	-1.07	59	279	21.1	-9.96	1	9	11.1	+8.00
Cheltenham	33	180	18.3	+39.51	33	295	11.2	-104.42	1	5	20	-2.00
Worcester	16	49	32.7	+0.17	41	164	25	-13.97	3	12	25	-6.93
Exeter	16	75	21.3	-20.47	35	215	16.3	-72.58	2	12	16.7	+40.91
Plumpton	13	31	41.9	+1.29	33	116	28.4	-4.70	1	2	50	+1.00
Ascot	20	57	35.1	+30.08	26	97	26.8	+78.51	0	3	0	-3.00
Chepstow	11	61	18	-19.53	28	151	18.5	-25.25	4	12	33.3	+4.00
Fontwell	4	33	12.1	-17.60	35	133	26.3	-13.94	4	14	28.6	-0.21
Stratford	8	50	16	-26.48	32	108	29.6	-0.73	0	2	0	-2.00
Newbury	10	52	19.2	-20.77	24	105	22.9	-19.24	4	11	36.4	+1.41
Warwick	14	43	32.6	-10.60	19	103	18.4	+1.98	2	10	20	-0.75
Hereford	9	27	33.3	-8.65	25	82	30.5	-6.42	1	3	33.3	+1.50
Uttoxeter	9	36	25	-7.92	26	120	21.7	-48.64	0			
Market Rasen	9	30	30	-5.14	24	78	30.8	+5.02	0	2	0	-2.00
Sandown	11	50	22	+19.38	18	72	25	-10.91	0			
Wincanton	5	39	12.8	-18.43	23	122	18.9	-5.27	1	11	9.1	-4.50
Ludlow	4	21	19	-6.25	23	84	27.4	-13.43	1	6	16.7	-4.33
Haydock	7	37	18.9	-17.43	15	97	15.5	-40.46	2	4	50	-1.21
Bangor	4	20	20	-4.68	17	77	22.1	-30.61	0	5	0	-5.00
Leicester	4	15	26.7	-3.90	13	51	25.5	-11.61	0			
Kempton	8	57	14	-16.20	8	72	11.1	-45.67	0	5	0	-5.00
Folkestone	1	4	25	-1.25	14	25	56	+1.65	1	3	33.3	+1.00
Aintree	4	85	4.7	-60.39	10	95	10.5	-24.67	1	3	33.3	+0.25
Towcester	0	10	0	-10.00	10	26	38.5	+2.90	3	5	60	+2.98
Southwell	3	20	15	-14.36	8	43	18.6	-26.07	1	1	100	+3.33
Wolverhampton	3	7	42.9	-3.31	9	23	39.1	+7.34	0			
Doncaster	5	14	35.7	+5.50	6	15	40	+11.03	0	2	0	-2.00
Sedgefield	4	7	57.1	+9.17	5	11	45.5	+7.97	0	1	0	-1.00
Lingfield	7	8	87.5	+9.19	1	9	11.1	-4.50	0			
Huntingdon	2	10	20	-5.20	5	29	17.2	-17.86	0	1	0	-1.00
Cartmel	1	5	20	-2.25	5	11	45.5	+2.84	0			
Ayr	1	23	4.3	-2.00	2	19	10.5	-12.83	0			
Perth	0	1	0	-1.00	2	5	40	+0.85	0			
Fakenham	0				1	3	33.3	+1.00	1	2	50	+2.00
Wetherby	0	5	0	-5.00	2	10	20	-7.30	0			
Catterick	0				1	2	50	+0.50	0			
Newcastle	0				0	1	0	-1.00	0			

Race type

	Chases				Hurdles			
	W	R	%	£1 stake	W	R	%	£1 stake
Handicap	172	850	20.2	-38.97	40	228	17.5	-52.61
Novice	177	496	35.7	+72.12	112	398	28.1	+22.51
Maiden	8	22	36.4	-1.51	10	64	15.6	-24.98
Selling	0	3	0	-3.00	6	17	35.3	+5.00
Claiming	-	-	-	-	4	14	28.6	+2.06
Amateur	4	32	12.5	-12.17	5	19	26.3	-0.74

Class of race

	Chases				Hurdles				Bumpers			
	W	R	%	£1 stake	W	R	%	£1 stake	W	R	%	£1 stake
A	47	263	17.9	-49.09	12	85	14.1	-2.46	2	8	25	+9.00
B	56	268	20.9	+51.79	14	74	18.9	-12.78	0	2	0	-2.00
C	55	206	26.7	-19.55	17	82	20.7	-11.93	-	-	-	-
D	109	368	29.6	-9.08	37	141	26.2	-22.02	-	-	-	-
E	77	231	33.3	+39.99	68	261	26.1	-14.49	-	-	-	-
F	16	59	27.1	+10.56	14	51	27.5	+8.00	-	-	-	-
G	0	3	0	-3.00	6	18	33.3	+4.00	-	-	-	-
H	15	35	42.9	+9.05	-	-	-	-	20	94	21.3	-18.16

Winning jockeys

	Chases				Hurdles				Bumpers			
	W	R	%	£1 stake	W	R	%	£1 stake	W	R	%	£1 stake
J Tizzard	132	531	24.9	-69.41	62	246	25.2	-18.69	3	25	12	-14.50
T J Murphy	63	228	27.6	+18.68	27	103	26.2	+7.36	6	17	35.3	+10.50
R Walsh	45	158	28.5	+26.62	21	84	25	+19.82	8	19	42.1	+15.60
M A Fitzgerald	26	80	32.5	+16.57	3	17	17.6	-6.56	1	1	100	+2.25
S Stronge	17	70	24.3	+5.34	9	48	18.8	-12.68	2	4	50	+2.50
R P McNally	11	39	28.2	-1.61	12	37	32.4	+2.54	1	7	14.3	-1.00
A P McCoy	9	34	26.5	-7.60	2	11	18.2	-3.67	0	3	0	-3.00
C Williams	9	39	23.1	-15.18	1	4	25	-2.71	0	1	0	-1.00
R Thornton	9	31	29	+12.05	0	10	0	-10.00	0	1	0	-1.00
P J Brennan	1	7	14.3	-3.50	8	36	22.2	-8.25	0	10	0	-10.00

By month

	Chases				Hurdles				Bumpers			
	W	R	%	£1 stake	W	R	%	£1 stake	W	R	%	£1 stake
January	32	120	26.7	-5.62	13	72	18.1	-9.55	1	2	50	+1.00
February	42	167	25.1	-9.81	12	71	16.9	-21.51	3	8	37.5	+9.41
March	38	163	23.3	-9.55	19	83	22.9	-10.90	3	10	30	+3.50
April	57	213	26.8	+14.98	35	119	29.4	+25.92	6	22	27.3	+2.50
May	29	113	25.7	+23.61	12	63	19	-21.02	1	18	5.6	-13.67
June	5	32	15.6	+2.50	4	13	30.8	+2.38	0	2	0	-2.00
July	7	23	30.4	+8.13	3	7	42.9	+6.12	1	1	100	+2.25
August	9	25	36	+14.68	3	7	42.9	-0.42	1	5	20	-3.33
September	7	29	24.1	-7.28	3	10	30	+6.50	0			
October	44	126	34.9	+9.83	19	56	33.9	+4.84	4	13	30.8	-3.06
November	65	225	28.9	+48.14	27	117	23.1	-15.81	2	16	12.5	-1.75
December	40	199	20.1	-61.93	18	94	19.1	-18.22	0	7	0	-7.00

Not forgetting ...

	Chases				Hurdles				Bumpers			
	W	R	%	£1 stake	W	R	%	£1 stake	W	R	%	£1 stake
Favourites	205	505	40.6	-28.08	92	208	44.2	+14.79	13	34	38.2	+1.01
After a break	66	229	28.8	+34.72	31	132	23.5	-10.34	7	22	31.8	+6.69

Sponsored by Stan James

All runners

	Wins	Runs	%	2nd	3rd	rest	Win prize	Total prize	£1 Stake
Chases	375	1435	26.1	244	172	644	3,959,773.16	6,249,192.70	+27.68
Hurdles	168	712	23.6	133	91	320	893,772.44	1,393,210.00	-51.68
Bumpers	22	104	21.2	16	9	55	69,638.50	105,190.00	-12.16
Totals	565	2251	25.1	393	272	1019	4,923,184.10	7,747,592.70	-36.16

Paul Nicholls

RUNNER-UP to Pipe in the championship for the last five years, Paul Nicholls has said that he'll never win it because he can't match his main adversary for numbers of runners.

But Nicholls does significantly better than Pipe in the most valuable races (in the last five years, he's won 47 Class A chases to Pipe's 30) and, since the championship is decided by prizemoney won, this gives him some hope of winning it one day.

His operation is geared to chasing – not only does he have many more runners over fences than hurdles, but his strike-rate with his chasers is better at most levels.

His chasers can be backed with confidence at Wincanton, Chepstow, Fontwell (oddly) and Sandown.

Course records

	Chases				Hurdles				Bumpers			
	W	R	%	£1 stake	W	R	%	£1 stake	W	R	%	£1 stake
Wincanton	44	133	33.1	+47.67	32	114	28.1	-3.44	3	9	33.3	+1.00
Chepstow	35	97	36.1	+26.27	20	77	26	+0.01	4	11	36.4	+3.65
Fontwell	32	82	39	+26.79	12	42	28.6	+6.20	1	8	12.5	-5.25
Taunton	22	70	31.4	+9.09	16	72	22.2	+4.75	2	9	22.2	-4.71
Newton Abbot	22	76	28.9	+11.72	10	33	30.3	+9.69	1	13	7.7	-2.00
Cheltenham	19	148	12.8	-53.01	10	47	21.3	+2.25	1	5	20	-1.00
Exeter	16	81	19.8	-1.45	13	48	27.1	-8.84	0	10	0	-10.00
Sandown	25	86	29.1	+42.22	2	13	15.4	-8.42	0			
Plumpton	16	41	39	-0.67	5	17	29.4	-4.30	1	2	50	-0.09
Uttoxeter	12	61	19.7	-10.55	8	21	38.1	+2.46	1	2	50	+3.00
Kempton	16	67	23.9	+2.84	4	22	18.2	+5.25	0	1	0	-1.00
Worcester	11	34	32.4	+13.25	3	13	23.1	+1.10	2	6	33.3	-1.08
Warwick	13	35	37.1	+7.61	1	18	5.6	-13.00	1	1	100	+2.25
Newbury	11	55	20	-19.99	2	25	8	-18.09	1	3	33.3	+10.00
Ayr	7	29	24.1	-2.64	5	12	41.7	+4.42	1	1	100	+4.50
Stratford	7	42	16.7	-3.01	4	10	40	+9.13	0			
Ascot	9	39	23.1	-5.52	1	12	8.3	-10.27	0	1	0	-1.00
Folkestone	7	16	43.8	-0.40	3	10	30	-3.59	0	1	0	-1.00
Ludlow	6	28	21.4	-16.34	2	14	14.3	-9.80	1	9	11.1	-5.25
Aintree	7	59	11.9	-29.90	1	14	7.1	+20.00	0	1	0	-1.00
Wetherby	5	18	27.8	-5.94	3	11	27.3	-5.05	0			
Hereford	3	15	20	-7.79	3	15	20	-8.22	1	5	20	-0.67
Perth	5	15	33.3	+6.30	0	2	0	-2.00	1	1	100	+2.50
Southwell	3	8	37.5	+6.50	3	5	60	+4.13	0			
Bangor	4	9	44.4	+5.12	1	3	33.3	-1.56	0	2	0	-2.00
Fakenham	5	9	55.6	+6.13	0	3	0	-3.00	0			
Market Rasen	3	11	27.3	+3.67	1	3	33.3	+2.50	0	1	0	-1.00
Haydock	3	21	14.3	-5.64	0	11	0	-11.00	0			
Doncaster	3	13	23.1	+2.00	0	3	0	-3.00	0			
Leicester	2	9	22.2	-1.42	1	3	33.3	-1.75	0			
Sedgefield	1	5	20	-3.60	1	2	50	+1.25	0			
Kelso	1	2	50	-0.64	0	1	0	-1.00	0			
Lingfield	0	2	0	-2.00	1	5	20	+2.50	0			
Cartmel	0	1	0	-1.00	0				0			
Carlisle	0	2	0	-2.00	0				0			
Newcastle	0	5	0	-5.00	0				0			
Towcester	0	1	0	-1.00	0	2	0	-2.00	0			
Huntingdon	0	10	0	-10.00	0	8	0	-8.00	0	2	0	-2.00
Wolverhampton	0				0	1	0	-1.00	0			

Race type

	Chases				Hurdles			
	W	R	%	£1 stake	W	R	%	£1 stake
Handicap	130	763	17	-86.83	123	766	16.1	-60.49
Novice	95	364	26.1	+46.87	170	704	24.1	-112.58
Maiden	1	6	16.7	-2.50	15	93	16.1	-39.93
Selling	2	4	50	+0.63	11	46	23.9	+5.31
Claiming	-	-	-	-	3	19	15.8	-8.50
Amateur	2	15	13.3	-9.92	6	39	15.4	-5.75

Class of race

	Chases				Hurdles				Bumpers			
	W	R	%	£1 stake	W	R	%	£1 stake	W	R	%	£1 stake
A	10	95	10.5	+16.75	16	117	13.7	+4.88	0	7	0	-7.00
B	17	136	12.5	-41.42	25	130	19.2	-18.82	1	3	33.3	+1.50
C	24	151	15.9	-19.71	14	119	11.8	-24.68	-	-	-	-
D	83	344	24.1	-31.72	80	359	22.3	-48.14	-	-	-	-
E	49	208	23.6	+14.24	129	514	25.1	-36.68	-	-	-	-
F	23	116	19.8	+3.23	28	197	14.2	-44.80	-	-	-	-
G	2	4	50	+0.63	11	50	22	+1.31	-	-	-	-
H	1	3	33.3	-1.20	-	-	-	-	31	146	21.2	-16.06

Winning jockeys

	Chases				Hurdles				Bumpers			
	W	R	%	£1 stake	W	R	%	£1 stake	W	R	%	£1 stake
R Johnson	77	338	22.8	+19.81	120	457	26.3	-18.71	16	49	32.7	+11.90
P Flynn	23	150	15.3	-47.19	42	222	18.9	-5.66	7	32	21.9	+4.62
R Widger	31	189	16.4	+12.55	35	256	13.7	-86.81	2	29	6.9	-23.58
A P McCoy	20	56	35.7	+14.20	16	48	33.3	+1.89	1	3	33.3	0.00
A Bateman	3	42	7.1	-22.00	9	60	15	-16.90	1	9	11.1	-2.00
G Tormey	1	10	10	+1.00	10	47	21.3	+20.25	0	3	0	-3.00
A Thornton	7	22	31.8	+0.60	4	17	23.5	-0.52	0	1	0	-1.00
D O'Meara	3	9	33.3	+24.50	5	27	18.5	-15.44	2	6	33.3	+2.00
A Honeyball	3	10	30	-2.08	4	15	26.7	+19.50	0			
S Durack	3	19	15.8	+1.50	3	15	20	-3.47	0	2	0	-2.00

By month

	Chases				Hurdles				Bumpers			
	W	R	%	£1 stake	W	R	%	£1 stake	W	R	%	£1 stake
January	19	108	17.6	-7.18	22	133	16.5	-40.74	1	12	8.3	-10.90
February	19	89	21.3	+8.89	16	140	11.4	-43.90	3	21	14.3	-6.50
March	19	114	16.7	-32.10	26	145	17.9	+31.15	6	30	20	-6.00
April	19	120	15.8	+29.65	34	157	21.7	-23.53	4	15	26.7	+14.75
May	18	79	22.8	+16.67	25	131	19.1	-15.86	2	10	20	-3.00
June	7	41	17.1	+7.13	17	82	20.7	-0.07	0	2	0	-2.00
July	7	37	18.9	-10.33	18	52	34.6	+18.44	1	2	50	-0.20
August	18	54	33.3	+20.17	23	91	25.3	-9.58	1	5	20	-3.33
September	10	44	22.7	-7.99	22	74	29.7	+1.14	0	1	0	-1.00
October	27	98	27.6	-15.10	30	127	23.6	-12.68	5	17	29.4	-1.75
November	27	143	18.9	-28.08	43	178	24.2	-18.74	9	29	31	+9.37
December	20	131	15.3	-38.43	27	176	15.3	-52.57	0	12	0	-12.00

Not forgetting ...

	Chases				Hurdles				Bumpers			
	W	R	%	£1 stake	W	R	%	£1 stake	W	R	%	£1 stake
Favourites	97	287	33.8	-41.59	172	447	38.5	-35.68	21	37	56.8	+20.19
After a break	31	143	21.7	+4.37	41	233	17.6	-60.18	4	19	21.1	-10.75

Sponsored by Stan James

All runners

	Wins	Runs	%	2nd	3rd	rest	Win prize	Total prize	£1 Stake
Chases	210	1058	19.8	175	163	510	1,625,702.37	2,559,346.00	-56.71
Hurdles	303	1486	20.4	241	181	761	1,708,392.31	2,687,266.00	-166.93
Bumpers	32	156	20.5	21	16	86	68,159.10	99,357.00	-22.56
Totals	545	2700	20.2	437	360	1357	3,402,253.78	5,345,969.00	-246.20

Philip Hobbs

SOMERSET'S third-best trainer, Hobbs may be rather fed-up with his prolific neighbours.

Martin Pipe wins much more money, Paul Nicholls has a better strike-rate (Hobbs has saddled 20 per cent more runners than Nicholls over the last five years, but they've yielded fewer wins and 30 per cent less prizemoney).

But, surprisingly, he does much the best of the three at local Exeter, where his chasers have proved profitable for level-stakes backers. And punters should make friends with the unglamorous Hobbs when it comes to the biggest races – alone among the top 20 trainers, his runners in Class A contests have re-turned level-stakes profits.

As with Nicholls, his good results over fences appear to derive from novice races rather than handicaps. He does well with his chasers throughout the summer, though his hurdlers seem to peak in July for some reason. Though his strike-rate dips in April, he does well at Aintree.

Course records

	Chases				Hurdles				Bumpers			
	W	R	%	£1 stake	W	R	%	£1 stake	W	R	%	£1 stake
Exeter	26	99	26.3	+34.04	34	156	21.8	-30.15	3	9	33.3	-3.10
Newton Abbot	20	82	24.4	-10.50	28	132	21.2	-37.07	3	11	27.3	+6.55
Stratford	19	55	34.5	+17.01	20	70	28.6	+8.86	1	3	33.3	+0.75
Taunton	11	61	18	-20.25	22	120	18.3	-21.06	2	7	28.6	+0.75
Chepstow	16	62	25.8	+12.24	17	76	22.4	+5.99	2	9	22.2	-1.25
Wincanton	7	54	13	-28.38	23	100	23	+12.43	5	15	33.3	+17.50
Worcester	10	54	18.5	-3.67	20	92	21.7	-8.86	1	8	12.5	-6.33
Ludlow	12	37	32.4	+0.50	11	48	22.9	-13.70	3	19	15.8	-9.40
Cheltenham	9	69	13	-17.25	15	107	14	-18.10	2	10	20	-2.25
Fontwell	12	37	32.4	+25.01	10	56	17.9	-19.35	0	7	0	-7.00
Hereford	4	35	11.4	-19.60	15	69	21.7	+4.24	2	5	40	+0.10
Uttoxeter	9	40	22.5	-1.80	11	48	22.9	+4.74		0		
Kempton	8	40	20	-2.88	5	44	11.4	-21.55	1	6	16.7	-1.00
Newbury	7	40	17.5	+8.78	5	62	8.1	-36.67	1	9	11.1	-5.75
Sandown	3	34	8.8	-21.75	9	46	19.6	+12.23	1	7	14.3	-5.20
Warwick	5	33	15.2	-7.25	7	33	21.2	-2.00	1	11	9.1	-9.43
Aintree	5	35	14.3	+10.00	5	29	17.2	+19.00	0	4	0	-4.00
Ascot	5	32	15.6	-16.13	3	46	6.5	-37.93	0	3	0	-3.00
Perth	2	15	13.3	-10.25	6	16	37.5	+4.14		0		
Huntingdon	3	19	15.8	-13.23	5	17	29.4	+16.51	0	4	0	-4.00
Ayr	3	18	16.7	+46.50	3	6	50	+5.00	1	1	100	+4.00
Bangor	3	16	18.8	-1.10	3	23	13	-16.27	1	3	33.3	+3.00
Plumpton	3	17	17.6	0.00	4	15	26.7	-2.76		0		
Haydock	2	17	11.8	-6.50	4	25	16	-8.75	0	1	0	-1.00
Towcester	3	17	17.6	+3.50	1	7	14.3	-4.38	2	2	100	+9.50
Southwell	0	3	0	-3.00	5	8	62.5	+12.55		0		
Folkestone	1	4	25	-1.00	4	10	40	+2.80	0	1		-1.00
Wetherby	0	2	0	-2.00	3	4	75	+7.85		0		
Lingfield	0	3	0	-3.00	2	5	40	+3.67		0		
Doncaster	0	6	0	-6.00	1	3	33.3	+0.25		0		
Leicester	1	10	10	-8.56	0	6	0	-6.00		0		
Musselburgh	1	2	50	-0.20		0				0		
Market Rasen	0	5	0	-5.00	1	5	20	-3.60		0		
Wolverhampton		0			1	2	50	+1.00		0		
Kelso	0	1	0	-1.00		0				0		
Carlisle		0				0			0	1	0	-1.00
Newcastle	0	4	0	-4.00		0				0		

Race type

	Chases				Hurdles			
	W	R	%	£1 stake	W	R	%	£1 stake
Handicap	70	412	17	+25.81	111	581	19.1	+123.67
Novice	61	277	22	-12.68	114	568	20.1	-88.96
Maiden	0	2	0	-2.00	5	54	9.3	-36.08
Selling	1	1	100	+5.00	4	36	11.1	-7.75
Claiming	-	-	-	-	3	9	33.3	+5.88
Amateur	2	12	16.7	+25.00	2	13	15.4	+1.00

Class of race

	Chases				Hurdles				Bumpers			
	W	R	%	£1 stake	W	R	%	£1 stake	W	R	%	£1 stake
A	6	43	14	-17.42	24	84	28.6	+70.84	3	12	25	+25.25
B	15	72	20.8	+61.58	15	89	16.9	+18.99	0	2	0	-2.00
C	11	75	14.7	-29.24	21	102	20.6	+24.31	-	-	-	-
D	39	203	19.2	-52.51	74	320	23.1	+17.59	-	-	-	-
E	27	140	19.3	-11.27	65	365	17.8	-77.54	-	-	-	-
F	19	90	21.1	+41.62	17	149	11.4	-46.07	-	-	-	-
G	1	1	100	+5.00	4	38	10.5	-9.75	-	-	-	-
H	0				-	-	-	-	28	145	19.3	-33.06

Winning jockeys

	Chases				Hurdles				Bumpers			
	W	R	%	£1 stake	W	R	%	£1 stake	W	R	%	£1 stake
L Cooper	21	126	16.7	-16.15	75	416	18	-2.01	9	54	16.7	-16.50
A P McCoy	28	86	32.6	+9.18	27	84	32.1	+12.42	0	8	0	-8.00
R McGrath	19	128	14.8	-29.33	26	156	16.7	-32.80	5	29	17.2	-8.67
A Dobbin	9	36	25	+12.08	16	48	33.3	+22.65	0	2	0	-2.00
T J Phelan	0	1	0	-1.00	14	52	26.9	+35.71	1	6	16.7	-3.50
N Williamson	3	15	20	+2.25	9	33	27.3	-10.63	3	8	37.5	-2.15
R Johnson	7	26	26.9	+13.75	6	41	14.6	+26.50	0	4	0	-4.00
B Hitchcott	2	17	11.8	-1.67	7	40	17.5	-2.54	3	7	42.9	+12.50
B J Geraghty	1	7	14.3	-3.50	9	26	34.6	+25.98	0			
J R Kavanagh	2	28	7.1	-22.84	4	19	21.1	+21.90	2	4	50	+0.88

By month

	Chases				Hurdles				Bumpers			
	W	R	%	£1 stake	W	R	%	£1 stake	W	R	%	£1 stake
January	7	76	9.2	-43.08	26	139	18.7	+0.66	2	13	15.4	-5.00
February	15	79	19	-7.69	28	149	18.8	-3.57	3	23	13	-10.00
March	11	66	16.7	+17.02	24	124	19.4	-13.42	7	26	26.9	-6.29
April	10	42	23.8	+29.33	18	83	21.7	+73.21	4	16	25	+21.00
May	13	41	31.7	+19.25	15	70	21.4	+0.38	1	8	12.5	-5.00
June	4	20	20	-2.84	5	34	14.7	-11.75	0	2	0	-2.00
July	2	8	25	+28.00	3	31	9.7	-17.50	0	4	0	-4.00
August	3	17	17.6	+1.25	10	56	17.9	-19.87	1	3	33.3	+4.00
September	4	19	21.1	-2.25	6	38	15.8	-7.08	2	3	66.7	+5.00
October	15	73	20.5	-4.23	30	128	23.4	+35.48	5	22	22.7	+6.91
November	21	100	21	-22.50	29	169	17.2	-58.17	4	21	19	-4.88
December	13	83	15.7	-14.50	26	126	20.6	+20.00	2	18	11.1	-9.56

Not forgetting ...

	Chases				Hurdles				Bumpers			
	W	R	%	£1 stake	W	R	%	£1 stake	W	R	%	£1 stake
Favourites	49	148	33.1	-23.47	111	262	42.4	+40.46	17	41	41.5	+4.44
After a break	18	100	18	-20.16	19	155	12.3	-45.96	9	33	27.3	+12.57

Sponsored by Stan James

All runners

	Wins	Runs	%	2nd	3rd	rest	Win prize	Total prize	£1 Stake
Chases	118	624	18.9	108	84	314	976,814.95	1,517,957.00	-2.25
Hurdles	220	1147	19.2	149	123	655	1,511,082.37	2,412,712.00	-1.62
Bumpers	31	159	19.5	26	22	80	93,457.89	143,827.00	-9.81
Totals	369	1930	19.1	283	229	1049	2,581,355.21	4,074,496.00	-13.68

Jonjo O'Neill

SINCE moving to Jackdaws Castle near Cheltenham, Jonjo O'Neill has enjoyed a rapid improvement in the quality of his string.

Though he won one less race last season than he had the season before, his prizemoney haul increased by almost 60 per cent, partly due to Mini Sensation's Welsh National and three winners at the Festival.

Jonjo's runners have returned level-stakes profits at both his local track and at Aintree. At a more prosaic level, look out for his raids on Ludlow.

Handicaps are his thing, and you could have made a decent return backing him blindly in such races.

Course records

	Chases				Hurdles				Bumpers			
	W	R	%	£1 stake	W	R	%	£1 stake	W	R	%	£1 stake
Bangor	6	32	18.8	-8.42	19	59	32.2	+38.59	0	4	0	-4.00
Carlisle	7	54	13	-18.95	12	62	19.4	+16.13	4	10	40	+6.25
Wetherby	6	27	22.2	-10.41	16	66	24.2	+21.72	1	5	20	-2.63
Perth	9	29	31	+23.13	10	44	22.7	-8.96	3	5	60	+6.50
Uttoxeter	9	37	24.3	+3.36	12	63	19	-24.01	1	3	33.3	-0.25
Haydock	2	23	8.7	-19.02	17	62	27.4	+2.51	1	5	20	-2.50
Cheltenham	7	32	21.9	+27.20	10	66	15.2	+10.14	1	6	16.7	-2.75
Aintree	8	18	44.4	+32.80	5	26	19.2	+40.91	1	4	25	+22.00
Kelso	7	29	24.1	+2.58	6	21	28.6	+8.83	0			
Stratford	5	16	31.3	+11.25	8	37	21.6	+2.39	0			
Doncaster	2	12	16.7	+0.91	10	33	30.3	+15.83	0	2	0	-2.00
Ludlow	5	18	27.8	+8.41	5	15	33.3	+30.50	1	2	50	-0.17
Warwick	2	13	15.4	-7.50	6	30	20	+2.83	3	7	42.9	+6.88
Market Rasen	6	31	19.4	+2.03	5	48	10.4	-32.55	0	7	0	-7.00
Huntingdon	6	12	50	+13.55	4	18	22.2	-7.15	0	10	0	-10.00
Ayr	3	31	9.7	-13.75	6	50	12	-24.25	0	10	0	-10.00
Kempton	1	20	5	-17.25	7	32	21.9	+0.58	1	3	33.3	0.00
Chepstow	1	12	8.3	-3.00	7	35	20	-2.08	1	8	12.5	-6.09
Newcastle	2	25	8	-12.50	7	34	20.6	+27.10	0	5	0	-5.00
Southwell	2	9	22.2	-2.13	6	23	26.1	+3.81	1	4	25	+1.00
Sedgefield	1	16	6.3	-14.09	7	27	25.9	+11.33	1	3	33.3	+5.00
Hexham	2	14	14.3	-3.63	4	20	20	-0.75	2	5	40	+2.50
Newbury	2	14	14.3	-2.00	4	31	12.9	-20.16	1	5	20	+3.00
Sandown	0	9	0	-9.00	6	37	16.2	+1.25	1	5	20	+2.00
Worcester	0	6	0	-6.00	5	32	15.6	-8.29	2	10	20	+1.50
Catterick	3	11	27.3	+1.50	2	26	7.7	-15.50	1	2	50	+1.00
Musselburgh	3	4	75	+17.50	3	22	13.6	-10.00	0	4	0	-4.00
Ascot	3	12	25	+1.60	0	16	0	-16.00	2	5	40	-0.50
Exeter	0	2	0	-2.00	2	13	15.4	-2.50	1	4	25	+4.00
Leicester	2	9	22.2	+2.33	1	9	11.1	-7.39	0			
Towcester	1	10	10	-6.00	2	8	25	-2.09	0	1	0	-1.00
Newton Abbot	0	4	0	-4.00	2	8	25	+9.50	1	2	50	-0.56
Fakenham	1	2	50	+0.50	1	4	25	-1.13	0	1	0	-1.00
Fontwell	1	3	33.3	+1.50	1	8	12.5	-5.13	0	1	0	-1.00
Wincanton	1	10	10	-6.75	1	18	5.6	-16.27	0	4	0	-4.00
Wolverhampton	1	1	100	+20.00	1	6	16.7	-3.38	0			
Hereford	1	8	12.5	+3.00	0	5	0	-5.00	0	3	0	-3.00
Cartmel	0	3	0	-3.00	0	21	0	-21.00	0			
Taunton	0				0	2	0	-2.00	0	1	0	-1.00
Plumpton	0	4	0	-4.00	0	4	0	-4.00	0	1	0	-1.00
Folkestone	0	2	0	-2.00	0	6	0	-6.00	0	2	0	-2.00

Race type

	Chases				Hurdles			
	W	R	%	£1 stake	W	R	%	£1 stake
Handicap	44	281	15.7	-42.45	49	387	12.7	-45.57
Novice	78	238	32.8	-21.53	131	560	23.4	-73.94
Maiden	4	15	26.7	-3.89	17	77	22.1	-33.36
Selling		0				0		
Claiming	-	-	-	-	1	4	25	+1.00
Amateur	2	8	25	+23.50	3	10	30	+15.50

Class of race

	Chases				Hurdles				Bumpers			
	W	R	%	£1 stake	W	R	%	£1 stake	W	R	%	£1 stake
A	16	121	13.2	-46.26	22	163	13.5	-41.89	2	15	13.3	-5.50
B	25	107	23.4	+8.19	17	125	13.6	-23.38	0	4	0	-4.00
C	12	63	19	-18.18	29	156	18.6	+13.67	-	-	-	-
D	52	162	32.1	+7.89	66	286	23.1	-15.54	-	-	-	-
E	29	96	30.2	+13.51	63	271	23.2	-80.15	-	-	-	-
F	1	8	12.5	+3.00	7	34	20.6	+11.53	-	-	-	-
G		0				0			-	-	-	-
H	2	7	28.6	+4.00	-	-	-	-	47	200	23.5	-15.62

Winning jockeys

	Chases				Hurdles				Bumpers			
	W	R	%	£1 stake	W	R	%	£1 stake	W	R	%	£1 stake
M A Fitzgerald	109	413	26.4	+1.47	148	655	22.6	-137.68	35	110	31.8	+20.88
M Foley	8	33	24.2	-9.06	20	91	22	+76.03	6	38	15.8	-11.38
J R Kavanagh	9	51	17.6	-20.75	16	154	10.4	-71.96	5	35	14.3	-11.63
N Williamson	1	7	14.3	+2.00	8	25	32	+7.30	0	1	0	-1.00
R Johnson	3	13	23.1	-0.13	3	13	23.1	+4.25	0	1	0	-1.00
A P McCoy	3	5	60	+5.30	2	5	40	-1.70	0	3	0	-3.00
J P McNamara		0			2	4	50	+9.50	0	1	0	-1.00
P Flynn		0				0			1	3	33.3	+5.00
R Walsh	0	2	0	-2.00	0	2	0	-2.00	1	1	100	+1.25
A Dobbin	1	1	100	+0.57	0	1	0	-1.00		0		

By month

	Chases				Hurdles				Bumpers			
	W	R	%	£1 stake	W	R	%	£1 stake	W	R	%	£1 stake
January	16	73	21.9	+0.09	29	131	22.1	-15.07	7	24	29.2	-2.38
February	22	81	27.2	-27.13	25	150	16.7	-9.88	6	30	20	+0.13
March	17	78	21.8	+15.54	22	161	13.7	-87.96	7	36	19.4	-3.70
April	9	71	12.7	-33.20	13	135	9.6	-90.75	5	30	16.7	-12.75
May	5	32	15.6	-6.60	14	78	17.9	-19.08	8	28	28.6	+4.04
June	3	12	25	+4.50	8	29	27.6	-3.94	2	12	16.7	-4.33
July	4	12	33.3	-3.68	0	8	0	-8.00	2	4	50	+2.25
August	0	1	0	-1.00	0	3	0	-3.00	0	2	0	-2.00
September	0	5	0	-5.00	3	7	42.9	+0.10	0	2	0	-2.00
October	9	19	47.4	+27.35	7	39	17.9	-7.48	2	7	28.6	+4.00
November	19	78	24.4	-16.89	34	123	27.6	+39.10	6	20	30	-1.13
December	33	102	32.4	+18.18	49	171	28.7	+70.20	4	24	16.7	-7.25

Not forgetting ...

	Chases				Hurdles				Bumpers			
	W	R	%	£1 stake	W	R	%	£1 stake	W	R	%	£1 stake
Favourites	80	197	40.6	-12.43	111	287	38.7	-44.09	29	78	37.2	-2.12
After a break	42	121	34.7	+53.09	39	186	21	+15.60	1	20	5	-17.50

Sponsored by Stan James

All runners

	Wins	Runs	%	2nd	3rd	rest	Win prize	Total prize	£1 Stake
Chases	137	564	24.3	85	68	274	1,371,060.35	2,150,611.00	-27.85
Hurdles	204	1035	19.7	162	114	554	1,416,406.55	2,262,409.00	-135.76
Bumpers	49	219	22.4	41	28	101	116,714.30	172,379.00	-25.12
Totals	390	1818	21.5	288	210	929	2,904,181.20	4,585,399.00	-188.73

Nicky Henderson

IF a big-race winner goes back to Lambourn in triumph this season, chances are it'll be the Seven Barrows yard that hosts the party.

For some years now, Nicky Henderson has been the only consistently big-time trainer in the area – the next best last season was Charlie Mann, eighteenth in the prizemoney list.

But Henderson maintains his level of performance from one year to the next. Though his total number of winners last season was possibly a little disappointing, he broke through the £1m barrier for the first time and his team for this season seems well up to scratch (see page 11).

Of course, Henderson's consistency is a problem for punters, because everyone knows they've got a chance of drawing if they follow him, so his runners don't usually start at value prices.

But he has the best strike-rate of the top 20 trainers with chasers absent for 120 days or more, and a healthy profit can be made by backing such horses.

His focus on getting good chasers means that his hurdlers don't usually make profits but it's interesting that they do just that at Kempton and Newbury.

Course records

	Chases				Hurdles				Bumpers			
	W	R	%	£1 stake	W	R	%	£1 stake	W	R	%	£1 stake
Kempton	18	62	29	+2.27	20	98	20.4	+22.07	5	15	33.3	+11.88
Newbury	8	43	18.6	-12.43	30	133	22.6	+30.86	2	17	11.8	-3.25
Cheltenham	14	64	21.9	+28.10	12	102	11.8	-33.33	2	14	14.3	-5.00
Sandown	11	44	25	+15.50	11	61	18	-3.77	4	9	44.4	+7.80
Huntingdon	5	21	23.8	-0.30	10	46	21.7	-16.09	5	18	27.8	+4.50
Ascot	7	45	15.6	-27.09	10	62	16.1	-15.77	1	5	20	-1.25
Ludlow	6	14	42.9	+2.95	6	25	24	-5.65	5	15	33.3	+4.25
Wincanton	5	14	35.7	-2.56	8	35	22.9	-5.83	3	8	37.5	+8.10
Doncaster	8	12	66.7	+4.05	7	21	33.3	+8.25	0	3	0	-3.00
Hereford	4	12	33.3	+2.65	7	23	30.4	+19.71	3	9	33.3	+2.63
Plumpton	4	9	44.4	+12.75	9	25	36	+8.45	0			
Folkestone	6	11	54.5	+8.17	6	18	33.3	-0.86	1	5	20	-3.60
Fakenham	2	5	40	-0.30	5	18	27.8	-5.47	5	8	62.5	+2.74
Worcester	3	14	21.4	+5.10	4	26	15.4	-10.56	5	20	25	-6.53
Leicester	8	29	27.6	-2.90	3	6	50	+7.75	0			
Fontwell	3	12	25	+2.30	7	34	20.6	+0.85	0	14	0	-14.00
Towcester	2	10	20	-4.38	4	18	22.2	+3.48	2	7	28.6	-2.38
Bangor	2	7	28.6	-4.30	3	21	14.3	-14.32	2	7	28.6	+1.00
Taunton	2	5	40	+2.63	4	25	16	-10.60	1	4	25	-1.75
Warwick	2	13	15.4	-8.77	5	22	22.7	-3.15	0	4	0	-4.00
Chepstow	0	17	0	-17.00	5	35	14.3	-21.28	2	9	22.2	+2.25
Wetherby	3	6	50	+6.23	4	13	30.8	+6.62	0	2	0	-2.00
Stratford	2	13	15.4	-2.75	4	20	20	+2.75	0	1	0	-1.00
Ayr	2	6	33.3	-1.00	3	10	30	-2.50	0	2	0	-2.00
Aintree	2	29	6.9	-15.00	1	41	2.4	-38.13	1	5	20	-2.50
Market Rasen	1	10	10	-8.20	3	8	37.5	-2.49	0	2	0	-2.00
Newton Abbot	3	5	60	+6.75	1	10	10	-8.56	0	6	0	-6.00
Haydock	1	9	11.1	-5.00	2	16	12.5	-9.90	0	3	0	-3.00
Windsor	1	1	100	+2.25	2	4	50	+1.07	0			
Uttoxeter	0	13	0	-13.00	3	23	13	-11.43	0	2	0	-2.00
Exeter	1	4	25	-1.80	1	15	6.7	-12.90	0	3	0	-3.00
Lingfield	0	1	0	-1.00	2	8	25	-5.10	0			
Perth	0	1	0	-1.00	1	6	16.7	-4.75	0	1	0	-1.00
Newcastle	0				1	1	100	+0.80				
Southwell	1	3	33.3	-0.75	0	4	0	-4.00	0	1	0	-1.00
Wolverhampton	0				0	2	0	-2.00	0			

Race type

	Chases				Hurdles			
	W	R	%	£1 stake	W	R	%	£1 stake
Handicap	45	321	14	-51.53	18	151	11.9	+5.62
Novice	69	307	22.5	+52.23	60	400	15	-22.32
Maiden	0	12	0	-12.00	3	37	8.1	-26.92
Selling	0	1	0	-1.00	0	2	0	-2.00
Claiming	-	-	-	-	0	1	0	-1.00
Amateur	0	7	0	-7.00	0	8	0	-8.00

Class of race

	Chases				Hurdles				Bumpers			
	W	R	%	£1 stake	W	R	%	£1 stake	W	R	%	£1 stake
A	19	100	19	-10.62	1	39	2.6	-37.64	0	10	0	-10.00
B	8	65	12.3	-27.26	4	48	8.3	-17.70	2	4	50	+10.25
C	17	93	18.3	+4.21	3	43	7	-25.09	-	-	-	-
D	45	226	19.9	-23.61	34	155	21.9	-9.54	-	-	-	-
E	23	122	18.9	-3.68	28	232	12.1	-42.25	-	-	-	-
F	4	28	14.3	-5.38	3	20	15	+37.75	-	-	-	-
G	0	2	0	-2.00	0	3	0	-3.00	-	-	-	-
H	4	14	28.6	-0.13	-	-	-	-	13	112	11.6	-26.70

Winning jockeys

	Chases				Hurdles				Bumpers			
	W	R	%	£1 stake	W	R	%	£1 stake	W	R	%	£1 stake
J Culloty	90	401	22.4	+13.29	46	319	14.4	-84.46	9	70	12.9	+2.30
A P McCoy	10	29	34.5	+10.35	1	9	11.1	-7.47	1	1	100	+2.25
T J Murphy	5	31	16.1	+22.00	4	17	23.5	-2.15	0	1	0	-1.00
M Batchelor	0	9	0	-9.00	7	48	14.6	+30.25	0	9	0	-9.00
R Biddlecombe	0	10	0	-10.00	3	30	10	-24.54	4	17	23.5	+2.00
L Cummins	1	5	20	-2.63	5	11	45.5	+54.12	0			
C Rafter		0			2	8	25	+8.00		0		
A Dempsey	2	7	28.6	-2.25	0	1	0	-1.00		0		
A Thornton	1	8	12.5	-5.50	1	5	20	-3.67	0	1	0	-1.00
C Llewellyn	0	2	0	-2.00	1	3	33.3	+0.75	1	2	50	+3.00

By month

	Chases				Hurdles				Bumpers			
	W	R	%	£1 stake	W	R	%	£1 stake	W	R	%	£1 stake
January	9	63	14.3	-7.29	11	67	16.4	-27.13	1	6	16.7	-4.00
February	10	69	14.5	-31.94	7	56	12.5	+9.79	3	16	18.8	+11.00
March	8	71	11.3	-28.17	5	55	9.1	-0.71	2	22	9.1	-7.00
April	11	69	15.9	-18.80	7	62	11.3	-33.45	0	15	0	-15.00
May	15	68	22.1	+34.39	7	47	14.9	-2.93	0	11	0	-11.00
June	0	10	0	-10.00	0	2	0	-2.00		0		
July		0			0	1	0	-1.00		0		
August	0	2	0	-2.00	1	1	100	+3.50		0		
September	1	12	8.3	-4.00	1	6	16.7	0.00		0		
October	18	56	32.1	+4.86	8	57	14	-27.46	1	8	12.5	+0.50
November	34	129	26.4	+29.13	14	100	14	-31.15	5	29	17.2	+0.30
December	14	101	13.9	-34.63	13	88	14.8	+15.17	3	19	15.8	-1.25

Not forgetting ...

	Chases				Hurdles				Bumpers			
	W	R	%	£1 stake	W	R	%	£1 stake	W	R	%	£1 stake
Favourites	52	137	38	-8.12	38	82	46.3	-4.45	4	19	21.1	-10.45
After a break	29	124	23.4	+1.56	11	85	12.9	-21.42	1	12	8.3	-3.50

Sponsored by Stan James

All runners

	Wins	Runs	%	2nd	3rd	rest	Win prize	Total prize	£1 Stake
Chases	120	650	18.5	115	67	348	1,586,093.94	2,592,965.00	-68.45
Hurdles	74	542	13.7	70	64	334	302,240.40	457,142.00	-97.37
Bumpers	15	126	11.9	16	11	84	45,957.50	68,300.00	-26.45
Totals	209	1318	15.9	201	142	766	1,934,291.84	3,118,407.00	-192.27

Henrietta Knight

THE most significant stat relating to this yard in 2003-04 is that Henrietta Knight is just 2-1 to become the first trainer of a triple Gold Cup winner in 38 years.

She's the ideal trainer to ensure that a champion of the quality of Best Mate can retain his ability for years. Famous for looking after her horses, she raced 83 horses a total of 284 times last season, averaging less than three and a half outings per runner (less than any of those above her in the prizemoney list).

Punters have latched onto her ability with chasers and our level-stakes statistics show how hard it is to turn a profit by backing them blindly, except at a handful of smaller tracks. However, as you'd expect, she prepares her novices well and combines a good strike-rate with a very healthy return on such runners.

Her hurdlers are generally infrequent winners – but just look at that outrageous profit on her runners over timber at Hereford.

MATES: Hen and her star

Course records

	Chases				Hurdles				Bumpers			
	W	R	%	£1 stake	W	R	%	£1 stake	W	R	%	£1 stake
Huntingdon	16	58	27.6	+8.00	3	27	11.1	-21.33	3	19	15.8	+4.50
Hereford	5	20	25	-1.38	11	35	31.4	+110.65	2	8	25	+3.50
Wincanton	8	26	30.8	-6.43	9	50	18	-2.64	0	9	0	-9.00
Ludlow	6	31	19.4	+16.82	8	34	23.5	-12.91	2	11	18.2	-4.20
Exeter	9	44	20.5	+5.12	6	45	13.3	-11.73	0	4	0	-4.00
Kempton	8	54	14.8	-18.25	5	34	14.7	-12.17	1	7	14.3	-2.00
Cheltenham	12	73	16.4	-5.30	0	37	0	-37.00	2	13	15.4	+6.50
Sandown	8	45	17.8	-18.75	3	26	11.5	-16.63	1	8	12.5	+5.00
Stratford	7	36	19.4	+21.25	4	20	20	+3.57	0			
Taunton	7	26	26.9	+1.11	2	15	13.3	-10.09	1	2	50	0.00
Bangor	5	10	50	+9.55	3	9	33.3	-4.27	0	3	0	-3.00
Doncaster	3	12	25	+11.75	2	23	8.7	-16.14	1	2	50	+4.00
Towcester	6	20	30	+8.98	0	11	0	-11.00	0	1	0	-1.00
Newbury	2	19	10.5	-0.25	3	31	9.7	-4.00	0	9	0	-9.00
Warwick	2	18	11.1	-7.00	3	26	11.5	-5.50	0	4	0	-4.00
Ascot	2	20	10	-12.25	0	11	0	-11.00	2	7	28.6	+5.25
Aintree	2	16	12.5	+1.50	2	16	12.5	-10.64	0	3	0	-3.00
Fontwell	1	9	11.1	-6.50	3	13	23.1	+3.50	0	1	0	-1.00
Leicester	3	30	10	-17.13	1	4	25	-2.47	0			
Market Rasen	4	11	36.4	-0.55	0	2	0	-2.00	0	1	0	-1.00
Uttoxeter	1	18	5.6	-15.00	2	22	9.1	-16.20	0	1	0	-1.00
Windsor	0	2	0	-2.00	2	9	22.2	-2.89	0			
Haydock	0	6	0	-6.00	1	9	11.1	-5.50	0	1	0	-1.00
Plumpton	0	9	0	-9.00	1	9	11.1	+25.00	0			
Wetherby	1	6	16.7	-1.50	0				0			
Lingfield	1	4	25	-0.75	0	3	0	-3.00	0			
Southwell	1	2	50	+0.50	0	1	0	-1.00	0			
Ayr	0				0	3	0	-3.00	0	1	0	-1.00
Chepstow	0	8	0	-8.00	0	4	0	-4.00	0	3	0	-3.00
Worcester	0	8	0	-8.00	0	3	0	-3.00	0	3	0	-3.00
Folkestone	0	2	0	-2.00	0	4	0	-4.00	0	2	0	-2.00
Newton Abbot	0	7	0	-7.00	0	6	0	-6.00	0	3	0	-3.00

Race type

		Chases				Hurdles		
	W	R	%	£1 stake	W	R	%	£1 stake
Handicap	95	533	17.8	-31.27	45	308	14.6	-72.94
Novice	69	256	27	-48.22	101	385	26.2	-61.86
Maiden	3	11	27.3	+0.85	17	102	16.7	-45.44
Selling	0				0	1	0	-1.00
Claiming	-	-	-	-	0	1	0	-1.00
Amateur	1	15	6.7	-4.00	0	11	0	-11.00

Class of race

		Chases				Hurdles				Bumpers		
	W	R	%	£1 stake	W	R	%	£1 stake	W	R	%	£1 stake
A	19	116	16.4	-8.73	7	85	8.2	-48.17	0	8	0	-8.00
B	21	118	17.8	-12.99	10	79	12.7	-31.24	1	4	25	+5.00
C	27	124	21.8	-10.69	15	75	20	-16.81	-	-	-	-
D	49	216	22.7	-29.24	49	212	23.1	-49.40	-	-	-	-
E	32	145	22.1	-45.16	73	276	26.4	-36.78	-	-	-	-
F	12	53	22.6	+18.95	6	46	13	-7.50	-	-	-	-
G	0				0	1	0	-1.00	-	-	-	-
H	3	8	37.5	+8.38	-	-	-	-	30	121	24.8	+11.55

Winning jockeys

		Chases				Hurdles				Bumpers		
	W	R	%	£1 stake	W	R	%	£1 stake	W	R	%	£1 stake
N Williamson	81	278	29.1	+50.66	60	246	24.4	-16.97	7	32	21.9	-1.83
B J Crowley	37	256	14.5	-67.69	44	235	18.7	-47.72	9	34	26.5	+7.88
A P McCoy	13	48	27.1	-7.47	12	42	28.6	-15.33	3	12	25	-3.53
S Kelly	1	8	12.5	-5.80	12	49	24.5	-6.67	2	9	22.2	0.00
R Johnson	4	31	12.9	-9.21	9	29	31	-4.51	0	0	0	0.00
F Windsor Clive	1	12	8.3	-1.00	3	24	12.5	-11.50	6	24	25	+11.25
A O'Keeffe	4	30	13.3	-11.00	2	24	8.3	-19.83	0	6	0	-6.00
A Dobbin	2	6	33.3	-0.33	2	7	28.6	+0.67	0			
R Farrant	0	3	0	-3.00	3	6	50	+6.07	1	1	100	+3.00
A Thornton	2	6	33.3	+0.75	2	10	20	-5.54	0	1	0	-1.00

By month

		Chases				Hurdles				Bumpers		
	W	R	%	£1 stake	W	R	%	£1 stake	W	R	%	£1 stake
January	31	133	23.3	-16.66	32	103	31.1	+22.86	1	7	14.3	-5.20
February	21	102	20.6	-24.94	20	121	16.5	-56.94	2	8	25	-1.25
March	21	104	20.2	-24.19	14	115	12.2	-54.94	7	16	43.8	+11.91
April	11	101	10.9	-54.76	15	100	15	-43.32	3	21	14.3	+2.50
May	9	47	19.1	+15.62	16	71	22.5	+10.77	3	13	23.1	+8.00
June	3	16	18.8	-7.60	3	20	15	-8.50	2	5	40	+0.25
July	2	8	25	-1.75	7	18	38.9	+1.69	0	3	0	-3.00
August	0	6	0	-6.00	3	14	21.4	-7.89	0	1	0	-1.00
September	2	7	28.6	-1.00	4	10	40	-0.32	1	1	100	+0.80
October	14	37	37.8	+2.08	11	34	32.4	-11.90	3	5	60	+12.25
November	22	97	22.7	+20.61	19	90	21.1	-31.09	4	28	14.3	-13.58
December	27	123	22	+18.10	16	78	20.5	-11.32	5	25	20	-3.13

Not forgetting ...

		Chases				Hurdles				Bumpers		
	W	R	%	£1 stake	W	R	%	£1 stake	W	R	%	£1 stake
Favourites	78	232	33.6	-31.32	102	255	40	-26.27	17	43	39.5	+4.30
After a break	35	153	22.9	-2.29	22	126	17.5	-40.74	4	20	20	+6.75

All runners

	Wins	Runs	%	2nd	3rd	rest	Win prize	Total prize	£1 Stake
Chases	163	781	20.9	109	109	400	1,488,936.87	2,329,745.00	-80.49
Hurdles	160	774	20.7	96	97	421	797,925.20	1,231,424.00	-190.9
Bumpers	31	133	23.3	18	13	71	67,199.40	97,586.00	+8.55
Totals	354	1688	21.0	223	219	892	2,354,061.47	3,658,755.00	-262.84

Venetia Williams

HAVING made her name as a trainer with an exceptional strike-rate, Venetia Williams has struggled to maintain that image in recent seasons.

Also, punters have latched onto her as a capable trainer, reducing the chances of getting value about one of her runners. The best call may be to focus on her chasers in November and December. Though the yard has tended to hold its form into January, the profits have not held up.

Course records

	Chases				Hurdles				Bumpers			
	W	R	%	£1 stake	W	R	%	£1 stake	W	R	%	£1 stake
Haydock	12	33	36.4	+6.49	9	37	24.3	-6.61	0	2	0	-2.00
Cheltenham	10	64	15.6	-3.83	10	52	19.2	-11.67	1	4	25	+5.00
Fontwell	11	34	32.4	+1.25	8	23	34.8	+0.86	0	8	0	-8.00
Towcester	13	32	40.6	+27.34	5	23	21.7	-3.89	0	6	0	-6.00
Uttoxeter	6	31	19.4	-2.10	11	49	22.4	-25.99	0	2	0	-2.00
Bangor	6	31	19.4	-8.46	7	28	25	-7.48	2	6	33.3	+5.38
Chepstow	6	31	19.4	+21.83	8	28	28.6	+6.45	1	7	14.3	-1.00
Taunton	8	26	30.8	+11.25	5	33	15.2	-8.25	1	3	33.3	+1.00
Stratford	7	23	30.4	+7.83	5	18	27.8	-7.76	2	3	66.7	+1.28
Folkestone	3	18	16.7	-8.83	6	14	42.9	+7.08	4	6	66.7	+7.80
Newbury	8	21	38.1	+14.90	4	36	11.1	-18.09	0	5	0	-5.00
Hereford	3	24	12.5	-6.50	8	37	21.6	-18.31	1	9	11.1	-5.00
Plumpton	7	28	25	-10.63	5	29	17.2	-18.75	0	4	0	-4.00
Kempton	7	31	22.6	-3.63	4	24	16.7	+4.08	0	2	0	-2.00
Southwell	3	8	37.5	+1.57	4	11	36.4	-2.57	3	4	75	+7.50
Huntingdon	3	20	15	-5.75	5	12	41.7	+13.83	2	6	33.3	+5.50
Market Rasen	3	13	23.1	-2.50	6	21	28.6	-10.40	1	1	100	+10.00
Exeter	3	15	20	-3.63	5	17	29.4	+1.29	1	1	100	+2.75
Fakenham	3	12	25	-5.23	5	14	35.7	+7.33	1	2	50	+0.88
Wincanton	5	29	17.2	-10.27	3	24	12.5	-12.75	1	4	25	+2.00
Ludlow	2	25	8	-17.40	5	33	15.2	-14.22	1	12	8.3	-9.25
Aintree	4	39	10.3	-12.50	3	28	10.7	-13.67	1	5	20	-1.00
Wetherby	4	15	26.7	-1.79	4	13	30.8	-2.02	0			
Leicester	4	19	21.1	-7.26	4	19	21.1	-12.52	0			
Newton Abbot	4	13	30.8	+2.82	3	20	15	-9.38	1	7	14.3	-5.33
Warwick	3	20	15	-7.75	1	18	5.6	-15.63	3	7	42.9	+5.25
Worcester	0	5	0	-5.00	5	20	25	+14.45	2	9	22.2	+2.50
Ascot	6	30	20	-7.27	0	21	0	-21.00	0	2	0	-2.00
Perth	3	18	16.7	-7.96	1	15	6.7	-11.00	0	1	0	-1.00
Sandown	3	38	7.9	-13.50	1	19	5.3	-13.50	0	1	0	-1.00
Ayr	0	8	0	-8.00	3	6	50	+5.50	0			
Lingfield	1	5	20	-2.00	1	5	20	+8.00	1	2	50	+6.50
Wolverhampton	1	3	33.3	+0.50	2	5	40	+5.36	0			
Doncaster	1	13	7.7	-8.50	1	9	11.1	-7.20	0			
Cartmel	0				1	4	25	0.00	0			
Windsor	0				1	1	100	+6.50	0			
Carlisle	0	1	0	-1.00	0				1	1	100	+0.80
Catterick	0				1	2	50	+7.00	0			
Kelso	0	1	0	-1.00	0				0			
Hexham	0				0	1	0	-1.00	0			
Newcastle	0	2	0	-2.00	0	2	0	-2.00	0			
Sedgefield	0	2	0	-2.00	0	1	0	-1.00	0			
Musselburgh	0				0	2	0	-2.00	0	1	0	-1.00

Race type

	Chases				Hurdles			
	W	R	%	£1 stake	W	R	%	£1 stake
Handicap	85	531	16	+79.61	53	385	13.8	+38.98
Novice	44	306	14.4	-26.57	46	414	11.1	-31.57
Maiden	1	16	6.3	-11.50	4	40	10	-20.75
Selling	1	3	33.3	+10.00	3	54	5.6	-8.00
Claiming	-	-	-	-	1	12	8.3	-9.90
Amateur	0	9	0	-9.00	3	16	18.8	+9.00

Class of race

	Chases				Hurdles				Bumpers			
	W	R	%	£1 stake	W	R	%	£1 stake	W	R	%	£1 stake
A	3	36	8.3	+2.50	2	15	13.3	-5.50	0	4	0	-4.00
B	11	56	19.6	+46.75	3	30	10	-8.50	0			
C	10	70	14.3	+2.75	11	52	21.2	+20.25	-	-	-	-
D	42	244	17.2	-22.18	26	180	14.4	-8.27	-	-	-	-
E	38	236	16.1	+15.21	38	304	12.5	-20.57	-	-	-	-
F	13	117	11.1	-20.50	8	96	8.3	-32.65	-	-	-	-
G	1	3	33.3	+10.00	3	58	5.2	-12.00	-	-	-	-
H	0	10	0	-10.00	-	-	-	-	7	108	6.5	-47.59

Winning jockeys

	Chases				Hurdles				Bumpers			
	W	R	%	£1 stake	W	R	%	£1 stake	W	R	%	£1 stake
D Elsworth	28	138	20.3	+43.36	19	162	11.7	-31.59	4	32	12.5	-9.59
J Crowley	28	143	19.6	+53.92	18	102	17.6	+32.22	0	18	0	-18.00
S Durack	23	182	12.6	-4.83	21	125	16.8	+20.05	1	17	5.9	-11.00
W Marston	15	65	23.1	+46.63	17	61	27.9	+38.49	0	4	0	-4.00
R Wilkinson	8	129	6.2	-84.92	7	126	5.6	-68.50	0	8	0	-8.00
G F Ryan	4	28	14.3	-6.50	2	21	9.5	-10.00	0	4	0	-4.00
P Whelan	2	12	16.7	-6.00	2	25	8	+5.00	0	2	0	-2.00
Miss S Beddoes	4	11	36.4	+10.00	0	2	0	-2.00	0	3	0	-3.00
S Stronge	3	7	42.9	+13.38	0	2	0	-2.00	0			
P Madden	0				2	8	25	+9.10	0			

By month

	Chases				Hurdles				Bumpers			
	W	R	%	£1 stake	W	R	%	£1 stake	W	R	%	£1 stake
January	5	60	8.3	-11.75	3	63	4.8	-14.71	1	7	14.3	+14.00
February	4	53	7.5	-25.00	5	58	8.6	-17.50	2	10	20	+4.91
March	8	61	13.1	-34.58	15	73	20.5	+46.63	1	17	5.9	-11.00
April	5	52	9.6	-20.00	8	67	11.9	-5.00	0	13	0	-13.00
May	16	85	18.8	+28.58	6	75	8	-42.09	0	3	0	-3.00
June	13	54	24.1	+38.75	6	34	17.6	-1.50	1	9	11.1	-6.00
July	8	51	15.7	+0.50	3	45	6.7	-34.96	0	5	0	-5.00
August	13	58	22.4	+57.63	5	48	10.4	-17.25	0	6	0	-6.00
September	5	38	13.2	-11.25	5	29	17.2	+17.00	1	4	25	+0.50
October	15	77	19.5	+26.40	10	61	16.4	+29.29	0	7	0	-7.00
November	16	105	15.2	-2.15	11	93	11.8	-35.12	0	19	0	-19.00
December	10	79	12.7	-23.58	14	89	15.7	+7.98	1	12	8.3	-1.00

Not forgetting ...

	Chases				Hurdles				Bumpers			
	W	R	%	£1 stake	W	R	%	£1 stake	W	R	%	£1 stake
Favourites	28	87	32.2	-3.14	27	65	41.5	+8.41	3	6	50	+3.41
After a break	12	74	16.2	+7.60	12	107	11.2	+1.50	0	14	0	-14.00

All runners

	Wins	Runs	%	2nd	3rd	rest	Win prize	Total prize	£1 Stake
Chases	118	773	15.3	107	101	447	785,299.10	1,209,018.00	+23.54
Hurdles	91	735	12.4	85	72	487	373,806.54	564,188.00	-67.24
Bumpers	7	112	6.3	15	10	80	12,111.80	17,279.00	-51.59
Totals	216	1620	13.3	207	183	1014	1,171,147.44	1,790,485.00	-95.29

Sue Smith

ONE of four trainers in our top 20 to make a level-stakes profit with her chasers over the five-year period, Sue Smith has plenty to offer loyal followers.

In terms of a percentage return on total stakes, it's hard not to like her record with chasers at Class B level. With a strike-rate of fractionally below one in five, she's produced profits of over 80 per cent with such runners.

Her novices have not have been over-priced, and it's with her handicap chasers that Smith has generated those profits. Interestingly, though the returns on her hurdlers have generally been poor, her handicappers over timber have also made profit.

Unusually, Smith's top four jockeys have all returned profits when riding for her (particularly Jim Crowley and Warren Marston), and she's had precious few wins when anyone else has been on board.

The yard's runners over fences have made solid profits through the summer months.

JIM CROWLEY

Course records

	Chases				Hurdles				Bumpers			
	W	R	%	£1 stake	W	R	%	£1 stake	W	R	%	£1 stake
Wetherby	15	72	20.8	+34.35	11	78	14.1	-16.71	0	9	0	-9.00
Market Rasen	14	71	19.7	+7.69	7	77	9.1	-40.50	1	8	12.5	-3.50
Haydock	7	29	24.1	+25.00	11	45	24.4	+67.68	1	8	12.5	-6.09
Southwell	5	31	16.1	+7.50	12	53	22.6	+13.54	0	4	0	-4.00
Hexham	10	51	19.6	+6.25	5	52	9.6	-19.90	1	5	20	-2.00
Carlisle	9	56	16.1	-5.70	7	37	18.9	-9.25	0	11	0	-11.00
Worcester	9	51	17.6	+13.00	5	38	13.2	-21.71	0	19	0	-19.00
Sedgefield	5	41	12.2	-23.17	6	32	18.8	+25.75	0	4	0	-4.00
Towcester	6	20	30	+11.33	3	23	13	+1.10	0	4	0	-4.00
Cartmel	6	25	24	+21.50	1	21	4.8	-13.00		0		
Catterick	1	41	2.4	-37.25	4	57	7	-33.52	2	12	16.7	+7.00
Newcastle	2	32	6.3	-25.59	4	43	9.3	+3.00	1	5	20	+16.00
Uttoxeter	5	34	14.7	+1.50	2	16	12.5	-3.50		0		
Stratford	4	20	20	-0.25	2	15	13.3	-3.00		0		
Kelso	2	21	9.5	-6.38	3	18	16.7	-7.00		0		
Perth	4	7	57.1	+40.00	0	5	0	-5.00	0	1	0	-1.00
Bangor	1	38	2.6	-35.25	2	39	5.1	-9.00	1	5	20	+6.00
Doncaster	2	27	7.4	-13.00	2	22	9.1	+30.00	0	5	0	-5.00
Ayr	2	13	15.4	-2.50	1	5	20	+6.00	0	2	0	-2.00
Aintree	3	28	10.7	-3.00	0	12	0	-12.00	0	5	0	-5.00
Warwick	2	5	40	+31.00	0	1	0	-1.00		0		
Huntingdon	0	15	0	-15.00	2	15	13.3	+7.29	0	2	0	-2.00
Sandown	0	4	0	-4.00	1	5	20	-0.50		0		
Hereford	1	6	16.7	+7.00	0	2	0	-2.00		0		
Plumpton	1	2	50	+4.00		0				0		
Cheltenham	1	12	8.3	-5.50	0	7	0	-7.00	0	2	0	-2.00
Wolverhampton	1	6	16.7	+7.00	0	7	0	-7.00		0		
Ascot	0	1	0	-1.00	0	4	0	-4.00				
Newbury	0	5	0	-5.00	0	2	0	-2.00	0	1	0	-1.00
Chepstow	0	1	0	-1.00	0	1	0	-1.00				
Leicester	0	5	0	-5.00	0	2	0	-2.00		0		
Musselburgh	0	3	0	-3.00	0	1	0	-1.00		0		

Race type

	Chases				Hurdles			
	W	R	%	£1 stake	W	R	%	£1 stake
Handicap	88	498	17.7	-33.60	131	851	15.4	-127.74
Novice	71	320	22.2	-71.47	95	547	17.4	-146.05
Maiden	4	17	23.5	+19.00	11	55	20	-10.90
Selling	0				25	143	17.5	-20.73
Claiming	-	-	-	-	13	51	25.5	+2.60
Amateur	2	5	40	+2.58	4	22	18.2	-9.65

Class of race

	Chases				Hurdles				Bumpers			
	W	R	%	£1 stake	W	R	%	£1 stake	W	R	%	£1 stake
A	3	47	6.4	-38.25	3	55	5.5	-38.59	1	7	14.3	0.00
B	14	89	15.7	-31.48	16	114	14	-45.18	0	2	0	-2.00
C	17	97	17.5	+1.14	27	155	17.4	-26.94	-	-	-	-
D	58	255	22.7	+30.15	59	364	16.2	-87.41	-	-	-	-
E	48	194	24.7	-2.37	72	403	17.9	-54.66	-	-	-	-
F	14	82	17.1	-21.59	37	207	17.9	-16.26	-	-	-	-
G		0			27	148	18.2	-18.40	-	-	-	-
H	0	3	0	-3.00	-	-	-	-	30	204	14.7	-58.66

Winning jockeys

	Chases				Hurdles				Bumpers			
	W	R	%	£1 stake	W	R	%	£1 stake	W	R	%	£1 stake
A Dempsey	59	254	23.2	+22.62	88	467	18.8	-62.16	7	50	14	-27.50
A Ross	29	117	24.8	+38.62	20	123	16.3	-52.59	5	17	29.4	+11.71
P Aspell	12	45	26.7	+12.20	9	72	12.5	+6.25	0	17	0	-17.00
G Lee	3	25	12	-10.00	17	64	26.6	+1.63	0	7	0	-7.00
M H Naughton	0	1	0	-1.00	16	100	16	-19.17	4	16	25	+1.63
F King	10	36	27.8	-8.33	7	57	12.3	-4.10	0	10	0	-10.00
A Garrity	5	29	17.2	+9.50	7	45	15.6	-4.42	0	2	0	-2.00
T Eaves	0				2	23	8.7	-10.00	6	26	23.1	-2.25
A Thornton	3	30	10	-16.20	5	28	17.9	+9.82	0	4	0	-4.00
Mr B Murphy	0	3	0	-3.00	6	27	22.2	-3.08	1	5	20	+1.00

By month

	Chases				Hurdles				Bumpers			
	W	R	%	£1 stake	W	R	%	£1 stake	W	R	%	£1 stake
January	26	103	25.2	+6.93	33	166	19.9	-2.38	6	26	23.1	+3.09
February	18	78	23.1	-25.74	19	149	12.8	-36.41	3	28	10.7	-18.05
March	14	77	18.2	+3.78	10	130	7.7	-74.55	1	20	5	-17.00
April	9	72	12.5	-32.25	13	112	11.6	-55.74	1	22	4.5	-18.00
May	10	52	19.2	-9.14	18	129	14	-35.30	3	17	17.6	-0.33
June	3	27	11.1	-13.83	7	50	14	-22.20	2	7	28.6	-1.00
July	1	23	4.3	-19.50	3	47	6.4	-32.70	1	3	33.3	0.00
August	2	19	10.5	-7.00	8	47	17	-9.87	0	2	0	-2.00
September	6	25	24	+14.75	10	70	14.3	-31.28	0	4	0	-4.00
October	16	62	25.8	+31.94	28	134	20.9	-23.67	2	20	10	-12.59
November	25	125	20	-27.94	53	223	23.8	+9.95	6	35	17.1	-13.15
December	24	104	23.1	+12.61	39	190	20.5	+25.73	6	29	20.7	+22.38

Not forgetting ...

	Chases				Hurdles				Bumpers			
	W	R	%	£1 stake	W	R	%	£1 stake	W	R	%	£1 stake
Favourites	81	224	36.2	-18.68	134	371	36.1	-27.92	15	48	31.3	-12.33
After a break	12	86	14	-17.26	9	111	8.1	-55.25	6	36	16.7	-8.92

All runners

	Wins	Runs	%	2nd	3rd	rest	Win prize	Total prize	£1 Stake
Chases	154	767	20.1	91	109	413	907,310.95	1,404,359.00	-65.39
Hurdles	241	1447	16.7	193	202	811	889,246.35	1,328,730.00	-288.42
Bumpers	31	213	14.6	24	22	136	62,337.20	91,020.00	-60.66
Totals	426	2427	17.6	308	333	1360	1,858,894.50	2,824,109	-414.47

Mary Reveley

WHEN analysing stats, it's a good idea to put your faith in those derived from samples of a reasonable size.

Mary Reveley's chasers, when broken down by the class of race they've contested, show that she's reliably profitable at Class D level. With 255 runners, the largest sample in her 'Class Of Race' section, the stat looks solid, and her level-stakes profit is over 10 per cent.

As with Sue Smith, Reveley seems to put up a very limited number of jockeys on her winning chasers – Alan Dempsey, Tony Ross and Paddy Aspell have shared nearly all her chase wins between them.

The yard's runners hit form in about September and seem to hold their form through most of the jumps season until February, though, predictably, the level of profit falls off by the end of that period.

As is well known, Reveley's runners struggle to make an impact at the big southern tracks.

Course records

	Chases				Hurdles				Bumpers			
	W	R	%	£1 stake	W	R	%	£1 stake	W	R	%	£1 stake
Wetherby	23	89	25.8	21.79	33	191	17.3	-23.83	6	20	30	-1.98
Newcastle	12	49	24.5	-9.80	26	133	19.5	+31.13	5	29	17.2	+1.24
Sedgefield	16	68	23.5	-21.25	22	151	14.6	-71.74	3	10	30	-0.34
Catterick	14	61	23	-7.06	16	100	16	-24.68	2	13	15.4	+2.00
Market Rasen	14	70	20	-25.19	14	105	13.3	-34.33	2	7	28.6	-0.25
Kelso	8	50	16	-9.10	21	86	24.4	+12.33	0			
Huntingdon	7	32	21.9	-8.90	12	58	20.7	-11.46	3	23	13	-10.67
Musselburgh	5	17	29.4	-2.87	13	47	27.7	+22.96	4	14	28.6	+15.75
Ayr	10	53	18.9	-23.70	7	50	14	-24.15	1	17	5.9	-12.00
Doncaster	10	46	21.7	+23.63	7	81	8.6	-32.76	0	14	0	-14.00
Carlisle	8	31	25.8	+19.29	8	36	22.2	-5.94	0	9	0	-9.00
Perth	3	19	15.8	+4.67	11	44	25	+1.62	1	3	33.3	+1.33
Haydock	1	12	8.3	+14.00	14	78	17.9	-7.45	0	6	0	-6.00
Uttoxeter	6	38	15.8	-2.83	8	46	17.4	-6.61	0	5	0	-5.00
Bangor	3	9	33.3	+2.83	2	16	12.5	-6.00	0	4	0	-4.00
Cartmel	1	3	33.3	+6.00	4	12	33.3	+2.43	0			
Newbury	3	12	25	+0.50	1	20	5	-14.00	0	4	0	-4.00
Plumpton	1	1	100	+3.50	3	5	60	+2.07	0			
Southwell	2	13	15.4	+5.00	2	12	16.7	-0.50	0	3	0	-3.00
Ludlow	1	2	50	+1.25	2	10	20	-5.79	0	4	0	-4.00
Aintree	1	13	7.7	0.00	2	23	8.7	-8.00	0	2	0	-2.00
Kempton	0	8	0	-8.00	3	21	14.3	+1.25	0	1	0	-1.00
Worcester	0	7	0	-7.00	0	13	0	-13.00	3	5	60	+9.25
Ascot	2	6	33.3	+5.00	0	8	0	-8.00	0	1	0	-1.00
Hexham	1	13	7.7	-8.50	1	24	4.2	-21.75	0	4	0	-4.00
Warwick	0	2	0	-2.00	2	6	33.3	+1.33	0	3	0	-3.00
Chepstow	0	1	0	-1.00	1	5	20	-2.75	1	2	50	+5.00
Leicester	1	4	25	-2.00	1	7	14.3	+1.00	0			
Towcester	0	1	0	-1.00	2	6	33.3	-2.71	0	1		-1.00
Cheltenham	1	19	5.3	-14.67	1	21	4.8	-14.50	0	5	0	-5.00
Fontwell		0			1	3	33.3	-1.09	0			
Stratford	0	6	0	-6.00	1	12	8.3	-6.50	0			
Exeter	0	1	0	-1.00	0	1	0	-1.00	0			
Sandown	0	9	0	-9.00	0	12	0	-12.00	0			
Fakenham	0	1	0	-1.00	0	3	0	-3.00	0	2	0	-2.00
Hereford	0					0			0	2	0	-2.00
Wincanton	0	1	0	-1.00	0	1	0	-1.00	0			

Race type

	Chases				Hurdles			
	W	R	%	£1 stake	W	R	%	£1 stake
Handicap	66	499	13.2	-161.31	26	289	9	-117.59
Novice	56	288	19.4	-24.94	63	443	14.2	-164.48
Maiden	7	23	30.4	+1.57	12	72	16.7	+25.00
Selling	1	4	25	0.00	5	64	7.8	-35.75
Claiming	0			-	0	12	0	-12.00
Amateur	2	19	10.5	-9.50	6	28	21.4	+29.38

Class of race

	Chases				Hurdles				Bumpers			
	W	R	%	£1 stake	W	R	%	£1 stake	W	R	%	£1 stake
A	5	70	7.1	-33.63	1	22	4.5	-18.50	0	3	0	-3.00
B	9	84	10.7	-42.99	2	27	7.4	-14.50	0	1	0	-1.00
C	13	68	19.1	-5.63	3	34	8.8	+1.00	-	-	-	-
D	36	214	16.8	-38.97	19	159	11.9	-71.37	-	-	-	-
E	37	220	16.8	-29.89	55	360	15.3	-62.59	-	-	-	-
F	20	115	17.4	-34.93	10	107	9.3	-54.13	-	-	-	-
G	1	4	25	0.00	5	65	7.7	-36.75	-	-	-	-
H	0				-	-	-	-	12	114	10.5	-36.53

Winning jockeys

	Chases				Hurdles				Bumpers			
	W	R	%	£1 stake	W	R	%	£1 stake	W	R	%	£1 stake
J P McNamara	25	173	14.5	-35.20	20	159	12.6	-73.31	4	35	11.4	-7.90
D N Russell	8	89	9	-47.08	10	82	12.2	-21.88	2	10	20	+11.00
A O'Keeffe	1	16	6.3	-12.50	6	26	23.1	+24.63	1	2	50	+2.50
A Dobbin	5	23	21.7	+0.08	1	9	11.1	-4.00	0	1	0	-1.00
A P McCoy	3	12	25	+1.75	1	5	20	-3.75	0	2	0	-2.00
I Jardine	1	6	16.7	-2.00	3	29	10.3	-16.13	0	5	0	-5.00
N P Mulholland	2	10	20	+7.00	2	13	15.4	-0.50	0	4	0	-4.00
J P Byrne	2	9	22.2	+0.25	1	13	7.7	-5.00	0	1	0	-1.00
G Lee	1	7	14.3	-4.25	1	4	25	-2.09	0			
A Thornton	1	6	16.7	-4.82	1	8	12.5	-4.50	0	2	0	-2.00

By month

	Chases				Hurdles				Bumpers			
	W	R	%	£1 stake	W	R	%	£1 stake	W	R	%	£1 stake
January	16	101	15.8	-24.52	7	87	8	-55.80	2	11	18.2	-3.13
February	13	81	16	-4.75	16	88	18.2	-2.99	1	12	8.3	-1.00
March	10	82	12.2	-43.34	10	61	16.4	+0.42	1	17	5.9	-2.00
April	10	98	10.2	-44.25	13	85	15.3	+15.64	5	25	20	+1.50
May	13	50	26	+20.25	10	78	12.8	-34.50	0	8	0	-8.00
June	5	30	16.7	-7.07	7	33	21.2	-14.82	0	1	0	-1.00
July	1	11	9.1	-7.75	1	13	7.7	-7.00	0	3	0	-3.00
August	0	10	0	-10.00	2	15	13.3	-5.00	0	1	0	-1.00
September	1	4	25	+1.50	1	11	9.1	+10.00	0			
October	8	51	15.7	-20.94	6	61	9.8	-16.50	0	10	0	-10.00
November	20	141	14.2	-56.43	12	130	9.2	-75.26	2	13	15.4	-6.90
December	24	116	20.7	+11.26	10	112	8.9	-71.03	1	17	5.9	-6.00

Not forgetting ...

	Chases				Hurdles				Bumpers			
	W	R	%	£1 stake	W	R	%	£1 stake	W	R	%	£1 stake
Favourites	57	137	41.6	+18.80	37	127	29.1	-46.42	4	12	33.3	-0.53
After a break	19	140	13.6	-61.49	13	148	8.8	-86.19	0	11	0	-11.00

Sponsored by Stan James

All runners

	Wins	Runs	%	2nd	3rd	rest	Win prize	Total prize	£1 Stake
Chases	121	775	15.6	98	97	459	843,887.74	1,332,176.00	-186.03
Hurdles	95	774	12.3	103	93	483	321,512.10	478,721.00	-256.84
Bumpers	12	118	10.2	12	14	80	23,266.00	33,505.00	-40.53
Totals	228	1667	13.7	213	204	1022	1,188,665.84	1,844,402.00	-483.40

Ferdy Murphy

WITH a yard like this, level-stakes followers are going to have to be a bit inventive to avoid doing their brains. Ferdy Murphy has not been a great generator of income for loyal backers.

However, one interesting trend is flagged up by his strike-rate from month to month. By the end of the jumps season proper, in March and April, it's beginning to tail off . . . then, when his number of runners drops dramatically (May for the chasers, June for the hurdlers), the strike-rate goes back up to a very healthy level, with the chasers producing a perfectly respectable profit.

Murphy's maidens have done well under both codes, though the smallness of the samples involved doesn't invite much faith.

His returns at Uttoxeter, and with his fencers at Towcester, Ayr and Hereford, are worth a second look.

Course records

	Chases				Hurdles				Bumpers			
	W	R	%	£1 stake	W	R	%	£1 stake	W	R	%	£1 stake
Sedgefield	9	82	11	-37.95	11	67	16.4	+6.92	1	7	14.3	-4.63
Musselburgh	7	30	23.3	+5.32	11	51	21.6	-0.07	0	6	0	-6.00
Hexham	4	34	11.8	-12.25	11	51	21.6	-13.10	1	9	11.1	-3.00
Carlisle	8	42	19	-8.22	4	36	11.1	-18.83	4	13	30.8	+13.50
Ayr	8	34	23.5	+5.42	5	30	16.7	-17.90	1	8	12.5	-1.50
Perth	5	25	20	-1.65	7	31	22.6	+35.92	0	2	0	-2.00
Fakenham	7	29	24.1	-4.32	4	24	16.7	+9.50	0	4	0	-4.00
Newcastle	6	54	11.1	-21.23	5	75	6.7	-59.09	0	12	0	-12.00
Kelso	6	37	16.2	-19.92	4	31	12.9	-12.19	0			
Wetherby	6	40	15	-19.19	3	45	6.7	-31.75	1	6	16.7	-0.50
Catterick	7	38	18.4	-10.00	3	44	6.8	-19.00	0	2	0	-2.00
Huntingdon	7	41	17.1	-15.95	3	40	7.5	-28.75	0	10	0	-10.00
Market Rasen	6	22	27.3	+1.83	4	25	16	-7.63	0	3	0	-3.00
Haydock	5	24	20.8	-5.28	2	29	6.9	-21.75	1	7	14.3	+4.00
Uttoxeter	5	16	31.3	+18.63	3	10	30	+6.25	0			
Hereford	6	19	31.6	+0.38	0	12	0	-12.00	0	1	0	-1.00
Cheltenham	4	39	10.3	-12.00	2	19	10.5	-6.50	0	3	0	-3.00
Towcester	3	7	42.9	+15.50	1	12	8.3	-8.25	1	3	33.3	+3.50
Aintree	3	28	10.7	-14.90	1	10	10	+11.00	0	1	0	-1.00
Cartmel	2	11	18.2	+4.50	2	12	16.7	-4.63	0			
Folkestone	2	5	40	+3.25	0	4	0	-4.00	2	2	100	+11.10
Doncaster	2	27	7.4	+10.00	1	27	3.7	-25.50	0	6	0	-6.00
Ascot	0	6	0	-6.00	2	7	28.6	+10.50	0			
Kempton	1	10	10	+1.00	1	4	25	-0.50	0	1	0	-1.00
Plumpton	2	6	33.3	+6.00	0	2	0	-2.00	0			
Ludlow	0	5	0	-5.00	1	9	11.1	-1.50	0	2	0	-2.00
Warwick	0	4	0	-4.00	1	13	7.7	-6.50	0	1	0	-1.00
Fontwell	0	5	0	-5.00	1	5	20	+3.00	0			
Worcester	0	4	0	-4.00	1	11	9.1	-6.50	0	2	0	-2.00
Wolverhampton	0				1	3	33.3	+3.00	0			
Bangor	0	4	0	-4.00	0	5	0	-5.00	0	3	0	-3.00
Exeter	0	1	0	-1.00	0				0			
Newbury	0	11	0	-11.00	0	3	0	-3.00	0	2	0	-2.00
Sandown	0	6	0	-6.00	0	4	0	-4.00	0			
Chepstow	0	3	0	-3.00	0	1	0	-1.00	0			
Leicester	0	7	0	-7.00	0	7	0	-7.00	0			
Southwell	0	14	0	-14.00	0	12	0	-12.00	0	2	0	-2.00
Stratford	0	5	0	-5.00	0	3	0	-3.00	0			

Race type

		Chases				Hurdles		
	W	R	%	£1 stake	W	R	%	£1 stake
Handicap	58	351	16.5	+45.20	9	137	6.6	-71.63
Novice	48	257	18.7	-88.74	35	320	10.9	-51.20
Maiden	0	5	0	-5.00	0	48	0	-48.00
Selling	0	2	0	-2.00	1	6	16.7	-4.09
Claiming	-	-	-	-	0	1	0	-1.00
Amateur	3	11	27.3	+6.25	0	5	0	-5.00

Class of race

		Chases				Hurdles				Bumpers		
	W	R	%	£1 stake	W	R	%	£1 stake	W	R	%	£1 stake
A	8	42	19	+20.00	2	14	14.3	-3.50	0	2	0	-2.00
B	9	51	17.6	-8.30	4	17	23.5	+22.63	0			
C	10	69	14.5	-28.34	3	38	7.9	-25.17	-	-	-	-
D	41	210	19.5	-9.51	12	150	8	-71.88	-	-	-	-
E	28	155	18.1	+2.61	23	214	10.7	-28.28	-	-	-	-
F	4	33	12.1	-3.00	2	27	7.4	-11.50	-	-	-	-
G	0	2	0	-2.00	1	6	16.7	-4.09	-	-	-	-
H	0	1	0	-1.00	-	-	-	-	7	89	7.9	-35.00

Winning jockeys

		Chases				Hurdles				Bumpers		
	W	R	%	£1 stake	W	R	%	£1 stake	W	R	%	£1 stake
R Johnson	45	226	19.9	-4.86	20	144	13.9	-4.91	0	16	0	-16.00
M Bradburne	21	134	15.7	-22.89	11	102	10.8	-4.06	2	18	11.1	-11.50
A Thornton	7	37	18.9	+23.00	2	38	5.3	-30.75	0	2	0	-2.00
S Wynne	6	48	12.5	-14.13	1	40	2.5	-35.50	1	13	7.7	-4.00
R Farrant	6	26	23.1	-10.70	1	17	5.9	-10.50	0	2	0	-2.00
M A Fitzgerald	3	8	37.5	+1.48	1	7	14.3	-5.20	0			
L Wyer	0				2	2	100	+15.88	0			
A P McCoy	0	5	0	-5.00	1	5	20	-2.00	1	1	100	+4.00
J Tizzard	1	5	20	+1.00	1	15	6.7	-10.50	0	3	0	-3.00
W Marston	1	7	14.3	+1.00	1	5	20	+16.00	0			

By month

		Chases				Hurdles				Bumpers		
	W	R	%	£1 stake	W	R	%	£1 stake	W	R	%	£1 stake
January	11	85	12.9	+3.35	6	61	9.8	-2.50	0	10	0	-10.00
February	14	84	16.7	-13.44	6	64	9.4	-24.38	1	15	6.7	-6.00
March	21	79	26.6	+60.69	7	71	9.9	-29.33	1	18	5.6	-15.25
April	8	40	20	-3.63	7	47	14.9	-9.13	1	9	11.1	-4.00
May	5	31	16.1	-3.75	2	36	5.6	-20.75	1	2	50	+1.50
June	0	7	0	-7.00	0	10	0	-10.00	0	1	0	-1.00
July	1	4	25	+9.00	0	3	0	-3.00	0			
August	0	3	0	-3.00	0	3	0	-3.00	0			
September	0	5	0	-5.00	0	3	0	-3.00	0			
October	6	40	15	-1.50	3	30	10	-11.75	0	3	0	-3.00
November	15	91	16.5	-35.61	8	76	10.5	+1.48	1	16	6.3	+5.00
December	19	94	20.2	-29.66	8	62	12.9	-6.43	2	17	11.8	-4.25

Not forgetting ...

		Chases				Hurdles				Bumpers		
	W	R	%	£1 stake	W	R	%	£1 stake	W	R	%	£1 stake
Favourites	44	118	37.3	-4.17	15	55	27.3	-16.87	3	10	30	0.00
After a break	15	98	15.3	+15.75	10	83	12	+1.23	0	4	0	-4.00

Sponsored by Stan James

All runners

	Wins	Runs	%	2nd	3rd	rest	Win prize	Total prize	£1 Stake
Chases	100	563	17.8	99	67	297	841,870.45	1,318,679.00	-29.54
Hurdles	47	466	10.1	49	51	318	211,142.44	319,974.00	-121.79
Bumpers	7	91	7.7	10	13	61	14,342.10	20,418.00	-37.00
Totals	154	1120	13.8	158	131	676	1,067,354.99	1,659,071	-188.33

Henry Daly

HIS old boss would be proud. Henry Daly learned his craft from Captain Tim Forster, for whom hurdles races were nothing but a means to an end, and the same holds true for Daly.

The Ludlow trainer's strike-rate varies dramatically, depending on the size of obstacles his charges are tackling. As for the bumpers, forget it.

He certainly knows what he's doing in handicap chases, returning a 13 per cent profit on investment for level-stakes backers over the last five years. He's also good at getting his charges fit when they've been off the track for a while – even his hurdlers make a profit in our 'after a break' section.

Interestingly, Daly's strike-rate and profit stats both peak in March – clearly, his two wins at the last Festival were very much part of the plan.

CAPTAIN TIM FORSTER

Course records

	Chases				Hurdles				Bumpers			
	W	R	%	£1 stake	W	R	%	£1 stake	W	R	%	£1 stake
Towcester	13	40	32.5	+6.52	2	29	6.9	-22.38	0	7	0	-7.00
Ludlow	8	51	15.7	-9.54	3	45	6.7	-14.09	1	9	11.1	0.00
Hereford	4	33	12.1	-0.25	7	35	20	-1.50	1	7	14.3	-3.25
Warwick	5	30	16.7	-11.38	6	35	17.1	+19.93	0	12	0	-12.00
Uttoxeter	6	30	20	+22.74	4	40	10	-22.52	0	5	0	-5.00
Cheltenham	7	27	25.9	+24.75	2	19	10.5	+5.00	0	2	0	-2.00
Chepstow	6	27	22.2	-8.25	2	23	8.7	-6.50	0	4	0	-4.00
Stratford	6	30	20	-6.85	1	20	5	-13.50	1	3	33.3	-0.25
Huntingdon	7	39	17.9	-6.81	1	26	3.8	-22.75	0	6	0	-6.00
Bangor	5	31	16.1	+0.75	1	23	4.3	-19.00	0	5	0	-5.00
Exeter	4	23	17.4	-4.86	1	13	7.7	-10.75	1	2	50	+3.00
Haydock	5	26	19.2	+19.87	1	30	3.3	-25.00	0	8	0	-8.00
Southwell	2	9	22.2	-3.75	4	12	33.3	+19.94	0	1	0	-1.00
Taunton	2	10	20	+0.75	3	8	37.5	+10.50	0	1	0	-1.00
Worcester	2	20	10	-5.50	1	14	7.1	+1.00	2	2	100	+22.50
Ascot	1	8	12.5	0.00	3	12	25	+14.83	0	1	0	-1.00
Kempton	3	14	21.4	+2.10	0	7	0	-7.00	0	1	0	-1.00
Newbury	3	17	17.6	+5.00	0	15	0	-15.00	0	1	0	-1.00
Sandown	2	12	16.7	-3.75	1	5	20	+0.50	0	2	0	-2.00
Wetherby	3	10	30	+1.75	0	2	0	-2.00	0	3	0	-3.00
Leicester	2	23	8.7	-15.39	1	15	6.7	-4.00	0			
Wincanton	1	9	11.1	-5.75	1	6	16.7	+5.00	1	3	33.3	+6.00
Carlisle	1	9	11.1	-6.00	1	7	14.3	+8.00	0			
Perth	1	3	33.3	+5.00	0	2	0	-2.00	0			
Lingfield	1	3	33.3	-1.70	0	1	0	-1.00	0			
Market Rasen	0	2	0	-2.00	1	4	25	+0.50	0			
Ayr	0				0	1	0	-1.00	0			
Kelso	0	1	0	-1.00	0				0			
Aintree	0	10	0	-10.00	0	3	0	-3.00	0	2	0	-2.00
Windsor	0				0	1	0	-1.00	0			
Fontwell	0	2	0	-2.00	0	1	0	-1.00	0			
Doncaster	0	9	0	-9.00	0	8	0	-8.00	0	4	0	-4.00
Newcastle	0	2	0	-2.00	0				0			
Newton Abbot	0	3	0	-3.00	0	4	0	-4.00	0			

Race type

	Chases				Hurdles			
	W	R	%	£1 stake	W	R	%	£1 stake
Handicap	60	358	16.8	+3.38	64	439	14.6	-9.99
Novice	29	182	15.9	-48.39	54	435	12.4	-182.80
Maiden	2	3	66.7	+13.00	10	78	12.8	-28.57
Selling	2	5	40	+2.25	14	47	29.8	+20.32
Claiming	-	-	-	-	8	25	32	+3.38
Amateur	0	12	0	-12.00	1	11	9.1	-3.00

Class of race

	Chases				Hurdles				Bumpers			
	W	R	%	£1 stake	W	R	%	£1 stake	W	R	%	£1 stake
A	1	11	9.1	-2.00	0	22	0	-22.00	0	1	0	-1.00
B	6	43	14	+9.75	4	57	7	-36.50	0			
C	13	62	21	+7.50	4	65	6.2	-32.50	-	-	-	-
D	21	134	15.7	-27.25	32	231	13.9	-42.83	-	-	-	-
E	26	135	19.3	-31.26	52	332	15.7	-35.12	-	-	-	-
F	15	111	13.5	-5.50	21	137	15.3	-37.77	-	-	-	-
G	2	5	40	+2.25	16	51	31.4	+22.82	-	-	-	-
H	0				-	-	-	-	4	87	4.6	-47.50

Winning jockeys

	Chases				Hurdles				Bumpers			
	W	R	%	£1 stake	W	R	%	£1 stake	W	R	%	£1 stake
D R Dennis	17	131	13	-40.50	42	253	16.6	-15.22	1	23	4.3	-17.00
R Wakley	16	106	15.1	-14.00	32	211	15.2	-37.83	0	14	0	-14.00
S Durack	18	87	20.7	-3.09	11	96	11.5	-43.42	0	3	0	-3.00
A P McCoy	8	20	40	+5.17	6	18	33.3	-5.89	0	1	0	-1.00
G Tormey	0	5	0	-5.00	6	35	17.1	-12.50	0	5	0	-5.00
M A Fitzgerald	4	16	25	+0.66	2	8	25	+2.50	0			
A Dobbin	2	14	14.3	-3.00	2	13	15.4	-1.67	0	1	0	-1.00
H Oliver	3	10	30	+14.00	1	17	5.9	-14.90	0			
R Johnson	0	11	0	-11.00	4	23	17.4	+4.00	0	2	0	-2.00
W Hutchinson	2	4	50	+7.75	2	9	22.2	+15.50	0			

By month

	Chases				Hurdles				Bumpers			
	W	R	%	£1 stake	W	R	%	£1 stake	W	R	%	£1 stake
January	2	33	6.1	-28.00	5	62	8.1	-29.50	1	5	20	+16.00
February	3	39	7.7	-21.27	8	81	9.9	-2.67	1	9	11.1	-3.00
March	15	60	25	+23.98	11	91	12.1	-41.09	0	15	0	-15.00
April	17	74	23	+21.50	11	100	11	-19.43	0	14	0	-14.00
May	10	52	19.2	-8.07	13	87	14.9	-9.67	0	9	0	-9.00
June	5	33	15.2	-3.38	9	49	18.4	+12.73	0	2	0	-2.00
July	3	23	13	-11.38	6	44	13.6	-19.59	1	3	33.3	+5.00
August	1	12	8.3	-3.00	15	54	27.8	-0.27	1	1	100	+3.50
September	7	21	33.3	+4.98	8	36	22.2	-6.83	0			
October	5	40	12.5	-11.25	20	90	22.2	+13.99	0	5	0	-5.00
November	9	57	15.8	-0.25	14	117	12	-44.58	0	17	0	-17.00
December	7	57	12.3	-10.38	9	84	10.7	-38.98	0	8	0	-8.00

Not forgetting ...

	Chases				Hurdles				Bumpers			
	W	R	%	£1 stake	W	R	%	£1 stake	W	R	%	£1 stake
Favourites	29	92	31.5	-10.09	57	130	43.8	+24.14	0			
After a break	17	64	26.6	+17.89	17	144	11.8	-5.78	1	15	6.7	-10.5

Sponsored by Stan James

All runners

	Wins	Runs	%	2nd	3rd	rest	Win prize	Total prize	£1 Stake
Chases	84	501	16.8	72	64	281	490,002.00	750,927.00	-46.51
Hurdles	129	895	14.4	101	90	575	407,646.65	604,902.00	-185.90
Bumpers	4	88	4.5	6	6	72	8,193.50	11,705.00	-48.50
Totals	217	1484	14.6	179	160	928	905,842.15	1,367,534.00	-280.91

Ian Williams

HIS chasers definitely peak in the spring, though the Festival doesn't seem to have had much to do with that, as can be seen from Williams' Cheltenham statistics.

The Birmingham trainer's hurdlers follow a different pattern, hitting their purple patch in high summer, a fact that is also reflected in his level-stakes profit for hurdlers at Market Rasen, home to lots of summer jumping.

Huntingdon and Ludlow have been happy hunting grounds for Williams followers in recent seasons, while he's also done well with his chasers after a break.

Course records

	Chases				Hurdles				Bumpers			
	W	R	%	£1 stake	W	R	%	£1 stake	W	R	%	£1 stake
Huntingdon	10	38	26.3	+11.02	13	62	21	+16.83	1	11	9.1	-6.50
Ludlow	8	42	19	+11.50	10	53	18.9	+6.13	1	10	10	+11.00
Market Rasen	4	35	11.4	-24.13	15	60	25	+34.22	0	6	0	-6.00
Hereford	6	34	17.6	+1.16	8	46	17.4	-9.95	0	4	0	-4.00
Warwick	3	21	14.3	-1.50	9	61	14.8	-15.85	0	7	0	-7.00
Worcester	1	20	5	-10.00	8	38	21.1	+15.60	1	8	12.5	0.00
Plumpton	4	8	50	+13.73	4	13	30.8	+6.00	0			
Newton Abbot	3	13	23.1	+0.25	5	24	20.8	-8.38	0			
Bangor	2	9	22.2	+9.00	5	29	17.2	+13.43	0	4	0	-4.00
Southwell	3	15	20	-2.75	4	21	19	-13.32	0			
Stratford	2	14	14.3	-2.38	5	51	9.8	-22.25	0	1	0	-1.00
Fakenham	4	15	26.7	+0.23	2	10	20	-4.33	0			
Towcester	4	22	18.2	+3.25	2	18	11.1	+20.00	0	3	0	-3.00
Sedgefield	3	10	30	+2.83	3	13	23.1	-5.42	0			
Exeter	2	11	18.2	-2.00	3	24	12.5	-13.60	0			
Fontwell	1	7	14.3	-3.75	4	14	28.6	-6.81	0	2	0	-2.00
Uttoxeter	2	16	12.5	-10.25	3	38	7.9	-15.00	0	1	0	-1.00
Ayr	4	9	44.4	+23.75	0	6	0	-6.00	0	1	0	-1.00
Ascot	2	10	20	+2.75	0	14	0	-14.00	1	4	25	+2.00
Perth	1	5	20	+0.50	2	10	20	-5.68	0			
Newbury	2	7	28.6	+5.25	1	20	5	-14.00	0	3	0	-3.00
Taunton	0	8	0	-8.00	3	20	15	-0.63	0			
Chepstow	0	2	0	-2.00	3	22	13.6	-10.75	0	2	0	-2.00
Wetherby	1	10	10	-8.60	2	22	9.1	-15.25	0	2	0	-2.00
Doncaster	1	14	7.1	-11.63	2	26	7.7	-6.00	0	2	0	-2.00
Cheltenham	0	22	0	-22.00	3	43	7	-27.00	0	2	0	-2.00
Wolverhampton	1	4	25	+2.00	2	8	25	+1.91	0			
Aintree	0	6	0	-6.00	2	18	11.1	-9.17	0	3	0	-3.00
Haydock	1	9	11.1	+2.00	1	25	4	-17.50	0	5	0	-5.00
Carlisle	2	3	66.7	+5.25	0				0			
Catterick	1	4	25	-1.25	1	1	100	+2.25	0			
Newcastle	2	4	50	+2.75	0	7	0	-7.00	0			
Wincanton	1	12	8.3	-9.50	1	19	5.3	-15.00	0	3	0	-3.00
Kelso	1	2	50	+4.00	0	5	0	-5.00	0			
Hexham	1	3	33.3	+4.00	0	1	0	-1.00	0			
Cartmel	0				1	4	25	+0.50	0			
Kempton	0	8	0	-8.00	1	16	6.3	-3.00	0	2	0	-2.00
Sandown	1	9	11.1	+2.00	0	10	0	-10.00	0	1	0	-1.00
Folkestone	0	6	0	-6.00	1	9	11.1	-6.90	0	1	0	-1.00
Leicester	0	11	0	-11.00	0	14	0	-14.00	0			
Lingfield	0	1	0	-1.00	0				0			
Musselburgh	0	2	0	-2.00	0				0			

Race type

	Chases W	R	%	£1 stake	Hurdles W	R	%	£1 stake
Handicap	47	216	21.8	+28.79	91	483	18.8	+15.72
Novice	32	130	24.6	-36.74	89	413	21.5	-115.96
Maiden	3	6	50	+1.49	10	58	17.2	-2.03
Selling	0	2	0	-2.00	12	37	32.4	+66.25
Claiming	-	-	-	-	2	6	33.3	+2.75
Amateur	2	12	16.7	+13.33	4	18	22.2	-5.88

Class of race

	Chases W	R	%	£1 stake	Hurdles W	R	%	£1 stake	Bumpers W	R	%	£1 stake
A	0	10	0	-10.00	4	24	16.7	+11.00	2	6	33.3	-0.75
B	2	19	10.5	+5.75	11	50	22	+8.82	0	1	0	-1.00
C	7	33	21.2	-3.61	10	57	17.5	-25.21	-	-	-	-
D	38	131	29	-22.13	43	198	21.7	-27.22	-	-	-	-
E	21	78	26.9	+12.87	69	366	18.9	-91.51	-	-	-	-
F	7	39	17.9	+14.75	22	138	15.9	-34.61	-	-	-	-
G	0	2	0	-2.00	13	39	33.3	+68.00	-	-	-	-
H	1	3	33.3	-1.39	-	-	-	-	31	130	23.8	-10.23

Winning jockeys

	Chases W	R	%	£1 stake	Hurdles W	R	%	£1 stake	Bumpers W	R	%	£1 stake
A Dobbin	35	97	36.1	+25.63	76	195	39	+54.78	9	32	28.1	-9.38
B Gibson	8	49	16.3	+3.58	29	224	12.9	-73.96	8	45	17.8	-17.23
W Dowling	1	3	33.3	+10.00	28	190	14.7	+18.49	7	27	25.9	+13.98
G Berridge	1	3	33.3	+2.00	6	59	10.2	-34.86	4	16	25	-7.85
B Harding	3	18	16.7	-6.60	3	19	15.8	-7.90	0			
A P McCoy	0	1	0	-1.00	4	4	100	+7.44	0			
G Lee	1	2	50	+1.50	2	7	28.6	-3.29	0			
J Crowley	1	2	50	+6.00	1	1	100	+20.00	0			
R Garritty	0				2	4	50	+0.50	0			
P Flynn	0				1	1	100	+2.75	0			

By month

	Chases W	R	%	£1 stake	Hurdles W	R	%	£1 stake	Bumpers W	R	%	£1 stake
January	8	47	17	-20.89	23	98	23.5	-6.78	2	28	7.1	-19.00
February	8	34	23.5	-2.13	9	106	8.5	-72.98	2	11	18.2	-4.90
March	10	32	31.3	+14.21	19	109	17.4	+42.18	6	20	30	+3.25
April	4	35	11.4	-17.89	23	90	25.6	-3.41	4	24	16.7	-10.08
May	5	30	16.7	+8.00	23	93	24.7	+26.55	1	8	12.5	-4.00
June	2	12	16.7	+1.00	9	37	24.3	+11.69	0	1	0	-1.00
July	1	3	33.3	+4.50	1	5	20	+2.00	0			
August	2	3	66.7	+1.80	1	6	16.7	-2.00	0			
September	1	2	50	+2.00	4	7	57.1	+10.75	0			
October	1	12	8.3	-8.50	13	63	20.6	-19.48	2	7	28.6	+8.63
November	15	59	25.4	-12.87	26	153	17	-48.00	9	20	45	+15.04
December	19	46	41.3	+25.00	21	105	20	-31.24	7	18	38.9	+0.09

Not forgetting ...

	Chases W	R	%	£1 stake	Hurdles W	R	%	£1 stake	Bumpers W	R	%	£1 stake
Favourites	45	115	39.1	-7.97	107	212	50.5	+53.08	23	45	51.1	+11.52
After a break	8	42	19	-10.31	15	150	10	-75.57	6	18	33.3	-2.51

All runners

	Wins	Runs	%	2nd	3rd	rest	Win prize	Total prize	£1 Stake
Chases	76	315	24.1	48	27	164	392,874.60	589,140.00	-5.76
Hurdles	172	872	19.7	94	78	528	728,869.55	1,102,404.00	-90.72
Bumpers	33	137	24.1	15	23	66	86,033.50	129,730.00	-11.98
Totals	281	1324	21.2	157	128	758	1,207,777.65	1,821,274.00	-108.46

Len Lungo

HE'S broken the record for most wins in a season by a Scottish trainer, but Len Lungo hasn't done so by spreading his horses all round the country.

As can be seen from the table below, the Dumfriesshire man has kept to a very limited field of endeavour in recent seasons, only rarely venturing south to the big tracks, and mostly mopping up little races round the northern gaffs.

Still, it can't be denied that he seems to know what he's doing when he sends one to Cheltenham or Aintree, and he's produced level-stakes profits on all runners at both. Ayr is the only track north of the border where

you couldn't have made money backing all his runners.

Lungo has a very respectable record in handicaps and generates excellent returns when Tony Dobbin is jocked up. Selling hurdles have also proved a forte.

He may be short of top-class chasers, but you can rely on his favourites over timber.

Course records

	Chases				Hurdles				Bumpers			
	W	R	%	£1 stake	W	R	%	£1 stake	W	R	%	£1 stake
Ayr	21	67	31.3	-3.67	25	128	19.5	-57.61	7	29	24.1	-3.23
Kelso	9	32	28.1	-4.08	28	116	24.1	+16.45		0		
Carlisle	12	41	29.3	-5.98	16	91	17.6	-14.75	4	16	25	-1.83
Newcastle	6	24	25	-4.18	17	107	15.9	-24.75	4	14	28.6	+0.29
Musselburgh	7	17	41.2	+28.91	13	45	28.9	-3.06	3	15	20	-5.70
Perth	4	18	22.2	-3.95	17	61	27.9	+33.42	1	8	12.5	-4.00
Hexham	2	24	8.3	-8.50	15	71	21.1	-5.38	3	8	37.5	+0.07
Sedgefield	8	22	36.4	+25.57	8	43	18.6	-13.81	2	6	33.3	+9.63
Wetherby	1	12	8.3	-10.50	11	54	20.4	-11.20	2	4	50	+9.50
Catterick	2	12	16.7	-3.50	4	26	15.4	-1.88	3	7	42.9	+3.88
Haydock	0	9	0	-9.00	6	52	11.5	-18.09	1	13	7.7	-11.20
Aintree	0	4	0	-4.00	2	14	14.3	+13.50	2	5	40	+0.63
Cheltenham	1	8	12.5	+13.00	2	8	25	+16.50	0	2	0	-2.00
Market Rasen	1	11	9.1	-7.25	2	15	13.3	0.00	0	1	0	-1.00
Sandown		0			2	7	28.6	+1.50		0		
Doncaster	0	1	0	-1.00	2	8	25	-4.36	0	3	0	-3.00
Bangor	1	9	11.1	-6.25	0	8	0	-8.00	0	3	0	-3.00
Chepstow		0			0	1	0	-1.00	1	2	50	0.00
Hereford		0			1	1	100	+0.80		0		
Leicester	1	1	100	+1.63		0				0		
Uttoxeter	0	2	0	-2.00	1	4	25	+3.00	0	1	0	-1.00
Cartmel		0			0	5	0	-5.00		0		
Newbury	0	1	0	-1.00	0	3	0	-3.00		0		
Southwell		0			0	2	0	-2.00		0		
Worcester		0			0	2	0	-2.00		0		

'He's a progressive four-year-old with several good placed efforts over hurdles and fences to his name. Ian Williams is in a good position with this one and will exploit his potential to the full'

Which horse? See Dave Nevison, page 115

Race type

	Chases				Hurdles			
	W	R	%	£1 stake	W	R	%	£1 stake
Handicap	23	197	11.7	-27.42	21	193	10.9	-9.93
Novice	20	98	20.4	+15.23	46	274	16.8	-25.92
Maiden	0	3	0	-3.00	7	42	16.7	-13.88
Selling	0				1	4	25	-1.00
Claiming	-	-	-	-	0	2	0	-2.00
Amateur	0	2	0	-2.00	0	2	0	-2.00

Class of race

	Chases				Hurdles				Bumpers			
	W	R	%	£1 stake	W	R	%	£1 stake	W	R	%	£1 stake
A	2	30	6.7	-18.50	5	56	8.9	-29.89	0	4	0	-4.00
B	5	60	8.3	-41.25	4	59	6.8	-28.75	0	2	0	-2.00
C	8	44	18.2	+8.75	10	56	17.9	+8.63	-	-	-	-
D	15	89	16.9	-12.70	24	127	18.9	-15.61	-	-	-	-
E	4	43	9.3	-13.67	25	160	15.6	-3.97	-	-	-	-
F	4	20	20	+21.50	3	30	10	+10.50	-	-	-	-
G		0			1	5	20	-2.00	-	-	-	-
H	3	3	100	+2.23	-	-	-	-	6	62	9.7	-5.00

Winning jockeys

	Chases				Hurdles				Bumpers			
	W	R	%	£1 stake	W	R	%	£1 stake	W	R	%	£1 stake
R Thornton	15	106	14.2	-3.45	29	186	15.6	-1.46	1	13	7.7	-7.50
R Johnson	18	103	17.5	-24.92	26	142	18.3	-18.12	0			
O McPhail	2	32	6.3	-19.50	4	50	8	-9.50	4	19	21.1	+28.00
W Marston	1	8	12.5	+7.00	9	61	14.8	-22.01	0			
Mr F Hutsby	3	4	75	+1.23		0			0			
W Hutchinson	1	4	25	+9.00	1	13	7.7	-9.00	1	13	7.7	-8.50
G Supple	0				1	1	100	+10.00	0			
R Massey	0				1	10	10	-2.00	0	7	0	-7.00
J A McCarthy	1	2	50	+6.00	0	3	0	-3.00	0			
James Davies	0				1	1	100	+20.00	0			

By month

	Chases				Hurdles				Bumpers			
	W	R	%	£1 stake	W	R	%	£1 stake	W	R	%	£1 stake
January	8	45	17.8	-3.49	8	72	11.1	-29.40	1	7	14.3	+27.00
February	4	30	13.3	-21.44	10	80	12.5	-32.75	0	8	0	-8.00
March	3	30	10	-8.00	13	65	20	+1.76	3	16	18.8	-2.50
April	2	30	6.7	-20.20	7	64	10.9	-1.89	0	9	0	-9.00
May	6	22	27.3	+29.88	8	35	22.9	+8.38	0	1	0	-1.00
June	1	7	14.3	-2.00	4	11	36.4	-2.07	0	1	0	-1.00
July	0	3	0	-3.00	0	3	0	-3.00	0	1	0	-1.00
August	0	5	0	-5.00	0	2	0	-2.00	1	1	100	+4.50
September	0	5	0	-5.00	0	4	0	-4.00	0	1	0	-1.00
October	3	17	17.6	+3.75	3	24	12.5	-0.50	0			
November	6	40	15	-7.50	9	60	15	-0.50	1	10	10	-6.00
December	8	55	14.5	-12.63	10	73	13.7	+4.88	0	13	0	-13.00

Not forgetting ...

	Chases				Hurdles				Bumpers			
	W	R	%	£1 stake	W	R	%	£1 stake	W	R	%	£1 stake
Favourites	13	45	28.9	-11.51	25	76	32.9	-17.34	0	4	0	-4.00
After a break	4	47	8.5	-20.00	6	75	8	-43.26	0	2	0	-2.00

Sponsored by Stan James

All runners

	Wins	Runs	%	2nd	3rd	rest	Win prize	Total prize	£1 Stake
Chases	41	289	14.2	51	40	157	249,095.45	381,992.75	-54.63
Hurdles	72	493	14.6	75	64	282	424,895.04	662,122.00	-61.09
Bumpers	6	68	8.8	9	5	48	14,014.00	20,020.00	-11.00
Totals	119	850	14.0	135	109	487	688,004.49	1,064,134.75	-126.72

Alan King

LAST season was significantly better than the one before in terms of numbers of winners and total prizemoney won for Alan King.

But it has to be said that we might have expected better by now from the man who worked for so long as David Nicholson's assistant, and who seemed to have had a successful future assured for him when he took over.

Let's not forget that the Duke is the only trainer other than Martin Pipe to have been champion in the last fifteen years.

King is light years from a title bid and there are some suggestions among the stats on these pages that it's not just lack of material that's holding him back. Whether we're talking about hurdlers or chasers, he has the worst record of our 20 featured

trainers with horses coming back from a break – for King, they win just eight per cent of the time.

Insofar as his yard may be said to hit form at all, the good times have usually come in May, for both chasers and hurdlers. King also seems to do well in novice chases, returning a level-stakes profit.

His Class F runners are worth a look, under either code.

Course records

	Chases				Hurdles				Bumpers			
	W	R	%	£1 stake	W	R	%	£1 stake	W	R	%	£1 stake
Kempton	3	17	17.6	-6.95	7	35	20	+0.25	0	2	0	-2.00
Hereford	2	10	20	+0.75	8	32	25	+13.66	0	4	0	-4.00
Huntingdon	5	17	29.4	+6.81	3	15	20	+3.62	0	10	0	-10.00
Wincanton	5	17	29.4	+17.38	2	27	7.4	-11.38	0	3	0	-3.00
Haydock	2	6	33.3	+3.50	3	20	15	+5.00	1	7	14.3	+27.00
Newbury	1	12	8.3	-5.00	4	26	15.4	-5.79	1	8	12.5	-4.00
Stratford	2	12	16.7	-0.50	4	16	25	-3.80	0	2	0	-2.00
Ascot	1	15	6.7	-9.00	4	30	13.3	-7.00	0			
Bangor	1	9	11.1	-7.00	3	10	30	+28.50	1	1	100	+3.50
Doncaster	3	16	18.8	+12.00	2	21	9.5	-11.75	0			
Uttoxeter	1	10	10	-7.63	4	24	16.7	-7.95	0	1	0	-1.00
Exeter	2	5	40	+19.00	2	20	10	-12.75	0			
Sandown	1	15	6.7	-8.50	3	11	27.3	+4.25	0			
Taunton	1	3	33.3	+5.00	2	15	13.3	-8.89	1	3	33.3	+1.00
Cheltenham	1	26	3.8	-23.50	3	40	7.5	-16.00	0	4	0	-4.00
Warwick	2	11	18.2	-1.13	1	28	3.6	-17.00	0	3	0	-3.00
Wetherby	2	7	28.6	+2.83	1	8	12.5	-1.50	0			
Southwell	2	6	33.3	+2.00	0	7	0	-7.00	1	1	100	+4.00
Market Rasen	1	1	100	+7.00	2	3	66.7	+2.62	0	2	0	-2.00
Newton Abbot	0	6	0	-6.00	2	5	40	+4.94	1	4	25	+1.50
Ludlow	0	12	0	-12.00	2	13	15.4	+2.75	0	4	0	-4.00
Aintree	0	7	0	-7.00	2	18	11.1	-7.00	0			
Chepstow	1	6	16.7	-0.50	1	14	7.1	-4.00	0	2	0	-2.00
Fakenham	1	4	25	+1.00	1	4	25	+17.00	0	1	0	-1.00
Ayr	1	6	16.7	-4.20	0	3	0	-3.00	0			
Fontwell	0	1	0	-1.00	1	17	5.9	-11.00	0	2	0	-2.00
Plumpton	0	3	0	-3.00	1	5	20	-2.25	0	2	0	-2.00
Leicester	0	9	0	-9.00	1	8	12.5	-1.50	0			
Lingfield	0				1	1	100	+2.50	0			
Towcester	0	4	0	-4.00	1	8	12.5	-5.63	0			
Worcester	0	6	0	-6.00	1	3	33.3	+5.00	0	2	0	-2.00
Hexham	0				0	1	0	-1.00	0			
Newcastle	0	1	0	-1.00	0	1	0	-1.00	0			
Folkestone	0	8	0	-8.00	0	4	0	-4.00	0			
Wolverhampton	0	1	0	-1.00	0				0			

Race type

	Chases				Hurdles			
	W	R	%	£1 stake	W	R	%	£1 stake
Handicap	62	583	10.6	-146.43	58	550	10.5	-62.41
Novice	55	318	17.3	-70.80	79	667	11.8	-231.50
Maiden	1	9	11.1	-4.67	8	77	10.4	-56.29
Selling	2	6	33.3	+3.33	3	40	7.5	-16.00
Claiming	-	-	-	-	1	6	16.7	+5.00
Amateur	2	25	8	-10.38	7	33	21.2	+5.93

Class of race

	Chases				Hurdles				Bumpers			
	W	R	%	£1 stake	W	R	%	£1 stake	W	R	%	£1 stake
A	9	96	9.4	-37.42	10	96	10.4	-45.99	1	16	6.3	+5.00
B	7	96	7.3	-48.92	8	96	8.3	-28.80	0	7	0	-7.00
C	13	107	12.1	-32.48	17	116	14.7	+8.72	-	-	-	-
D	38	251	15.1	-50.11	33	281	11.7	-100.41	-	-	-	-
E	24	168	14.3	-51.01	41	393	10.4	-236.65	-	-	-	-
F	12	97	12.4	-15.46	21	157	13.4	+28.03	-	-	-	-
G	2	6	33.3	+3.33	4	43	9.3	-9.00	-	-	-	-
H	0	5	0	-5.00	-	-	-	-	30	254	11.8	-74.94

Winning jockeys

	Chases				Hurdles				Bumpers			
	W	R	%	£1 stake	W	R	%	£1 stake	W	R	%	£1 stake
C Llewellyn	71	524	13.5	-212.82	98	708	13.8	-133.17	12	102	11.8	-18.52
J Goldstein	11	108	10.2	-28.92	8	145	5.5	-93.93	13	64	20.3	+17.96
T Scudamore	4	30	13.3	-5.50	10	77	13	-41.41	4	32	12.5	-12.38
R Biddlecombe	3	32	9.4	-3.00	4	21	19	-1.00	0	5	0	-5.00
Antony Evans	1	19	5.3	-6.00	4	37	10.8	+10.50	1	31	3.2	-27.00
A P McCoy	1	1	100	+3.33	1	2	50	+0.25	0			
G Tormey	1	3	33.3	+4.00	0	1	0	-1.00	0			
A Dempsey	1	1	100	+3.00	0				0			
J Culloty	1	1	100	+20.00	0	1	0	-1.00	0			
R Bellamy	0				1	2	50	+5.00	0			

By month

	Chases				Hurdles				Bumpers			
	W	R	%	£1 stake	W	R	%	£1 stake	W	R	%	£1 stake
January	5	74	6.8	-36.67	13	135	9.6	-41.65	1	21	4.8	-14.00
February	9	77	11.7	-13.47	8	124	6.5	-79.93	0	31	0	-31.00
March	8	79	10.1	-8.63	11	126	8.7	-55.63	2	29	6.9	+3.00
April	13	101	12.9	-3.17	18	124	14.5	+10.83	3	31	9.7	-7.50
May	9	59	15.3	+2.17	14	115	12.2	-34.36	4	32	12.5	-8.25
June	0	12	0	-12.00	7	39	17.9	+26.63	0	3	0	-3.00
July	3	18	16.7	+2.00	2	23	8.7	-2.50	2	9	22.2	-1.43
August	3	14	21.4	-5.59	1	16	6.3	-7.00	1	5	20	0.00
September	12	30	40	+23.66	11	38	28.9	+1.05	0	4	0	-4.00
October	21	109	19.3	-40.75	14	147	9.5	-100.61	12	37	32.4	+23.91
November	13	144	9	-87.37	22	164	13.4	-31.44	2	42	4.8	-34.67
December	9	109	8.3	-57.25	13	133	9.8	-71.50	4	33	12.1	0.00

Not forgetting ...

	Chases				Hurdles				Bumpers			
	W	R	%	£1 stake	W	R	%	£1 stake	W	R	%	£1 stake
Favourites	46	153	30.1	-31.01	55	138	39.9	-4.06	9	37	24.3	-10.27
After a break	25	127	19.7	-2.37	14	154	9.1	-87.72	4	24	16.7	-1.00

Sponsored by Stan James

All runners

	Wins	Runs	%	2nd	3rd	rest	Win prize	Total prize	£1 Stake
Chases	105	826	12.7	123	100	498	1,114,750.70	1,785,351.60	-237.06
Hurdles	134	1184	11.3	146	137	767	727,974.45	1,123,504.00	-386.10
Bumpers	31	277	11.2	34	31	181	56,912.25	82,606.00	-76.94
Totals	270	2287	11.8	426	268	1446	1,899,637.40	2,991,461.60	-700.10

Nigel Twiston-Davies

DESPITE his reputation for doing well with staying chasers and novices, Nigel Twiston-Davies would be an expensive trainer for any punter to follow.

When this yard is off-form, they're really off-form, and this has impacted on the low, low strike-rates that appear so frequently on these pages. None of our 20 featured trainers has a lower strike-rate over fences, and only a couple do worse (in percentage terms) with their hurdlers.

In strike-rate terms, the pick of his stats are novice chasers, all runners in September, chasers in October, favourites, and chasers after a break – but you'll be struggling to get any of these groups to pay on a consistent basis.

Course records

	Chases				Hurdles				Bumpers			
	W	R	%	£1 stake	W	R	%	£1 stake	W	R	%	£1 stake
Worcester	6	34	17.6	-9.01	11	60	18.3	-19.52	4	23	17.4	-7.18
Bangor	10	30	33.3	+38.74	5	45	11.1	-5.75	4	18	22.2	+3.91
Exeter	9	41	22	+4.74	9	71	12.7	-27.83	1	7	14.3	-3.00
Hereford	8	54	14.8	-4.07	6	78	7.7	-50.08	2	20	10	-11.17
Uttoxeter	5	39	12.8	+7.67	11	65	16.9	-31.34	0	5	0	-5.00
Newbury	7	37	18.9	+6.90	8	55	14.5	+5.60	0	14	0	-14.00
Chepstow	6	43	14	-30.63	5	67	7.5	-44.63	2	12	16.7	+15.50
Towcester	4	45	8.9	-25.77	7	46	15.2	-4.88	2	11	18.2	+2.00
Perth	6	17	35.3	+17.58	6	21	28.6	+19.70		0		
Cheltenham	2	79	2.5	-72.88	7	109	6.4	-71.75	1	19	5.3	-12.00
Kempton	1	26	3.8	-18.00	8	48	16.7	+19.63	0	11	0	-11.00
Warwick	4	37	10.8	-9.25	4	45	8.9	-7.00	1	20	5	-9.00
Ludlow	4	38	10.5	-4.50	1	53	1.9	-50.63	3	22	13.6	+4.00
Haydock	3	43	7	-26.00	4	47	8.5	-31.73	1	7	14.3	-4.00
Sandown	3	19	15.8	-6.25	5	26	19.2	+15.50	0	6	0	-6.00
Huntingdon	3	19	15.8	-10.52	4	44	9.1	-19.50	1	20	5	-16.00
Newton Abbot	2	15	13.3	-5.00	4	20	20	-1.64	1	8	12.5	-3.50
Ascot	4	20	20	-5.87	2	38	5.3	-20.00	0	4	0	-4.00
Stratford	2	28	7.1	-13.50	4	49	8.2	+6.16	0	2	0	-2.00
Aintree	2	35	5.7	-7.00	3	24	12.5	+18.00	0	8	0	-8.00
Southwell	2	7	28.6	+2.13	3	7	42.9	+16.94	0	3	0	-3.00
Hexham	2	4	50	+1.83	2	5	40	-2.36		0		
Taunton	0	15	0	-15.00	3	31	9.7	-10.25	1	4	25	-0.50
Ayr	0	10	0	-10.00	1	4	25	-1.75	2	5	40	+14.00
Plumpton	2	6	33.3	+1.25	1	7	14.3	-3.25	0	1	0	-1.00
Leicester	2	12	16.7	-5.04	1	12	8.3	-9.50		0		
Lingfield	1	1	100	+5.00	2	6	33.3	+4.00	0	1	0	-1.00
Market Rasen	1	7	14.3	-4.00	0	5	0	-5.00	2	2	100	+8.00
Carlisle	1	12	8.3	-9.00	1	9	11.1	-6.25	0	5	0	-5.00
Fontwell	1	9	11.1	-6.00	1	19	5.3	-17.00	0	6	0	-6.00
Wetherby	0	6	0	-6.00	2	16	12.5	-8.75	0	1	0	-1.00
Doncaster	1	9	11.1	+8.00	0	15	0	-15.00	1	2	50	+5.00
Sedgefield	1	3	33.3	-1.60	0	3	0	-3.00	1	1	100	+4.00
Fakenham	0	5	0	-5.00	0	2	0	-2.00	1	2	50	+7.00
Wincanton	0	12	0	-12.00	1	21	4.8	-17.50	0	3	0	-3.00
Folkestone	0	4	0	-4.00	1	6	16.7	-2.25	0	3	0	-3.00
Wolverhampton	0	1	0	-1.00	1	4	25	-0.50		0		
Kelso	0	1	0	-1.00		0				0		
Windsor	0	1	0	-1.00		0				0		
Catterick	0	1	0	-1.00	0	1	0	-1.00	0	1	0	-1.00
Newcastle	0	1	0	-1.00		0				0		

Race type

	Chases				Hurdles			
	W	R	%	£1 stake	W	R	%	£1 stake
Handicap	14	98	14.3	-17.80	25	188	13.3	+9.73
Novice	12	48	25	+6.05	27	169	16	-71.74
Maiden	0	1	0	-1.00	7	40	17.5	+5.50
Selling	1	2	50	+9.00	5	23	21.7	+42.63
Claiming	-	-	-	-	0	2	0	-2.00
Amateur	0	2	0	-2.00	1	6	16.7	+5.00

Class of race

	Chases				Hurdles				Bumpers			
	W	R	%	£1 stake	W	R	%	£1 stake	W	R	%	£1 stake
A	3	16	18.8	-1.75	1	17	5.9	-14.13	0	1	0	-1.00
B	2	13	15.4	+4.50	3	21	14.3	+17.00	0			
C	4	17	23.5	-4.63	2	21	9.5	-6.00	-	-	-	-
D	7	27	25.9	-4.07	17	86	19.8	-27.05	-	-	-	-
E	4	25	16	+5.75	26	157	16.6	-24.22	-	-	-	-
F	3	31	9.7	-17.30	0	50	0	-50.00	-	-	-	-
G	1	2	50	+9.00	5	25	20	+40.63	-	-	-	-
H	1	4	25	+30.00	-	-	-	-	10	46	21.7	-2.38

Winning jockeys

	Chases				Hurdles				Bumpers			
	W	R	%	£1 stake	W	R	%	£1 stake	W	R	%	£1 stake
R Johnson	14	41	34.1	+10.93	16	80	20	-22.83	1	7	14.3	-3.75
W Marston	4	21	19	+1.70	17	99	17.2	-31.24	4	12	33.3	+8.13
J Mogford	0	2	0	-2.00	6	39	15.4	-6.68	3	7	42.9	+1.25
C Llewellyn	3	13	23.1	+15.50	3	11	27.3	+12.00	0	2	0	-2.00
J A McCarthy	0	9	0	-9.00	3	19	15.8	-3.75	1	1	100	+3.50
M A Fitzgerald	1	4	25	-1.13	2	4	50	+3.23	0			
A Dobbin	0	1	0	-1.00	1	2	50	+24.00	0			
P Robson	0				1	1	100	+12.00	0			
S Curran	0	6	0	-6.00	1	18	5.6	-15.50	0	1	0	-1.00
O McPhail	0	1	0	-1.00	0	8	0	-8.00	1	4	25	+3.50

By month

	Chases				Hurdles				Bumpers			
	W	R	%	£1 stake	W	R	%	£1 stake	W	R	%	£1 stake
January	3	13	23.1	+6.88	5	50	10	-23.32	1	6	16.7	-3.75
February	3	12	25	+3.50	6	46	13	-19.47	0	2	0	-2.00
March	3	15	20	-6.55	6	48	12.5	-26.88	4	8	50	+6.50
April	2	18	11.1	-10.50	6	53	11.3	+11.00	0	9	0	-9.00
May	1	15	6.7	+19.00	5	32	15.6	+2.00	1	5	20	+6.00
June	4	10	40	+5.10	5	27	18.5	+4.23	1	4	25	-0.75
July	1	5	20	-0.50	3	14	21.4	-6.77	0			
August	1	8	12.5	-5.80	2	12	16.7	-7.99	0			
September	0	3	0	-3.00	2	10	20	+5.10	0			
October	4	9	44.4	+29.38	2	12	16.7	-2.00	0			
November	2	13	15.4	-5.00	5	38	13.2	-11.38	1	6	16.7	+1.50
December	1	14	7.1	-11.00	7	35	20	+11.70	2	7	28.6	-1.88

Not forgetting ...

	Chases				Hurdles				Bumpers			
	W	R	%	£1 stake	W	R	%	£1 stake	W	R	%	£1 stake
Favourites	14	35	40	+9.50	27	64	42.2	+10.88	6	9	66.7	+8.38
After a break	2	22	9.1	-7.13	12	80	15	-2.88	1	8	12.5	-5.25

All runners

	Wins	Runs	%	2nd	3rd	rest	Win prize	Total prize	£1 Stake
Chases	25	135	18.5	25	21	64	269,329.59	442,270.00	+21.50
Hurdles	54	377	14.3	42	49	232	232,256.40	353,843.00	-63.77
Bumpers	10	47	21.3	2	7	28	16,932.30	24,189.00	-3.38
Totals	89	559	15.9	69	77	324	518,518.29	820,302.00	-45.65

Richard Phillips

AS we get further down the list of our top 20 trainers, the danger of making strong conclusions out of small samples becomes greater, but it's highly encouraging that Richard Phillips has turned a five-year profit from all his chasers.

Narrowing this down a bit, we can see he does particularly well with novices, while Richard Johnson is clearly a positive booking, as is Carl Llewellyn.

His string seem at their brightest and best from January to March and can be confidently backed under both codes at Class B level.

Course records

	Chases				Hurdles				Bumpers			
	W	R	%	£1 stake	W	R	%	£1 stake	W	R	%	£1 stake
Worcester	1	7	14.3	-4.63	4	14	28.6	-2.27	0	3	0	-3.00
Folkestone	1	6	16.7	+2.00	1	15	6.7	-13.27	3	5	60	+4.50
Market Rasen	2	4	50	+0.73	2	15	13.3	-3.75	1	3	33.3	+0.25
Newton Abbot	0	6	0	-6.00	5	20	25	+9.01	0	1	0	-1.00
Ayr	2	6	33.3	-3.30	2	4	50	+0.83	0	1	0	-1.00
Ludlow	1	9	11.1	+12.00	3	18	16.7	+5.63	0	8	0	-8.00
Kempton	2	7	28.6	+2.00	2	12	16.7	+2.00	0	3	0	-3.00
Taunton	1	4	25	+0.50	3	15	20	+26.50	0			
Warwick	0	2	0	-2.00	2	18	11.1	-5.00	2	2	100	+8.75
Hereford	1	4	25	+7.00	3	16	18.8	-8.02	0	1	0	-1.00
Uttoxeter	0	5	0	-5.00	4	13	30.8	-0.74	0			
Haydock	1	4	25	+8.00	1	11	9.1	-6.00	1	1	100	+2.50
Sandown	1	4	25	+1.00	2	7	28.6	+4.88	0	2	0	-2.00
Leicester	1	4	25	+1.00	2	8	25	-1.80	0			
Newcastle	0	1	0	-1.00	3	5	60	+7.50	0			
Stratford	1	4	25	-1.80	2	11	18.2	-1.63	0			
Cheltenham	2	13	15.4	-5.25	1	12	8.3	+14.00	0			
Sedgefield	1	2	50	+1.50	2	5	40	+1.63	0			
Aintree	2	5	40	+6.50	0	8	0	-8.00	0			
Chepstow	1	2	50	+0.88	1	6	16.7	+5.00	0	2	0	-2.00
Plumpton	0	2	0	-2.00	2	16	12.5	-1.50	0			
Doncaster	1	3	33.3	-0.63	1	14	7.1	-11.25	0	2	0	-2.00
Wincanton	1	3	33.3	-0.50	1	17	5.9	-11.00	0	2	0	-2.00
Huntingdon	1	5	20	+29.00	0	18	0	-18.00	1	3	33.3	+0.25
Kelso	0				1	1	100	+5.00	0			
Bangor	0	4	0	-4.00	1	10	10	+3.00	0			
Exeter	0	2	0	-2.00	0	13	0	-13.00	1	2	50	+9.00
Hexham	0				1	2	50	+1.25	0			
Newbury	0	2	0	-2.00	1	11	9.1	-8.75	0			
Fontwell	0	3	0	-3.00	1	10	10	-4.00	0	2	0	-2.00
Towcester	0	2	0	-2.00	0	6	0	-6.00	1	1	100	+1.38
Wolverhampton	1	1	100	+3.50	0				0			
Ascot	0	2	0	-2.00	0	8	0	-8.00	0			
Perth	0	2	0	-2.00	0	3	0	-3.00	0			
Windsor	0				0	1	0	-1.00	0			
Carlisle	0	1	0	-1.00	0	1	0	-1.00	0	1	0	-1.00
Fakenham	0	1	0	-1.00	0	3	0	-3.00	0			
Wetherby	0	2	0	-2.00	0	3	0	-3.00	0	1	0	-1.00
Catterick	0				0	1	0	-1.00	0			
Lingfield	0				0	2	0	-2.00	0			
Southwell	0	1	0	-1.00	0	3	0	-3.00	0	1	0	-1.00
Musselburgh	0				0	1	0	-1.00	0			

Race type

	Chases				Hurdles			
	W	R	%	£1 stake	W	R	%	£1 stake
Handicap	34	243	14	-33.87	52	401	13	-1.71
Novice	20	111	18	+36.92	52	338	15.4	+25.36
Maiden	1	3	33.3	+14.00	13	67	19.4	-3.92
Selling	0				1	3	33.3	+4.50
Claiming	-	-	-	-	0	1	0	-1.00
Amateur	1	7	14.3	-4.50	2	11	18.2	-6.31

Class of race

	Chases				Hurdles				Bumpers			
	W	R	%	£1 stake	W	R	%	£1 stake	W	R	%	£1 stake
A	4	38	10.5	-12.75	1	43	2.3	-32.00	0	4	0	-4.00
B	1	29	3.4	-24.67	4	53	7.5	-18.20	0	1	0	-1.00
C	6	49	12.2	-17.50	10	89	11.2	+27.88	-	-	-	-
D	19	108	17.6	+28.91	37	237	15.6	-0.58	-	-	-	-
E	15	89	16.9	-0.19	49	264	18.6	+62.95	-	-	-	-
F	3	26	11.5	-7.75	14	81	17.3	-0.22	-	-	-	-
G	0				1	3	33.3	+4.50	-	-	-	-
H	0				-	-	-	-	4	42	9.5	+7.63

Winning jockeys

	Chases				Hurdles				Bumpers			
	W	R	%	£1 stake	W	R	%	£1 stake	W	R	%	£1 stake
N Fehily	35	201	17.4	+13.27	55	331	16.6	+55.91	1	24	4.2	-21.38
J Magee	1	30	3.3	-4.00	22	143	15.4	+21.29	0			
C Rafter	0	4	0	-4.00	14	79	17.7	+8.80	2	14	14.3	+20.00
D Crosse	6	30	20	+10.08	5	58	8.6	+21.50	0	2	0	-2.00
D Gallagher	0				8	33	24.2	+11.73	0			
A Dobbin	1	4	25	-0.50	0	1	0	-1.00	0			
J Culloty	0	3	0	-3.00	1	5	20	+4.00	0	1	0	-1.00
R Johnson	0	4	0	-4.00	1	7	14.3	-5.78	0			
C Llewellyn	1	5	20	-1.00	0	5	0	-5.00	0			
M Bradburne	0				1	1	100	+0.44	0			

By month

	Chases				Hurdles				Bumpers			
	W	R	%	£1 stake	W	R	%	£1 stake	W	R	%	£1 stake
January	3	36	8.3	-5.00	7	88	8	-27.33	0	4	0	-4.00
February	2	33	6.1	-22.00	8	100	8	+34.50	0	5	0	-5.00
March	3	32	9.4	-15.50	6	72	8.3	-48.00	0	6	0	-6.00
April	1	27	3.7	-22.67	7	59	11.9	-7.25	1	5	20	-2.38
May	3	18	16.7	-6.25	20	72	27.8	+70.53	2	4	50	+22.00
June	3	19	15.8	+5.50	6	45	13.3	+1.28	0			
July	1	11	9.1	-7.00	8	42	19	-10.00	0			
August	2	7	28.6	+1.50	12	40	30	+9.13	0			
September	3	11	27.3	+3.38	5	32	15.6	+2.57	0			
October	4	24	16.7	+9.93	6	54	11.1	-8.00	0	3	0	-3.00
November	14	59	23.7	+14.33	18	90	20	+45.41	0	11	0	-11.00
December	9	62	14.5	+8.83	13	77	16.9	-19.50	1	9	11.1	+12.00

Not forgetting ...

	Chases				Hurdles				Bumpers			
	W	R	%	£1 stake	W	R	%	£1 stake	W	R	%	£1 stake
Favourites	18	63	28.6	-11.87	42	105	40	+11.57	1	5	20	-2.38
After a break	8	44	18.2	+23.83	12	122	9.8	+30.28	0	6	0	-6.00

Sponsored by Stan James

All runners

	Wins	Runs	%	2nd	3rd	rest	Win prize	Total prize	£1 Stake
Chases	48	339	14.2	66	56	169	284,941.65	438,536.00	-34.95
Hurdles	116	771	15	110	105	440	446,996.54	674,341.00	+43.32
Bumpers	4	47	8.5	6	2	35	7,149.50	10,190.00	+2.63
Totals	168	1157	14.5	182	163	644	739,087.69	1,123,067.00	+11.00

Charlie Mann

HERE'S a turn-up for the books. The slightly unexpected truth of the matter is that Charlie Mann is the only one of our featured 20 trainers to have produced a level-stakes profit on all runners over the last five-years.

Arguably, that ought to make him every punter's hero (it compares favourably with, say, Martin Pipe's deficit of over 660 times your unit stake) but let's not go overboard.

The profit in question is, after all, just one per cent of the total invested.

Mann is also the only featured trainer to return a profit on his hurdlers, which win at a slightly better rate than his chasers. His hurdlers have done best at Class E level, producing a profit of almost a quarter of total stakes.

Mann peaks from August to November and generates profits with horses coming back from a break.

Course records

	Chases				Hurdles				Bumpers			
	W	R	%	£1 stake	W	R	%	£1 stake	W	R	%	£1 stake
Worcester	1	10	10	-2.00	12	36	33.3	+19.00	1	1	100	+12.00
Fontwell	2	13	15.4	-7.50	11	56	19.6	+33.04	0	1	0	-1.00
Huntingdon	3	15	20	-2.75	8	36	22.2	-7.20	1	2	50	+11.00
Market Rasen	5	23	21.7	+3.00	7	37	18.9	-3.81		0		
Uttoxeter	2	15	13.3	+14.75	8	33	24.2	+5.01	0	2	0	-2.00
Newbury	6	27	22.2	+4.21	3	47	6.4	+3.00	0	3	0	-3.00
Stratford	3	15	20	-0.25	6	39	15.4	-10.03	0	1	0	-1.00
Plumpton	6	21	28.6	+23.13	2	16	12.5	-3.75	0	2	0	-2.00
Bangor	0	12	0	-12.00	6	21	28.6	+12.04		0		
Warwick	2	5	40	+19.25	2	18	11.1	-9.00	2	4	50	+19.63
Wincanton	2	12	16.7	+2.50	4	31	12.9	+17.00	0	1	0	-1.00
Newton Abbot	2	6	33.3	+11.50	4	32	12.5	-12.60		0		
Ascot	2	20	10	-12.42	3	26	11.5	-5.00	0	1	0	-1.00
Kempton	3	18	16.7	+3.70	2	34	5.9	+4.00	0	5	0	-5.00
Hereford	2	6	33.3	+13.50	3	22	13.6	+15.50		0		
Leicester	0	5	0	-5.00	5	9	55.6	+29.08		0		
Sandown	0	11	0	-11.00	4	23	17.4	-1.75	0	1	0	-1.00
Cheltenham	0	10	0	-10.00	4	38	10.5	+8.50	0	5	0	-5.00
Folkestone	1	8	12.5	-2.50	3	16	18.8	-5.50	0	3	0	-3.00
Perth	2	5	40	+1.00	1	9	11.1	-2.00		0		
Taunton	0	4	0	-4.00	3	34	8.8	-19.50		0		
Chepstow	1	19	5.3	-11.00	2	22	9.1	-9.50	0	4	0	-4.00
Southwell	2	7	28.6	-3.07	1	11	9.1	-8.50		0		
Ludlow	0	7	0	-7.00	2	23	8.7	+30.75	0	5	0	-5.00
Haydock	0	7	0	-7.00	2	16	12.5	-4.25	0	2	0	-2.00
Doncaster	0	3	0	-3.00	2	20	10	+11.50	0	1	0	-1.00
Towcester	0	4	0	-4.00	2	9	22.2	+5.50	0	1	0	-1.00
Fakenham	0	5	0	-5.00	1	7	14.3	-5.43	0	1	0	-1.00
Catterick		0			1	3	33.3	-1.67		0		
Lingfield	0	3	0	-3.00	1	4	25	-1.63				
Sedgefield	0	2	0	-2.00	1	3	33.3	+0.50				
Wolverhampton	1	1	100	+3.00	0	2	0	-2.00		0		
Ayr		0			0	3	0	-3.00		0		
Exeter	0	4	0	-4.00	0	13	0	-13.00	0	1	0	-1.00
Aintree	0	8	0	-8.00	0	11	0	-11.00		0		
Cartmel	0	1	0	-1.00	0	2	0	-2.00		0		
Windsor		0			0	1	0	-1.00		0		
Wetherby	0	7	0	-7.00	0	6	0	-6.00		0		
Musselburgh		0			0	2	0	-2.00		0		

Race type

	Chases				Hurdles			
	W	R	%	£1 stake	W	R	%	£1 stake
Handicap	81	538	15.1	-20.19	16	136	11.8	-29.58
Novice	36	249	14.5	-29.52	43	262	16.4	+29.97
Maiden	0	3	0	-3.00	3	49	6.1	-31.75
Selling	0				0	3	0	-3.00
Claiming	-	-	-	-	1	2	50	-0.43
Amateur	9	25	36	+29.83	2	13	15.4	-6.25

Class of race

	Chases				Hurdles				Bumpers			
	W	R	%	£1 stake	W	R	%	£1 stake	W	R	%	£1 stake
A	3	16	18.8	-2.00	3	14	21.4	-2.88	0	2	0	-2.00
B	3	55	5.5	-39.50	1	17	5.9	-7.00	0	1	0	-1.00
C	17	98	17.3	+57.70	5	32	15.6	+11.50	-	-	-	-
D	26	251	10.4	-116.00	16	138	11.6	-40.44	-	-	-	-
E	34	194	17.5	+11.31	33	200	16.5	+3.95	-	-	-	-
F	23	99	23.2	+35.43	3	30	10	-10.43	-	-	-	-
G	0				0	4	0	-4.00	-	-	-	-
H	0	5	0	-5.00	-	-	-	-	3	108	2.8	-75.00

Winning jockeys

	Chases				Hurdles				Bumpers			
	W	R	%	£1 stake	W	R	%	£1 stake	W	R	%	£1 stake
A Thornton	62	336	18.5	+27.12	35	217	16.1	-19.89	3	50	6	-17.00
R Walford	20	118	16.9	+16.17	4	63	6.3	-13.00	0	20	0	-20.00
R Widger	7	43	16.3	-8.97	1	8	12.5	-2.50	0	5	0	-5.00
J P McNamara	4	28	14.3	+9.25	4	28	14.3	+3.50	0	4	0	-4.00
A P McCoy	1	6	16.7	-1.50	3	5	60	+6.19	0	4	0	-4.00
Mr J D Moore	3	11	27.3	+10.00	1	2	50	+0.75	0	3	0	-3.00
R Johnson	2	7	28.6	+7.00	1	7	14.3	-3.25	0	3	0	-3.00
T J Murphy	0	3	0	-3.00	2	4	50	+13.00	0			
M A Fitzgerald	1	8	12.5	-2.50	1	5	20	-1.00	0			
S Wynne	0	4	0	-4.00	1	1	100	+8.00	0			

By month

	Chases				Hurdles				Bumpers			
	W	R	%	£1 stake	W	R	%	£1 stake	W	R	%	£1 stake
January	9	68	13.2	-1.85	5	45	11.1	-8.56	0	4	0	-4.00
February	6	46	13	-23.94	4	50	8	-33.50	0	12	0	-12.00
March	11	76	14.5	-20.04	7	72	9.7	-20.34	1	23	4.3	-8.00
April	10	82	12.2	+28.38	6	54	11.1	+9.00	1	12	8.3	+1.00
May	4	73	5.5	-53.42	5	28	17.9	-0.50	0	7	0	-7.00
June	2	10	20	+6.00	1	9	11.1	-7.17	0	2	0	-2.00
July	0	9	0	-9.00	1	3	33.3	+2.50	0			
August	0	11	0	-11.00	2	5	40	-1.60	0	2	0	-2.00
September	4	22	18.2	-8.50	2	13	15.4	-5.42	0	4	0	-4.00
October	16	83	19.3	-6.07	11	41	26.8	+9.54	1	6	16.7	-1.00
November	27	133	20.3	+32.53	8	57	14	+7.13	0	28	0	-28.00
December	17	106	16	+7.85	9	58	15.5	-0.38	0	11	0	-11.00

Not forgetting ...

	Chases				Hurdles				Bumpers			
	W	R	%	£1 stake	W	R	%	£1 stake	W	R	%	£1 stake
Favourites	32	124	25.8	-25.56	19	50	38	+2.58	0	5	0	-5.00
After a break	24	113	21.2	+30.53	9	63	14.3	+33.25	1	9	11.1	-4.00

All runners

	Wins	Runs	%	2nd	3rd	rest	Win prize	Total prize	£1 Stake
Chases	106	719	14.7	107	109	397	571,926.15	874,899.00	-59.06
Hurdles	61	435	14	46	44	283	260,628.13	400,564.00	-49.29
Bumpers	3	111	2.7	10	12	86	6,654.50	9,475.00	-78.00
Totals	170	1265	13.4	163	165	766	839,208.78	1,284,938.00	-186.35

Robert Alner

THE man who trained Cool Dawn is certainly capable of springing an upset on the more fashionable stables in the biggest races, but doesn't have the talent at his disposal to do so on a consistent basis.

Just look at his stats for chasers, broken down by class of race. Despite a respectable three-from-16 record at the highest level, the profits here are in backing Alner runners in races of Class C, E and F.

His relatively poor showing in Class D races is possibly a reflection of his moderate novice chase form. That said, his novice hurdlers have done a bit better and, perhaps because his reputation isn't usually linked to such horses, they've generated a level-stakes profit.

Alner doesn't often leave his runners short of fitness and they produce good profits after a break, particularly his hurdlers (over 50 per cent of total stakes).

GOLD: after Cool Dawn won

Course records

	Chases				Hurdles				Bumpers			
	W	R	%	£1 stake	W	R	%	£1 stake	W	R	%	£1 stake
Wincanton	17	99	17.2	-4.25	5	85	5.9	-55.75	0	10	0	-10.00
Exeter	6	54	11.1	+10.50	9	50	18	-6.97	1	10	10	+3.00
Plumpton	8	47	17	-1.75	6	23	26.1	+31.63	0	2	0	-2.00
Taunton	7	44	15.9	-1.83	3	42	7.1	-24.75	1	7	14.3	-2.00
Chepstow	5	29	17.2	+18.00	5	33	15.2	+6.00	1	11	9.1	+4.00
Hereford	8	39	20.5	-2.88	1	18	5.6	-14.25	0	4	0	-4.00
Kempton	6	46	13	+3.00	2	17	11.8	+7.00	0	6	0	-6.00
Fontwell	4	35	11.4	-23.54	4	25	16	-10.00	0	6	0	-6.00
Folkestone	5	31	16.1	-6.40	2	9	22.2	+2.50	0	10	0	-10.00
Ludlow	5	34	14.7	+6.50	1	9	11.1	-1.00	0	4	0	-4.00
Uttoxeter	4	18	22.2	-4.75	2	10	20	+0.50	0			
Newton Abbot	4	28	14.3	-3.55	2	15	13.3	-7.67	0	6	0	-6.00
Towcester	2	11	18.2	-4.00	3	8	37.5	+13.25	0	1	0	-1.00
Cheltenham	4	22	18.2	+10.83	1	10	10	-6.00	0	1	0	-1.00
Leicester	4	24	16.7	-6.77	0	3	0	-3.00	0			
Southwell	2	8	25	-0.75	2	4	50	+0.82	0			
Huntingdon	2	13	15.4	-6.25	2	5	40	+6.63	0	5	0	-5.00
Ascot	2	17	11.8	+9.00	1	10	10	-5.50	0	2	0	-2.00
Haydock	1	5	20	-1.75	2	8	25	+14.50	0	1	0	-1.00
Newbury	1	16	6.3	-11.00	2	17	11.8	-6.00	0	9	0	-9.00
Sandown	3	20	15	-2.50	0	4	0	-4.00	0	3	0	-3.00
Warwick	1	9	11.1	-6.25	2	8	25	+7.25	0	3	0	-3.00
Lingfield	1	4	25	+0.33	2	2	100	+20.44	0	1	0	-1.00
Stratford	2	24	8.3	-9.00	0	8	0	-8.00	0			
Market Rasen	0	2	0	-2.00	2	2	100	+3.08	0	1	0	-1.00
Bangor	1	13	7.7	+2.00	0	2	0	-2.00	0	2	0	-2.00
Windsor	1	2	50	+5.00	0	1	0	-1.00	0			
Ayr	0	1	0	-1.00	0				0			
Aintree	0	5	0	-5.00	0	1		-1.00	0	1	0	-1.00
Wetherby	0	1	0	-1.00	0				0			
Doncaster	0	2	0	-2.00	0	2	0	-2.00	0			
Worcester	0	15	0	-15.00	0	4	0	-4.00	0	5		-5.00
Wolverhampton	0	1	0	-1.00	0				0			

Race type

	Chases				Hurdles			
	W	R	%	£1 stake	W	R	%	£1 stake
Handicap	43	246	17.5	+49.78	14	136	10.3	-11.00
Novice	42	218	19.3	+28.38	29	282	10.3	-141.96
Maiden	2	15	13.3	+4.00	1	49	2	-42.00
Selling	0	2	0	-2.00	0	1	0	-1.00
Claiming	-	-	-	-	0			
Amateur	2	6	33.3	+2.50	0			

Class of race

	Chases				Hurdles				Bumpers			
	W	R	%	£1 stake	W	R	%	£1 stake	W	R	%	£1 stake
A	3	39	7.7	-15.75	1	26	3.8	-9.00	0	8	0	-8.00
B	15	65	23.1	+43.50	3	29	10.3	-5.00	0	1	0	-1.00
C	11	66	16.7	-21.73	4	41	9.8	-8.75	-	-	-	-
D	30	155	19.4	+36.98	9	126	7.1	-61.92	-	-	-	-
E	21	105	20	+12.86	21	166	12.7	-74.79	-	-	-	-
F	3	22	13.6	-7.00	1	34	2.9	-24.00	-	-	-	-
G	0	2	0	-2.00	0	1	0	-1.00	-	-	-	-
H	0	1	0	-1.00	-	-	-	-	19	161	11.8	+19.08

Winning jockeys

	Chases				Hurdles				Bumpers			
	W	R	%	£1 stake	W	R	%	£1 stake	W	R	%	£1 stake
J A McCarthy	21	151	13.9	+10.89	12	139	8.6	-75.66	0	19	0	-19.00
T Doyle	5	38	13.2	-17.12	5	42	11.9	-15.25	0	12	0	-12.00
A Thornton	7	39	17.9	+4.46	1	17	5.9	-15.92	1	3	33.3	+8.00
J P Byrne	5	22	22.7	+18.75	1	35	2.9	-28.00	2	29	6.9	-11.00
R Garritty	4	33	12.1	+0.75	1	20	5	-13.00	2	11	18.2	+10.50
N Williamson	4	8	50	+6.75	0	4	0	-4.00	1	1	100	+12.00
M A Fitzgerald	5	14	35.7	-3.54	0	5	0	-5.00	0	2	0	-2.00
P Flynn	2	4	50	+2.88	0	1	0	-1.00	0			
Mr M Baldock	1	4	25	+1.00	0				1	7	14.3	+14.00
M Foley	1	4	25	+1.00	0	1	0	-1.00	0			

By month

	Chases				Hurdles				Bumpers			
	W	R	%	£1 stake	W	R	%	£1 stake	W	R	%	£1 stake
January	9	59	15.3	-14.13	4	49	8.2	-24.18	5	26	19.2	+1.25
February	10	45	22.2	+47.30	3	44	6.8	-24.50	4	33	12.1	-16.42
March	6	39	15.4	-7.87	10	53	18.9	-4.35	3	24	12.5	+6.00
April	8	50	16	+6.32	4	51	7.8	-15.00	2	26	7.7	+6.00
May	6	35	17.1	+6.00	3	31	9.7	-10.00	2	15	13.3	+23.00
June	7	27	25.9	+20.53	0	15	0	-15.00	0	1	0	-1.00
July	2	15	13.3	-7.60	2	9	22.2	+12.00	0	1	0	-1.00
August	4	13	30.8	-0.40	1	12	8.3	-4.50	0	1	0	-1.00
September	1	10	10	-5.50	0	6	0	-6.00	0	2	0	-2.00
October	9	25	36	+8.94	1	27	3.7	-25.50	0	8	0	-8.00
November	6	62	9.7	-32.45	3	59	5.1	-45.88	2	14	14.3	+20.00
December	15	75	20	+24.71	8	67	11.9	-21.55	1	19	5.3	-16.75

Not forgetting ...

	Chases				Hurdles				Bumpers			
	W	R	%	£1 stake	W	R	%	£1 stake	W	R	%	£1 stake
Favourites	33	69	47.8	+12.78	14	28	50	-0.29	2	15	13.3	-10.50
After a break	16	79	20.3	+31.10	8	77	10.4	-23.38	0	19	0	-19.00

Sponsored by Stan James

All runners

	Wins	Runs	%	2nd	3rd	rest	Win prize	Total prize	£1 Stake
Chases	83	455	18.2	61	54	257	562,542.25	859,008.80	+45.86
Hurdles	39	423	9.2	41	44	299	164,952.80	252,792.00	-184.46
Bumpers	19	170	11.2	12	21	118	32,025.00	45,530.00	+10.08
Totals	141	1048	13.5	114	119	674	759,520.05	1,157,330.80	-128.52

Paul Webber

FOR Webber, more than any other trainer in our list, chasers matter a sight more than hurdlers – that can be the only explanation for the fact that his runners over fences are twice as likely to win as those over the smaller obstacles.

He does an excellent job with his fencers, maintaining high strike-rates and profits in handicaps and novice contests, and in most Class bands, though he doesn't usually get the talent to compete at the highest level.

His chasers peak in December, run well after a break and must be respected at Newbury.

Course records

	Chases				Hurdles				Bumpers			
	W	R	%	£1 stake	W	R	%	£1 stake	W	R	%	£1 stake
Bangor	4	19	21.1	+3.57	4	24	16.7	-6.93	3	9	33.3	+37.00
Huntingdon	7	26	26.9	+8.16	3	22	13.6	-1.63	1	12	8.3	+5.00
Kempton	5	20	25	+1.00	3	22	13.6	+6.00	1	5	20	+0.50
Newbury	6	19	31.6	+15.57	2	28	7.1	-12.00	0	9	0	-9.00
Wetherby	6	27	22.2	+8.63	2	13	15.4	-3.67	0	2	0	-2.00
Leicester	8	36	22.2	+19.01	0	6	0	-6.00		0		
Market Rasen	7	29	24.1	-3.10	1	12	8.3	-10.50	0	4	0	-4.00
Ludlow	3	21	14.3	+13.00	1	24	4.2	-22.50	3	13	23.1	+2.75
Towcester	2	9	22.2	+3.25	1	11	9.1	-9.92	3	12	25	+18.50
Haydock	2	9	22.2	+5.80	1	7	14.3	-3.25	2	4	50	+10.75
Warwick	3	13	23.1	-3.75	2	19	10.5	-1.50	0	7	0	-7.00
Stratford	4	17	23.5	+14.88	1	15	6.7	-5.00		0		
Uttoxeter	3	23	13	-15.69	2	20	10	-16.14	0	4	0	-4.00
Folkestone	3	10	30	+11.63	1	7	14.3	-4.00	1	11	9.1	-8.75
Plumpton	2	11	18.2	-4.13	2	10	20	-1.75	0	3	0	-3.00
Wincanton	1	14	7.1	+12.00	3	18	16.7	+13.00	0	3	0	-3.00
Sandown	1	15	6.7	-11.25	0	20	0	-20.00	2	5	40	+5.00
Chepstow	2	10	20	+18.00	0	13	0	-13.00	1	10	10	+3.00
Hereford	1	10	10	-7.25	1	9	11.1	-2.00	1	4	25	+17.00
Doncaster	2	19	10.5	-4.00	1	18	5.6	-16.09	0	6	0	-6.00
Worcester	2	14	14.3	+2.00	1	19	5.3	-12.50	0	6	0	-6.00
Aintree	2	14	14.3	+5.50	0	7	0	-7.00	0	1	0	-1.00
Lingfield	1	5	20	-1.75	1	4	25	+3.00	0	2	0	-2.00
Cheltenham	1	23	4.3	-20.00	1	23	4.3	-18.00	0	9	0	-9.00
Musselburgh	1	2	50	+5.00	1	3	33.3	-1.09		0		
Ayr	0	4	0	-4.00	1	2	50	+15.00	0	3	0	-3.00
Ascot	1	9	11.1	-6.25	0	16	0	-16.00	0	6	0	-6.00
Perth	1	3	33.3	-0.90		0				0		
Hexham		0			1	1	100	+1.00		0		
Fakenham		0			0	3	0	-3.00	1	5	20	-0.67
Fontwell	1	4	25	-0.50	0	2	0	-2.00	0	6	0	-6.00
Southwell	1	6	16.7	-4.56	0	5	0	-5.00		0		
Newton Abbot	0	7	0	-7.00	1	2	50	+5.00	0	2	0	-2.00
Wolverhampton	0	1	0	-1.00	1	1	100	+10.00		0		
Kelso		0			0	1	0	-1.00		0		
Exeter		0			0	2	0	-2.00		0		
Taunton	0	4	0	-4.00	0	11	0	-11.00	0	5	0	-5.00
Windsor		0			0	1	0	-1.00		0		
Carlisle		0				0			0	1	0	-1.00
Catterick	0	1	0	-1.00	0	1	0	-1.00	0	1	0	-1.00
Sedgefield	0	1	0	-1.00	0	1	0	-1.00		0		

Race type

	Chases				Hurdles			
	W	R	%	£1 stake	W	R	%	£1 stake
Handicap	30	138	21.7	+4.55	23	155	14.8	-25.00
Novice	31	113	27.4	-28.74	26	157	16.6	-69.67
Maiden	1	6	16.7	+0.50	6	27	22.2	+11.67
Selling	0				4	10	40	+7.05
Claiming	-	-	-	-	1	3	33.3	+6.00
Amateur	1	4	25	+0.50	1	8	12.5	-4.00

Class of race

	Chases				Hurdles				Bumpers			
	W	R	%	£1 stake	W	R	%	£1 stake	W	R	%	£1 stake
A	0	11	0	-11.00	0	13	0	-13.00	0	4	0	-4.00
B	4	30	13.3	-9.50	2	12	16.7	-4.59	0			
C	6	29	20.7	+7.92	3	19	15.8	+10.50	-	-	-	-
D	23	83	27.7	+0.63	15	96	15.6	-15.79	-	-	-	-
E	20	66	30.3	-4.05	23	140	16.4	-45.63	-	-	-	-
F	3	19	15.8	+0.41	8	46	17.4	-13.67	-	-	-	-
G	0				4	10	40	+8.05	-	-	-	-
H	0				-	-	-	-	12	67	17.9	+21.25

Winning jockeys

	Chases				Hurdles				Bumpers			
	W	R	%	£1 stake	W	R	%	£1 stake	W	R	%	£1 stake
A Dobbin	31	127	24.4	-10.37	34	175	19.4	-29.04	7	35	20	+7.25
B Harding	14	63	22.2	+5.19	12	90	13.3	-22.50	0	13	0	-13.00
J Crowley	2	7	28.6	0.00	1	9	11.1	-0.50	3	5	60	+23.00
P Robson	3	5	60	+4.03	1	11	9.1	-2.00	0	2	0	-2.00
F King	0	3	0	-3.00	1	17	5.9	-13.00	1	3	33.3	-1.00
L Wyer	0	2	0	-2.00	2	4	50	+9.75	0			
D Elsworth	0				2	3	66.7	+3.17	0	1	0	-1.00
G Lee	0	1	0	-1.00	1	2	50	+0.50	0			
V T Keane	0				1	1	100	+2.50	0	1	0	-1.00
G Berridge	1	1	100	+1.25	0				0			

By month

	Chases				Hurdles				Bumpers			
	W	R	%	£1 stake	W	R	%	£1 stake	W	R	%	£1 stake
January	7	30	23.3	-8.51	5	44	11.4	-22.31	1	10	10	-3.00
February	3	24	12.5	-12.25	3	22	13.6	-14.90	5	7	71.4	+28.00
March	3	23	13	-18.46	7	33	21.2	+11.67	0	16	0	-16.00
April	2	21	9.5	-16.50	8	48	16.7	+9.05	2	12	16.7	-4.75
May	9	21	42.9	+32.48	6	26	23.1	+7.50	0			
June	5	12	41.7	+5.25	2	17	11.8	-6.50	0	1	0	-1.00
July	2	4	50	-1.07	1	5	20	+2.00	0	3	0	-3.00
August	5	14	35.7	+7.91	2	10	20	-4.00	0	2	0	-2.00
September	1	5	20	-1.50	4	12	33.3	+2.63	0			
October	6	16	37.5	+1.00	4	32	12.5	-14.50	0	3	0	-3.00
November	8	40	20	+13.00	10	57	17.5	-20.79	3	12	25	+22.75
December	5	28	17.9	-16.94	3	30	10	-24.96	1	5	20	-1.75

Not forgetting ...

	Chases				Hurdles				Bumpers			
	W	R	%	£1 stake	W	R	%	£1 stake	W	R	%	£1 stake
Favourites	35	75	46.7	+10.66	23	59	39	-6.63	4	11	36.4	-0.25
After a break	11	39	28.2	+50.44	12	71	16.9	-13.33	0	5	0	-5.00

Sponsored by Stan James

All runners

	Wins	Runs	%	2nd	3rd	rest	Win prize	Total prize	£1 Stake
Chases	56	238	23.5	35	25	122	293,589.00	452,047.00	-15.59
Hurdles	55	336	16.4	45	31	205	187,436.60	277,637.00	-75.13
Bumpers	12	71	16.9	14	6	39	19,828.00	28,200.00	+16.25
Totals	123	645	19.1	94	62	366	500,853.60	757,884.00	-74.47

Nicky Richards

AS the son of the great Gordon Richards, trainer of One Man and Hallo Dandy, Nicky Richards ought to know what he's doing, but he hasn't made a major splash in his first few seasons, which may explain the amount of value seemingly on offer about his runners.

Most interesting of all are his stats relating to chasers after a break. Only Henderson and Nicholls have better strike-rates with such runners, but neither can touch Richards in terms of profitability, the Greystoke man re-turning a profit of 130 per cent on total stakes. He has also done well with his handicappers.

Though the samples are not large, Richards has generally kept up a steady strike-rate from May to January with his fencers. Admittedly, the profits they generate tail off badly by the end of that period.

Richards has an enviable record in bumpers, with an overall profit for level-stakes punters. This is largely due to his four wins from 12 at Ayr, at an average SP of over 6-1.

WITH TONY DOBBIN

Course records

	Chases				Hurdles				Bumpers			
	W	R	%	£1 stake	W	R	%	£1 stake	W	R	%	£1 stake
Ayr	8	35	22.9	-9.61	8	43	18.6	-26.26	4	12	33.3	+17.25
Perth	4	18	22.2	-7.09	9	36	25	+21.50	0	1	0	-1.00
Hexham	6	17	35.3	+3.25	5	15	33.3	+7.25	0	4	0	-4.00
Carlisle	6	31	19.4	-15.25	4	33	12.1	-14.00	0	11	0	-11.00
Sedgefield	6	14	42.9	-2.28	3	22	13.6	-4.88	1	4	25	-2.00
Kelso	6	19	31.6	+17.51	3	27	11.1	-14.53	0			
Musselburgh	1	12	8.3	-7.50	6	20	30	+7.42	1	8	12.5	-4.75
Haydock	2	8	25	-2.00	4	19	21.1	-4.59	1	5	20	+12.00
Newcastle	3	14	21.4	+0.13	2	31	6.5	-6.25	1	3	33.3	+1.50
Cartmel	3	7	42.9	+10.25	2	11	18.2	-4.00	0			
Uttoxeter	3	7	42.9	+2.25	1	5	20	+1.00	1	1	100	+1.75
Bangor	1	7	14.3	+10.00	2	14	14.3	-4.50	1	4	25	+9.00
Wetherby	2	9	22.2	-0.75	2	10	20	+3.50	0			
Market Rasen	2	3	66.7	+3.00	1	4	25	-2.20	0	1	0	-1.00
Hereford	1	3	33.3	+1.00	1	3	33.3	-0.25	0			
Aintree	1	6	16.7	+4.00	0	6	0	-6.00	0	2	0	-2.00
Warwick	0				0	1	0	-1.00	1	1	100	+7.00
Catterick	0	4	0	-4.00	1	10	10	-8.33	0	3	0	-3.00
Doncaster	0	4	0	-4.00	0	7	0	-7.00	1	4	25	+3.50
Worcester	1	1	100	+4.50	0	2	0	-2.00	0	3	0	-3.00
Wolverhampton	0	1	0	-1.00	1	3	33.3	+4.00	0			
Ascot	0	2	0	-2.00	0				0			
Ludlow	0				0	1	0	-1.00	0	1	0	-1.00
Kempton	0	1	0	-1.00	0				0			
Newbury	0	1	0	-1.00	0	2	0	-2.00	0			
Sandown	0	3	0	-3.00	0				0			
Chepstow	0	1	0	-1.00	0				0			
Fakenham	0				0	1	0	-1.00	0			
Southwell	0				0	2	0	-2.00	0			
Stratford	0	3	0	-3.00	0	2	0	-2.00	0			
Cheltenham	0	7	0	-7.00	0	6	0	-6.00	0	3	0	-3.00

Outlook

Big-RACE RESULTS
May 2002 – April 2003

1 Merewood Homes Swinton Handicap
Hurdle (Grade 3) (2m)
Haydock May 4 (Good)
1 **Intersky Falcon** 5-11-10   L Cooper
2 **Gralmano** 7-10-0   G Lee
3 **Whistling Dixie** 6-10-5   A Dempsey
11-2, 6-1, 12-1. 1/2l, 3l. 11 ran. 3m 32.4
(b12.40) Interskyracing com & Mrs Jonjo
O'Neill (Jonjo O'Neill, Cheltenham)

Intersky Falcon had made his handicap debut off a mark of 109 at the end of February. Two wins and a second place later, he came into this on 148 and proved just up to the task, getting up in the dying strides. **Tucacas**, the 3-1 fav, found them going too quick for her over the last two and faded into a well-beaten sixth, while the previous year's winner **Milligan** never looked like getting the double.

2 Britannia Building Society Summer
Chase (Showcase Handicap)
(4m110yds)
Uttoxeter June 30 (Good to Firm)
1 **Stormez** 5-11-8   A P McCoy
2 **General Claremont** 9-10-9   R Walsh
3 **Ardent Scout** 10-10-6   S Durack
11-2, 9-2f, 20-1. nk, 1 1/2l. 14 ran. 8m 8.2
(b7.70) D A Johnson (M Pipe, Wellington)

Making his handicap debut after winning two from three in novice chases during May, **Stormez** was not the most polished fencer and edged left on the run-in but stayed well and proved a good battler. The form may amount to little, since **General Claremont** was 6lb higher than his most recent win, over a year earlier, but Stormez was giving lumps of weight to all bar the well-beaten **Mister One** and this was a doughty effort.

3 McCallum Corporate Consulting
Summer Handicap Hurdle
(2m1f110yds)
Market Rasen July 20 (Good to Soft)
1 **Puntal** 6-11-10   A P McCoy
2 **Loop The Loup** 6-10-11   P Aspell (5)
3 **Cotopaxi** 10-10-2   B J Crowley

4 **Whistling Dixie** 6-11-7   A Dempsey
6-1, 14-1, 14-1, 11-1. 4l, 4l, 3l. 16 ran. 4m
9.2 (a7.70) Terry Neill (M Pipe, Wellington)

Brought over from France, **Puntal** had made his UK debut when well beaten as an unfancied 33-1 shot in a Grade 1 for novices at Aintree in April. Unbeaten in four much weaker events since then, he had returned to France in June for a handicap hurdle at Auteuil, but fell on the Flat. Clearly, there were no ill effects, however, as he made all, drew clear three out and won as he liked. Fancied pair **Patriot Games** (sent over by Charlie Swan, and ridden by him) and **Spectrometer** never looked like landing a blow.

4 Tote Scoop6 Summer Plate Chase
(Showcase Handicap) (2m4f)
Market Rasen July 20 (Good to Soft)
1 **Chicuelo** 6-10-4   A P McCoy
2 **Star Jack** 7-10-5   P Robson (5)
3 **Logician** 11-11-10   M Bradburne
15-8f, 20-1, 14-1. 5l, 2 1/2l. 15 ran. 4m 56.9
(a7.90) Mrs Belinda Harvey (M Pipe, Wellington)

Another French import, **Chicuelo** had been brought over by Ian Williams the previous autumn and had since raced six times over fences without success, for three of which he'd been favourite. This was his first start for Pipe and he was well backed once more, but this time the backing was justified. Confidently ridden, he was still on the bit when taking it up before the last and won impressively. The unseasonably easy going went against **Logician**, **Phar From A Fiddle**, **Ei Ei** and **Demasta**.

5 Hewlett Packard Galway Plate Handicap Chase (Grade B) (2m6f)
Galway July 31 (Soft)
1 **Rockholm Boy** 9-10-10   K Hadnett (5)
2 **Wotsitooya** 10-10-6   D J Howard (5)
3 **Ridgewood Water** 10-9-10   P Moloney
4 **Risk Accessor** 7-11-5   R Walsh
20-1, 14-1, 25-1, 15-2. 3 1/2l, 3l, 1/2l. 22 ran.

5m 39.5 (a3.89) M G H Syndicate (M Hourigan, Ireland)

A course and distance winner the previous autumn, **Rockholm Boy** came into this on a 17lb higher mark. Having made steady progress, he took it up in the final furlong and stayed on for a workmanlike success. Hourigan afterwards reported that the horse had been in rare form for the race. Noel Meade's 7-1 favourite **Royal Jake** never got into the argument, while **Monty's Pass** was never nearer than his finishing position of sixth.

6 **Guinness Galway Handicap Hurdle (Grade B) (2m)**
Galway August 1 (Good to Soft)

1 **Say Again** 6-10-7		J L Cullen
2 **Mutakarrim** 5-10-3		B J Geraghty
3 **Just Our Job** 7-12-0		K A Kelly
4 **Touch Of Love** 6-9-11		J E Casey

16-1, 12-1, 25-1, 12-1. 2l, shd, 2¹/2l. 24 ran. 3m 56.1 (a3.76) Sean Duggan (P Nolan, Ireland)

Say Again was 32lb higher than on his handicap debut 10 months before but he'd shown great consistency, winning twice and only once finishing out of the places in ten outings (falling once). Prominent behind a steady pace, he cruised to the lead at the last and was always holding **Mutakarrim**, who nonetheless maintained his effort to the line.

7 **Guinness Kerry National Handicap Chase (Grade A) (3m)**
Listowel September 25 (Firm)

1 **Monty's Pass** 9-11-9		B J Geraghty
2 **Putsometnby** 6-9-10		G Cotter
3 **Native Performance** 7-9-11		G T Hutchinson (5)
4 **Sparkling Gold** 8-10-9		P J Crowley (5)

9-1, 20-1, 10-1, 16-1. 2l, nk, 4l. 18 ran. 5m 44.7 (b33.95)
Dee Racing Syndicate (J J Mangan, Ireland)

This was a sixth handicap win for **Monty's Pass**, off a mark 42lb higher than his first. As he'd been placed in this, as well as in the Topham and the Galway Plate, trainer James Mangan felt it was about time he won a big one. Close up throughout, he led two out and plugged on gamely. Mangan nominated Aintree's National as the target. This year's Plate winner **Rockholm Boy** was brought down at the first.

8 **John James McManus Memorial Hurdle (Grade 2) (2m)**
Tipperary October 6 (Good to Firm)

1 **Intersky Falcon** 5-11-12		L Cooper
2 **Bob What** 8-11-5		R Walsh
3 **In Contrast** 6-11-12		P Flynn

3-1, 14-1, 7-4f. 1¹/2l, 10l. 9 ran. 3m 45.2 (b13.52)
Intersky Racing/Mrs JJ O'Neill (Jonjo O'Neill, Cheltenham)

Having his first run since winning the Swinton *(1)*, **Intersky Falcon** was forced to make a lot of his own running when the early pace was steadied after the second. Although he should have beaten the runner-up further if the ratings were to be believed, he finished tired and in the circumstances probably did well to win at all. **In Contrast** and **Scottish Memories** were also well-regarded sorts making their debuts, and both ran a fair bit below their best.

9 **Anglo Irish Bank Munster National Handicap Chase (Grade C) (3m)**
Limerick October 13 (Good to Soft)

1 **More Than A Stroll** 10-10-0		C O'Dwyer
2 **Arctic Copper** 8-10-1		P Carberry
3 **Monty's Pass** 9-10-4		B J Geraghty

6-1, 5-2, 7-4f. 1l, 2¹/2l. 6 ran. 6m 3.2 (a8.97)
Mrs D Grehan (A L Moore, Ireland)

Up 7lb for his Kerry National win, **Monty's Pass** was bested by a couple of seasonal debutants, apparently confirming the previous impression that he's better going left-handed. This was **More Than A Stroll**'s first win since the previous year's Kerry National, and he was 10lb higher here. In a muddling race, he had to make a fair bit of the running, but kept on dourly.

10 **Velka Pardubicka Chase (4m2f)**
Pardubice October 13 (Heavy)

1 **Maskul** 8-10-7		P Gehm
2 **Decent Fellow** 7-10-7		D Andres
3 **Kedon** 7-10-7		J Vana

7l, 12l. 17 ran. 10m 22.1 (H Radek)

Kevin Prendergast must be kicking himself about having let a Pardubicka winner leave his yard – he trained **Maskul** as a two-year-old. The winner was always handy and German jockey Peter Gehm (winning the race for the second year in succession) drove him out for a tired win on very patchy ground. There was no British interest, after Celibate and Paddy's Return were withdrawn.

11 **Fieldspring Desert Orchid Limited Handicap Chase (Grade 2) (2m5f)**
Wincanton October 27 (Good)

1 **Valley Henry** 7-11-7		M A Fitzgerald
2 **Upgrade** 8-11-10		A P McCoy
3 **Celibate** 11-10-4		N Fehily (5)

4-5f, 7-2, 11-1. 7l, 6l. 6 ran. 5m 0.8 (b11.05)
Paul K Barber (P Nicholls, Shepton Mallet)

Valley Henry had finished his distinctly mixed novice season on an upward curve, winning twice. He walked through the first here, but his jumping was better after that. Still, it took him until the run-in to master **Upgrade**, who was conceding weight, and this effort was short of impressive.

12 Peterhouse Group Charlie Hall Chase (Grade 2) (3m1f)
Wetherby November 2 (Good to Soft)
1 **Marlborough** 10-11-0   M A Fitzgerald
2 **Hussard Collonges** 7-11-5   R Garritty
3 **Gingembre** 8-11-0   A Thornton
7-2, 9-1, 14-1. 2l, nk. 8 ran. 6m 22.6
Sir Robert Ogden (N Henderson, Lambourn)

A good field was significantly reduced at the sixth, where **What's Up Boys** fell (chipping a hock, which kept him on the sidelines for the rest of the season, though a full recovery is expected) and **Lord Noelie** unseated after swerving round the faller. In the melee, **Marlborough** lost his place completely, but Mick Fitzgerald patiently allowed him to find his rhythm again and work his way slowly back into the race. **Hussard Collonges** set a strong pace, jumping boldly, and had seen off all rivals before the winner collared him going to the last. Peter Beaumont, trainer of the runner-up, reckoned he'd be better for the run. **Gingembre** made an almighty howler at the second and did well to finish so close on his first run since winning the Scottish National 19 months before.

13 William Hill Haldon Gold Cup Chase (Showcase Handicap) (G 2) (2m1f110yds)
Exeter November 5 (Good)
1 **Edredon Bleu** 10-11-10   J Culloty
2 **Seebald** 7-10-13   A P McCoy
3 **Armaturk** 5-10-12   R Walsh
10-1, evensf, 5-2. 10l, 21l. 6 ran. 4m 10.5 (b6.00)
Jim Lewis (Miss H Knight, Wantage)

Edredon Bleu had been beaten on both previous attempts in this race, so, at the weights, it was easy to understand that punters looked past him in favour of the placed horses from the previous season's Arkle, but the veteran put in an exhibition round of jumping and had this sewn up with two to go. It's a credit to his trainer that he's held his form so well for so long.

14 Freephone Stanley 0808 100 1221 Handicap Hurdle (2m)
Down Royal November 9 (Heavy)
1 **Emotional Moment** 5-10-1 N Williamson
2 **Milkat** 4-10-5   R Walsh
3 **Spirit Leader** 6-11-1   B J Geraghty
4 **Czar Of Peace** 4-10-10   P Moloney
13-2, 8-1, 3-1f, 14-1. 1/2l, 21/2l, 8l. 16 ran. 3m 55.0 (a53.61)

Watercork Syndicate (T Taaffe, Ireland)

Emotional Moment had won four of his previous six, improving 37lb over 11 months. This turned into a battle over the last two flights, with the first three finishing 8l clear. **Spirit Leader** deserved the lion's share of credit, giving so much weight to the first two on such ground. The race may have left its mark on **Milkat**, who could manage no better than a distant tenth in four subsequent outings.

15 James Nicholson Wine Merchant Champion Chase (Grade 1) (3m)
Down Royal November 9 (Heavy)
1 **More Than A Stroll** 10-11-10 C O'Dwyer
2 **See More Business** 12-11-10   R Walsh
3 **Give Over** 9-11-10   Mr D N Russell
20-1, 2-1f, 8-1. 5l, 9l. 7 ran. 6m 29.1 (a27.80)
Mrs D Grehan (A L Moore, Ireland)

A major upset, but the race rather fell into the winner's lap. Fitter for landing the Munster National *(9)*, **More Than A Stroll** was held up at the back while the market leaders vied for the lead. As they tired, he closed up three out and won quite comfortably. It was 8-1 bar **See More Business**, **Florida Pearl** and **Foxchapel King**, all of whom were having their reappearance runs (the latter was reportedly lame after pulling up). Florida Pearl had been beaten in the last three renewals of the race, having landed the inaugural running in 1999.

16 Badger Brewery Handicap Chase (Listed Race) (3m1f110yds)
Wincanton November 9 (Good)
1 **Swansea Bay** 6-10-3   A Thornton
2 **Gola Cher** 8-10-10   R Thornton
3 **Itsonlyme** 9-10-0   B J Crowley
14-1, 4-1, 10-3f. 21/2l, 13l. 12 ran. 6m 26.2 (a8.80)
W J Evans (P Bowen, Haverfordwest)

Cheekpieces worked the oracle for **Swansea Bay**, as he landed his sixth handicap success from seven starts, from a 39lb higher mark than the first just four months before. Only one of those wins came on ground easier than good (and that was a poor three-runner affair). **Itsonlyme** was taking a big step up in class on his fifth run over fences and didn't cope well. After many mistakes, his saddle slipped on the run-in, but for which he'd have been closer.

17 Prix La Haye Jousselin (Group 1) (3m1f110yds)
Auteuil November 10 (Heavy)
1 **Sunny Flight** 8-10-8   P Sourzac
2 **Cerilly** 5-10-3   L Metais
3 **Innox** 6-10-8   T Doumen
6-1, 13-2, 15-2. 5l, 8l. 7 ran. 7m 29.0
P Boiteau (A Chaille-Chaille, France)

A fifth course win for **Sunny Flight**, who has since made it six. **Innox** blundered away his chance at the third-last.

18 Prix Renaud Du Vivier (Group 1) (2m4f110yds)

Auteuil November 10 (Heavy)

1 **Karly Flight** 4-10-1	P Sourzac
2 **Foreman** 4-10-6	T Doumen
3 **Kotkita** 4-10-1	C Pieux

11-10f, 15-2, 6-1. 5l, 1¹/2l. 7 ran. 5m 18.0
P Boiteau (A Chaille-Chaille, France)

The sixth of eight consecutive wins, all at this course, for **Karly Flight**, whose run was brought to an end only by the Willie Mullins-trained Nobody Told Me in the Grand Course De Haies (June 2003).

19 Tote Bookmakers Handicap Hurdle (Listed Race) (3m1f110yds)

Cheltenham November 16 (Good to Soft)

1 **Native Emperor** 6-10-4	L Cooper
2 **Yeoman's Point** 6-10-3	C F Swan
3 **It Takes Time** 8-11-12	A P McCoy

13-2, 10-3f, 4-1. 1¹/4l, ¹/2l. 11 ran. 6m 24.1 (b7.46)
R & E H Investments Ltd (Jonjo O'Neill, Cheltenham)

Springfield Scally set a strong pace, making this a real test of stamina, which found out **It Takes Time**, outstayed by the front two after travelling well throughout. **Yeoman's Point** had been an easy winner one week beforehand and ought to have had a fitness advantage over the reappearing winner, but the 9lb rise anchored him.

20 Intervet Trophy Handicap Chase (Listed Race) (3m3f110yds)

Cheltenham November 16 (Good to Soft)

1 **Stormez** 5-10-6	B J Geraghty
2 **Southern Star** 7-10-2	J Culloty
3 **Good Shuil** 7-10-0	P Aspell (5)

5-1, 4-1, 12-1. ³/4l, 4l. 10 ran. 7m 12.7 (a11.90)
D A Johnson (M Pipe, Wellington)

Up 9lb for his Summer National win (2), **Stormez** again stayed best of all. Taking it up four out, he was put under strong pressure by the runner-up but rallied well. In hindsight, the form wasn't strong – neither of the placed horses managed a win all season, while well-beaten favourite **Shooting Light** was on a mark 24lb higher than when he won at the same meeting a year before.

21 Thomas Pink Gold Cup Chase (Showcase Handicap) (Grade 3) (2m4f110yds)

Cheltenham November 16 (Good to Soft)

1 **Cyfor Malta** 9-11-9	B J Geraghty
2 **Poliantas** 5-10-9	T J Murphy
3 **Wave Rock** 7-10-2	R Wakley

16-1, 25-1, 16-1. 7l, 5l. 15 ran. 5m 13.8 (a6.55)
D A Johnson (M Pipe, Wellington)

The race that brought Barry Geraghty to the British public's attention as a big-race jockey – he later rode five winners at the Festival. **Chicuelo** was sent off 2-1 favourite after some serious hype but, in the words of one spectator, "he jumped as though he had diving boots on." He was pulled up two out. The hype had allowed his stablemate **Cyfor Malta**, once fancied for the Gold Cup and the winner of this race in 1998 off a 4lb lower mark, to go off at a big price – in fairness, the horse's only win in three and a half years had been in a Class B a year before. He showed here that he could still do the job when things fall right, though, and was always prominent before taking it up after two out and running on up the hill. Youngster **Poliantas** ran a fine race on his handicap debut.

22 Rehabilitation Of Racehorses Hurdle (Showcase Handicap) (2m110yds)

Cheltenham November 17 (Good to Soft)

1 **Rooster Booster** 8-11-12	S Durack
2 **Quazar** 4-10-8	L Cooper
3 **Dark'n Sharp** 7-10-0	J Mogford

7-1, 6-1, 13-2. 9l, 1¹/2l. 11 ran. 3m 58.1 (a2.60)
Terry Warner (P Hobbs, Minehead)

Up 11lb since his County Hurdle win over course and distance eight months before, **Rooster Booster** showed he'd made further progress by running away with this. He'd already coasted to a 4l lead when the last-flight fall of stablemate **In Contrast** left him clear. He was such a big price mainly because of **Dream With Me**, seeking a sixth successive win for the Pipe/McCoy team. Chucked up a stone for winning a lesser race on his latest start, he was sent off the 7-2 favourite but trailed in a distant sixth.

23 Edward Hanmer Memorial Limited Handicap Chase (Grade 2) (3m)

Haydock November 17 (Soft)

1 **Kingsmark** 9-11-10	D R Dennis
2 **Chives** 7-10-10	Richard Guest
3 **Bobby Grant** 11-10-12	R Garritty

10-3, 3-1f, 16-1. 1¹/2l, 19l. 9 ran. 6m 7.2 (a6.00)
Sir Robert Ogden (M Todhunter, Penrith)

Kingsmark was winning this for the third year in a row, off a mark 22lb higher than the first time. Though smaller than second-season chaser **Chives** (who was getting a stone), he outbattled that one on the run-in. **Bobby Grant** did well on his first run for a year.

24 **Pierse Contracting Troytown Handicap Chase (Grade B) (3m)**
Navan November 17 (Soft)
1 **Takagi** 7-10-4   N Williamson
2 **Arctic Copper** 8-10-5   P Carberry
3 **Lord Of The Turf** 9-10-5   B J Geraghty
4-1, 3-1, 4-1. 5l, 2¹/2l. 6 ran. 6m 29.3 (a28.67)
D Cox (E O'Grady, Ireland)

Behrajan's presence meant that only two of his rivals were able to run off their true marks, but he was a hugely disappointing 9-4 favourite. His jumping became increasingly erratic and a mistake five out finished his chances. **Takagi** didn't have to find much improvement to win off a 5lb higher mark than when he had been successful over course and distance the previous March.

25 **McCallum Corporate Consulting BBA Peterborough Chase (Grd2) (2m4f110yds)**
Huntingdon November 23 (Good to Soft)
1 **Best Mate** 7-11-10   J Culloty
2 **Douze Douze** 6-11-0   J Ricou
3 **Geos** 7-11-0   M A Fitzgerald
8-15f, 7-2, 8-1. 8l, 2¹/2l. 5 ran. 5m 6.4 (a7.10)
Jim Lewis (Miss H Knight, Wantage)

The Gold Cup winner didn't disappoint on his reappearance. Despite looking short of peak fitness, he made all and powered clear up the straight. **Douze Douze**, having his first run outside France, didn't cope well with the fences, diving at many of them, but was still in contention until running down the last.

26 **Tote Becher Chase (Showcase Handicap) (3m3f)**
Aintree November 24 (Good to Soft)
1 **Ardent Scout** 10-10-0   D Elsworth (3)
2 **Amberleigh House** 10-10-5   A Dobbin
3 **Blowing Wind** 9-11-8   A P McCoy
14-1, 9-2f, 5-1. 24l, 14l. 15 ran. 7m 13.1 (a25.40)
Mrs Alicia Skene & W S Skene (Mrs S J Smith, Bingley)

Having been second and fourth in the previous two runnings, **Ardent Scout** galloped away with this, aided by the falls of **Bindaree** and **Moor Lane**. Last year's winner **Amberleigh House** ran another good race off 9lb higher, while **Blowing Wind** was 7lb above the mark from which he'd been third in the previous two Grand Nationals.

27 **Hennessy Cognac Gold Cup Chase (Showcase Handicap) (Grade 3) (3m2f110yds)**
Newbury November 30 (Good to Soft)
1 **Be My Royal** 8-10-0   D J Casey
2 **Gingembre** 8-10-13   A Thornton
3 **Harbour Pilot** 7-10-3   P Carberry

4 **Whitenzo** 6-10-2   R Walsh
33-1, 16-1, 11-1, 25-1. ¹/2l, 1¹/2l, 2¹/2l. 25 ran.
6m 35.8 (b4.35)
Mrs V O'Leary (W P Mullins, Ireland)

Be My Royal had fallen or unseated in five of his first seven attempts over fences, but had finally seemed to get his act together, winning three from four before coming here. That said, he'd shown little to suggest he was in this class and raced from 3lb out of the handicap. Positioned close behind a strong pace, he made a couple of errors but rallied to lead on the run-in, just doing enough to hold off the renewed challenge of **Gingembre**. But connections had the cup of joy dashed from their lips in no uncertain terms. After the race, Be My Royal was found to have damaged a tendon so severely that he would be unable to race for at least two years, and it seems very likely that this was his final outing. Then, some weeks afterwards, it was revealed that the horse was one of a number to have ingested accidentally-contaminated feed, which resulted in a positive test for morphine after the race. Though the procedures are not yet complete, he seems sure to be disqualified as Hennessy winner. Gingembre will be a deserving substitute winner, since this was his second runner-up finish in the race (off a 16lb higher mark than the first time). **Harbour Pilot** was in front when smashing through the last, but for which he may well have won, while **Whitenzo** blundered away his chance at the fourth-last. Following these, there were stout efforts in one of the most competitive races of the season by **Hussard Collonges**, **Carbury Cross** and **Gunther McBride**. Whitbread winner **Bounce Back** was a disappointing favourite for the Pipe/McCoy combo, coming in 16th of 19 finishers, having not jumped well.

28 **Pertemps 'Fighting Fifth' Hurdle (Grade 2) (2m)**
Newcastle November 30 (Good to Soft)
1 **Intersky Falcon** 5-11-8   L Cooper
2 **The French Furze** 8-11-0   B Harding
3 **Marble Arch** 6-11-0   M Bradburne
11-10f, 9-1, 13-8. 6l, 8l. 6 ran. 3m 54.5 (a2.50)
Interskyracing com & Mrs Jonjo O'Neill (Jonjo O'Neill, Cheltenham)

Given that **Marble Arch** failed to run to form on this, his seasonal debut, **Intersky Falcon** was entitled to win easily, and duly did so.

29 **Boylesports Royal Bond Novice Hurdle (Grade 1) (2m)**
Fairyhouse December 1 (Soft)

1 **Hardy Eustace** 5-11-12   K A Kelly
2 **Back In Front** 5-11-12   N Williamson

3 **Macs Valley** 5-11-12   R Walsh
5-1, 4-1, 8-1. 1¹/2l, 9l. 10 ran. 4m 3.3 (a2.01)
Laurence Byrne (D Hughes, Ireland)

Two subsequent Festival winners fought out this usually informative race. **Back In Front**, making his hurdling bow, cruised to the lead two out and looked the winner but he lost momentum by clouting the last and got collared close home. **Hardy Eustace** did well to come back after looking beaten when dropping off the pace at the top of the straight. He finished strongly, as he'd done when winning a bumper at the same course the previous April.

30 **Pierse Group Drinmore Novice Chase (Grade 1) (2m4f)**
Fairyhouse December 1 (Soft)
1 **Le Coudray** 8-11-12   B J Geraghty
2 **Barrow Drive** 6-11-12   J Culloty
3 **Fiery Ring** 7-11-12   R Geraghty
evensf, 3-1, 14-1. 6l, dis. 9 ran. 5m 23.7 (b8.04)
JP McManus (C Roche, Ireland)

Le Coudray was a Grade 2-winning hurdler but had been off the course almost three years before going novice chasing the month before this. He fell when looking the likely winner first time, then won a modest race at Naas. This looked a lot more competitive, but he won easing down after most of his rivals became seriously tired in the conditions. Even he dived through the last.

31 **Ballymore Properties Hatton's Grace Hurdle (Grade 1) (2m4f)**
Fairyhouse December 1 (Soft)
1 **Limestone Lad** 10-11-12 B J Geraghty
2 **Scottish Memories** 6-11-12 P Carberry
3 **Ned Kelly** 6-11-12   N Williamson
8-15f, 7-2, 6-1. 8l, dis. 5 ran. 5m 7.7 (a10.58)
James Bowe (J Bowe, Ireland)

Limestone Lad's 33rd career win (he made it 35 before New Year) and his third in this race. Once again, he made all and powered away from leg-weary rivals. Neither of the two who chased him home were anything like as comfortable in the conditions.

32 **John Hughes Rehearsal Limited Handicap Chase (Listed Race) (3m2f110yds)**
Chepstow December 7 (Soft)
1 **See More Business** 12-11-10 A Thornton
2 **Bindaree** 8-10-4   C Llewellyn
3 **Rugged River** 7-10-4   R Walford
2-1j, 8-1, 7-2. 7l, 2l. 5 ran. 7m 12.1 (a21.10)
Paul K Barber & Sir Robert Ogden (P Nicholls, Shepton Mallet)

A race with a mixed history for **See More Business**, who'd won it twice but had also taken a crashing fall in the latest running, which left his career in doubt. He showed no memory of that, though, jumping cleanly and making all against an admittedly weak field. For **Bindaree**, this was a confidence-booster after falling in the Becher Chase (26) and unseating in the Hennessy (27). **Rugged River** did well from 11lb out of the handicap.

33 **Mitsubishi Shogun Tingle Creek Trophy Chase (Showcase) (Grade 1) (2m)**
Sandown December 7 (Soft)
1 **Cenkos** 8-11-7   R Walsh
2 **Edredon Bleu** 10-11-7   J Culloty
3 **Wahiba Sands** 9-11-7   A P McCoy
6-1, 13-2, 10-1. 14l, 15l. 6 ran. 3m 59.4 (a13.00)
Mrs J Stewart (P Nicholls, Shepton Mallet)

It's doubtful what **Cenkos** achieved here because, although he strung out a top-class field, his two main rivals, **Flagship Uberalles** and **Moscow Flyer**, cannoned into each other at the fifth, causing the latter to unseat. Flagship Uberalles never got back into the race, so the eventual winner only had the ageing pair **Edredon Bleu** and **Wahiba Sands** to beat. If Cenkos reproduced the form of his April win over course and distance, he was a shoo-in from that point, and he came home unchallenged.

34 **William Hill Handicap Hurdle (Listed Race) (2m110yds)**
Sandown December 7 (Soft)
1 **Spirit Leader** 6-10-0   N Williamson
2 **Moving On Up** 8-10-0   N Fehily
3 **Hawadeth** 7-10-0   J Culloty
9-2, 20-1, 16-1. 4l, 4l. 12 ran. 4m 6.9 (a14.08)
D Thompson (Mrs J Harrington, Ireland)

Though the pace was by no means strong, soft going exacts a toll at this track and it was notable that the first four home carried 10st or less, while the only two runners burdened with over 11st finished well back. **Spirit Leader**, while consistent, had been hard to win with in her native Ireland but showed great battling qualities here, holding off a strong challenge after blundering at the last. **Hawadeth** ran on well and was never nearer than at the line, while favourite **Samon** seemed to struggle in the conditions and may be poorly handicapped.

35 **John Durkan Memorial Punchestown Chase (Grade 1) (2m4f)**
Punchestown December 8 (Soft)
1 **Native Upmanship** 9-11-12 C O'Dwyer

2 **Rince Ri** 9-11-12 R Walsh
3 **First Gold** 9-11-12 T Doumen
5-4f, 5-1, 5-2. 3l, 1¹/2l. 5 ran. 5m 24.5 (a12.81)
Mrs John Magnier (A L Moore, Ireland)

Fair-enough performances from **Rince Ri** and **First Gold** on their seasonal reappearances, but this was very easy for **Native Upmanship**. **More Than A Stroll** nicked a Grade 1 (15) when last seen, but was shown up here.

36 Lombard Properties Handicap Chase (3m1f110yds)
Cheltenham December 13 (Good)
1 **Horus** 7-11-4 A P McCoy
2 **Bramblehill Duke** 10-10-11 B J Crowley
3 **Ballinclay King** 8-11-1 D N Russell
5-2f, 16-1, 16-1. 1¹/4l, 6l. 10 ran. 6m 44.7 (a19.65)
B A Kilpatrick (M Pipe, Wellington)

Horus was two wins from four when a hunter chaser with Martin Pipe's son David the previous season, but this made it three out of three in his new career as a pro for Pipe Snr, a run which is the more impressive because the horse isn't elligible for novice chases. This one was set up for him by a steady early pace, which allowed him to settle the argument with a burst of speed on the downhill run. He beat a field largely consisting of underachievers.

37 Doncaster Bloodstock Sales Future Champions Novices' Chase (2m5f)
Cheltenham December 14 (Good)
1 **Paxford Jack** 6-11-0 O McPhail
2 **Supreme Catch** 5-11-5 J Culloty
3 **Toulouse-Lautrec** 6-11-5 R Johnson
33-1, 13-8f, 16-1. 1l, 2¹/2l. 10 ran. 5m 25.4 (a11.90)
M Harris (M Harris, Banbury)

A moderate race for the course, which lost a deal of its competitiveness when the challenging **Dead-Eyed Dick** fell three out, bringing down **Pontius**. **Paxford Jack** made all and stayed on gamely.

38 Tripleprint Gold Cup Chase (Showcase Handicap) (Grade 3) (2m5f)
Cheltenham December 14 (Good)
1 **Fondmort** 6-10-5 M A Fitzgerald
2 **Foly Pleasant** 8-11-3 J Culloty
3 **Youlneverwalkalone** 8-10-1 C O'Dwyer
5-1, 7-1, 7-2. 6l, 6l. 9 ran. 5m 18.3 (a4.80)
W J Brown (N Henderson, Lambourn)

Fondmort had been stepped up to 2m5f for the first time for his handicap debut the week before, having been kept to 2m throughout his novice season. If anything, he'd seemed outpaced that time and he showed sound stami-

na here, galloping clear on the run to the last, where he put in a spectacular leap. **Foly Pleasant** could keep on only at the one pace and seems weighted up to his best, while **Youlneverwalkalone** was also short of pace. **Cyfor Malta** had been put up 10lb for his Thomas Pink win (21) and that was enough to stop him getting competitive – he finished 6l further back in fourth.

39 Victor Chandler Bula Hurdle (Grade 2) (2m1f)
Cheltenham December 14 (Good)
1 **Rooster Booster** 8-11-4 R Johnson
2 **Landing Light** 7-11-8 M A Fitzgerald
3 **Geos** 7-11-0 N Williamson
11-8f, 6-1, 7-1. 2¹/2l, hd. 9 ran. 4m 3.7 (a0.20)
Terry Warner (P Hobbs, Minehead)

A serious test of **Rooster Booster**'s championship pretensions, as he took on the second, fourth and fifth from the previous season's Champion Hurdle (respectively, **Marble Arch**, **Geos** and **Landing Light**). Travelling well throughout, he went to the front two out and, although he had to be driven thereafter, he never looked in any danger. On the face of it, this was almost as good a performance as that put up by Hors La Loi to win here in March.

40 Tommy Whittle Chase (Grade 2) (3m)
Haydock December 14 (Good)
1 **Sackville** 9-11-8 T J Murphy
2 **Bobby Grant** 11-10-12 R Garritty
3 **Kingsmark** 9-11-4 D R Dennis
3-1, 1-2, 8-11f. 1¹/2l, 1¹/2l. 4 ran. 6m 23.4 (a22.20)
Seamus O'Farrell (Miss F M Crowley, Ireland)

Sackville was briefly ante-post favourite for the Gold Cup after running away with the 2001 Charlie Hall Chase, but he lost his way and this was his first win since. It was a pretty soft one; they went a steady pace, with the winner taking it up a third of the way into the race and being allowed to dictate it from there. Neither **Bobby Grant** (having his third run in two years) nor **Take Control** are reliable yardsticks, so **Kingsmark** is the only way of judging this form, and he had at least two possible excuses, since he ideally wants the ground softer and his trainer Martin Todhunter felt this may have come too soon after his last run (23).

41 Cantor Sport Long Walk Hurdle (Grade 1) (3m1f110yds)
Ascot December 20 (Soft)
1 **Deano's Beeno** 10-11-7 A P McCoy
2 **Baracouda** 7-11-7 T Doumen
3 **Native Emperor** 6-11-7 L Cooper
14-1, 4-11f, 5-1. 1l, dis. 5 ran. 6m 42.4 (a49.22)

Axom (M Pipe, Wellington)

It's hard to begrudge **Deano's Beeno** his first Grade 1 success, after four wins at Grade 2 level and three seconds in this event, for two of which he was favourite. But **Baracouda** should not have lost this, his first defeat in 11 outings since November 2000. McCoy wanted a true pace and sent Deano's Beeno into a clear lead, which had stretched to 20l with 6f to run. That Thierry Doumen allowed this to happen shows the limitations of his tactical nous. Baracouda may be a tricky ride, in that he has to be played late, but there was no need to set him such a task, and the wonder of it is that he almost pulled it off, having almost caught the leader by the last. By that point, however, he'd run his race and could find no more.

42 cantorindex.co.uk Handicap Chase (2m)
Ascot December 21 (Soft)

1 **Young Devereaux** 9-10-1		R Walsh
2 **Seebald** 7-11-12		A P McCoy
3 **Shamawan** 7-10-4		L Cooper

3-1, 11-2, 11-4f. 1l, 2¹/2l. 7 ran. 4m 16.8 (a26.40)
Paul K Barber,Mick Coburn,Colin Lewis 2 (P Nicholls, Shepton Mallet)

A major training performance by Paul Nicholls. **Young Devereaux** had run once in 23 months, when second to Cyfor Malta at Newbury the previous December. His injury problems meant he'd been unable to school until the day before this, and he had to run 14kg above his ideal racing weight. Just the same, he battled well to hold off **Seebald**, though his task was made easier by the falls of **Dark'n Sharp** and **Get Real**, who was still there when coming down at the second-last. Tragically, Get Real shattered a hock and had to be put down. Four of his eight wins had been at Ascot, where his ashes were subsequently buried.

43 cantorsport.co.uk Silver Cup Handicap Chase (Listed Race) (3m110yds)
Ascot December 21 (Heavy)

1 **Behrajan** 7-11-12		R Johnson
2 **Exit To Wave** 6-10-6		R Walsh
3 **Zafarabad** 8-10-9		A P McCoy

7-1, 6-1, 15-2. nk, dis. 7 ran. 6m 42.3 (a39.70)
The Behrajan Partnership (H Daly, Ludlow)

This was cast wide open when 2-1 favourite **Truckers Tavern** capsized at the first – the other six runners were all returned between 6-1 and 15-2. There were only two possible winners from a long way out, though. **Behrajan** led for most of the way and was clear with seven to go, at which point **Exit To Wave** was sent after him. A battle ensued, with Behrajan de-

fying a hefty weight concession and giving a much better impression than on his reappearance (24).

44 Ladbroke Hurdle (Showcase Handicap) (Listed Race) (2m110yds)
Ascot December 21 (Heavy)

1 **Chauvinist** 7-10-0		N Williamson
2 **Idaho D'ox** 6-10-3		G Supple
3 **Benbyas** 5-10-10		P J Brennan (5)
4 **Tikram** 5-10-2		T J Murphy

15-2, 50-1, 20-1, 12-1. 15l, ¹/2l, 1l. 20 ran. 4m 24.4 (a34.22)
Mrs E Roberts & Nick Roberts (N Henderson, Lambourn)

Nicky Henderson had reckoned **Chauvinist** would be his best novice last season but he "never put it all together" and was beaten all three starts. On his reappearance, a month before this, he easily won a decent-looking maiden race and was clearly much-improved. He confirmed that here, though it also helped that he coped with the gluey conditions much better than most of his rivals. **Whistling Dixie** appeared to be going as well as the winner when coming down at the second-last. Norman Williamson, riding Chauvinist, didn't realise that he'd been left so far clear and pushed his horse right out to the line, saying afterwards that he couldn't have won by an inch further. Henderson's stable jockey Mick Fitzgerald was on **Valerio**, who, like the Irish-trained 4-1 favourite **Holy Orders**, didn't handle the ground.

45 Pertemps Aviation Resources Feltham Novices' Chase (Grade 1) (3m)
Kempton December 26 (Soft)

1 **Jair Du Cochet** 5-11-7		J Ricou
2 **Le Sauvignon** 8-11-7		R Walsh
3 **Bold Investor** 5-11-7		A P McCoy

5-2, 2-1f, 7-2. 6l, 5l. 7 ran. 6m 19.0 (a31.00)
Mrs F Montauban (G Macaire, France)

Jair Du Cochet may be based in France, but his increasingly anglophile trainer Guillaume Macaire seems happy to run him almost exclusively in Britain – by the end of this season, 11 of his last 13 outings had been on this side of the Channel. This was his fourth chase win from as many starts, and easily his most impressive to date. **Le Sauvignon** had also been a top class staying hurdler in France, who'd looked a chaser with a future on his fencing debut, and he cruised up to challenge his younger rival at the top of the straight, but the physically imposing Jair Du Cochet rallied well and was clear before making a mistake at the last (his jockey reported that he slipped on the approach).

46 Pertemps Christmas Hurdle (Grade 1) (2m)
Kempton December 26 (Soft)

1 **Intersky Falcon** 5-11-7   C F Swan
2 **Santenay** 4-11-7   T J Murphy
3 **Davenport Milenium** 6-11-7   R Walsh
evensf, 20-1, 11-2. 3l, 6l. 6 ran. 3m 58.0 (a12.40)
Interskyracing com & Mrs Jonjo O'Neill (Jonjo O'Neill, Cheltenham)

Impressive stuff from **Intersky Falcon**, who led from the third and went clear three out, only to tire approaching the last. **Santenay**, who would have been almost 2st better off in a handicap, joined him at the last but Intersky Falcon found more. His performance drew high praise from Charlie Swan, a triple Champion Hurdle winner with Istabraq, who said; "I couldn't believe how much he found. He's not the biggest horse but jumps so well. Small horses don't usually improve, but he's very tough." **Davenport Milenium** reportedly blew up on the turn for home but there were no obvious excuses for **Hors La Loi** and **Marble Arch**, who seemed to devalue the Bula Hurdle (39) form by running so poorly.

47 Pertemps King George VI Chase (Showcase Race) (Grade 1) (3m)
Kempton December 26 (Soft)

1 **Best Mate** 7-11-10   A P McCoy
2 **Marlborough** 10-11-10   T J Murphy
3 **Bacchanal** 8-11-10   M A Fitzgerald
11-8f, 14-1, 10-3. 1¼l, 4l. 10 ran. 6m 17.7 (a29.70)
Jim Lewis (Miss H Knight, Wantage)

This race last season was the last time **Best Mate** had suffered defeat, when worries about his ability to see out the trip led Tony McCoy to adopt conservative tactics that, arguably, caused his downfall. McCoy was back in the saddle (the horse's regular partner Jim Culloty was serving a three-day ban) and made no mistake this time, taking it up five out and getting a response when **Marlborough** challenged from two out. The runner-up only gave best on the run-in, giving what might fairly be regarded as a career-best performance. **Bacchanal** ran a solid race to be third for the second year running but **Florida Pearl** and **Native Upmanship** couldn't last home on such a soft surface. **Douze Douze** ruined his chance by pulling too hard, while **Flagship Uberalles**, **Shooting Light** and **Lord Noelie** were never in the hunt.

48 Denny Gold Medal Novice Chase (Grade 1) (2m1f)
Leopardstown December 26 (Heavy)

1 **Le Coudray** 8-11-12   B J Geraghty
2 **Bust Out** 6-11-12   P Carberry
3 **Ricardo** 8-11-12   G Cotter
8-13f, 5-2, 10-1. ¹/2l, 20l. 5 ran. 4m 35.1 (a14.22)
JP McManus (C Roche, Ireland)

Three from four over fences for **Le Coudray**, who fell on his debut, and this was his second Grade 1 success – but the field was weak and **Bust Out** was the only one to make a race for it, with Le Coudray outfighting him despite untidy jumps at the last two. Bust Out had run Istabraq to a head over hurdles the previous season, but was then off for a year before landing a beginners' chase by a distance at Fairyhouse. This was a highly creditable effort on only his second chase run.

49 skybet.com Castleford Chase (Grade 2) (2m)
Wetherby December 26 (Soft)

1 **Geos** 7-10-12   J R Kavanagh
2 **Armaturk** 5-11-3   S Stronge
3 **Davoski** 8-11-4   G Lee
8-11f, 4-1, 7-1. 8l, dis. 4 ran. 4m 18.4 (a23.20)
Thurloe Finsbury (N Henderson, Lambourn)

A poor field for the prize, allowing **Geos** to win his first chase in the UK, and his first race of any kind for over two years. **Armaturk**, so promising as a novice, had been well beaten on both starts this term. **Redemption** was still in the race when falling three out.

50 Western Daily Press Finale Juvenile Hurdle (Grade 1) (2m110yds)
Chepstow December 27 (Heavy)

1 **Nas Na Riogh** 3-10-9   M Foley
2 **Lewis Island** 3-11-0   C Llewellyn
3 **Lougaroo** 3-11-0   C Gombeau
5-1, 10-3, 9-2. 11l, 19l. 8 ran. 4m 20.8 (a24.85)
Brian Twojohns Partnership (N Henderson, Lambourn)

Lewis Island rather set this up for **Nas Na Riogh** by blazing off in front. None of his rivals chased him, reckoning he'd come back, and so he did, though only Nas Na Riogh had enough energy to go past. She coped well with the testing conditions, as did Lewis Island, though he'd have been third if **Le Duc** had not come down at the last.

51 Coral Welsh National Chase (Showcase Handicap) (Grade 3) (3m5f110yds)
Chepstow December 27 (Heavy)

1 **Mini Sensation** 9-10-4   A Dobbin
2 **Chives** 7-11-12   Richard Guest
3 **Gunner Welburn** 10-10-6   B Fenton
4 **Frosty Canyon** 9-11-7   T Doyle
8-1, 10-1, 5-2f, 20-1. 7l, 13l, 1³/4l. 16 ran. 8m

15.5 (a41.20)
JP McManus (Jonjo O'Neill, Cheltenham

Mini Sensation had won his first two novice chases the previous season, after which his form had rather tailed off, though he was a distant second in the Midlands National. After a no-show on his reappearance when last of four, he ran here off the same mark as in the Midlands and was well backed, touching 14-1 at the course before going off at 8s. He closed up four out, went on near the last and won with plenty in hand. Market leader **Gunner Welburn**, who'd won at the track earlier in the month, ran a fine race but pre-race fears about his stamina proved justified. **Chives** was easily best at the weights and looked suited by this kind of marathon but his reward was a further 4lb rise in his rating. **Rugged River**, who'd run so well here on his last outing *(32)*, was effectively 11lb lower this time, but was never going and was pulled up four out.

52 Pertemps Employment Alliance Handicap Chase (3m)
Kempton December 27 (Soft)
1 **Carryonharry** 8-11-8   G Supple
2 **Ask The Natives** 8-11-7   R Walsh
3 **Handyman** 8-11-7   R Johnson
16-1, 11-2, 13-2. 1¹/₄l, nk. 11 ran. 6m 25.9 (a37.90)
Drs' D Silk J Castro M Gillard P Walker (M Pipe, Wellington)

Sent off favourite on his seasonal debut, **Carryonharry** ran well enough until stumbling on landing at a crucial stage. Here, he made no such mistake but would surely have given best if the novice **Ask The Natives** had put in a cleaner round of jumping.

53 Ericsson Chase (Grade 1) (3m)
Leopardstown December 28 (Heavy)
1 **Beef Or Salmon** 6-11-9   T J Murphy
2 **Colonel Braxton** 7-12-0   N Williamson
3 **Harbour Pilot** 7-12-0   P Carberry
5-1, 20-1, 6-1. 6l, shd. 7 ran. 6m 41.2 (b4.04)
B J Craig (M Hourigan, Ireland)

Michael Hourigan could hardly be accused of keeping **Beef Or Salmon** wrapped in cotton wool. Feeling from the first that this was a top class chaser, he pitched him into a Group 2 against more experienced rivals for the horse's first run over fences, which he duly won. A second win in a Grade 3 followed and this was the horse's third outing over the larger obstacles. Making easy progress when asked, he took it off **Colonel Braxton** on the run-in and looked easily best in the race, despite the wealth of veteran talent up against him. **Harbour Pilot** ran well considering he didn't jump as fluently as the first two but market leaders **Rince Ri** and **First Gold** were highly disappointing in last and second-last. The latter was thought to have suffered a respiratory tract infection.

54 Evening Herald December Festival Hurdle (Grade 1) (2m)
Leopardstown December 29 (Heavy)
1 **Liss A Paoraigh** 7-11-7   B J Geraghty
2 **Stage Affair** 8-11-12   R Walsh
3 **Turtleback** 4-11-7   N Williamson
11-10f, 9-4, 4-1. 25l, 20l. 5 ran. 4m 16.6 (a10.34)
Mrs N Flynn (J Kiely, Ireland)

Liss A Paoraigh maintained her record of winning a Graded race each season over hurdles but the race wasn't the fiercest contest. The starter was afterwards cautioned as to his responsibilities, having let them go when apparently only the winner was ready – she got a flyer and never looked like being headed.

55 Paddy Power Handicap Chase (Grade B) (3m)
Leopardstown December 29 (Heavy)
1 **Coq Hardi Diamond** 8-10-0G T Hutchinson (3)
2 **Satcoslam** 7-10-8   G Cotter
3 **Clonmel's Minella** 11-9-10 R P McNally (3)
4 **Bennie's Pride** 6-10-6   N Williamson
14-1, 25-1, 14-1, 16-1. 7l, 14l, 14l. 21 ran. 6m 55.7 (a10.46)
Mrs Catherine Howard (N Meade, Ireland)

Gruelling conditions, with only nine finishers from the 21 who set out. **Coq Hardi Diamond** was a second-season chaser still looking for his first success since landing his first novice contest. He'd come down 10lb from his highest rating and was much the best at handling these conditions.

56 Unicoin New Homes Chase (Showcase Handicap) (2m5f)
Cheltenham January 1 (Heavy)
1 **Ballinclay King** 9-10-11   D N Russell
2 **Katarino** 8-11-7   M A Fitzgerald
3 **Grey Abbey** 9-11-12   B Harding
7-2, 3-1f, 10-1. 6l, ³/₄l. 7 ran. 5m 50.9 (a37.40)
I Guise, B Leatherday & N L Spence (F Murphy, Leyburn)

A collection of horses who find it hard to get home in front (except **Halexy**, who came here looking for a hat-trick but unseated shortly after halfway), with **Ballinclay King** finding it suspiciously easy to get his first success for almost two years, and his first outside novice company. On the other hand, he'd run well here on his two previous visits and copes well with the track.

57 Grand Prix de La Ville De Nice (Group 3) (2m7f)
Cagnes Sur Mer January 11 (Soft)
1 **Billy De Bessac** 8-10-6   JC Meignant
2 **Double Ange** 5-10-3   L Metais
3 **Grand Charles** 9-11-3   D Berra

11-1, 9-1, 1-2. hd, 4l. 11 ran. 0.0
J-p Senechal (T Civel, France)

58 Pierse Leopardstown Handicap Chase (Grade B) (3m)
Leopardstown January 12 (Soft)
1 **Youlneverwalkalone** 9-10-5B J Geraghty
2 **Foxchapel King** 10-12-0   D J Casey
3 **Eskimo Jack** 7-10-2   C O'Dwyer
7-2, 13-2, 5-2f. 1l, 3¹/2l. 11 ran. 6m 35.1
(b10.14)
JP McManus (C Roche, Ireland)

Having been the subject of huge amounts of hype as a novice hurdler, and again (albeit to a lesser extent) as a novice chaser, **Youlneverwalkalone** finally started putting it together in his second season over fences. Following a reappearance win in a minor contest, he was third in the Tripleprint (38) and then took this, battling well when he had to and thus belying his reputation as a shirker. This was a grand weight-carrying performance by **Foxchapel King**, but **Rince Ri** ran poorly under 1lb less.

59 Pierse Handicap Hurdle (Grade A) (2m)
Leopardstown January 12 (Soft)
1 **Xenophon** 7-10-11   M A Fitzgerald
2 **Colourful Life** 7-10-6   A Dobbin
3 **Camden Tanner** 7-10-12   D N Russell
4 **Emotional Moment** 6-11-2 N Williamson
12-1, 25-1, 16-1, 11-1. 2l, ³/4l, ³/4l. 28 ran.
3m 56.8 (b9.46)
Lane Syndicate (A J Martin, Ireland)

Xenophon turned out to be a highly talented handicap hurdler and Tony Martin did well to get him here in peak condition and yet so unexposed. He had three runs in maiden hurdles the previous season, winning at the third attempt against a big field. Made favourite for a strong handicap at Punchestown on his reappearance, his first run for ten months, he ran on to be a never-nearer second. Up 3lb for this, he was a comfortable winner, moving up smoothly to take it up on the run to the last. Only two British yards sent runners, but Mary Reveley's **Colourful Life** ran on into second from a long way back at the last. Up 6lb for her Sandown win (34), **Spirit Leader** ran another fine race in fifth, her first finish outside the first four in 16 career starts.

60 Premier Stayers' Hurdle (Grade 2) (2m7f110yds)
Haydock January 18 (Good to Soft)
1 **Lord Transcend** 6-11-0   A Dobbin
2 **Deano's Beeno** 11-11-8   A P McCoy
3 **Stromness** 6-11-4   R Thornton
8-1, 5-6f, 2-1. nk, 20l. 6 ran. 6m 10.3 (a30.72)

Transcend (Hair & Beauty) Limited (J Howard Johnson, Crook)

Howard Johnson's found a new stable star. This was a serious step up for **Lord Transcend**, after three strong-finishing wins in lesser company over 2m. A physically imposing sort, plainly destined to make a chaser, he coped well with mistakes three out and at the last and outgunned a seasoned battler.

61 Bet Direct Peter Marsh Limited Handicap Chase (Grade 2) (3m)
Haydock January 18 (Good to Soft)
1 **Truckers Tavern** 8-10-9   D N Russell
2 **Hussard Collonges** 8-11-10   R Garritty
3 **Goguenard** 9-10-4   W Marston
9-2, 3-1f, 20-1. 2¹/2l, 10l. 9 ran. 6m 24.1
(a22.90)
Mrs M B Scholey (F Murphy, Leyburn)

Fans of **Truckers Tavern** had their hearts in their mouths when he threatened to repeat his first-fence exit of his last outing (43). But he got over that and went on to duel up the straight with **Hussard Collonges**. Both deserved plenty of credit but the race lacked strength in depth, with **Barton** and **Whitenzo** in particular running well below their best.

62 Red Square Vodka Champion Hurdle Trial (Grade 2) (2m)
Haydock January 18 (Good to Soft)
1 **Flame Creek** 7-11-6   S Durack
2 **October Mist** 9-11-2   A Dempsey
3 **Ilnamar** 7-11-10   A P McCoy
9-4, 14-1, 11-10f. 13l, nk. 7 ran. 3m 57.2
(a12.40)
Martin Wesson Partners (N Chance, Upper Lambourn)

A championship trial in name only, the progressive **Flame Creek** not being hard pressed to see off failed chaser **October Mist**. **Ilnamar** and **The French Furze** both ran below their best.

63 Tote Exacta Limited Handicap Chase (Grade 2) (2m)
Kempton January 18 (Good)
1 **Young Devereaux** 10-10-4   R Walsh
2 **Seebald** 8-11-5   R Greene
3 **Dark'n Sharp** 8-10-11   R Johnson
9-2, 11-2, 10-3j. 1l, 9l. 9 ran. 3m 52.5 (b0.50)
Paul K Barber,Mick Coburn,Colin Lewis 2 (P Nicholls, Shepton Mallet)

It's testament to **Young Devereaux**'s injury problems that, at the age of ten, he was having only his sixth run over fences, and only his tenth outing of any kind. Up 12lb from his Ascot win (42), for which he was 10lb worse off for a length with **Seebald**, and on ground which he'd have wanted softer, he did well to win here. He cruised up to lead three out looking like an easy winner, but he found the runner-up hard to shake and was all out by the finish. **Fondmort** was ridden but still in the race when falling heavily three out.

64 Tote Scoop6 Lanzarote Hurdle (Showcase Handicap) (2m)
Kempton January 18 (Good)

1 **Non So** 5-11-5		J P McNamara
2 **Hawadeth** 8-11-3		A Bateman (5)
3 **Miss Cool** 7-11-3		Mr J E Moore (7)
4 **Monkerhostin** 6-11-9		S Stronge

9-1, 14-1, 25-1, 16-1. 2¹/2l, 1³/4l, ¹/2l. 21 ran. 3m 52.0 (a6.40)
ROA Dawn Run Partnership (N Henderson, Lambourn)

Nicky Henderson, so good with his handicap hurdlers, had another progressive type on his hands with **Non So**. A dual novice winner before pulling up in the Triumph the previous season, he had excuses for a poor reappearance, since when he'd won over this track and trip in December. Up 6lb for that, he was always travelling here and could be named the winner some way out. **Hawadeth** ran on strongly but had left it too late to challenge the winner, while **Gin Palace** ran an encouraging race further back.

65 Tote Tolworth Hurdle (Grade 1) (2m)
Wincanton January 18 (Good to Soft)

1 **Thisthatandtother** 7-11-7		T J Murphy
2 **Puntal** 7-11-7		B J Geraghty
3 **Self Defense** 6-11-7		F Keniry

11-4, 4-6f, 25-1. 2¹/2l, 14l. 7 ran. 3m 51.1 (a11.10)
C G Roach (P Nicholls, Shepton Mallet)

Puntal had been punted for the Champion Hurdle at fancy prices early in the season but those looked optimistic wagers after this, his second consecutive odds-on defeat. But there was no disgrace in losing to another highly-rated novice, though **Thisthatandtother**'s primary objective after this race was said to be the 2004 Arkle Chase.

66 IAWS Thyestes Handicap Chase (Grade B) (3m)
Gowran Park January 23 (Heavy)

1 **Be My Belle** 7-10-0		T J Murphy
2 **Takagi** 8-10-7		B J Geraghty
3 **Kirmar** 8-10-0		K P Gaule

4-1, 3-1f, 20-1. 2¹/2l, 5l. 13 ran. 6m 27.2 (a24.62)
Mrs M Aherne (S Treacy, Ireland)

Only four ran from their proper handicap marks here, but **Be My Belle** took the prize from 9lb 'wrong'. Four times a winner at 3m or further over hurdles and fences, she was well suited by this stamina test and was a cosy winner of her first handicap chase. **Takagi** put up another sound effort, while **Foxchapel King** lugged 12st into fourth.

67 Byrne Bros Cleeve Hurdle (Grade 1) (2m5f110yds)
Cheltenham January 25 (Good to Soft)

1 **Classified** 7-11-8		A P McCoy
2 **Mr Cool** 9-11-8		T Scudamore
3 **Sudden Shock** 8-11-8		B J Geraghty

8-11f, 11-1, 9-1. 1l, 16l. 6 ran. 5m 30.9 (a21.30)
D A Johnson (M Pipe, Wellington)

Classified had been a beaten favourite on both his previous attempts at this course and distance, and it really looked like he was about to hit an unwanted hat-trick. **Mr Cool** set a good pace and was clear two out, with Classified working hard to bridge the gap – but the hill changed it all, the leader tiring and Classified running on strongly to hit the front in the last 75 yards.

68 Pillar Property Chase (Grade 2) (3m1f110yds)
Cheltenham January 25 (Good to Soft)

1 **Behrajan** 8-11-6		R Johnson
2 **Foly Pleasant** 9-11-6		J Culloty
3 **Gingembre** 9-11-0		A Thornton

9-2, 7-1, 11-2. 14l, dis. 6 ran. 6m 54.9 (a29.85)
The Behrajan Partnership (H Daly, Ludlow)

Given an uncontested lead, **Behrajan** is seriously hard to pass, and these rivals never even caught up with him. **Gingembre** and **Valley Henry** were completely unsuited by the sticky ground and ran way below what they're usually capable of, while **Foly Pleasant** was trying this trip for the first time and, while he stayed on creditably, he never looked a danger. **Cyfor Malta** might have been in the shake-up but for unseating just after halfway. **Bacchanal**, who fell earlier in the race, broke a hind leg and was put down.

69 Ladbroke Trophy Handicap Chase (Listed Race) (2m5f)
Cheltenham January 25 (Good to Soft)

1 **Lady Cricket** 9-11-12		A P McCoy
2 **Shamawan** 8-10-4		N Fehily
3 **Hermes III** 8-10-5		R Johnson

9-2f, 11-1, 13-2. nk, 3¹/2l. 15 ran. 5m 30.5 (a17.00)

D A Johnson (M Pipe, Wellington)

Lady Cricket's third course win, a year after she was second in the same race off a 9lb lower mark. She was arguably lucky to keep this, though, having edged across the runner-up on the run-in, forcing him to switch. **Shamawan** rallied so strongly that there was a case for saying the interference cost him the race, but the stewards would have had to be sure before throwing out a Pipe/McCoy favourite.

70 skybet.com Great Yorkshire Listed Chase (Showcase Handicap) (3m)

Doncaster January 25 (Good)
1 **Barryscourt Lad** 9-10-1   R Greene
2 **Ryalux** 10-11-4   R McGrath
3 **Tonoco** 10-10-0   D Elsworth (3)
4 **Donnybrook** 10-10-0   P Whelan (3)
9-2, 14-1, 9-1, 66-1. hd, 9l, 3l. 18 ran. 6m 13.2 (a14.40) Roseberry Racing (M Pipe, Wellington)

Barryscourt Lad had been hunter chasing for David Pipe the previous season, showing ability in five runs for an amateur rider without breaking his duck. He'd looked the likely winner on his debut for Pipe Snr but fell at the last, for which he was put up 7lb – which nearly cost him here. A strong, galloping type, he led from before halfway but conceded the lead to **Ryalux** at the last with a less than fluent leap. Improbably, he managed to get his momentum back in time to snatch the verdict on the line. Novice **Shardam** ran well until hitting three out, while **Gunner Welburn** threw in a stinker.

71 Baileys Arkle Perpetual Challenge Cup Novice Chase (Grade 1) (2m1f)

Leopardstown January 26 (Soft)
1 **Bust Out** 7-11-12   B J Geraghty
2 **Native Scout** 7-11-12   K Hadnett
3 **Rathgar Beau** 7-11-12   T J Murphy
11-10f, 12-1, 16-1. 1l, 2l. 8 ran. 4m 33.9 (a13.02)
B B Horse Racing Club (Mrs J Harrington, Ireland)

Bust Out looked likely to win easily at the top of the straight but was bustled up in the end, having idled in front. He was reckoned to be Ireland's leading Arkle hope after this, but subsequently suffered an aggravation of an old leg injury and was said to be facing at least a year on the sidelines.

72 AIG Europe Champion Hurdle (Grade 1) (2m)

Leopardstown January 26 (Good to Soft)
1 **Like-A-Butterfly** 9-11-5   C F Swan

2 **Limestone Lad** 11-11-10 B J Geraghty
3 **Stage Affair** 9-11-10   D J Casey
6-4f, 15-8, 10-1. hd, 13l. 5 ran. 4m 1.8 (b4.46)
JP McManus (C Roche, Ireland)

A fine tussle between two tough animals. Still, Christy Roche gave some indication of the worth of the form when saying he'd have been disappointed if **Like-A-Butterfly** hadn't been able to beat **Limestone Lad** over 2m, even though this was her first run for nine months. She only just managed to hold off the veteran and had to survive a stewards' inquiry, so the excitement of the race possibly clouded objective views of a performance that was below championship standard. On the other hand, this was the runner-up's first defeat in six starts this season.

73 Scilly Isles Novices' Chase (Grade 1) (2m4f110yds)

Sandown February 1 (Heavy)
1 **Tarxien** 9-11-6   A P McCoy
2 **Farmer Jack** 7-11-6   A Thornton
3 **Ground Ball** 6-11-6   D J Casey
15-8f, 2-1, 10-1. 3l, 15l. 4 ran. 5m 33.8 (a37.57)
B A Kilpatrick (M Pipe, Wellington)

Tarxien had won his first two over fences by wide margins, and was only just pipped by Joss Naylor in his third. He just had **Farmer Jack** to beat after **Telemoss** burst a blood vessel, and did so convincingly, running on strongly.

74 Tote Scoop6 Sandown Handicap Hurdle (Grade 3) (2m6f)

Sandown February 1 (Heavy)
1 **Chopneyev** 5-10-5   R Johnson
2 **Camden Tanner** 7-10-12   J Culloty
3 **Whistling Dixie** 7-11-2   A Dempsey
15-8f, 11-2, 11-1. ³/4l, 6l. 13 ran. 5m 58.9 (a48.70)
Mrs Claire Smith (R Phillips, Moreton-in-Marsh)

Chopneyev was up 12lb since winning his first handicap by 9l in December and was plainly progressive. Despite the desperate going, he was cruising until belting the penultimate flight, after which this became a struggle, but **Camden Tanner**, third in the Pierse Hurdle (59) off a 5lb lower mark, gives the form a solid look.

75 Agfa Diamond Handicap Chase (3m110yds)

Sandown February 1 (Heavy)
1 **Iris Bleu** 7-11-2   T Scudamore
2 **Frosty Canyon** 10-11-8   T Doyle
3 **Lord Jack** 7-10-13   P Robson (3)
12-1, 15-2, 11-2. 23l, ³/4l. 14 ran. 6m 42.3 (a47.05)
D A Johnson (M Pipe, Wellington)

It had taken **Iris Bleu** until his 15th attempt to win a race in Britain, but he finally got off the mark in an amateurs' race at Cheltenham in November on his last start prior to coming here. Up 7lb for that, he looked a different horse, taking it up four out and quickly going well clear of a decent field. He was never going to be caught from two out and won as he pleased. **Gunther McBride** was a disappointing favourite and seemed handicapped up to his best.

76 Singer & Friedlander National Trial Showcase Handicap Chase (3m4f)

Uttoxeter February 1 (Heavy)
1 **Mini Sensation** 10-11-3   B J Geraghty
2 **Ardent Scout** 11-10-13   W Marston
3 **Historg** 8-10-10   D N Russell
5-2, 7-1, 2-1f. 12l, 14l. 7 ran. 8m 31.9
JP McManus (Jonjo O'Neill, Cheltenham)

Mini Sensation defied an 11lb hike for his Welsh National win *(51)* but this was pretty uncompetitive stuff considering the money on offer, and only **Ardent Scout** ever looked like making a race for it. **Historg** was made favourite on the strength of a last-time win at Cheltenham, but he never landed a blow. Bizarrely, the winner went up 12lb for this, more than he had for winning the Welsh National, which was enough to kill his chances in the two other handicaps he contested later in the season.

77 Sodexho Prestige Game Spirit Chase (Grade 2) (2m1f)

Newbury February 8 (Good)
1 **Kadarann** 6-11-4   J Tizzard
2 **Cenkos** 9-11-10   R Walsh
3 **Lady Cricket** 9-11-5   A P McCoy
5-1, 5-6f, 2-1. 8l, 4l. 5 ran. 4m 4.2 (b9.95)
Notalotterry (P Nicholls, Shepton Mallet)

Something of a turn-up, as **Kadarann** ran away from his much more fancied stablemate. The winner had been backed at big prices for the Champion Chase in the week before, though Paul Nicholls told the press that he had no doubt Cenkos was working much the better of the two at home. If **Cenkos** had run to his form, this would have been an improvement of about a stone from Kadarann, suggesting that the favourite ran some way below his best – Nicholls himself pointed out afterwards that the horse was dull in his coat. This trip looks very sharp for **Lady Cricket** these days.

78 Tote Gold Trophy Hurdle (Showcase Handicap) (Grade 3) (2m110yds)

Newbury February 8 (Good)
1 **Spirit Leader** 7-10-0   N Williamson
2 **Non So** 5-10-0   M Foley (3)

3 **Tikram** 6-10-0   L Aspell
4 **In Contrast** 7-10-13   R Johnson
14-1, 9-2f, 25-1, 6-1. 1¹/2l, 3¹/2l, 1l. 27 ran. 3m 50.2 (b11.53)
D Thompson (Mrs J Harrington, Ireland)

In her lastest run, **Spirit Leader** had run fourth in the highly competitive Pierse Hurdle *(59)*, the first time in her career she'd been worse than fourth. Having gone up another 3lb for that, it was arguable that the handicapper had caught up with her, but she thoroughly disproved that notion by landing just about the toughest handicap hurdle of the year. Coping well with a better surface than she was used to, she travelled well apart from the odd jumping error down the back, and fought it out with **Non So** from before the last. The latter also looks highly progressive, running here off a mark 13lb higher than when he won his first handicap six weeks before. **Benbyas** set a strong pace and stuck on admirably for fifth, while **Monkerhostin** finished strongly from a long way back to be sixth.

79 AON Chase (Grade 2) (3m)

Newbury February 8 (Good)
1 **Valley Henry** 8-11-6   B J Geraghty
2 **Chives** 8-11-0   Richard Guest
3 **Truckers Tavern** 8-11-6   D N Russell
4-1, 3-1, 5-1. 2¹/2l, 7l. 6 ran. 5m 53.9 (b6.10)
Paul K Barber (P Nicholls, Shepton Mallet)

Marlborough was 6-4 favourite, coming here fresh from his King George second *(47)*, but he was third at best when falling at the last. This was a welcome return to form for **Valley Henry**, who'd won four in a row and looked highly progressive before flopping on sticky ground at Cheltenham *(68)*. Neither **Chives** nor **Truckers Tavern**, both of whom prefer some cut, had the pace to land a blow.

80 Deloitte And Touche Novice Hurdle (Grade 1) (2m2f)

Leopardstown February 9 (Good to Soft)
1 **Solerina** 6-11-5   P Carberry
2 **Hardy Eustace** 6-11-10   K A Kelly
3 **Nil Desperandum** 6-11-10   R Walsh
11-10f, 9-4, 13-2. 2l, 14l. 6 ran. 4m 43.1 (a10.21)
John P Bowe (J Bowe, Ireland)

Seven wins from eight hurdle runs in three months for **Solerina**, who made all and won comfortably, being eased at the finish. **Hardy Eustace** had been unbeaten in three and appeared to run his race, with the pair finishing clear, so the form looks solid. Remarkably, Solerina is from the same three-horse yard as Limestone Lad, that of James Bowe. Connections reckon she's too small to go chasing, or even to try her hand at handicap hurdles. Unfortunately, she developed a leg infection that meant this was her final outing for the season.

81 Dr. P.J. Moriarty Novice Chase (Grade 1) (2m5f)

Leopardstown February 9 (Good to Soft)

1 **Barrow Drive** 7-11-12		J Culloty
2 **Nomadic** 9-11-12		P Carberry
3 **BallyAmber** 8-11-12		R Walsh

6-1, 16-1, 14-1. dis, nk. 7 ran. 5m 50.0 (a13.59)
Mrs B Lenihan (A Mullins, Ireland)

Barrow Drive set a strong pace but looked beaten when 8-15 favourite **Le Coudray** went past after the second-last. He was back on level terms by the last, though, and it would have been an interesting battle if Le Coudray hadn't crashed out at the final fence, his first jumping error of the race. Barrow Drive had been well beaten by Le Coudray in the Drinmore *(30)*.

82 Hennessy Cognac Gold Cup Chase (Grade 1) (3m)

Leopardstown February 9 (Good to Soft)

1 **Beef Or Salmon** 7-12-0		T J Murphy
2 **Colonel Braxton** 8-12-0		N Williamson
3 **Harbour Pilot** 8-12-0		P Carberry

evensf, 7-2, 6-1. 4l, nk. 5 ran. 6m 37.7 (b7.54)
B J Craig (M Hourigan, Ireland)

A remarkably similar race to the Ericsson *(53)*, run over the same course and distance six weeks before. Then, **Beef Or Salmon** had been held up, had made ground smoothly over the last few fences and had taken it up on the run-in to beat **Colonel Braxton** and **Harbour Pilot** by 6l and a short-head, with **Rince Ri** and First Gold disappointing in rear. He ran a precisely similar race here to beat the same two horses by similar distances, with Rince Ri further back and **Florida Pearl** pulled up. Like First Gold on the former occasion, Florida Pearl was afterwards said to have suffered a respiratory infection. The most noticable difference between the races was that Beef Or Salmon was on level terms with his rivals here, having enjoyed a 5lb concession in the Ericsson. For a horse having only his fourth run over fences, it was also impressive that he was so readily able to confirm superiority over battle-hardened opponents. The consensus afterwards was that he was the main threat to Best Mate's Cheltenham crown.

83 William Hill Handicap Hurdle (2m4f)

Ascot February 15 (Good to Soft)

1 **Korelo** 5-10-8		A P McCoy
2 **Chopneyev** 5-11-6		R Johnson
3 **Formal Bid** 6-10-8		J Culloty

4-1, 5-2f, 16-1. 1¹/4l, 12l. 12 ran. 5m 23.0 (a35.00)
D A Johnson (M Pipe, Wellington)

A decent-sized field but the ex-French novices **Korelo** and **Chopneyev** had this to themselves from a fair way out. Having had just three muddling runs in Britain, Korelo was hard to weigh up for punters but he looked very progressive in beating a triple winner here, even allowing for the fact that the runner-up was up 11lb for his Sandown win *(74)*.

84 Ritz Club Ascot Chase (Grade 1) (2m3f110yds)

Ascot February 15 (Good to Soft)

1 **Tiutchev** 10-11-7		A P McCoy
2 **Geos** 8-11-7		M A Fitzgerald
3 **Tresor De Mai** 9-11-7		R Greene

15-8f, 11-2, 12-1. 12l, 1¹/4l. 7 ran. 5m 12.8 (a23.81)
The Liars Poker Partnership (M Pipe, Wellington)

For the third straight season, **Tiutchev** managed a single win, each time in February. This was impressive, as he took it up four out and romped home unchallenged, though the opposition was some way short of championship standard. The fragile **Young Devereaux** was held in third when breaking down before the last – he was reportedly fine the next day but this was his final run of the season.

85 Red Mills Trial Hurdle (Grade 2) (2m)

Gowran Park February 15 (Soft)

1 **Sacundai** 6-11-9		C F Swan
2 **Liss A Paoraigh** 8-11-6		B J Geraghty
3 **Calladine** 7-11-9		Mr A P Crowe

7-4, 4-6f, 14-1. 1¹/2l, 13l. 6 ran. 4m 4.8 (a11.43)
Malm Syndicate (E O'Grady, Ireland)

It was 12-1 bar two and so it proved, though the punters made the wrong one odds-on. **Liss A Paoraigh** attempted to make all but, perhaps feeling the effects of a seven-week layoff due to a lung infection, she ran out of puff between the last two.

86 Country Gentlemen's Association Chase (Listed Race) (3m1f110yds)

Wincanton February 15 (Good to Soft)

1 **See More Business** 13-11-12		R Walsh
2 **Iris Bleu** 7-11-12		T Scudamore
3 **First Gold** 10-11-12		T Doumen

7-4, 13-8f, 9-4. 9l, 1l. 5 ran. 6m 31.9 (a14.50)
Paul K Barber & Sir Robert Ogden (P Nicholls, Shepton Mallet)

Iris Bleu was sent off favourite, despite having 16lb to make up on **See More Business** on Official Ratings – in the end, that was an accurate reflection of the gap between them. **First Gold** ran well for a long way but mistakes at two of the last three cost him second place. Interestingly, 11 of See More Business's 15 chase wins have now come in fields of six or fewer, whereas he's been beaten on his last eight runs in bigger fields, suggesting he doesn't cope well with being crowded.

87 Axminster Kingwell Hurdle (Grade 2) (2m)
Wincanton February 15 (Good to Soft)

1 **Rhinestone Cowboy** 7-11-6   N Williamson
2 **Thisthatandtother** 7-11-6   R Walsh
3 **Hors La Loi III** 8-11-10   A Dobbin
8-11f, 7-2, 10-3. 1³/4l, 14l. 6 ran. 3m 43.4 (a3.40)
Mrs John Magnier (Jonjo O'Neill, Cheltenham)

For the fourth time in his four hurdles outings, **Rhinestone Cowboy** won cheekily and very easily. When he joined **Thisthatandtother** between the last two, it looked as though there might be a race on, but amazingly the winner came right back on the bridle and appeared to win at his leisure, with **Hors La Loi**, the reigning Champion hurdler and twice successful in this race, a distant third. When a horse wins like this, it's impossible to know how much or how little he might have in hand, but this race certainly left no room for anyone to doubt that Rhinestone Cowboy was a serious championship contender.

88 Collins Stewart National Spirit Hurdle (Grade 2) (2m4f)
Fontwell February 17 (Good to Soft)

1 **Classified** 7-11-10   A P McCoy
2 **Telimar Prince** 7-11-2   L Aspell
3 **Comex Flyer** 6-11-2   R Walsh
8-13f, 7-1, 10-1. 1¹/2l, 2l. 7 ran. 5m 3.4
D A Johnson (M Pipe, Wellington)

Hardly a trial for the Stayers', having been run at a married man's gallop early on. Given the lack of emphasis on stamina, **Classified** did well to hold off his challengers, but the worth of the form is practically nil.

89 betfair.com Rendlesham Hurdle (Grade 2) (3m110yds)
Kempton February 21 (Good)

1 **Deano's Beeno** 11-11-10   A P McCoy
2 **Palua** 6-11-2   B Fenton
3 **Stromness** 6-11-6   R Thornton
evensf, 4-1, 10-3. 12l, 8l. 5 ran. 6m 1.8 (a10.22)
Axom (M Pipe, Wellington)

Deano's Beeno rarely makes it look easy and

he was being driven for most of the second circuit here, but kept running and outgalloped his rivals, as indeed he ought to have done at the weights.

90 Racing Post Chase (Showcase Handicap) (Grade 3) (3m)
Kempton February 22 (Good)

1 **La Landiere** 8-11-7   W Marston
2 **Gunther Mcbride** 8-10-8   R Johnson
3 **Ryalux** 10-11-0   R McGrath
5-1j, 5-1j, 14-1. 3l, 1l. 14 ran. 5m 53.8 (a5.80)
Mrs R J Skan (R Phillips, Moreton-in-Marsh)

By the end of the season, her first over fences, **La Landiere** had suffered but a single defeat, when second to Impek on her debut in May, at a 2m trip that, in hindsight, was on the sharp side. This was her sixth win, and her third in a handicap, the first having been over 2m4f at this track in December. She was 25lb higher here, the price of two easy handicap successes, but won impressively after taking it up three out, on her first try beyond 2m5f. **Gunther McBride** ran a fine race off a stone higher mark than when he'd won here the previous season and these conditions seem ideal for him, while this was also a good run from **Ryalux** off a mark 11lb higher than he'd ever won off. **Fondmort** was still in the race when hitting three out, after which he faded into seventh. **Chicuelo** had managed to win a couple of softish races since his Thomas Pink debacle *(21)* but his jumping went to bits in this company.

91 Paddy & Helen Cox Memorial Newlands Chase (Grade 2) (2m)
Naas February 23 (Good to Soft)

1 **Arctic Copper** 9-11-7   P Carberry
2 **Fadoudal Du Cochet** 10-11-12 C O'Dwyer
3 **Go Roger Go** 11-11-10   N Williamson
7-2, 6-1, 3-1f. ¹/2l, 5l. 8 ran. 4m 18.4 (b10.38)
Grand Alliance Racing Club (N Meade, Ireland)

Rathbawn Prince set a good pace (at a trip short of his best, this looked like an attempt to bring stamina into the issue) and, although overhauled, kept on well to be fourth. **Arctic Copper** is another who's more usually associated with further these days but he had enough pace.

92 Red Square Vodka Gold Cup Chase (Showcase Handicap) (Gr 3) (3m4f110yds)
Haydock March 1 (Good)

1 **Shotgun Willy** 9-11-12   R Walsh
2 **You're Agoodun** 11-10-12   R Thornton
3 **Iris Bleu** 7-11-6   T Scudamore
4 **Wonder Weasel** 10-10-5   D Flavin (5)
10-1, 40-1, 13-2f, 10-1. ³/4l, shd, 5l. 17 ran. 7m 25.8 (a21.15)

C G Roach (P Nicholls, Shepton Mallet)

This was **Shotgun Willy**'s first success since landing the AON Chase as a novice over two years before. Then again, it was his first outing since he'd been second (beaten half a length off a mark just 1lb lower than here) in the Scottish National the previous April. His whole aim this season was said to be the Grand National, but he was certainly fit for this – having looked beaten when coming under pressure four out, he rallied well to lead near the line. **Iris Bleu** ran on, despite wanting it softer, but looks to have nothing in hand over the assessor on this mark.

93 E.B.F. 'NH' Novices' Handicap Hurdle Final (Grade 3) (2m4f110yds)
Sandown March 8 (Heavy)

1	**Tana River**	7-11-12	B Fenton
2	**Nonantais**	6-11-10	M Batchelor
3	**Benbecula**	6-11-6	J A McCarthy

7-1, 12-1, 11-1. 9l, 1¹/2l. 12 ran. 5m 32.4 (a41.30)
The Frisky Fillies (Miss E Lavelle, Andover)

Terrible racing conditions, with half the field pulling up and the remainder finishing exhausted. **Tana River** was labouring in eighth at the second-last, but kept on galloping as the others ran out of steam and surged clear after the last. He looks extremely tough and his record in five hurdle runs now reads 22111, with only two well respected novices getting the better of him.

94 Sunderlands Imperial Cup Hurdle (Showcase Handicap) (2m110yds)
Sandown March 8 (Heavy)

1	**Korelo**	5-11-6	A P McCoy
2	**Newhall**	5-11-2	F J Flood
3	**Lawz**	9-10-13	N Fehily
4	**Canada**	5-10-11	R Greene

9-4f, 16-1, 33-1, 14-1. 6l, 2¹/2l, 1¹/2l. 17 ran. 4m 22.1 (a29.28)
D A Johnson (M Pipe, Wellington)

Martin Pipe has an amazing record in this race, which led punters to back his runner down to 9-4 in such an apparently competitive race, despite the 13lb raise he'd suffered for winning at Ascot (83). Two out, there were plenty of worried faces in the stands, as **Korelo** appeared to be struggling, but this was a serious stamina test on such going and, as a 2m4f winner on soft ground, he was always likely to be running on better than most. **Lawz**, who set the pace, did amazingly well to hold on for third. Korelo's main market rival was **Talarive**, who weakened rapidly from three out and pulled up.

95 Gerrard Wealth Management Supreme Novices' Hurdle (Grade 1) (2m110yds)
Cheltenham March 11 (Good)

1	**Back In Front**	6-11-8	N Williamson
2	**Kicking King**	5-11-8	B J Geraghty
3	**Chauvinist**	8-11-8	M A Fitzgerald

3-1f, 13-2, 20-1. 10l, 4l. 19 ran. 3m 56.7 (a1.20)
D Cox (E O'Grady, Ireland)

Also: 4 Keltic Bard, 5 Thisthatandtother, 6 Limerick Boy, 7 Jaboune, 8 Inca Trail, 9 Mutakarrim, 10 Rosaker

He may not have impressed all paddockwatchers, but **Back In Front** could have done nothing more in the race itself. Always travelling, he led two out and accelerated clear of his rivals in a race that usually sees a much tighter finish. **Kicking King** had only previously been beaten by Solerina in four hurdles outings – he is reckoned to be a chaser in the making. Of the others that finished to the fore, **Chauvinist** and **Thisthatandtother** deserve plenty of credit, since underfoot conditions were on the fast side for their liking.

96 Irish Independent Arkle Challenge Trophy Chase (Grade 1) (2m)
Cheltenham March 11 (Good)

1	**Azertyuiop**	6-11-8	R Walsh
2	**Impek**	7-11-8	J Culloty
3	**Isio**	7-11-8	M A Fitzgerald

5-4f, 6-1, 10-1. 11l, 1l. 9 ran. 3m 56.6 (b5.48)
J Hales (P Nicholls, Shepton Mallet)

Also: 4 Farmer Jack, 5 Hand Inn Hand, 6 Stage Affair, 7 Ricardo

Le Roi Miguel went off at a rate of knots under Tony McCoy but fell at the third, leaving **Azertyuiop** in the lead – where he stayed. He fiddled two out but jumped well otherwise and came clear in the straight to win easily, already looking the main challenger to Moscow Flyer for next year's 2m championship. **Isio** was beaten after a mistake two out and gave up second on the run-in but impressed for a horse with just three previous runs over fences, none of which had involved a battle. Trainer Seamus Mullins was talking up **Farmer Jack** as a future Gold Cup horse, but it's hard to see how such a claim could be justified by reference only to the horse's form.

97 Smurfit Champion Hurdle Challenge Trophy (Showcase) (Gr 1) (2m110yds)
Cheltenham March 11 (Good)

| 1 | **Rooster Booster** | 9-12-0 | R Johnson |
| 2 | **Westender** | 7-12-0 | R Greene |

3 **Rhinestone Cowboy** 7-12-0 N Williamson
9-2, 33-1, 5-2f. 11l, 3l. 17 ran. 3m 54.5 (b1.00)
Terry Warner (P Hobbs, Minehead)

Also: 4 Self Defense, 5 Intersky Falcon, 6 In
Contrast, 7 Landing Light, 8 Holy Orders, 9 Santenay, 10 Like-A-Butterfly

It had looked likely that we'd see a new
champion crowned, but that was made a
certainty when the tape went up and **Hors
La Loi** refused to race. The form of his championship win the year before was rather un-
dermined when the second and fifth from
that race, **Marble Arch** and **Landing Light**,
were comprehensively outpointed here,
but that may be slightly unfair, as Marble Arch
had already seemed to lose his form over
hurdles before this, while Landing Light had
only run one good race in the intervening
year. **Intersky Falcon** set a strong pace,
which suited the winner ideally, as **Rooster Booster** was cruising until asked to go
and win his race before the last, when he
found a serious turn of foot to go clear. **Westender** lost many lengths with a slow start
and was also hampered by the fall of
Copeland (second and not yet beaten when
coming down three out), so he did well to
run on past the others, while **Self Defense**
also came from a long way back, having
lacked the pace to lie handy. It was possibly no surprise that the novice **Rhinestone
Cowboy**, who'd never had to shift at this
pace in his few races so far, should have
made the odd mistake. He was never travelling as well as expected, but earned new
admirers by fighting his way into third place
and is clearly no 'bridle horse'. **Like-A-Butterfly** was beaten a long way out and seems
to lack the pace for 2m at this level on decent ground.

98 William Hill National Hunt Handicap Chase (Grade 3) (3m110yds)
Cheltenham March 11 (Good)

1 **Youlneverwalkalone** 9-10-11   B J Geraghty
2 **Haut Cercy** 8-10-0   R Johnson
3 **Ad Hoc** 9-11-0   R Walsh
4 **Maximize** 9-10-1   T J Murphy
7-1, 10-1, 5-1j, 20-1. 3/4l, 9l, 1 1/4l. 18 ran. 6m
16.7 (b4.80)
JP McManus (C Roche, Ireland)

Also: 5 Djeddah, 6 Historg, 7 Bramblehill Duke,
8 Southern Star, 9 Royal Auclair, 10 The Bun-
ny Boiler

Novice chaser **Joss Naylor** was joint-
favourite with **Ad Hoc** and travelled well for
much of the race but folded quickly from
four out. **Youlneverwalkalone** made it

three wins from four starts, with his other
effort being a third place in the Tripleprint
here in December *(38)*. Up 6lb for his latest win, he battled well to go past **Haut Cercy** on the run-in, finally looking something
like the horse he was always supposed to
be. For the runner-up, this was his twelfth
run over fences since October 2000, but he
remained technically a novice, having won
over obstacles for the first time just two
months before. Up 11lb for that, despite having since been stuffed by Keen Leader in
a Grade 2 novices chase, he now looks to
be progressing well. Having made a howler
at the fourth-last, he appeared to recover
quickly, but that mistake must have taken
something out of him and probably cost him
the race. He deserves plenty of credit for
finishing 9l clear of the third in a race as competitive as this. Ad Hoc had been kept to
hurdles for his four outings this season, and
it was hardly a secret that he was being campaigned for the Grand National. He was third
here for the second successive year and ran
a solid, if uninspiring, trial.

99 Fulke Walwyn Kim Muir Handicap Chase (Amateur Riders) (3m110yds)
Cheltenham March 11 (Good)

1 **Royal Predica** 9-11-6 Mr S McHugh (7)
2 **Ibis Rochelais** 7-10-8 Mr L McGrath (3)
3 **Rathbawn Prince** 11-11-11   Mr R
Loughran (3)
4 **Montreal** 6-11-1   Mr J E Moore (3)
33-1, 4-1f, 40-1, 12-1. 10l, 3/4l, 1/2l. 23 ran.
6m 23.1 (a1.60)
P A Deal, J S Dale & A Stennett (M Pipe,
Wellington)

Also: 5 Katarino, 6 Carryonharry, 7 Samuel
Winderspin, 8 Ifni Du Luc, 9 Tom Costalot, 10
Spinofski

Royal Predica, running for the first time since
the previous April, looked the first horse beat-
en. He trailed the field for the first circuit,
and the picture only changed from four out,
when he moved forward rapidly to pass the
entire field, and he was clear before the last.
The novices **Ibis Rochelais** and **Montreal**
both put up sound efforts in a strong field
for the race, while **Rathbawn Prince** did well
under a hefty burden.

100 Pertemps Final Handicap Hurdle (Listed Race) (3m1f110yds)
Cheltenham March 11 (Good)

1 **Inching Closer** 6-11-2   B J Geraghty
2 **Royal Emperor** 7-11-9 D Elsworth (3)
3 **Tribal Venture** 5-10-6   D N Russell
4 **Ravenswood** 6-11-3   T Scudamore
6-1f, 14-1, 33-1, 7-1. shd, 12l, 1 3/4l. 24 ran.

6m 20.8 (b10.76)
Mrs N L Spence (Jonjo O'Neill, Cheltenham)

Also: 5 Guard Duty, 6 Creon, 7 Dubai Seven Stars, 8 Carlovent, 9 Rostropovich, 10 Ballysicyos

The ground was probably on the lively side for a few of these slow old staying hurdlers but the front two coped well. **Inching Closer** had run only once since finishing down the field in the previous year's Royal & SunAlliance Hurdle. Reappearing at Haydock in February, he'd won a moderate handicap easily and been put up 8lb. He made rapid headway to challenge **Royal Emperor** but needed all of the run-in to get on top and will have nothing in hand once he's raised for this, although he retains plenty of Flat-race speed. Royal Emperor had been hurdling for a couple of years but enjoyed no success until switching from Jonjo O'Neill to Sue Smith for the start of this season. After a couple of novice wins, he took a couple of handicaps and ran here 23lb higher than when landing the first of those. Clearly, Smith's found the key to him, though it'll be surprising if there's much more to come.

101 Royal & SunAlliance Novices' Hurdle (Grade 1) (2m5f)
Cheltenham March 12 (Good)

1 **Hardy Eustace** 6-11-7   K A Kelly
2 **Pizarro** 6-11-7   N Williamson
3 **Lord Sam** 7-11-7   W Marston
6-1, 2-1f, 10-1. 1l, 3$\frac{1}{2}$l. 19 ran. 5m 5.7 (b1.95)
Laurence Byrne (D Hughes, Ireland)

Also: 4 Foreman, 5 Sh Boom, 6 Nil Desperandum, 7 Supreme Prince, 8 Little Sport, 9 Texas Ranger, 10 Double Honour

Plenty of strength in depth here. **Pizarro** came in for heavy support, which wasn't entirely justified by his achievments in winning two hurdles starts from three outings to date. Much was made of how well his win in the previous season's bumper had worked out, when he beat Rhinestone Cowboy, Back In Front, Thisthatandtother and Iris's Gift. He ran well but was found one-paced when it mattered, as **Hardy Eustace** and **Coolnagorna** fought it out. The latter, who'd led from halfway, edged left and interfered with his rival two out – although he finished second, he was disqualified and placed last. Hardy Eustace had only been beaten by Solerina in four starts over hurdles, but all his form was on a softer surface than this, so he deserves even more credit for having produced a career-best effort here. **Lord Sam** would have finished closer but for some sloppy jumping.

102 Royal & SunAlliance Chase (Grade 1) (3m110yds)
Cheltenham March 12 (Good)

1 **One Knight** 7-11-4   R Johnson
2 **Jair Du Cochet** 6-11-4   Jacques Ricou
3 **Barrow Drive** 7-11-4   B J Geraghty
15-2, 4-1, 9-1. 1$\frac{3}{4}$l, 10l. 9 ran. 6m 14.8 (b6.70)
R Gibbs (P Hobbs, Minehead)

Also: 4 Sea Drifting, 5 Keen Leader, 6 It Takes Time

One Knight must be about the least convincing jumper to have won this prize but he was allowed an uncontested lead and had the toughness to keep on galloping, despite his lack of fluency. He had won three from four coming into this, including a defeat of Le Roi Miguel, but had showed a similar tendency to make mistakes on his only run at Newbury and will need to get his act together if he's to win races in his second season. French jockeys are often unfairly criticised in the British press but it would be hard to defend the ride given **Jair Du Cochet** by Jacques Ricou. He held this relentless galloper at the back of the field and didn't ask him to chase the winner until the run to the last – had he made more use of the horse, he could well have won. **Keen Leader** and **It Takes Time** were the punters' favourites but both disappointed. Keen Leader didn't jump well enough in this company – he had fallen on his only two previous visits to Cheltenham, including in a hurdle race at the previous Festival.

103 Queen Mother Champion Chase (Grade 1) (2m)
Cheltenham March 12 (Good)

1 **Moscow Flyer** 9-12-0   B J Geraghty
2 **Native Upmanship** 10-12-0   C O'Dwyer
3 **Cenkos** 9-12-0   R Walsh
7-4f, 12-1, 7-1. 7l, 3l. 11 ran. 3m 53.7 (b8.38)
Brian Kearney (Mrs J Harrington, Ireland)

Also: 4 Geos, 5 Flagship Uberalles, 6 Edredon Bleu, 7 Kadarann, 8 Florida Pearl

Moscow Flyer remains unbeaten in nine completed runs over fences (though he'd fallen twice and unseated once prior to this, and unseated again at Punchestown on his run following this). This could have been a lot closer – he was going well but still had two serious challengers when **Seebald** and **Latalomne** when both fell independently at the second-last. Seebald was being pushed along at the time and looked booked for third at best but Latalomne was still travelling, so this was heartbreaking for his connections and supporters, who'd had to endure the same agony at the same fence the previous year. **Native Upmanship** hasn't won at this trip since November 2000 (and that was on heavy ground), so this was a classy effort from him, though it was hard to be impressed with many of those he beat. **Cenkos**, **Flagship Uberalles** and **Edredon Bleu** are now the old guard of 2m chasing, and it looks as though they've had their day. **Geos** has never been good enough at this level, while the gamble of running **Florida Pearl** here rather than in the Gold Cup did not pay off – he was never going to be quick enough. **Kadarann** didn't jump well enough to get into contention.

104 Coral Cup Hurdle (Showcase Handicap) (Grade 3) (2m5f)
Cheltenham March 12 (Good)

1 **Xenophon** 7-11-0	M A Fitzgerald
2 **Samon** 6-11-3	D J Casey
3 **Spectrometer** 6-11-8	R Johnson
4 **Emotional Moment** 6-11-4B	J Geraghty

4-1f, 25-1, 10-1, 7-1. 3¹/2l, 1l, 3l. 27 ran. 5m 4.2 (b3.45)
Lane Syndicate (A J Martin, Ireland)

Also: 5 Korelo, 6 Moving On Up, 7 Bow Strada, 8 Persian Waters, 9 Aimees Mark, 10 Anatar

"With a horse like this there is no point in going for Micky Mouse races – one big one makes up for ten little ones." Tony Martin was entitled to be on good terms with himself – he'd produced **Xenophon** to win this on only his sixth start, the horse having already won the valuable Pierse Hurdle (59). He came straight here from the Leopardstown race, for which he'd been raised 13lb, but it clearly wasn't anything like enough to stop him. Always travelling behind a predictably strong pace, he was asked to go past on the run-in and charged up the hill. Reportedly, he will go chasing next season. **Samon**, also on his sixth start, was rather more exposed than the winner but is capable of very good form on the right day. It was asking a lot of **Korelo** to take this just four days after a gruelling race in the Imperial Cup, and under a 7lb penalty, but he ran his race and would probably have done even better if he'd had his favoured bottomless conditions again.

105 National Hunt Challenge Cup Novices' Chase (Amateur Riders') (4m)
Cheltenham March 12 (Good)

1 **Sudden Shock** 8-11-7	Mr D W Cullen
2 **Stormez** 6-12-0	Mr J E Moore
3 **Young Ottoman** 7-11-11	Mr J M Pritchard

25-1, 7-4f, 10-1. 1l, 13l. 24 ran. 8m 21.7 (a7.30)

Darren C Mercer (Jonjo O'Neill, Cheltenham)

Also: 4 High Cotton, 5 Moorlands Again, 6 Lucky Bay, 7 Ask Henry, 8 Majed, 9 Druid's Glen, 10 Clonmel's Minella

Fatuously, **Stormez** was touted as many people's "banker of the meeting", as if there could ever be such a thing as a banker at the Cheltenham Festival, never mind a novice chaser in a race for amateur riders. Still, the horse is unbelievably tough for one so young and inexperienced and, despite a number of early blunders, he clawed his way to the front two out. Hard at work on the run-in, he was caught by a strong finishing run from **Sudden Shock**. Despite some useful form over hurdles, this winner was hard to foresee – he'd fallen in his first two chases early in the season and although he'd subsequently managed to complete round Wincanton and Kempton, he'd never looked like actually winning over fences and had indeed been stuffed by Stormez on the latter occasion. The beaten favourite doesn't look the easiest ride for an amateur but young Jamie Moore impressed and should have a future.

106 Mildmay Of Flete Challenge Cup Handicap Chase (Listed Race) (2m4f110yds)
Cheltenham March 12 (Good)

1 **Young Spartacus** 10-10-9	R Johnson
2 **Fondmort** 7-10-13	M A Fitzgerald
3 **Scots Grey** 8-10-0	Mr A Tinkler (7)
4 **Cregg House** 8-10-0	R M Power (5)

16-1, 11-2, 16-1, 25-1. 4l, 4l, 3l. 19 ran. 5m 5.0 (b2.25)
B G Hellyer (H Daly, Ludlow)

Also: 5 Lady Cricket, 6 Horus, 7 Fadalko, 8 Armaturk, 9 Blowing Wind, 10 Arctic Copper

Henry Daly pronounced himself "gobsmacked" by this result, saying he'd only run the horse because there was no other suitable race for such a highly-rated animal. **Young Spartacus** had last been succesful in the Racing Post Chase over two years before. Leg trouble meant this was just his fifth start since, and he'd been stuffed every time, but a consequence was that he ran here off just a 1lb higher mark than for the Kempton win. He was perhaps lucky, though, because **Goguenard** was still going well in front when Warren Marston fell off two out. **Fondmort** continues to progress, running an excellent second back at the scene of his Tripleprint success (38) off an 8lb higher mark, and just 1lb less than when well beaten in the Racing Post Chase (90). Last year's winner **Blowing Wind** was disappointing off just 1lb higher and his enthusiasm must now

Sponsored by Stan James

be called into question.

107 Weatherbys Champion Bumper Standard Open NH Flat (Grade 1) (2m110yds)
Cheltenham March 12 (Good)

1 **Liberman** 5-11-6 A P McCoy
2 **Trabolgan** 5-11-6 S Durack
3 **Widemouth Bay** 5-11-6 R Johnson
2-1f, 50-1, 33-1. ¹/2l, 1l. 25 ran. 3m 52.2 (b1.28)
D A Johnson (M Pipe, Wellington)

Also: 4 Bold Bishop, 5 Miller's Bay, 6 Bourbon Manhattan, 7 Govamix, 8 Kim Fontaine, 9 He's The Boss, 10 Royal Alphabet

It's amazing how many future stars have come out of this race and this renewal looks likely to produce its share. **Liberman** has been highly consistent in five bumpers, winning three and running second in the others, all but one of which featured fields of 16 or more. This was only his second run since joining Pipe from Paddy Mullins, his British debut having been four months before, yet he gave little sign of greenness and battled right to the line – it'll be a big surprise if he doesn't do well over hurdles. **Widemouth Bay** deserves plenty of credit, having run on strongly from off a moderate pace and finishing close up despite being hampered inside the final furlong. The first four finished 5l clear.

108 JCB Triumph Hurdle (Grade 1) (2m1f)
Cheltenham March 13 (Good)

1 **Spectroscope** 4-11-0 B J Geraghty
2 **Well Chief** 4-11-0 A P McCoy
3 **Golden Cross** 4-11-0 C F Swan
20-1, 7-1, 11-2f. hd, 5l. 27 ran. 3m 59.4 (b4.10)
Mrs G Smith (Jonjo O'Neill, Cheltenham)

Also: 4 Lilium De Cotte, 5 Mughas, 6 Le Duc, 7 Newlands Gold, 8 Mutineer, 9 Red Wine, 10 Dashing Home

There isn't much of **Spectroscope** and what there is suffered a bit of a fright when he was brought down on a previous visit here in November. He didn't jump too confidently when beaten next time but Geraghty was put up for the first time when the horse won his prep for this and the pair went well together again. **Well Chief** set a strong pace and still had the strength to fight when the winner challenged from the last but wasn't quite good enough. **Golden Cross**, who would want it softer than this, stayed on takingly, while **Le Duc** also ran respectably, considering he was hampered in a melee three from home.

109 Bonusprint Stayers' Hurdle (Grade 1) (3m)
Cheltenham March 13 (Good)

1 **Baracouda** 8-11-10 T Doumen
2 **Iris's Gift** 6-11-10 B J Geraghty
3 **Limestone Lad** 11-11-10 P Carberry
9-4j, 7-1, 9-4j. ³/4l, 5l. 11 ran. 5m 41.3 (a1.25)
JP McManus (F Doumen, France)

Also: 4 Classified, 5 Liss A Paoraigh, 6 Deano's Beeno, 7 Galileo, 8 Brother Joe, 9 Palua

Despite the fact that staying hurdlers are a select band of specialists, **Baracouda** was the first back-to-back winner for 15 years. Indeed, were it not for poor judgement on the part of his jockey, the horse would be unbeaten in his last dozen races – in any event, he deserves to be recognised as a great champion for maintaining his form at the highest level over three seasons. Unfortunately for English jumps fans, this was **Limestone Lad**'s first run outside Ireland since he was runner-up to Bacchanal in this race three years before. He ran a similar race to the one he ran then, leading at a strong pace but setting the race up for a classier rival, whose pace he couldn't match on this ground. **Iris's Gift** made a fight of it and ran an extraordinary race for a novice. This was his only defeat in seven hurdles outings through the season, but there may be better to come, as he looks a chaser. **Galileo**, running for the first time since winning the Royal & SunAlliance Novices Hurdle at last year's Festival, appeared not to stay, while the enigmatic **Brother Joe** ran no sort of race in first-time blinkers.

110 Tote Cheltenham Gold Cup Chase (Showcase Race) (Grade 1) (3m2f110yds)
Cheltenham March 13 (Good)

1 **Best Mate** 8-12-0 J Culloty
2 **Truckers Tavern** 8-12-0 D N Russell
3 **Harbour Pilot** 8-12-0 P Carberry
13-8f, 33-1, 40-1. 10l, 2¹/2l. 15 ran. 6m 39.1 (b6.15)
Jim Lewis (Miss H Knight, Wantage)

Also: 4 Valley Henry, 5 Behrajan, 6 Commanche Court, 7 Chives, 8 See More Business, 9 You're Agoodun, 10 Colonel Braxton

Best Mate proved himself a long way clear of his contemporaries in becoming the first dual winner of the Gold Cup since 1971, and only the second since Arkle. He also became the first horse to win the King George and the Gold Cup in the same season since Desert Orchid. That he's remained sound and held his form so well is thanks to the patience of Henrietta Knight, who makes no bones about keeping her star lightly-raced, in order to maximize the length of his career. No trainer would be more likely to produce the horse fit and ready to try for the hat-trick next March. The eight-year-old was held up some way off a strong pace, cut out by **Behrajan** and **See More Business**. As Best Mate made progress towards the leaders about six from home, his stablemate **Chives** sailed into the lead and continued the unrelenting gallop, outpacing those who'd led up 'til then. At the third-last, the champ made his move and, by the next, he was clear and the race was over bar a fall. Of those behind, only **Valley Henry** ever looked like making a race of it, closing up to challenge three out when everything else was off the bridle. But Best Mate got away from him easily and Valley Henry got very tired on the run to the last. Some critics have attempted to undermine the worth of this win by pointing out that the second and third are little better than good handicappers. This seems unfair to the winner – both are tough stayers who ran on into the frame because the rest were left reeling with fatigue trying to keep up. **Beef Or Salmon** was sent off second-favourite, but novices have an abysmal record in this race; before this renewal, only two of the nine to have run since 1986 had even completed, with Dorans Pride running third in 1997. Despite his undoubted ability, Beef Or Salmon underlined this statistic by falling at the third.

111 Christie's Foxhunter Chase Challenge Cup (3m2f110yds)
Cheltenham March 13 (Good)

1 **Kingscliff** 6-12-0   Mr R Young
2 **Bright Approach** 10-12-0Miss P Gundry
3 **Last Option** 11-12-0   Mrs F Needham
11-4f, 20-1, 16-1. 2^1/2l, ^{1}/2l. 24 ran. 6m 49.5 (a4.25)
A J Sendell (Mrs S Alner, Blandford Forum)

Also: 4 Earthmover, 5 County Derry, 6 Spot Thedifference, 7 Araminta, 8 Sheltering, 9 Jabiru, 10 Polaris Flame

A highly impressive performance by **Kingscliff**, who outpointed the older hunters as comprehensively as Best Mate had bested his peers shortly before. Having reportedly won both his point-to-points on the bridle, he was initially put to the test in a hunter chase at Wincanton, where he won by 30l from a decent field despite a couple of errors. He again clouted one here and got tired on the run-in but still won with plenty in hand. This was his final outing of the season and he will be campaigned in handicaps next term. With former winners **Last Option** and **Earthmover** running their races, the form looks solid, but the race was

entirely marred by the fatal fall of **Dorans Pride**. The hardy chestnut won 30 races on the Flat, over hurdles and over fences, including four Grade 1 chases, and he was twice placed in the Gold Cup itself, having previously won the Stayers' Hurdle at the Festival. Why he was still racing at 14 years of age is anyone's guess.

112 Grand Annual Handicap Chase Challenge Cup (Listed Race) (2m110yds)
Cheltenham March 13 (Good)

1 **Palarshan** 5-10-0   M Bradburne
2 **Risk Accessor** 8-10-1   S Durack
3 **Dark'n Sharp** 8-11-2   R Johnson
4 **Vol Solitaire** 5-10-8   R Walsh
8-1, 20-1, 13-2, 7-1. 3l, ^{3}/4l, ^{3}/4l. 21 ran. 3m 58.6 (b7.15)
Mrs A L Wood (H Daly, Ludlow)

Also: 5 Ross Moff, 6 Red Ark, 7 Native Scout, 8 Exit Swinger, 9 Korakor, 10 Royal Jake

Henry Daly's second winner at the meeting, with a scopey, tough young chaser that is typical of the yard. **Palarshan** had never been out of the first three in four chase runs, but those were small-field novice races and the most significant piece of form to his name may have been a win round here over hurdles on his British debut the previous April. He strung out a competitive field here, despite swerving away from the whip on the run-in, and should still be a force in handicaps after reassessment.

113 Cathcart Challenge Cup Chase (Grade 2) (2m5f)
Cheltenham March 13 (Good)

1 **La Landiere** 8-10-12   R Johnson
2 **Irish Hussar** 7-11-0   M A Fitzgerald
3 **Macs Gildoran** 9-11-3   R Walsh
5-4f, 14-1, 25-1. 1^1/2l, 5l. 9 ran. 5m 12.5 (b1.00)
Mrs R J Skan (R Phillips, Moreton-in-Marsh)

Also: 4 Le Coudray, 5 Poliantas, 6 Barton, 7 Regal Exit, 8 Iznogogud

La Landiere was top on Official Ratings but, because of the terms of this race, was getting weight from the entire field. Her chance was obvious and she duly brought the layers to their knees by becoming the tenth wiining favourite at the Festival. Her main rival, judged on both ratings and the betting market, was **Tarxien**, who clouted the third, fourth and fifth before tipping up at the sixth, an effort that was the more disappointing because the pace was only moderate by the standards of this meeting. When it came to the crunch, the first two had much better acceleration than the rest. La Landiere proved toughest and extended her winning run to seven. Both **Macs Gildoran** and **Le Coudray** could have used some cut, while **Barton** can't seem to recapture his old form.

114 Vincent O'Brien County Handicap Hurdle (Grade 3) (2m1f)
Cheltenham March 13 (Good)

1 **Spirit Leader** 7-11-7	B J Geraghty
2 **Balapour** 5-10-5	M F Mooney (5)
3 **Through The Rye** 7-10-9	G Lee
4 **Non So** 5-11-5	M A Fitzgerald

10-1, 25-1, 66-1, 10-1. nk, shd, 5l. 28 ran.
3m 58.2 (b5.30)
D Thompson (Mrs J Harrington, Ireland)

Also: 5 Jaboune, 6 Direct Bearing, 7 Turtleback, 8 Polar Red, 9 Idaho d'Ox, 10 Never

This was **Spirit Leader**'s third major British handicap success this season, following battling wins in the William Hill Hurdle *(34)* and the Tote Gold Trophy *(78)*, an outstanding achievement, particularly for an Irish raider. She has held her form in the face of a spiralling handicap mark (up 18lb since her Sandown win), has only once finished outside the first four in 18 career starts, when fifth in the Pierse Hurdle *(59)*, and seems well-suited by a strongly-run race. Her willingness to fight was again shown here, as she was being pushed from three out, when it seemed that most of the field still had a winning chance. Edging ahead on the run-in, she was challenged on both sides but always looked like holding on. **Balapour** finished strongly, having run on into second in the previous year's Triumph Hurdle, while **Non So** upheld the Tote Gold Trophy form, for which he'd been raised 7lb. A couple of other Irish raiders started at shorter prices than the winner – both **Direct Bearing** and **Mise Rafturai** looked to have been laid out for the race and were arguably well handicapped. The former ran his race in sixth but the latter, sent off 5-1 favourite for his first run in four months, faded from three out and was pulled up.

115 John Smith's Midlands Grand National Chase Showcase Handicap (4m2f)
Uttoxeter March 15 (Soft)

1 **Intelligent** 7-10-10	R M Power (5)
2 **Akarus** 8-10-4	Mr J E Moore (7)
3 **Jurancon II** 6-10-1	R Johnson
4 **River Bug** 9-10-0	L Cummins

6-1, 33-1, 8-1, 25-1. 1¹/₂l, 28l, 18l. 17 ran.
9m 26.6 (a1m6.80)
Norman Moore (Mrs J Harrington, Ireland)

No stable was in quite the form of Jessica Harrington's coming into this, she having won with both her runners at the Cheltenham Festival. **Intelligent** was only a novice but, being Irish, he'd had plenty of experience of slogging through heavy ground and he stayed on strongly. His rider, Robert Power, was scarcely more experienced but didn't want for stamina as his mount got the better of a protracted battle with the runner-up on the run to the last. **Jurancon II** ran a grand race considering this was only his second attempt over fences. Eleven of the seventeen starters were pulled up, including Welsh National winner **Mini Sensation** and Scottish National winner **Take Control**.

116 Ashleybank Investments Scottish Borders National H'cap Chase (4m)
Kelso March 21 (Good)

1 **A Piece Of Cake** 10-11-12	A Dempsey
2 **Interdit** 7-10-0	K Renwick
3 **Tarbolton Moss** 8-10-0	J Crowley

20-1, 25-1, 8-1. 5l, 4l. 13 ran. 8m 37.0 (a21.00)
Lightbody Celebration Cakes Ltd (Mrs M Reveley, Saltburn)

Jonjo O'Neill's **Putsometnby** had been touted for a race at the Cheltenham Festival, having unseated when 12l up at Doncaster early in the month. He came here instead, which ought to have been a lot easier, so he was duly sent off favourite but jumping errors again cost him. **A Piece Of Cake** had never won beyong 2m6f before but good ground and weak opposition meant he was good enough this time.

117 EBF Crandon Park Stud Mares Novices Handicap Hurdle (Listed) (2m5f)
Newbury March 22 (Good)

1 **Ar Muin Na Muice** 7-11-10B	J Geraghty
2 **Glenmoss Tara** 5-11-0	B Harding
3 **Blue Ride** 6-10-13	P J Brennan (5)
4 **Spaghetti Junction** 5-10-5	A Thornton

11-8f, 11-2, 4-1, 33-1. 2¹/₂l, 4l, 10l. 16 ran.
4m 59.5 (b7.10)
Mrs G Smith (Jonjo O'Neill, Cheltenham)

Ar Muin Na Muice was touted as a possible Gold Cup runner by her trainer when running in bumpers in Ireland. Since joining O'Neill, she'd only been beaten once over hurdles, and then only by a useful sort, but her races have not exactly been competitive and it's not clear what she beat here either. However, the first three, who were top on Official Ratings, finished clear. **Glenmoss Tara** had been unbeaten in three hurdles outings, while **Blue Ride** was two wins from three and went on to land a Cheltenham handicap off a 6lb higher mark.

118 sportingoptions.co.uk Long Distance Hurdle (Grade 2) (3m)
Ascot April 2 (Good)

1 **Deano's Beeno** 11-11-10   A P McCoy
2 **Frosty Canyon** 10-11-2   T Doyle
3 **Stromness** 6-11-6   R Thornton
5-4f, 20-1, 12-1. 8l, 5l. 7 ran. 5m 55.0 (a14.20)
Axom (M Pipe, Wellington)

Deano's Beeno's eleventh hurdles success and his seventh at Graded level. As usual, he needed plenty of driving but was able to dominate and ran away from his rivals up the straight. **Galileo** and **Brother Joe**, stuffed in the Stayers' Hurdle *(109)*, were again disappointing. **Landing Light** ought to have been able to travel well at this trip but was never going with any enthusiasm.

119 Martell Cognac Nisa Today's Handicap Hurdle (Listed Race) (3m110yds)
Aintree April 3 (Good)

1 **Carlovent** 8-10-11   A P McCoy
2 **Rostropovich** 6-10-12   N Williamson
3 **Keepatem** 7-10-2   D J Casey
4 **Fairwood Heart** 6-10-0   R M Power (5)
16-1, 16-1, 8-1, 12-1. 1^1/2l, ^{1}/2l, 1^1/2l. 22 ran. 6m 9.8 (a14.55)
C M, B J & R F Batterham (M Pipe, Wellington)

Carlovent hadn't won since landing this race off a 12lb higher mark two years before. He's said to keep a bit to himself but he'd also gone up a stone within two runs of that last success and had taken a long time to come down to a more reasonable level. **Rostropovich** had also proved hard to win with but seemed to appreciate the sound surface.

120 Martell Cognac Cup Chase (Grade 2) (3m1f)
Aintree April 3 (Good)

1 **First Gold** 10-11-2   T Doumen
2 **Lady Cricket** 9-11-7   A P McCoy
3 **Commanche Court** 10-11-6   R Walsh
14-1, 6-1, 10-3. 14l, ^{3}/4l. 7 ran. 6m 22.5 (a11.00)
JP McManus (F Doumen, France)

Like Carlovent, **First Gold** was winless since landing this self-same race in 2001, but in his case the fall from grace was the more lamentable because he'd looked a highly impressive King George winner that season. Since then, he'd had trouble getting near any winner, in various types of race, and had been a beaten favourite four times. The difference here appeared to be first-time blinkers. Leading from the second, First Gold attacked his fences,

bowled clear before the straight and won as he pleased. It's tempting to conclude that **Valley Henry** and **Marlborough** didn't run their races (many horses don't produce their best at Aintree, especially if they've been on the go all season) but the placed horses are still useful yardsticks and this remains a highly encouraging return to form by the winner, who beat Rince Ri to land a Grade 1 at Punchestown in similar fashion later in the month.

121 Martell Safeway Red Rum Chase (Showcase Handicap) (Listed) (2m)
Aintree April 3 (Good)

1 **Golden Alpha** 9-10-13   A P McCoy
2 **Dark'n Sharp** 8-11-10   R Johnson
3 **Risk Accessor** 8-10-11   S Durack
4 **Log On Intersky** 7-10-2   G Lee
7-1, 4-1f, 7-1, 10-1. 10l, 1^1/4l, 6l. 16 ran. 3m 56.3 (a1.42)
D A Johnson (M Pipe, Wellington)

There were some revealing post-race comments from Tony McCoy regarding the winner, who'd been travelling well when falling three out in Palarshan's race at the Festival *(112)*. McCoy said **Golden Alpha** "isn't a very strong finisher and that's why he tends to fall late on," (the horse had unseated two out on a previous visit to Cheltenham). He was a good jumper, McCoy continued, if you left him alone, but he'd had to ask for a big jump at the Festival, and the horse didn't cope. This flat track showed him to better effect and he quickened well when asked to win his race between the last two. **Dark'n Sharp** ran well off a mark 13lb higher than when winning this last year.

122 Ember Inns Anniversary 4YO Novices' Hurdle (Grade 2) (2m110yds)
Aintree April 3 (Good)

1 **Le Duc** 4-11-0   R Walsh
2 **Spectroscope** 4-11-4   B J Geraghty
3 **Well Chief** 4-11-4   A P McCoy
33-1, 8-1, 2-1f. hd, 2^1/2l. 19 ran. 4m 4.1 (a11.45)
Mrs J Stewart (P Nicholls, Shepton Mallet)

Cheltenham form may not always stand up at Aintree, but the Triumph Hurdle form was almost repeated here, with the first, second and fifth from the Festival finishing second, third and sixth here, in the same order. The crucial difference was that the Cheltenham sixth, **Le Duc**, managed to improve five places for his first win in eight attempts over hurdles. He's reckoned to be a chaser in the making, which would explain why he's taken time to mature. He didn't get a clear run in the Triumph, but Paul Nicholls said after this that he wouldn't have

Sponsored by Stan James

won in any case. Here, it was his turn to inflict interference, as he hung across the runner-up on the run-in, though this probably didn't affect the outcome. **Moneytrain** ran out of steam halfway up the straight after travelling well.

123 St Austell Brewery Mersey Novices' Hurdle (Grade 2) (2m4f)
Aintree April 3 (Good)

1 **Leinster** 6-11-0		K A Kelly
2 **Crystal d'Ainay** 4-10-7		R Thornton
3 **Aine Dubh** 6-10-9		C F Swan

12-1, 14-1, 66-1. 7l, 17l. 15 ran. 5m 1.1 (a15.10)
Cathal M Ryan (D Hughes, Ireland)

Although this was his first win over obstacles, **Leinster** had never been worse than fourth in four big-field maiden hurdles in Ireland, and Dessie Hughes reported afterwards that he needs good ground, which he hadn't had since winning his bumper. This fell into his lap when 11-10 favourite **Coolnagorna** suffered a fatal fall three out, and it must be doubtful if he beat much of quality, but he clearly has ability and will be an interesting handicapper in the right conditions.

124 Martell Cognac V.S. Thresher Handicap Chase (3m1f)
Aintree April 4 (Good)

1 **Master Tern** 8-11-1		A Dobbin
2 **Shardam** 6-10-8		C Llewellyn
3 **Ross Moff** 10-11-1		M A Fitzgerald

5-1, 11-1, 9-2f. 1¼l, 7l. 14 ran. 6m 33.7 (a22.20)
JP McManus (Jonjo O'Neill, Cheltenham)

Master Tern has done well to win three over fences, considering he doesn't jump at all well. He has class, though, having also won the County Hurdle at the Cheltenham Festival, and was able to see this out despite smashing through the last. Nigel Twiston-Davies does well with his novice chasers in handicaps and **Shardam** fairly flew from an unpromising position to take second.

125 Laurel Pub Company Top Novices' Hurdle (Grade 2) (2m110yds)
Aintree April 4 (Good)

1 **Limerick Boy** 5-11-0		A Dobbin
2 **Man O'Mystery** 6-11-0		T Doyle
3 **Lirfox** 6-11-0		R Greene

5-1, 11-2, 12-1. 4l, 12l. 12 ran. 4m 10.3 (a17.65)
Favourites Racing (Miss V Williams, Hereford)

The winner ran a decent race in sixth to Back

In Front at the Festival *(95)*. Though he didn't travel so well this time, and was under plenty of pressure by halfway, he kept on finding and outbattled **Man O'Mystery**, who wasn't the easiest to win with on the Flat.

126 Martell Cognac Melling Chase (Grade 1) (2m4f)
Aintree April 4 (Good)

1 **Native Upmanship** 10-11-10		C O'Dwyer
2 **Seebald** 8-11-10		A P McCoy
3 **Kadarann** 6-11-10		J Tizzard

5-4f, 4-1, 12-1. 1l, 18l. 6 ran. 5m 8.9 (a14.30)
Mrs John Magnier (A L Moore, Ireland)

A sixth Grade 1 win for **Native Upmanship**, of which all but the first have been at this trip. He was never troubled, taking it up between the last two and winning cheekily, still on the bridle. **Cenkos** had never won beyond 2m1f before and, after setting the pace, he faded tamely from two out.

127 Martell Cognac Sainsbury's Topham Chase (Showcase Handicap) (2m5f110yds)
Aintree April 4 (Good)

1 **Clan Royal** 8-10-2		L Cooper
2 **Macs Gildoran** 9-11-8		R Walsh
3 **Exit Swinger** 8-11-12		A P McCoy
4 **Mr Bossman** 10-10-8		H Oliver

12-1, 5-1f, 12-1, 12-1. 2½l, 3½l, 2½l. 29 ran. 5m 39.3 (a31.50)
JP McManus (Jonjo O'Neill, Cheltenham)

Clan Royal had gone up a stone for winning a couple of moderate handicaps but he relished this test over the longest trip he'd tackled. Leading eight fences from home, he was only briefly headed by the eventual sixth **Quality First** two from home. **Macs Gildoran** stuck on well but didn't have the acceleration to catch the winner. Best finisher was **Falcon Du Coteau**, who made the running in the race the year before until falling at Valentine's – this time, he never got into it, but made up five places on the run-in to be fifth.

128 Martell Cognac Sefton Novices' Hurdle (Grade 1) (3m110yds)
Aintree April 4 (Good)

1 **Iris's Gift** 6-11-4		B J Geraghty
2 **Royal Emperor** 7-11-4		D Elsworth
3 **Supreme Prince** 6-11-4		P Flynn

10-11f, 12-1, 12-1. 8l, 12l. 9 ran. 6m 22.6 (a27.35)
Robert Lester (Jonjo O'Neill, Cheltenham)

Iris's Gift didn't have to be anything like as good as he was at Cheltenham *(109)* to take this, and he won without fuss. Leading from halfway, he was clear with three to jump and would have won much further if he hadn't idled in front. Disappointment of the race was **Hardy Eustace**, tailed off in fifth on his first attempt beyond 2m5f. This was his seventh outing of the season and may have been a bridge too far.

129 Happy Shopper Mildmay Novices' Chase (Grade 2) (3m1f)
Aintree April 4 (Good)

1 **Irish Hussar** 7-11-2   M A Fitzgerald
2 **It Takes Time** 9-11-7   A P McCoy
3 **Joly Bey** 6-11-7   R Walsh
3-1, 15-8f, 6-1. 5l, 7l. 9 ran. 6m 34.9 (a23.40)
Major Christopher Hanbury (N Henderson, Lambourn)

It Takes Time had been very disappointing at Cheltenham (102) but the Pipe/McCoy combo were having such a good time at this Aintree meeting that he was sent off favourite. When he went past the pace-setting **Irish Hussar** four out, it looked as though their faith was to be rewarded, but his rival had plenty of reserves left and went past again on the run to the last, winning in style to underline the worth of La Landiere's Cathcart win (113).

130 Clark's Brewery Handicap Hurdle (Listed Race) (2m4f)
Aintree April 4 (Good)

1 **Patriot Games** 9-10-4   C F Swan
2 **Gralmano** 8-10-6   G Lee
3 **Canada** 5-10-0   R Greene
4 **Emotional Moment** 6-11-1B J Geraghty
16-1, 10-1, 16-1, 3-1f. 1¹/₂l, 5l, 6l. 16 ran. 5m 6.3 (a20.30)
JP McManus (C Swan, Ireland)

A pretty good training and riding performance from Charlie Swan to land this competitive event with a cripple. **Patriot Games** is a fast-ground specialist with dodgy limbs – he has a chip in one knee and a pin in one leg. Plus, he'd been off the course for six months before this. It would have been hard to tell, though, as he cruised past the field on the wide outside, taking it up two out and holding on well, but sadly he finished lame and it's not known if or when he'll make it back. **Emotional Moment** and **Samon**, fifth, both look in the handicapper's grip.

131 Cordon Bleu Handicap Hurdle (Listed Race) (2m110yds)
Aintree April 5 (Good)

1 **Risky Reef** 6-10-7   R Walsh
2 **Altay** 6-10-2   P Whelan (3)
3 **Brooklyn's Gold** 8-10-7James Davies (7)
4 **Edmo Heights** 7-10-0   D O'Meara
20-1, 7-1, 16-1, 40-1. 1³/4l, 3l, 1l. 19 ran. 3m 56.5 (a3.85)
Ergon Syndicate (A Lee, Ireland)

Having shown promise in six hurdles outings to date, **Risky Reef** put it all together in his first handicap over obstacles, and his first hurdles run in Britain. He was always going well (connections say a fast pace on a flat track are his ideal conditions) and, making his challenge between runners at the last, showed grit to take the lead and hold it. **Altay** couldn't go with him but the lightly-raced sort showed the worth of the form when winning a valuable handicap hurdle off a 6lb higher mark the following month. **Non So** ought to have gone close, having been raised just 1lb for his County Hurdle fourth, but those at the upper end of the weights have a poor record in this race and he could manage only tenth.

132 Martell Maghull Novices' Chase (Grade 1) (2m)
Aintree April 5 (Good)

1 **Le Roi Miguel** 5-11-1   R Walsh
2 **Vol Solitaire** 5-11-1   J Tizzard
3 **Impek** 7-11-4   J Culloty
9-4, 10-3, 6-4f. 11l, hd. 5 ran. 3m 52.5 (b2.38)
Mrs J Stewart (P Nicholls, Shepton Mallet)

Not the hottest of races as it turned out, with **Rathgar Beau** and **Tysou** falling, while 6-4 favourite **Impek** lacked the pace to get competitive in these conditions. Still, **Le Roi Miguel** looked the part, jumping cleanly on only his fourth run over fences and bounding clear when asked. He gave no sign of having lost any confidence through his Cheltenham fall (96) and went on to beat Impek again in a Grade 1 for novices at Punchestown the next month.

133 Martell Cognac Aintree Hurdle (Grade 1) (2m4f)
Aintree April 5 (Good)

1 **Sacundai** 6-11-7   R Walsh
2 **Rooster Booster** 9-11-7   R Johnson
3 **Like-A-Butterfly** 9-11-2   C F Swan
9-1, 5-4f, 11-2. hd, 7l. 11 ran. 4m 51.8 (a5.80)
Malm Syndicate (E O'Grady, Ireland)

Rooster Booster hadn't been beaten in five runs since this race last year. He might be said to have run well when fourth that day, having been merely the winner of the County Hurdle and a 12-1 shot to boot, but this time round he was the champion hurdler and 5-4 favourite, so second place was a let-down. He had his excuses, having never won beyond 2m1f, while

96

Richard Johnson dropped his whip with a furlong to run – but this last factor is of doubtful relevance, as he's a willing horse who looks as though he gives his all, so **Sacundai** may well have worn him down in any case. The winner has usually kept good company in Ireland and came into this on a run of three wins, but this was still his best form by some way. Notably, he'd been a 3l fifth to **Like-A-Butterfly**, a distant third here, at the 2001 Festival. **Lord Transcend** looks a staying chaser, so he ran well above himself here and deserves credit for his fifth place, despite meeting defeat for the first time.

134 Martell Cognac Grand National Chase (Showcase Handicap) (Grade 3) (4m4f)
Aintree April 5 (Good)

1 **Monty's Pass**	10-10-7	B J Geraghty
2 **Supreme Glory**	10-10-2	L Aspell
3 **Amberleigh House**	11-10-4	G Lee
4 **Gunner Welburn**	11-10-2	B Fenton

16-1, 40-1, 33-1, 16-1. 12l, 2l, 14l. 40 ran. 9m 21.7 (a43.30)
Dee Racing Syndicate (J J Mangan, Ireland)

Irish raiders had no luck in this between L'Escargot in 1975 and Bobbyjo in 1999 but this was their third victory in five years. Both Bobbyjo and 2000's successful raider Papillon had their final prep runs over hurdles, and so it was with **Monty's Pass**. Following his Kerry National win in September (7) and his third in the Munster National (9), he was kept off the course until March. He warmed up by getting stuffed in a couple of novice hurdles – uninspiring, perhaps, but after two such clear precedents, punters had no excuse for not seeing what was coming. Monty's Pass was the subject of an almighty gamble from 66-1 down, with one of his part-owners quoted as saying he'd won over £800,000. In the race, he got an ideal run, staying prominent throughout, taking it off **Gunner Welburn** two out and going clear with little obvious effort. Having never won beyond 3m before, he had his stamina to prove, but saw out the trip in style. The same cannot be said of Gunner Welburn, who got very tired after the last, having coped well with the course once again, with the exception of a slow jump at The Chair. **Supreme Glory** and **Amberleigh House** stayed on dourly but lacked the winner's class. Notably, the first four, together with fifth-placed **Montifault** and the sixth **Bindaree**, were all aimed at this race throughout the season, and all missed Cheltenham. As so often here in the past, a couple of class horses were weighted out of it, even though compression of the handicap ought to have favoured them;

both **Shotgun Willy** and **Gingembre** started backpedalling early on the second circuit. **Ad Hoc** was called unlucky for getting brought down the previous year, but he had no one to blame but himself when dropping his jockey at the first ditch on the second circuit. Those with excuses included **Chives**, pulled up on the first circuit after breaking a blood vessel, **Iris Bleu**, pulled up lame before halfway, and **Youlneverwalkalone**, who broke down on the run to the twelfth.

135 Samsung Electronics Scottish Champion Handicap Hurdle (Grade 2) (2m)
Ayr April 12 (Good)

1 **In Contrast**	7-10-13	R Johnson
2 **Thisthatandtother**	7-10-12	R Walsh
3 **Westender**	7-11-10	A P McCoy

2-1, 6-1, 11-8f. 2½l, 6l. 5 ran. 3m 38.5 (a0.10)
Tony Staple (P Hobbs, Minehead)

Having benefitted from the fast pace in the Champion Hurdle (97), **Westender** had to make his own running here, which didn't suit nearly so well. He set this up for the front two, with the more experienced of the pair getting the verdict. With fast ground and a left-handed track, **In Contrast** had his ideal conditions.

136 Gala Casinos Daily Record Scottish National Handicap Chase (4m1f)
Ayr April 12 (Good)

1 **Ryalux**	10-10-5	R McGrath
2 **Stormez**	6-10-10	A P McCoy
3 **Spendid**	11-10-5	R Thornton
4 **Kerry Lads**	8-10-0	K Renwick

15-2, 6-1, 12-1, 40-1. nk, 20l, ¾l. 19 ran. 8m 12.5 (a4.10)
William Lomas (A Crook, Leyburn)

Ryalux has long been a consistent handicapper, if workmanlike, but this saved him from being labelled a 'nearly' horse – he'd been second or third in 13 of his previous 18 starts, winning just three times, including once when he would have been third if the front two hadn't knocked each other sideways at the last. But he looked well suited by a marathon on this first try beyond 3m1f, running on strongly to peg back **Stormez** near the line. The runner-up was only 3lb higher than when winning in November (20), so was entitled to go close, but **Gunther McBride** is firmly in the handicapper's grip – conditions should have been perfect for him, but he was held in fourth when unseating two out. **Shotgun Willy** ran from a 6lb higher mark than when pulled up in the Grand National (134) just a week before, and in the circumstances put up a blinding effort to be fifth in first-time blinkers.

137 Faucets For Mira Showers Trophy Limited Handicap Chase (Gr2) (2m5f)
Cheltenham April 16 (Good)

1 **Poliantas**	6-11-1	R Walsh
2 **Fondmort**	7-11-10	M A Fitzgerald
3 **Upgrade**	9-11-8	T J Murphy

6-1, 9-4j, 25-1. 10l, 9l. 7 ran. 5m 8.5 (b5.00)
Mark Tincknell (P Nicholls, Shepton Mallet)

Poliantas started the season with a couple of blinding runs, when second here in the Thomas Pink *(21)* and beating Golden Goal and **Fondmort** at Wincanton. Three defeats later, he was back to the same handicap mark from which he'd enjoyed that win, and was 9lb better in with Fondmort, and he took full advantage, making all and going clear before the last.

138 Dan Moore Handicap Chase (2m1f)
Fairyhouse April 20 (Good to Firm)

1 **Killultagh Storm**	9-10-12	R Walsh
2 **Alcapone**	9-11-3	B J Geraghty
3 **Arctic Copper**	9-11-5	P Carberry

5-2f, 5-1, 3-1. hd, 3l. 6 ran. 4m 9.2 (b41.66)
Mrs Rose Boyd (W P Mullins, Ireland)

Competitive, with the three market-leaders fighting it out, and **Killultagh Storm** finding enough to go one better than he managed in the equivalent race the year before. Willie Mullins reckons the horse peaks in the spring on fast ground.

139 Menolly Homes Novice Hurdle (Grade 2) (2m)
Fairyhouse April 21 (Good to Firm)

1 **Glenhaven Nugget**	7-11-4N	Williamson
2 **Mutakarrim**	6-11-10	B J Geraghty
3 **Carlesimo**	5-11-6	P Carberry

9-4, 11-8f, 3-1. hd, 12l. 5 ran. 4m 5.0 (a3.71)
David Cahill (E O'Grady, Ireland)

The winner had been a distant fifth in a Grade 2 at Aintree *(125)*, but this was a lot less competitive and he only had to beat **Mutakarrim**, ninth in the Supreme Novices' Hurdle at Cheltenham *(95)*.

140 Powers Gold Label Irish Grand National Handicap Chase (Gr A) (3m5f)
Fairyhouse April 21 (Good)

1 **Timbera**	9-10-12	J Culloty
2 **Knock Knock**	6-10-2	M D Grant (3)
3 **Winning Dream**	9-10-5	A P McCoy
4 **Davids Lad**	9-12-0	T J Murphy

11-1, 20-1, 9-1, 10-1. hd, 2l, 2l. 21 ran. 7m
43.8 (b36.23)
Mrs J M Breen (D Hughes, Ireland)

This was **Timbera**'s fifth win at the track – he'd looked booked for the places in last year's renewal when falling two out. Effectively 6lb lower this time, he had plenty of supporters and didn't let them down, jumping fluently and running on to lead near the line. **Knock Knock** ran extremely well for a novice, having just his seventh run over fences (he'd won on both his previous handicap starts). He made one pretty bad error and, although that was a long way from home, it could easily have cost him the race. **Davids Lad** may be fairly handicapped, but top weight was always going to leave him vulnerable and he could manage only fourth.

141 Powers Gold Cup (Grade 1) (2m4f)
Fairyhouse April 22 (Good)

1 **Thari**	6-11-9	P Carberry
2 **One Night Out**	7-11-9	J R Barry

6-1, 5-1. 3l. 3 ran. 5m 3.4 (b28.34)
D P Sharkey (N Meade, Ireland)

The 'outsider of three' merchants copped a win here, but **Thari**'s was a highly fortunate success. The 30-100 favourite **Adamant Approach** was 2l up and looking all over the winner two out, when, for the second time in three races, he fell. In doing so, he seriously interfered with his stablemate **One Night Out**, gifting the race to the slowest runner.

142 Powers Gold Label Handicap Hurdle Series Final (Grade A) (2m)
Fairyhouse April 22 (Good)

1 **High Prospect**	5-10-0	N Williamson
2 **Junior Fontaine**	6-10-13D	J Howard (3)
3 **The Dark Flasher**	6-10-13	D J Casey
4 **Healy's Pub**	7-11-3	R C Colgan (7)

5-1f, 14-1, 16-1, 8-1. ^{1}/2l, ^{3}/4l, 2l. 18 ran. 3m
40.4 (b20.89)
Alec Scallan (P Nolan, Ireland)

High Prospect defied a 10lb penalty for his second handicap win since joining Paul Nolan earlier in the year. Given the fast time, it seems likely that the going was quicker than the official 'Good', yet the winner is said to be better with cut, so it'll be interesting to follow his campaign through the coming winter, when his target is said to be the Pierse Hurdle.

143 Goffs Land Rover Bumper (2m)
Fairyhouse April 22 (Good)

1 **Newmill**	5-11-7	Mr A FitzGerald

2 **Hardy Duckett** 4-11-0Mr R Loughran (5)
3 **Rushneeyriver** 5-11-7 Mr D F O'Regan (7)
10-1, 5-1, 25-1. 3¹/2l, ³/4l. 17 ran. 3m 38.3 (b17.26)
Mrs Mary T Hayes (T O'Leary, Ireland)

Not much to go on in terms of previous form here and the race may amount to little but the winner at least is bred to make a decent hurdler or chaser and he won this in some style, going clear early in the straight, having led before halfway.

144 Concept Hurdle (2m110yds)
Sandown April 25 (Good to Firm)

1 **Santenay** 5-11-6   R Walsh
2 **Copeland** 8-11-6   A P McCoy
3 **Ben Ewar** 9-11-6   A Thornton
7-4, 8-15f, 50-1. 7l, 14l. 6 ran. 3m 43.2 (b9.62)
The Hon Mrs Townshend (P Nicholls, Shepton Mallet)

It was 25-1 bar two. Although behind on Official Ratings, **Copeland** had looked likely to finish well ahead of **Santenay** in the Champion Hurdle (97) before falling and that, together with the irresistible Pipe/McCoy partnership, was enough to send him off favourite. But Paul Nicholls said after this that Santenay had been off-colour at Cheltenham, so, with the fast ground in his favour here, it was no surprise that he was able to take control on the run-in.

145 Press The Red Button To Bet attheraces Hurdle (3m)
Sandown April 26 (Good to Firm)

1 **Rostropovich** 6-11-5   N Williamson
2 **Deano's Beeno** 11-11-9   A P McCoy
3 **Carlovent** 8-11-5   T Scudamore
4-1, 8-13f, 8-1. shd, dis. 6 ran. 5m 39.1
M A Kilduff (M Morris, Ireland)

Again, as the market suggested, a two-horse race, with both of the principals having had aspersions cast on their resolution in the past. As usual, **Deano's Beeno** had to be driven along on the final circuit, while **Rostropovich** cruised along behind him. But, when it came to a battle, Rostropovich didn't go past as easily as had seemed likely and in the end he may not have won if the runner-up hadn't wandered right and left in the closing stages on ground that was too lively for him.

146 Queen Elizabeth The Queen Mother Celebration Chase (2m)
Sandown April 26 (Good to Firm)

1 **Seebald** 8-11-6   A P McCoy

2 **Cenkos** 9-11-10   R Walsh
3 **Wahiba Sands** 10-11-6   N Williamson
11-8, 5-4f, 33-1. 1¹/4l, 9l. 5 ran. 3m 49.7 (a3.30)
The Macca & Growler Partnership (M Pipe, Wellington)

Another two-horse race at this meeting produced a deserved first success of the season for **Seebald**, who'd been second in six of his previous seven races, a run that began in the previous season's Arkle Chase – the other race was this term's Champion Chase, when he was still upsides when falling two out. Here, he tracked his only serious rival and found enough acceleration to go past on the run-in. **Cenkos** looks on the downgrade now but the spring brings out the best in him, so this form merits respect.

147 attheraces Gold Cup Chase (Showcase Handicap) (Grade 3) (3m5f110yds)
Sandown April 26 (Good to Firm)

1 **Ad Hoc** 9-10-10   R Walsh
2 **Stormez** 6-10-12   A P McCoy
3 **Gunther Mcbride** 8-10-1   R Johnson
4 **Frosty Canyon** 10-10-2   T Doyle
7-1, 9-2f, 7-1, 9-1. 9l, 1¹/4l, ¹/2l. 16 ran. 7m 21.0 (a10.25)
Sir Robert Ogden (P Nicholls, Shepton Mallet)

Ad Hoc became the first to win this race twice since Topsham Bay 10 years before, off a mark 11lb higher than the one from which he took the 2001 renewal. He hadn't won in seven starts over fences since, though that run included two third places at the Cheltenham Festival, a fourth in this race in 2002 and two non-completions in the Grand National. Whereas he'd been brought down at Aintree in 2002, he only unseated this time, but came back badly cut and reportedly only came right again in the week before this. He didn't put a foot wrong in the race, following the leaders until asked to go on three from home, from which point he quickly went clear to win unchallenged. For **Stormez**, this was his twelfth outing since he'd started chasing the previous May, and it showed – he was never going and even got a reminder after the first. Last down the back straight on the final circuit, he ran on dourly to take second on the run-in, showing remarkable courage and toughness. Many of those who finished down the field look well held on their present handicap marks, notably **Gunther McBride**, **Bounce Back** (10lb higher than when he won in 2002) and **Foxchapel King**. Conditions ought to have been ideal for **Frosty Canyon**, so this was a disappointing effort from him. The fancied **Killusty** broke down on the first circuit.

Index

All horses placed or commented on in our 'Big-Race Results' section, with race numbers

Outlook
Ken Hussey 1928-2003

RACING journalism lost a true giant this autumn when Ken Hussey, a pioneer in the use of speed figures, passed away at the age of 75.

Taken on as a tipster by The Handicap Book in the early 1950s, Ken wrote for a number of publications over the years, including *The Sporting Chronicle*, *The Daily Star*, *The Sunday Mirror* and, of course, *Racing & Football Outlook*. In an obituary for RFO, his former colleague Tony Peach wrote: "It is debatable whether any racing correspondent tipped as many National winners or as many big-priced winners."

Ken also advised on the purchase of Tom Sharp, who went on to win the Cesarewitch at 40-1, having opened at 66s.

No-one could have been more dedicated to his work, nor more consistently successful than Ken, who is sadly missed by all at RFO. He is survived by his wife, Lilian, son Paul and daughter Gail.

As a final tribute, we reproduce Ken's top tens on speed figures from the last season.

	Chasers	Speed rating	Distance in furlongs	Going	Track	Date achieved
1	Best Mate	89	26	G	Cheltenham	Mar 13
2	Moscow Flyer	87	16	G	Cheltenham	Mar 12
3	Edredon Bleu	84	17	G	Exeter	Nov 5
4	Behrajan	82	24	Hy	Ascot	Dec 21
5	Marlborough	78	24	VS	Kempton	Dec 26
	Truckers Tavern	78	26	G	Cheltenham	Mar 13
7	Lady Cricket	77	16	Y	Cheltenham	Nov 15
	Native Upmanship	77	20	S	Aintree	Apr 4
9	Kadarann	76	17	G	Newbury	Feb 8
10	Azertyuiop	75	16	GY	Cheltenham	Mar 11

	Hurdlers	Speed rating	Distance in furlongs	Going	Track	Date achieved
1	Rooster Booster	89	16	G	Cheltenham	Mar 11
2	Baracouda	87	24	G	Cheltenham	Mar 13
3	Iris's Gift	85	24	G	Cheltenham	Mar 13
4	Intersky Falcon	80	16	VS	Kempton	Dec 26
5	Santenay	78	16	F	Sandown	Apr 25
6	Deano's Beeno	76	25	VS	Ascot	Dec 20
7	Limestone Lad	76	24	G	Cheltenham	Mar 13
8	Westender	76	16	G	Cheltenham	Mar 11
9	Landing Light	75	16	Y	Cheltenham	Dec 14
10	Spirit Leader	74	17	G	Cheltenham	Mar 13

Going key: H = hard, VF = very firm, F = firm, GF = good to firm, G = good, Y = yielding, S = soft

2003-2004 Preview

Ante-Post

by
Steffan Edwards

Take the profit and run

AS WE pointed out in this year's Flat Annual, betting exchanges have added a new dimension to ante-post punting. Having backed a horse at long odds some weeks or months before the big day, it is now possible to lay off the bet nearer the time if your fancy shortens in price, thereby ensuring a profit whether it eventually wins or loses – even if it doesn't turn up.

Of course, if you lay off and the horse wins, your profit will be a lot less than if you'd brazenly stuck to your guns. But the ability to 'close out' a bet in this way should reduce the importance of luck in long-term betting, and ensure that good judgement gets rewarded more consistently.

If you've plumped for a long shot many months in advance, and then its price drops through the floor as other johnny-come-latelys jump on your bandwagon, you've proved your skill at anticipating the market and deserve some return on your shrewdness. Nothing is more frustrating, after this happens, than still losing your money because the horse wasn't quite good enough on the day.

We've flagged up the chances of some impressive 'shorteners' in this feature. Recent annuals have included tips for Asian Heights (50-1 into 6-1 for the 2001 Derby), King Of Happiness (33-1 into 11-2 for the 2,000 Guineas of 2002), Hussard Collonges (66-1 into 8-1 for the 2003 Cheltenham Gold Cup), Intercontinental (25-1 into 5-1 for this year's 1,000 Guineas) and Alamshar (33-1 into 4-1 for this year's Derby).

Even without laying off, we made a ten-point profit from our tips in the last jumps annual. But, if you manage to get a fancy price about a runner who turns into a leading contender, you'd be well advised to take advantage of the exchanges – lay off part of the bet and make sure that, at the very least, you're not going to lose money if the worst comes to the worst.

Champion Hurdle

As has often been noted, the gap between the best handicap hurdlers and the Graded-class performers is not great.

The result is that it's far from unusual to see good handicappers progress to become Champion Hurdle contenders in a short space of time. In the past decade, Flakey Dove, Make A Stand and **Rooster Booster** have all gone from running big races in the Tote Gold Trophy to Champion Hurdle glory. The latter, of course, also won the County Hurdle at the Festival in the year preceding

his Champion Hurdle victory.

Last season, **SPIRIT LEADER** won both the Tote Gold Trophy and the County Hurdle. A tough mare, she did nothing but improve throughout the season; having begun the campaign rated 116, she ran off 140 when scoring at the Festival.

When Rooster Booster won the 2002 County Hurdle, he ran off a 4lb higher mark than that, but carried 6lb less in weight. There's no doubt that Spirit Leader will have to improve again this season if she is to

HARD AS NAILS: Spirit Leader fights off the opposition to win Cheltenham's County Hurdle

become a realistic challenger in March, but there are no signs of an end to her progress. A proven course winner (12 of the last 15 champion hurdlers had already won at Cheltenham), she will be ideally suited by the strong gallop which invariably characterises the race, and is a sporting bet to improve

her trainer's already outstanding record – four winners from nine runners at the past four Festivals – at Prestbury Park.

Second favourite in most lists is the Supreme Novices' winner **Back In Front**. He was impressive in landing that prize, but the race has not been a regular source of

	Bet365	Cashm'	Coral	Hills	Ladbs	PPower	SJames	Tote	VChandler
Smurfit Champion Hurdle Cheltenham, 16th March 2004									
Rooster Booster	5	9-2	5	5	5	4	5	5	9-2
Back In Front	6	6	**8**	7	6	7	7	13-2	7
Rhinestone Cowboy	8	7	**10**	8	**10**	**10**	7	9	**10**
Sporazene	14	12	14	**16**	14	**16**	12	**16**	12
Davenport Millenium	14	16	12	**20**	16	16	**20**	**20**	**20**
Sacundai	-	-	-	-	12	**20**	16	12	-
Specular	-	-	16	-	-	**20**	-	-	-
Westender	14	**33**	**33**	20	25	25	20	25	25
Intersky Falcon	20	**33**	16	20	20	16	16	20	20
Spectroscope	20	20	-	25	20	25	25	**33**	25
Well Chief	20	20	-	25	25	**33**	**33**	25	25
Spirit Leader	**33**	20	25	**33**	25	25	25	25	25
Like-A-Butterfly	25	-	25	25	-	25	25	**33**	25
In Contrast	-	25	**33**	**33**	-	-	-	**33**	-
Liberman	**33**	-	25	**33**	25	25	25	25	25
Our Vic	**33**	-	25	-	-	**33**	25	25	25
Landing Light	33	20	33	25	33	33	33	**40**	33
Lingo	20	-	20	25	-	25	20	33	**40**
Kicking King	**50**	-	20	**50**	-	20	-	-	25
Hasty Prince	25	-	33	33	25	40	-	**50**	-

each-way 1/4 odds, 1-2-3
Others on application, prices correct at time of going to press

future champions. It's run over the same course and distance as the Champion Hurdle, within two hours of the big race itself, and it's illuminating to compare the winning times, year by year, of both events over the past decade.

Only two winners of the Supreme Novices' have been able to better the time clocked by the Champion Hurdle winner later the same day – Montelado and Hors La Loi III.

Montelado's career was hampered by an injury which kept him off the track for the next two years, but Hors La Loi III went on to finish second to Istabraq the following year before going one better in the hurdling championship in 2002.

Back In Front recorded a time over two seconds slower than Rooster Booster's Champion, suggesting he may not be the exceptional novice some people think.

In what looked a fairly decent renewal, Rooster Booster won in fine style, showing an impressive turn of foot in the process. His ability to quicken off a fast pace is a valuable asset and, were it not for his age (he will be ten next year), he would probably be worth a saver. No horse older than nine has won the race in the past 20 years, so 5-1 is short enough.

Intersky Falcon is at his best on a flat track, while **Ned Kelly** needs soft ground and, in any case, rarely seems to be off the injury list. Another who spent most of last year on the sidelines is **Davenport Millenium**; as a rule, it's best to leave crocks alone until they've proven they're back to their best.

Although the Champion has been won by "Flat" horses in their first season over hurdles, I wouldn't be rushing to back horses like **Lingo** before they've even been seen over timber. The same goes for Champion Bumper winner **Liberman**.

Westender ran the race of his life to finish runner-up last season, and his record at Cheltenham (111232) suggests he reserves his best for his visits to the Cotswolds. He's fairly priced at 33-1, but is probably only an each-way play at best.

RHINESTONE COWBOY should improve past him. The subject of plenty of hype last season, he was sent off as 5-2 favourite for the Champion, which was hardly justified by his form, but he was far from disgraced in finishing third.

Early mistakes in a race run at an unfamiliarly fast pace put him on the back foot, but he didn't throw in the towel and stayed on well up the hill. He'll be more the finished article this time around and, given the price he started as a novice, the 10-1 available now looks good value.

The fact that no five-year-old has won the race since 1985, despite 65 having tried, suggests it's best to give last year's best juvenile hurdlers (**Spectroscope**, **Well Chief** and **Sporazene**) the swerve. In fact, Sporazene looks particularly short in the betting, considering that all he's done is win a weak four-runner affair at Ayr and a Punchestown race in which he was taking on rivals who had been on the go all season.

Sacundai is a talented horse, as he showed when just edging out Rooster Booster at Aintree, but that 2m4f trip probably suits him better than the minimum distance, and connections may be forced to move up to 3m if they are to taste Cheltenham glory with him.

Champion Chase

Last year, I was very sweet on the chances of *MOSCOW FLYER***, and he duly did the business on the big day.**

The manner of his victory last season was as impressive as his Arkle success the previous year, and he sets a high standard for the young guns to match. Unbeaten when completing over fences, his Achilles heel is that he does make the odd error. He unseated his rider twice last season (albeit through no fault of his own in the Tingle Creek), and hit the fourth-last at Cheltenham pretty hard. He does seem to reserve his best for the big occasion, though, and, with a similar campaign planned this season, he remains the one to beat.

Cenkos tends to have one big run in him per year, and for the past two seasons that performance has come at Sandown, although last year's runaway victory in the Tingle Creek was devalued by the early exit of both main rivals.

Third in the past two Champion Chases, it's difficult to see him finding the improvement required to win at the third attempt, especially if the ground is fast.

If the Champion Chase was run over 2m4f, **Native Upmanship** would have won a couple, but it isn't and, unless the ground is testing, he will once again struggle to go the pace.

Seebald is an admirable type – he's only once failed to finish in the first two in 15 starts over fences, and that was when falling at the second-last in last season's Champion Chase when still in with a major chance of a place. On all known form, he will struggle to beat Moscow Flyer, but he holds each-way prospects.

His stablemate **Tiutchev**, on the other hand, has had his problems and is probably best left alone, as his glory days are almost certainly behind him now.

Kadarann, who needs top of the ground, is at his best in a small field on a flat track and, last time I checked, Cheltenham wasn't that flat.

Latalomne hasn't won any race for two years but he's been in the process of running cracking races in the last two renewals of the Champion Chase when crashing out at the second-last both times.

He may run well again, but he's not the sort of horse who's going to shorten much in the betting prior to the big race if previous seasons are anything to go by, so he's not an ante-post play.

Little went right last season for the former champion **Flagship Uberalles**. First, he lost his chance when slipping badly in the Tingle Creek, then he was tried unsuccessfully over 3m in the King George.

Blinkered in the Champion Chase, he ran only a fair race to finish fifth, but he bounced back to form with the headgear left off at Punchestown. At his best, he is no 25-1 shot, but he has a history of back problems and cannot, therefore, be advised ante-post.

It's a tricky business trying to figure out whether last season's novices are going to cut the mustard when taking on the proven two-milers the following season, but a good place to start is by assessing the strength of the previous season's championship event for novices, the Arkle.

It's fascinating to note that, of the last 20 winners of the Arkle, 12 got to within a second of the time set by the Champion Chase winner over the same course and distance 24 hours later (a handful of those bettered the Champion's time).

The ground was softer for the 1989 and 2002 runnings of the Champion Chase than for the Arkles in those years but, in each of the other years, ground conditions appear to have been similar.

Working backwards, the "fast" Arkle winners include Moscow Flyer, Flagship

MOSCOW FLYER

Queen Mother Champion Chase								Cheltenham, 17th March 2004	
	Bet365	Cashm'	Coral	Hills	Ladbs	PPower	Skybet	StanleyVChandler	
Moscow Flyer	3	5-2	3	3	3	100-30	5-2	3	3
Azertyuiop	4	7-2	3	4	4	7-2	7-2	4	4
Le Roi Miguel	10	10	10	8	16	10	12	10	7
Flagship Uberalles	16	14	12	10	16	14	12	14	16
Tiutchev	16	-	-	12	16	-	10	14	-
Seebald	14	16	16	12	20	16	14	16	16
Native Upmanship	20	20	14	-	14	16	12	16	12
Cenkos	14	20	12	14	16	14	14	14	14
Impek	16	20	14	20	16	16	20	16	14
Kadarann	20	-	20	14	20	25	25	20	20
Adamant Approach	20	20	20	20	20	20	25	20	20
Isio	25	22	-	20	25	25		25	25
Farmer Jack	25	-	20	20	33	25	33	25	25
Latalomne	25	33	25	-	25	25	25	25	25
Geos	25	-	25	-	25	-	33	33	33

each-way 1/4 odds, 1-2-3
Others on application, prices correct at time of going to press

'All in all, I take the view that reigning champ Moscow Flyer remains head and shoulders above the current bunch of two-milers, and that the novices aren't the decent group everyone thinks'

Uberalles, Klairon Davis, Travado, Remittance Man and Waterloo Boy. The "slow" Arkle winners on the other hand include such world-beaters as Tiutchev, Champleve, Or Royal, Nakir and Young Pokey.

To this latter, unspectacular bunch we can now add the name of **Azertyuiop**, who clocked a time fully three seconds slower than that managed by Moscow Flyer a day later. Notwithstanding the impressive manner of his victory and his undoubted scope for improvement, he won the fifth-slowest Arkle in the past 20 years, relative to the times of the Champion Chases run at the same meetings.

History therefore suggests Paul Nicholls' stable star has a lot to prove and, at a best-priced 4-1, he makes little appeal.

Impek made the frame at all three of the spring festivals, showing himself to be one of the best novices around. He doesn't like being crowded in a big field, though, and all his wins have come on right-handed tracks, so the Tingle Creek might give him his best opportunity of a day in the sun, rather than Cheltenham.

Isio may well be a flat-track bully, although it's a little early to be certain about that. He ran well in the Arkle for one so inexperienced and, as a proven fast-ground performer open to improvement, 25-1 isn't a bad price.

The Irish were keen enough on **Adamant Approach**'s chance in the Arkle to send him off at 7-1, despite the fact that he had only had two previous starts over fences. His inexperience cost him dear and he was an early casualty, and he has since tipped over again at Fairyhouse. His fencing will need to improve a good deal if he is to make his mark over 2m this season, and there are signs that he will be better over further, like **Farmer Jack** for that matter.

Bust Out is a talented horse, but he has yet to race on ground faster than good to soft. He is also fragile. Forced to miss the Arkle after injuring the same leg which kept him out for most of the 2001-02 season, his

trainer expects him to be on the sidelines for another six to 12 months from the beginning of this season, and so he may not even make the gig.

The best play for trading purposes looks to be **Le Roi Miguel**. As short as 7s with Victor Chandler, he's a stand-out 16s with Ladbrokes. I personally don't believe he'll win in March, but he makes some modest appeal as an early trade to lay off after a couple of easy wins before Christmas.

He's always been talked up by Nicholls as being just as good as Azertyuiop at home, and his performances in the spring at Aintree and Punchestown did mark him down as an improving type.

However, those contests were not nearly as strongly-contested as the Arkle and, throughout the season, both as a four-year-old and later as a five-year-old, he benefited from generous allowances, something he won't enjoy this time round.

Only three six-year-olds have contested the past 10 Champion Chases, and two of them were sent off favourite. Each was beaten, though, and sloppy jumping was the reason on each occasion.

The case for **Palarshan** is flimsy at best. He scrambled home in the Grand Annual off a mark of 134; when Edredon Bleu won the same race in 1998, he ran off 139, carried 11st7lb, and won by three lengths, and he was beaten in the following year's Champion Chase, so Palarshan has to improve out of all recognition to take a hand.

Fifteen of the last 19 Champion Chase winners had won or been placed at the Festival before, so it's difficult to see from where other challengers will emerge.

All in all, I take the view that reigning champ Moscow Flyer remains head and shoulders above the current bunch of two-milers, and that the novices aren't the decent group everyone thinks they are.

The 100-30 isn't as tasty as last year's 5-1, but it's a fair price in a race which outsiders rarely win.

Sponsored by Stan James

Cheltenham Gold Cup

The problem with this Gold Cup as a betting medium is that it's dominated by one horse whose form is impossible to knock and, as with Istabraq in his heyday, one feels silly tipping anything to beat him.

Best Mate's repeat victory last season was impressive in every way and, on the face of it, it's difficult to see how any of those who finished behind him could reverse the form this time round. Yet to finish out of the first two in a career which has seen him take in a modest 16 races to date, he should get to Cheltenham in peak condition after another light campaign, and attempt to secure a place in history as the first horse since Arkle to complete a hat-trick in the race.

He deserves to be a short price, but the historical magnitude of the task before him makes 2-1 look decidedly skinny.

Truckers Tavern and **Harbour Pilot** ran fine races to finish in the frame last season, but it's 20 years since a placed horse went on to win the following year, and neither strikes me as good enough to take gold this time around. Truckers Tavern is a mud-lover who will need the heavens to open to go one better, while Harbour Pilot's jumping leaves plenty to be desired; he, too, has done all his winning on soft ground.

We were on **Hussard Collonges** at a massive 66-1 last season, so it was disappointing to see him run no sort of race on the day. Later, it transpired that he'd been suffering from a sore throat, so at least his lacklustre effort can be excused.

The performances of Harbour Pilot and Truckers Tavern, whom he had run close while giving them over a stone in, respectively, the Hennessy and the Peter Marsh Chase, suggest that a peak-form Hussard Collonges ought to have been a major contender for the places.

A superb stayer, his subsequent tumble at Punchestown was unfortunate, as he is normally a safe and accurate jumper, and at 25-1 I'm tempted to put him up again. However, there is a strong suspicion that he's at his best with cut in the ground, and in recent years the ground at the Festival has tended to ride on the fast side. So, reluctantly, he gets the swerve.

Valley Henry, who's done all his winning in small fields, failed to stay last year, and is one to avoid, along with **Commanche Court**, who's best days are behind him, and **Kingscliff**, who impressed many with his win in the Foxhunters last year but has a mountain to climb to get involved at this level in his first season in open company.

Top-class staying hurdlers **Baracouda** and **Iris's Gift** are in many of the bookmakers' lists for the Gold Cup, but anyone who had their fingers burnt by **Beef Or Salmon** last year will tell you that this is not

Tote Cheltenham Gold Cup

Cheltenham, 18th March 2004

	Bet365	Cashm'	Coral	Hills	Ladbs	PPower	SJames	Tote	VChandler
Best Mate	5-4	6-4	7-4	6-4	6-4	7-4	7-4	2	7-4
Beef Or Salmon	10	8	12	8	10	10	12	12	12
First Gold	10	16	12	12	12	12	11	10	12
Baracouda	-	20	16	16	-	20	20	14	16
Truckers Tavern	16	25	25	16	25	25	25	16	25
Hussard Collonges	25	25	25	16	25	25	20	25	25
Jair Du Cochet	16	25	20	20	25	25	25	25	25
Keen Leader	20	25	25	14	-	20	25	33	20
One Knight	16	25	20	20	33	25	25	20	25
La Landiere	16	25	20	-	20	25	20	33	25
It Takes Time	25	33	33	20	-	33	33	-	33
Valley Henry	25	25	33	-	25	33	25	25	25
Chives	33	-	25	33	-		25	33	33
Irish Hussar	33	25	-		25		-	-	-
Kingscliff	33	33	33	33	33	25	33	33	-

each-way 1/4 odds, 1-2-3 (except Hills, 1/4 odds 1-2-3-4)
Others on application, prices correct at time of going to press

Steeple Chase

THE BIG ONE: a spring-heeled One Knight, seen beating Jair Du Cochet at the Festival

a race in which to support a novice. Sixteen such horses have tried in the past 29 years, of whom many were quite well fancied, yet none have succeeded.

Michael Hourigan sent out Dorans Pride to finish third in the Gold Cup in his novice season, and made no secret of the fact that he rated Beef Or Salmon a better horse than his late stable stalwart. Following a string of victories in slowly-run, soft-ground chases in Ireland, he arrived at Cheltenham with plenty of confidence behind him, but the faster pace, quicker ground and stiffer fences found him out and he was a faller at the third.

That failure should not be held against him this time round, as he will be a far more experienced jumper by March, but what should count against him is the likelihood once again of fast ground. Hourigan has always maintained that Beef Or Salmon will be seen to better effect on fast ground, but

he hasn't exactly gone out of his way to run his stable star on that sort of surface – quite the opposite in fact. He was due to run the gelding in the Heineken Gold Cup at Punchestown, but pulled him out, having been informed by riders that the ground was on the fast side of good.

Until Beef Or Salmon proves that he can go on fast ground, I'll be looking elsewhere.

First Gold returned from injury looking a shadow of his former self and was pulled up in the Gold Cup, but a pair of blinkers and the adoption of positive tactics saw him return to something like his best at Aintree and Punchestown. A slick jumper at his best, he doesn't give his fences much air, and flat tracks have always suited him best. If he carries his form over from last spring, he will be a worthy contender in March, but the King George VI Chase on Boxing Day is more likely to be his big day.

Irish Hussar is a lightly-raced, improving sort who looks sure to win decent races this season. Any Gold Cup aspirations his connections may have are hindered by the fact that he suffers from sore shins, though, and consequently he needs soft ground.

Only four mares have ever won the Gold Cup (the last to achieve the feat was Dawn Run in 1986), so history suggests **La Landiere** faces a difficult task. A tough, progressive novice last term, she's only been beaten once over fences, and may well have further improvement in her this season, but the big question is whether she'll stay the Gold Cup trip.

She got 3m round Kempton's sharp track well enough to win the Racing Post Chase, but a stiff 3m2f is another matter altogether. If she stays, she will be difficult to keep out of the frame but, on balance, given that she looks so good over 2m4f, she's probably worth opposing.

As with last year, I feel that the Royal & SunAlliance Chase form has been underrated. Plenty was made of the fact that **Keen Leader** and **It Takes Time** ran below par, which supposedly devalued the result.

However, the former is a soft-ground horse whose record at Cheltenham prior to the race read 'FF', so he probably didn't deserve to be sent off at such a short price, while It Takes Time had his chance to make amends at Aintree but was surprisingly outstayed on that sharp track.

Both the Royal & SunAlliance winner *ONE KNIGHT*, and the runner-up **Jair Du Cochet** appeal as the likeliest candidates to emerge as challengers for Best Mate's crown.

One Knight was a Grade 2 winner over hurdles but has moved up another notch since switching to the larger obstacles. He gave Le Roi Miguel (now third-favourite for the Champion Chase) almost a stone and a beating on his fencing debut, and jumped notably well at Exeter on his final two starts prior to Cheltenham.

It was therefore surprising when his jumping proved less than fluent on the big day itself. Despite making numerous mistakes, though, he ran out a worthy winner, which suggests to me that, with another year on his back and further experience, he should be a serious tool come March.

He's probably best suited by some give, but he won well enough on good ground

at the Festival and, as he stays well and likes to run from the front, he should enjoy a clear view of his fences and thereby avoid any trouble in running.

Jacques Ricou received plenty of criticism for his ride of Jair Du Cochet at Cheltenham, much of which was justified. He gave his mount too much to do after holding him up at the rear of the field for most of the race and, when One Knight didn't come back to him up the hill, as he had expected, he was left with oeuf on his face.

The French gelding is talented enough to develop into a genuine Gold Cup contender but, with his trainer adamant that the dodgy Ricou keeps the ride, he is probably not worth chancing.

Save your Grand National money until the weights are published in early February, but keep an eye on the following candidates.

Scottish Grand National winner **Ryalux** jumps and stays well, is marvellously consistent, and is to be targeted at the race. **Bounce Back** and **Iznogoud** struggled last season after successful novice campaigns, but both have the necessary class to take a hand if campaigned with the race in mind.

Timbera appeals as the pick of the Irish for now. Winner of last season's Irish National, he's also finished second at the Cheltenham Festival in the past.

Frosty Canyon is consistent, **Haut Cercy** looks a progressive type and **Mini Sensation** would be a threat to all if it's soft.

Sponsored by Stan James

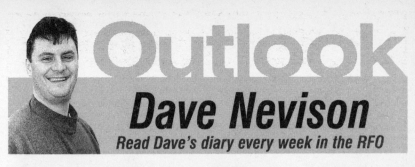

Imports looking useful

MOST RFO readers will know that I am essentially an All-Weather specialist nowadays, but if I have many more seasons like last winter's jumping, I may well be tempted to switch back.

I attended only about half a dozen jumps meetings all winter and made more money on those days than I did in the entire All-Weather season.

This year's Cheltenham Festival was amazing and must surely have been a one-off, as favourite after favourite obliged, with bookies on their knees by the end.

I have never seen as many punters walking around with so much money in their pockets on the last day of a big meeting and I feel the meeting worked out even better for those of us who were not too bogged down in the form.

More of the same would be very nice. I believe it is quite possible in the championship races and I have already backed the big three, **Rooster Booster**, **Moscow Flyer** and **Best Mate**, in a big ante-post treble out of last year's profits.

Even though he's rising ten, Rooster Booster looked a serious champion to me and it would only be a Group horse from the Flat who stands in his way this time. Moscow Flyer is inclined to miss one out but is otherwise just about unbeatable, while Best Mate is head and shoulders above the rest in the staying chase division.

If they all get to the Festival in one piece, the treble will be a lot less than the 66-1 it was paying this summer.

Last year, I called upon the leading bloodstock expert and leader of the 'Million In Mind' syndicates Anthony Bromley to give us a few dark horses for the winter, and he did exceptionally well. I am once again indebted to him for telling me a little bit about this year's midsummer purchases.

Bromley has made his name alongside David Minton as the top purchaser of bloodstock from abroad, and France in particular. This year, he has once again been in every dark corner and, judging by his enthusiasm, he has uncovered a few gems once more.

Mon Villez is now with Nicky Henderson after reaching the top of the four-year-old chasing division in France last season. He won the Champion three-year-old chase and was third in the spring champion four-year-old at the end of May.

ROOSTER
BOOSTER

'I am looking forward to my own horse Mercato. I'll be fed up if he doesn't win a novice or two'

Because he has not won a hurdle, it is expected that he will be campaigned in the best novice events up to 2m.

Garde Champetre won three from four on the Flat for Guillaume Macaire and was beaten a neck in the other race. He is jumps-bred and will also go for novice hurdles at first, though (given Paul Nicholls' preference for fences) he could well end up novice chasing before long.

Chockdee is another with Paul Nicholls and is a useful Flat horse from the south-west provinces. He is a maiden but has form with Group horses and is already reported to be schooling well over hurdles.

Lord Lington has won his last three on the Flat, including two in useful company in Paris. He is reckoned to be a seriously exciting jumping prospect.

Ian Williams is the new trainer of **Saint Reverian**, who is a progressive four-year-old with several good placed efforts over hurdles and fences to his name. Williams is in a good position with this one, a maiden under all codes, and will almost certainly exploit his potential to the full.

Kadoun is a winner of three Paris chases as a four-year-old and has now joined Henry Daly. Interestingly, he hasn't won a hurdle and he, too, is expected to be aimed at 2m novices in the first half of the season.

Bromley believes he is a useful front-running grey, who

LILIUM DE COTTE

could well be suited by the brush hurdles at Haydock, Worcester and Southwell.

J P McManus does not have many with Nicky Henderson but the Irishman has purchased last year's Triumph Hurdle fourth **Lilium De Cotte** and sent it to the Lambourn trainer. This one is apparently going 2m novice chasing, on the advice of previous trainer Guillaume Macaire.

Henderson, whose French import Saint-saire became one of the talking horses of last season, also takes charge of **Sleep Bal**, who won his only career start in impressive style. He was thrown in at the deep end in a valuable affair in Paris and came out with flying colours. He will initially go for intermediate hurdles and then over fences.

Freddy Crystal and **Le Royal** are two that Bromley did not manage to buy but would dearly have liked to. The latter is with Mary Reveley and won a French bumper from three starts last winter. He is closely related to the very useful Camitrov.

Freddy Crystal is a maiden but a very useful one and was a good third at Auteuil on his final start. He has joined Philip Hobbs and is owned by Terry Warner of Rooster Booster fame.

This select group should give us plenty to watch for over the winter but I must say I am most looking forward to my own horse **Mercato** giving me a lot of fun over fences. He would have lost his novice status but for tipping up at Huntingdon.

After that, he was switched back to hurdles, where he landed me a big touch in a showcase at Plumpton. He was fifth in the Imperial Cup and will hopefully give me my first runner at the Festival next March.

If he doesn't win a novice or two, I will be seriously fed up.

Outlook

Morning Mole
by Steve Mellish

Jonjo's the man again

AFTER THE loss of the Cheltenham Festival to foot and mouth in 2001, and with dire predictions being made about the effect a hunting ban would have on the sport, there was a time when a cloud hung over jump racing.

But the 2003 Festival was a roaring success, an extension of the meeting to four days is on the cards, and jumping folk seem on much better terms with themselves. As a punter who loves both branches of our sport, this is great news.

One concern I have, though, is where the next batch of stars, particularly hurdlers, will come from. With All-Weather racing getting bigger all the time, fewer and fewer horses are coming from the level to jump racing.

Champions like Alderbrook, Sea Pigeon, Collier Bay and Istabraq all went jumping after a Flat career. With the possibilities of continuing on the All-Weather, or even going abroad to race in countries like Dubai, fewer owners are taking the jumping option, with its inherent injury risks.

Obviously, bumpers will produce some champions, but these are mainly embryo chasers. I can only see this problem getting worse.

Never mind. Whatever the long-term future may bring, there's a good-looking season on the immediate horizon and I've been ruminating about how best to turn a profit from it. At this stage, my thoughts have crystallised around two trainers and six horses who should help us pay the fuel bills.

With three winners at last season's Festival and another four at Liverpool, **Jonjo O'Neill** confirmed his arrival in the top echelons of the training tree (as predicted in this space last year). As long as he has such wonderful facilities and the backing of JP McManus, he can only continue on the up.

Ironically, the man who was based at Jackdaws Castle before Jonjo's arrival, **Richard Phillips**, also had a good year. Many thought he'd struggle after having to move on, but he's proved those doubters wrong.

Dark'n Sharp was the flag-bearer two seasons ago, while last season it was La Landiere, a fabulous mare who won seven on the trot, including a first Festival success for Phillips in the Cathcart.

The way she maintained her form in the face of some tough assignments was a credit to her trainer and, if he doesn't get more horses on the back of this, then there's something wrong with the game.

RICHARD PHILLIPS

Le Roi Miguel
5 b g, Paul Nicholls

The 2004 Queen Mother Champion Chase looks like being one of the season's highlights. Reigning champ Moscow Flyer v Paul Nicholls is the way I see it.

Azertyuiop is rated by most observers as Nicholls's main contender, but it may prove costly to ignore that one's stable companion Le Roi Miguel. If there was a better-looking horse running last winter, I didn't see it.

A tall, rangy gelding who seems sure to improve with age, he's had five runs over fences and has looked more impressive each time. He ran in the Arkle, but only got as far as the third, where he over-jumped and paid the price. Don't worry about his fencing, though – this was mere exuberance.

Next time, in the Grade 1 Martell Novices Chase at Aintree, he fenced brilliantly and treated his rivals with contempt. He put up a repeat performance at Punchestown.

Impek, who finished behind him in both these races, had been second to Azertyuiop in the Arkle and, using him as a guide, there would appear to be little to choose between Nicholls' two stars.

Le Roi Miguel is getting better all the time and could have the edge by the spring.

Royal Rosa
4 ch g, Howard Johnson

In four bumper races, Royal Rosa did nothing but improve, culminating in a facile win in the Grade 1 Paddy Power Champion at Punchestown, where

LE ROI MIGUEL

he beat the cream of the Irish crop. This season, his attentions are turned to hurdling and it's not hard to imagine him starting among the favourites for one of the novice events at Cheltenham.

What his best trip will prove to be is hard to say, as he's bred to stay but hasn't looked short of pace so far, and he seems a novice to follow.

Howard Johnson certainly thinks a lot of him, having broken the record payment for a jumps horse at auction when going to 340,000gns to buy him out of Nicky Henderson's yard in May.

Trabolgan
5 b g, Nicky Henderson

When Mole was growing up, Lambourn was the volcanic core of jump racing. There's no doubt, however, that the balance of power has now shifted to the West Country, with the big battalions of Pipe, Hobbs and Nicholls based out there.

One Lambourn man bucks the trend, though. Nicky Henderson constantly produces good horses and has a Cheltenham Festival record most trainers would die for.

The tragic death of Bacchanal last season, taken together with Marlborough reaching the veteran stage, leaves Henderson looking for stars, but Trabolgan appeals as a horse with a future.

This gelding has finished runner-up in all three starts in bumpers, but his form has hardly stood still. Promising though his first two runs were, at Uttoxeter and Kempton, he still started a 50-1 chance for the Champion Bumper at the Festival and was considered very much his stable's second-string behind Back To Ben Alder, who started third-favourite.

He belied those odds with a sterling effort, running the hot favourite Liberman to half a length.

He's by King's Ride, an excellent National Hunt stallion, and has the size and breeding to make a chaser in time. That's for the future, though, as a hurdling career beckons first and he should take high rank amongst the novices this winter.

It would be no surprise if his

KEEN LEADER: *relaxing at Jackdaws Castle, this young chaser remains a fine prospect*

trainer gives him a couple more runs in bumpers first, to gain further experience. As a maiden with no penalty to carry, he'll be very hard to beat in that sphere.

Keen Leader
7 b g, Jonjo O'Neill

I put this horse in last year's list and, as he won three of his five starts in novice chases, he can hardly be deemed a failure.

Nonetheless, his season must be considered a shade disappointing, as he flopped the day it really mattered, when hot favourite for the Royal & SunAlliance Chase. It's hard to know why, but he could manage only a moderate fifth.

The ground probably wasn't as soft as he likes it and he made a few mistakes. One thing I know is that he's better than this and he's definitely got a big prize in him. He's rated by his trainer (who's had some good horses in his time) to be one of his finest ever prospects.

An early season target could be the Hennessy, as it's a race in which second-season chasers do well. His Cheltenham effort won't do his handicap mark any harm.

He has the pace for shorter trips if his trainer so chooses. A wet winter would be a plus.

Thisthatandtother
7 b g, Paul Nicholls

In two seasons, one in bumpers and one over hurdles, this gelding has shown himself to be useful but just below the best. It may be different now that his attentions are turned to fences.

He's always been thought of by his trainer as a top chaser in the making. A quick jumper of hurdles with a fine cruising speed, you can see this one running up a sequence in minor novice events before taking on the big guns.

The whole Nicholls set-up is geared towards chasing and, with the brilliant Ruby Walsh ever more closely associated with the yard, this could be the season Thisthatandtother realises his potential.

Royal Emperor
7 gr g, Sue Smith

What an admirable horse this is, and what an improved one too. Rated 102 at the start of last season, he began by winning a novice hurdle at Carlisle. On his seventh and final run, he finished second in the Grade 1 Martell Novices Hurdle at Aintree, his rating having soared to 148.

His season's record reads four wins and three seconds. Possibly his best performance was when beaten a short-head in the Pertemps Final at the Festival, carrying 11st9lb. There, he showed tremendous battling qualities, something which was a feature of his racing style throughout the year.

He's probably reached as far as he can go in hurdling and the plan now is to go chasing. By Roselier out of a Boreen mare, he could hardly be better bred for the job and, if he takes to the game, he can be expected to go to the very top.

Three miles plus with give in the ground is his ideal. If connections choose to cherry-pick, he should win plenty of novice races in the north before hopefully heading for the Festival to take on the stars.

Outlook's Horses to Follow

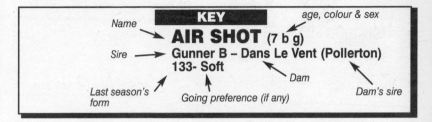

ALFA SUNRISE (6 b g)
Alflora – Gipsy Dawn (Lighter)
217- Good, good to soft

Below form on his third and last run, Alfa Sunrise had impressed the time before at Fontwell when zooming away with a bumper, beating a well-regarded horse of Oliver Sherwood's by 17l. The time of the race was 9.8secs faster than the other division. Bob Buckler reports the gelding to have strengthened up over the close season and he should be out soon. Novice hurdles are his for the taking on good and good to soft.

Bob Buckler, Bridport

BE FAIR (5 br g)
Blushing Flame – Tokyo (Mtoto)
11402-11

A terrific first season for the five-year-old, who, although losing out on the really big prizes, gobbled up three bumpers and two hurdle races. He ran atrociously in the Festival bumper but put his best foot forward at Aintree when runner-up to Classic Native. The third horse was 17l back, so that form looks solid and the first two are worth following. Be Fair is a big creature and will make a chaser. We suspect that he'll be kept hurdling in the first half of the season (he was unbeaten in two starts in May) before being tried over fences.

Don Cantillon, Carlton

BEFORE THE MAST (6 br g)
Broken Hearted – Kings Reserve (King's Ride)
3- Not firm

Was restricted to one run last season because of a host of problems but Noel Chance told *Racing & Football Outlook* that none of these problems was career-threatening and that Before The Mast will be ready to run soon. Last October, he went to Chepstow with a big reputation and was sent off 8-15 favourite in a field of 16 for a bumper. Fingers were burnt but we remain confident that the gelding will score over hurdles between 2m and 2m4f. He will avoid firm ground.

Noel Chance, Upper Lambourn

BOW STRADA (6 ch g)
Rainbow Quest – La Strada (Niniski)
2231714-

A useful stayer on the Flat and a fair hurdler, Bow Strada should come into his own when going chasing, if a run at Ascot in late March is to be believed. It was a only a Class D novice event but Bow Strada couldn't have been more impressive and had his rivals crispy-fried emerging from Swinley Bottom. After that it was just a question of how far as he cruised home up the straight. So it came as something of a surprise that he was beaten the length of Sauchiehall Street by Vol Solitaire in the Grade 2 Future Champion Novices Chase at Ayr next time. It was reported that he had a broken blood vessel, so the run is probably best overlooked.

Philip Hobbs, Minehead

CLASSIC NATIVE (5 b g)
Be My Native – Thats Irish (Furry Glen)
101-

Like many sons of Be My Native, this gelding is built for both hurdling and chasing. If things pan out, he's going to be a force for several seasons under both codes. Three runs so far, all in bumpers, have seen him shape with promise. He made a winning debut at Warwick, ran midfield in the Cheltenham Festival bumper and then won the Aintree equivalent. The field was well strung out at Liverpool and Classic Native got the better of Be Fair in a protracted duel. Jonjo O'Neill trained Iris's Gift to be second in this race the previous year. Classic Native could turn out at least as good.

Jonjo O'Neill, Cheltenham

FLAME CREEK (7 b g)
Shardari – Sheila's Pet (Welsh Term)
110P-11

Victory in the Champion Hurdle Trial at Haydock was as good as it got for Flame Creek. Thirteenth at Cheltenham (where he was a sick horse) and pulled up in the Scottish equivalent, he was sent fencing instead and picked up two small novice chases at Bangor and Wetherby. Noel Chance has mapped out the Independent Newspaper Novices Chase (won last year by Azertyuiop) at Cheltenham's Paddy Power meeting as his first target, the Arkle being the ultimate objective. He needs time between races, reckons Chance, so expect a sparing campaign.

Noel Chance, Upper Lambourn

FLIGHT COMMAND (5 ch g)
Gunner B – Wing On (Quayside)
1-

Peter Beaumont gets hardly any first-time-out winners, so this is a horse that has to be followed. Starting at 20-1 in a Perth bumper in April, Flight Command stayed on strongly to beat 16 others. He's big and workmanlike and, even if he spends this season over hurdles, he's one to keep in mind for the future – he'll make a chaser one day.

Peter Beaumont, Brandsby

GOT ONE TOO (6 ch g)
Green Tune – Gloria Mundi (Saint Cyrien)
12U10–

There should be plenty of opportunities for this gelding because he goes on ground ranging from heavy to good to firm. He wasn't asked to do too much last term, competing in four novice chases before being pitched into Cheltenham's 2m Grand Annual Chase, in which he finished mid-division. In the spring, he raced three times on the Flat, proving his pace by winning twice. Got One Too has the making of a cracking handicap chaser between 2m and 2m4f and the Tripleprint at Cheltenham in December could be a target.

Nicky Henderson, Lambourn

IRISH HUSSAR (7 b g)
Supreme Leader – Shuil Ard (Quayside)
1F121- Soft

So nearly took the Cathcart. Compensation came swiftly in the Mildmay Novices Chase at Aintree over 3m1f, where he came out on top in a thrilling finish with It Takes Time. The ground, officially good, was in fact very testing, so Irish Hussar, briefly headed by It Takes Time, deserves plenty of credit for fighting back to a 5l victory. He's a grand sort with a courageous attitude and is going to be up there with the best handicap chasers at 3m or more. Races like the Racing Post Chase spring to mind for him. Soft ground's a must.

Nicky Henderson, Lambourn

IRIS'S GIFT (6 gr g)
Gunner B – Shirley's Gift (Scallywag)
1111121-

It's with some embarrassment that Iris's Gift is included in this year's list – he really should have been in last year's, when bagging six wins from seven starts. In his first season hurdling, he won five on the spin, including three Grade 2s. Jonjo O'Neill then asked him a massive question when entering him for the Stayers' Hurdle at Cheltenham. The grey ran a cracker to be second to Baracouda, beaten less than a length. His Grade 1 reward came next time in the 3m1f novice hurdle at Aintree. Whether he goes chasing or stays hurdling, this sturdy grey is going to be brilliant to watch.

Jonjo O'Neill, Cheltenham

IZNOGOUD (7 b or br g)
Shafoun – Vancia (Top Dancer)
P5U85-7 Good to soft, soft

There's no doubt he has talent, even if he doesn't show it every time. Three seasons ago, he won the Grade 1 Tolworth Hurdle and last season he ran his best race in the Attheraces Gold Cup, when fifth to Ad Hoc. That was a great effort, considering he was taking such a step up in distance. He ran twice at the Cheltenham Festival, unseating in the William Hill and then showing no interest in the Cathcart two days later. He's a young horse who likes some cut in the ground and is potentially well handicapped if running to his best. A big staying chase could fall his way – perhaps even the Hennessy.

Martin Pipe, Wellington

JAZZ D'ESTRUVAL (6 gr g)
Bayolidaan – Caro d'Estruval (Caramo)
-1

One run, two years ago, in a maiden hurdle, one in a handicap hurdle (he won both) and it's straight to chasing for this taking grey. Perth was the scene of both victories; the most recent, in mid-May, was run at a good gallop and Jazz d'Estruval took it without coming off the bridle. Nicky Richards has a nice staying chaser on his hands.

Nicky Richards, Penrith

LILIUM DE COTTE (4 b g)
Ragmar – Vanille de Cotte (Italic)
3122414-

The Triumph Hurdle fourth has joined Nicky Henderson from Guillaume Macaire. Beaten 6l, he finished 4l ahead of the fifth home and was staying on strongly. Although he won one of the best trials for the Triumph, a juvenile event at Sandown, hurdling won't be his game and he'll go chasing, in Henderson's words "sooner rather than later". French-breds are so precocious that it will be no surprise if this one competes in Graded company, even at the age of four.

Nicky Henderson, Lambourn

L'OISEAU (4 br g)
Video Rock – Roseraie (Quart de Vin)
-2

Len Lungo is adept at running up sequences with his novice hurdlers. They seldom go off great prices but a string of short-priced winners never hurt the bank balance. L'Oiseau is just the type to notch an early-season hat-trick. His only ever run was at Kelso in May when he came second in a bumper. He travelled well and stayed on, looking as if the experience would do him good. It was a promising beginning and Lungo may start him off in a bumper.

Len Lungo, Carrutherstown

LORD LINGTON (4 b g)
Bulington – Tosca de Bussy (Le Riverain)
No jumps form

Arrived at Paul Nicholls's place in the summer, having had three runs on the Flat in France in non-thoroughbred company. Nicholls went over to France to watch him school before approving the purchase, so this looks likely to be the latest high-quality import for the yard.

Paul Nicholls, Shepton Mallet

"How the hell he didn't win last season, I'll never know. He's off an incredibly low mark and we'll have plenty of fun with him. He will run up a sequence."
Which trainer, which horse? Read Borderer, page 140

LORD TRANSCEND (6 gr g)
Aristocracy – Capincur Lady (Over The River)
1115- Soft, heavy

Our 'cover' horse, and not for aesthetic reasons; this one has looked highly progressive so far and could be a real star. He was initially rated 95 after scoring at 33-1 on his debut, in a novice hurdle at Newcastle, but ended the season on 150 after only four races. His neck defeat of Deano's Beeno in the Premier Stayers' Hurdle at Haydock was the clincher and the handicapper slapped 25lb on him immediately afterwards. Howard Johnson reckons this horse is up with the best that he's had (Morceli, Direct Route, Ushers Island) and he's clearly an exciting chase prospect. Lord Transcend stays 3m – he might get further – and can't have it soft enough.

Howard Johnson, Crook

MURPHY'S CARDINAL (7 b g)
Shernazar – Lady Swinford (Ardross)
1111-

Had a terrific season, winning four from four – a bumper and three hurdles. Now Noel Chance will send him chasing and has already mapped out an ambitious campaign. Ascot's Reynoldstown Chase (February) is the main target, but he may also take in Kempton's Feltham (December) and the Royal & SunAlliance Novices Chase at the Festival. He acts on bottomless ground, as he showed twice last year at Folkestone. In Chance's own words: "He's a proper, old-fashioned chasing type."

Noel Chance, Upper Lambourn

NAS NA RIOGH (4 b f)
King's Theatre – Abstraite (Groom Dancer)
212211F0-

Ended last season on a couple of low notes. She had quite a bit to do when falling three out in the Triumph Hurdle, and then went to Punchestown, where she trailed home 43l behind Sporazene in the Champion Four-Year-Old Hurdle. In retrospect, those disappointments were no surprise, as she had had a long season. She's a tough filly, though, and came through her juvenile/novice term with great credit. Her biggest prize was the Western Daily Press Finale Juvenile Hurdle at Chepstow on December 27, a Grade 1 affair. She could go novice chasing.

Nicky Henderson, Lambourn

NO COLLUSION (7 b g)
Buckskin – Miss Ironside (General Ironside)
51P21324- Good to soft, soft

This one, who joined Henrietta Knight during the summer, was quite highly tried by Noel Chance in his hurdling season. Knight is likely to send him novice chasing once the rains come and she should meet with plenty of success. Chance always thought of this one as a chaser, so it doesn't matter that his hurdling career was a bit patchy. He should stay 3m and is expected to need some cut.

Henrietta Knight, Wantage

ROSSLEA (5 b g)
Roselier – Burren Gale (Strong Gale)
P230-

Rosslea hasn't won a race yet but we don't anticipate that state of affairs lasting for too much longer. He was beaten 4l by one of Jonjo O'Neill's best novice hurdlers, Sh Boom, at Uttoxeter in December (it was 28l back to the third home in that field of 12). Next time, he ran third at Wincanton before finishing off with a 13th of 19 at the Cheltenham Festival. We don't expect to see Rosslea over timber again, because he has the make and shape of a chaser, and should prove a novice to follow.

Henrietta Knight, Wantage

ROYAL EMPEROR (7 gr g)
Roselier – Boreen Bro (Boreen)
1121122-

From being an interesting novice hurdler, Royal Emperor rose through the ranks at high speed to become one of the best in the land. Two wins at Carlisle and one at Wetherby hadn't marked him down as a world-beater, but his handicap debut was a revelation. He trounced a useful field at Haydock by 9l, revelling in the soft ground and the 3m trip. Next stop was the 3m2f Pertemps Final at the Cheltenham Festival, where he was beaten a short-head by Inching Closer, giving him 4lb. In his last race, he was runner-up to Iris's Gift at Aintree. He has all the makings of a top-notch chaser.

Sue Smith, Bingley

ROYAL ROSA (4 ch g)
Garde Royale – Crystalza (Crystal Palace)
1611-

Broke the record for a jumps horse sold at auction when fetching 340,000gns at Doncaster's spring sale. Formerly owned by the Million In Mind syndicate and trained by Nicky Henderson, he is now in the care of Howard Johnson. Last season, he ran in four bumpers, winning three of them. The last of them was a Grade 1 race at Punchestown at the end of April, when he beat Royal Alphabet by three and a half lengths. Henderson said after that: "He's a good horse and is going to be a very good one. He has already jumped hurdles and he is brilliant," so he must be gutted to have lost him.

Howard Johnson, Crook

SANTENAY (5 b g)
Mister Mat – Guigone (Esprit Du Nord)
11201-2

This five-year-old is typical of the best French imports, precocious and talented. It's difficult to believe that he has already won a Grade 2 hurdle at Wincanton, run midfield in the Champion Hurdle and picked up a Class B at Sandown . . . and he's not even six yet. Paul Nicholls has targeted the Arkle, which he won last season with Azertyuiop, as this season's objective. His defeat by Duke Of Buckingham when first put over fences in mid-May must go down as a fluke result. He's schooled well and has to be followed.

Paul Nicholls, Shepton Mallet

Sponsored by Stan James

SLEEPING NIGHT (7 b g)
Sleeping Car – Doll Night (Karkour)
No runs last season

Mary Reveley did really well with this French import in the one season she had him, even if he didn't get his head in front. A winning chaser in France, he had his first British run in the Charlie Hall Chase at Wetherby and came second to Sackville. Reveley also placed him over hurdles to be a length second to Baracouda in the Rendlesham at Kempton. Paul Nicholls has him now and will aim him at the top chase prizes over 3m plus whenever there is soft ground. There's an outside chance he could be a Grand National type and the trainer deserves a change of luck in that race.

Paul Nicholls, Shepton Mallet

SPORAZENE (4 gr g)
Cozzene – Sporades (Vaguely Noble)
3311– Good to soft, good

Joined Paul Nicholls from Andre Fabre last autumn and ran third in a couple of juvenile events before dotting up by 14l in a race at Ayr after a five-month break, during which he had been gelded. He was much improved for the operation and took the Grade 1 Champion Four-Year-Old Trophy at Punchestown next time out. There were some good horses behind him that day, including Triumph Hurdle winner Spectroscope. A fast-run 2m on decent ground suits and it's possible that he could go to the top of the hurdling tree.

Paul Nicholls, Shepton Mallet

STRONG FLOW (6 br g)
Over The River – Stormy Skies (Strong Gale)
21-11

Strong Flow has had a Martin Pipe-style first season. Pipe is known to throw his horses into the deep end in their first season and, increasingly, we are seeing Paul Nicholls adopting the same modus operandi. Strong Flow had two runs in novice hurdles before tackling, and winning, a novice chase at Worcester in May on good to soft. The very next race (his fourth career start) was in a handicap chase, at Kelso in May. In winning by 11l, he made some seasoned handicap chasers look second-rate. He's given the official assessor a real head-scratcher and should give punters some real profits.

Paul Nicholls, Shepton Mallet

SUPREME PRINCE (6 b g)
Supreme Leader – Strong Serenade (Strong Gale)
11173-

Has all the makings of a novice chaser and should stay 3m. Philip Hobbs gave him a whole year off, so that he could grow into his frame, before sending him over hurdles in October. Supreme Prince's subsequent hat-trick could hardly be described as brilliant but it earned him a place in the Royal & SunAlliance Novices Hurdle at Cheltenham, where he came seventh of 19 behind Hardy Eustace. His third to Iris's Gift at Aintree proved his stamina and ability to handle the soft.

Philip Hobbs, Minehead

TIGHTEN YOUR BELT (6 b g)
Phardante – Hi' Upham (Deep Run)
13-

This half-brother to Native Upmanship was well backed on his debut in a bumper at Stratford and didn't let his supporters down, quickening up to win without being shown the whip. The race took place just before the Cheltenham Festival, so the next stop was Aintree, where he finished about 20l behind Classic Native in the bumper. He's had plenty of time to mature and should be followed in novice hurdles. Soft ground will suit him.

Venetia Williams, Hereford

TRUCKERS TAVERN (8 ch g)
Phardante – Sweet Tulip (Beau Chapeau)
3F132-

Is included for the second year running in the belief that he has a realistic chance of toppling Best Mate. Fourth in the Arkle two seasons ago, he moved sweetly up to staying trips last term and took advantage of a decent weight when winning the Peter Marsh Chase in receipt of 15lb from Hussard Collonges. He was beaten 10l by Best Mate in the 3m2f Cheltenham Gold Cup, vindicating Ferdy Murphy's faith. That was the furthest he's tried, so nearly all the top staying chases are within his compass and soft ground is a bonus. A word of warning, however – he takes a lot of getting fit, so be cautious first time out.

Ferdy Murphy, Leyburn

TYSOU (6 b or br g)
Ajdayt – Pretty Point (Crystal Glitters)
1331F1- Good, Good to firm

His form figures look pretty good on the page but mean little. For instance, the last of his wins was a three-horse race in which the other two pulled up. It's the second win that catches the eye, even though there were only three others involved. The venue was Wincanton and the event was a 2m novice chase. Tysou made all the running and had his rivals cooked as they turned into the straight. The time was only 0.7secs outside standard. He should be a force in handicaps or Grade 3 company, and wants 2m and a fast surface.

Nicky Henderson, Lambourn

Outlook's 10 to follow

Flight Command	Royal Rosa
Iris's Gift	Sleeping Night
Iznogoud	Sporazene
Lilium De Cotte	Tighten Your Belt
Royal Emperor	Truckers Tavern

Berkshire by Downsman

NO PRIZES for guessing who takes star billing in this neck of the woods.

Forget all the negative talk concerning the quality of opposition in the 2003 Gold Cup. **Best Mate**'s performance in becoming the first horse in more than 30 years to defend his title was right out of the very top drawer, placing him firmly among the very best to wear chasing's most prestigious crown.

The question entertaining us now is just how high can he climb?

Many professionals feared *HENRIETTA KNIGHT* may have been enjoying one of her more eccentric moments when first mentioning this horse in the same breath as Arkle some three years ago, but he is now just one Gold Cup away from emulating Tom Dreaper's hero from the 1960s.

Of course, it will always be futile to compare the relative merits of two horses separated by such a distance in time, unless of course you believe that the clone-meisters will be able to recreate the Irish legend and make him race again.

Indeed, such is the remarkable resemblance between the pair, there are conspiracy theorists who believe the scientists have already been busy!

Arkle, would of course, find the chasing scene much changed from his heyday. Perhaps the biggest difference is the greater number of opportunities for the very best chasers in contemporary times.

The possibilities of winning valuable prizes both on the way to and after the Cheltenham Festival are bountiful nowadays and tempt many an owner and trainer fortunate enough to own a premier performer.

But not Henrietta Knight. She has steadfastly stuck to her plan to keep Best Mate's pre-Gold Cup appearances to a minimum and not even her most ardent critics can say that she's got

LEAPING INTO HISTORY: Best Mate (right) is one Gold Cup short of matching Arkle (left)

it wrong. To get any horse to Cheltenham fit to run is a feat in itself, but the Lockinge team have had their star ready for the sternest test in the sport two years running, and that is training of the highest calibre, a thorough vindication of his "reclusive" preparation.

Can he complete the hat-trick? Well, there's unlikely to be any great change in the training routine, that's for sure!

There is, however, a possibility that the venue for the first of his two intended runs before Cheltenham will change. Ascot are considering a new race, which might suit him as a warm-up for the King George, and he may head there rather than the Peterborough Chase at Huntingdon.

One race he will definitely miss is the Haldon Gold Cup. Although he hacked up in the Exeter feature two years ago, the 2m2f is too sharp for him now and it will be left to former 2m champ **Edredon Bleu** (another great example of his trainer's expert handling of chasers and the winner of the race last year) or her rising star **Impek**.

Impek took some flak for his attitude during his spell over timber, but the French-bred put his critics firmly back in their boxes with a lucrative first novice campaign over fences last season. His trainer is ever-mindful of the strength of the Paul Nicholls stable in 2m events this term, however, and intends to step him up in trip after his comeback effort.

Miss Knight has plenty of strength in all divisions to back her main players and there looks sure to be a first-class team of novice chasers for the forthcoming exchanges.

Inca Trail, Best Mate's brother, will be expected to improve on a slightly disappointing 2002-03 campaign. A throat problem was diagnosed as the root of the below-par performances and hopes are high he will do much better following corrective surgery on the breathing problem during the summer.

Rosslea's name was quick to his trainer's mind when she was asked for some potentially smart fencing prospects and his promising performances in a light hurdling season last term were only part of a learning curve.

No Collusion, who joins the Knight team after running some very good races in bumpers and hurdles for Noel Chance, will also take his chance over the larger obstacles, as will **Caribbean Cove**, an easy winner of a novice hurdle at Bangor in April.

Captain Flinders, a half-brother to Sheer Ability, is expected to grab a race or two, whilst **Fragrant Rose**, a winner of three hurdles races last term, should maintain her trainer's fine record in the 'Mares Only' chase series.

Miller's Bay, who was not far off the best bumper horses last season, and the unbeaten **Chelsea Bridge** will be trying their luck over hurdles. They should take their place on any list of potentially high-class novice hurdlers, along with mud-loving **Romantic Affair**, a useful performer on the Flat for John Dunlop.

From the wealth of young talent in Knight's care, the well-bred **Blazing Guns**, **Imperial Dream**, **Pointillism** and **Easter Present** are all names to conjure with.

NOEL CHANCE is another to enjoy the rare privilege of two Gold Cups wins and one has to take notice when he reveals there may be another potentially smart stayer housed at his Upper Lambourn base.

Murphy's Cardinal was something of a dark horse (even to his trainer) before he made his debut in a bumper at Folkestone in November, and it was a surprise when he proceeded to break his duck.

But he didn't stop improving thereafter and ended the campaign with three wins from as many starts over timber. He now works like a class performer and should continue his winning run when put to fences this term.

Chief Witness is another sure to do well when sent novice chasing this term, but he will need a real test of stamina to be seen to best advantage. He won three from three last term and also has plenty of scope for improvement.

'A throat problem was diagnosed as the root of Inca Trail's below-par performances and hopes are high he'll do much better following corrective surgery on the problem during the summer'

KELTIC BARD (furthest left): winning a novice handicap hurdle at Cheltenham in January

Over timber, **Sands Of Thyne** should win his novice hurdles and the trainer was anxious to make mention of the highly-rated **Before The Mast**, who was not right for much of last year. **River City**, who has done well, could be nicely handicapped, and a bumper horse to look out for is **Megapac**, an unraced son of Supreme Leader.

OLIVER SHERWOOD has the French-bred **Light Des Mulottes** near the top of his list of dark horses to look out for and one of the most interesting things to note about this chap is the fact that he came from Eddie Hales, Kim Bailey's former assistant.

Eddie, who now trains in Ireland, has been responsible for finding top-class performers for a number of trainers in recent years and the mere fact he has recommended him to his old pal Sherwood is a tip in itself.

Rhonehurst may find the novice hurdling division its most lucrative area this season, and there is much excitement concerning **Eric's Charm**, the winner of two bumpers last term before finishing a creditable fifth in a hot event at Aintree on his final start.

Musimaro, who landed a bumper at Ludlow, should also pay his way in similar events, whilst **The Lyme Volunteer** should win her novice chases. She improved throughout last

season and there seems no reason why she should not continue to progress.

Spud One did not quite convert his more-than-useful bumper form to novice hurdles, but his trainer has not given up and is more than hopeful he will not be too long in regaining the winning thread.

Keltic Bard was not far off the best novice hurdlers last season and he would have to be one of the Valley's leading hopes for top honours in novice chases. *CHARLIE MANN* reports he's in great form after his summer break and the trainer can't wait to get him on the schooling ground.

The Whitcoombe team are hoping for a lucrative season with their team of young fencers and a particular favourite of mine is **Abbot**, a classy juvenile two years ago. Unfortunately, a leg problem prevented him from appearing last season, but the enforced spell on the sidelines may have been a blessing in disguise because he has now furnished what was a pretty sparse frame.

Proper Squire, who, like Abbot, joined Mann from Brian Meehan's Flat-racing yard, has already shown plenty of aptitude for birch, but there is another less exposed type in the ex-Irish **Regal Act**. This one won over hurdles in his native land and should help continue his trainer's impressive record with imports from Ireland.

Merchants Friend won three in a row last autumn in his first season at Whitcoombe but one can't help feeling he should have won more. His jumping let him down more than once, but Mann and stable jockey Noel Fehily have worked hard on the problem and reckon they have straightened him out.

Gaora Bridge, a decent Irish bumper horse last season, is put forward by Mann as a youngster to note for novice hurdles.

Mann is getting a better grade of horse year on year, but he still has some way to travel to match *NICKY HENDERSON*, who, realistically, is the only trainer from this area to go anywhere near matching the big three West Country trainers on a regular basis.

The Seven Barrows handler loves to hold a strong hand in the novice chase department and he can once again call on a powerful team to do battle.

Chauvinist must be near the top of the shop after his stirring exploits over timber last term. A little disappointing over the smaller obstacles during 2001-02 (when he may have been a little weak), last term he reproduced what has always been top class home form, landing the ultra-competitive Ladbroke Handicap Hurdle at Ascot.

A powerfully-made sort, he looks a real chaser and will be at his best on soft ground.

Non So also paid his way in top handicaps over timber last season and should prove worth following, as will two quality novice hurdlers from last term, **Caracciola** and **Calling Brave**.

Henderson also reveals that **Landing Light** may have a try over birch in the wake of what has been a very good Flat campaign during the summer.

If this correspondent had to pick one name from the list, however, it would be **Nas Na Riogh**, a very consistent juvenile hurdler last term and the winner of a Grade 1 event at Chepstow. She has plenty of quality about her and loves very soft ground – furthermore, she will be getting the allowances for mares and four-year-olds.

Back To Ben Alder will be on many professionals' lists of novice hurdlers to follow after producing a high quality winning effort in a Kempton bumper, along with **Trabolgan**, who showed his class with a game second in the Festival Bumper at Cheltenham.

King Player and **Thames** are also thought good enough to make their presence felt around the Park courses.

Few trainers have done better with French imports in recent years, and Henderson is excited about the prospects for **Mon Villez**, who has already won a chase in his native country, despite being only a three-year-old. He will have a season over timber, and could be a very useful moneyspinner.

If there is a class second-season chaser at the Lambourn yard, then it is surely the handsome **Irish Hussar**, who had his training problems last term but intimated very good things may be to come with his victory over It takes Time in the valuable Mildmay Novices Chase at Aintree in April.

ALAN KING has some top quality animals in his care at Barbury Castle.

Novices again rule the roost for the yard and, in **Bourbon Manhattan**, he has one of our very best chances in novice hurdle events. He landed a nice touch for connections when scoring at both Taunton and Newbury in his first two bumpers and has already schooled well over hurdles.

Alf Lauren won on his only appearance in a bumper at Huntingdon towards the backend and is well-liked by connections after making some pleasing physical progress during the summer.

The tough **Jaboune** should fly the flag for the young trainer in novice events, as should the ex-Irish pointer **Fork Lightning** and **Lord's Best**. The last-named won four races over timber last term and seems to handle any ground.

Finally, King reveals that he may well have a crack at Chepstow's Tote Silver Trophy with the lightly-raced **Crystal d'Ainay**, a fine second in the Mersey Novices Hurdle at Aintree. King's old boss David Nicholson loved to win this early-season handicap hurdle and this highly-talented French import may just have it about him to land the prize.

The West by Hastings

THE WEALTH of jumping talent based in the West Country grows year-on-year and there's every chance of the region once again dominating the National Hunt season that lies ahead.

The record-breaking *MARTIN PIPE* is bidding for a remarkable fourteenth training title and, given the strength in depth at Pond House, it's firmly on the cards. Pipe bagged so many winners last term that he amassed a staggering £2.6m in prizemoney.

One of his most exciting charges is the exceptional chase prospect **Classified**, who rose to the upper echelons of the staying hurdle tree last winter.

The tough son of Roselier proved hard to beat in bumpers and as a novice hurdler, racking up an impressive six wins on the bounce. More recently, he proved his mettle when grinding down prolific stablemate Mr Cool in the Grade 1 Cleeve Hurdle at Cheltenham in January.

Although he was left trailing by Baracouda, Iris's Gift and Limestone Lad in the Stayers' Hurdle at the Festival, his fourth place was still a good effort from a horse whose future lies over fences.

Held in the highest esteem by his illustrious connections, he possesses the perfect conformation for a successful career as a chaser and his will to win is undoubted.

Seebald provided his owners, football aces Steve MacManaman and Robbie Fowler, with plenty of thrills and spills at the highest level last season, and looks the most likely challenger to champion two-miler Moscow Flyer come next March.

He was a multiple winner during a novice career that saw him finish second in the Arkle Chase, and kicked off last season with a creditable trio of seconds off ratings of 154 and 156.

Although he came a cropper two out in the Champion Chase, the fact he was upsides the eventual winner at the time bodes well for next year's bid. He proved his pride alone was dented by the Prestbury Park fall when beating smart subsequent winner Cenkos over 2m at Sandown in April.

Pipe is a master at picking up capable Flat recruits and he may have found a bargain in claiming **Forbearing** for 15,000gns out of Sir Mark Prescott's yard, following a ready win over 1m4f at Catterick in early August.

This son of Bering boasted placed efforts behind the likes of Ekraar and Island House as a three-year-old in 2000. Although not the same force since spending 2001 on the sidelines through injury, he's managed to win three times in lesser grades this year and has the build and stamina to make his mark over timber.

He's proven on all ground conditions and could well rack up a sequence this autumn.

Another less exposed member of Pipe's squad is French import **Akarus**, who's expected to make his mark in some of the top marathon events, a division that's been lacking quality in recent years.

The eight-year-old enjoyed a consistent and successful time when trained in the French provinces last year, picking up a valuable Auteuil purse along the way. He's taken time to acclimatise since arriving at his new home in Devon, and struggled to get competitive when thrown in the deep end on his first two starts.

The decision to dramatically step him up in trip proved the making of him in the Midlands National at Uttoxeter, when he finished a gallant second of six finishers in the 4m2f slog. Off his current attractive mark, he's an interesting candidate for the season's staying chases and he may find a place in the Grand National field.

PAUL NICHOLLS is the only trainer capable of giving Pipe a run for his money in the Champion Trainer Stakes. The Somerset man maintained a strike-rate of 27 per cent last season, despite sending out more runners than anyone except Martin Pipe.

One of his charges fancied to go right to the top of the hurdling ranks is the unexposed **Sporazene**, a tall, leggy French import who made giant strides in the juvenile division last spring.

A lack of fluency blunted his abundant Flat

SPORAZENE: highly-progressive hurdler is our pick from the talent in Paul Nicholls' yard

speed between the flights when he failed to justify market confidence on his first two sightings over British timber.

However, a subsequent gelding operation seemed to do the trick.

With confidence boosted markedly by an effortless success in a minor Class C event at Ayr in April, the youngster was sent across the Irish Sea to take on the big guns in a Grade 1 event at the Punchestown Festival. Having travelled well throughout, he quickened clear of Spectroscope and the well-backed Golden Cross (who'd been first and third in the Triumph Hurdle) in the style of a quality animal.

He could be a warm order for one or two top events this season.

Another exciting inmate expected to pay his way in the months to come is **Santenay**. Although bought from France to go chasing, it was over hurdles that he made his mark last winter.

A second to Intersky Falcon in Kempton's Christmas Hurdle was a highly respectable first run-out in the big league. However, Nicholls was far from happy with the state of Santaney's coat before the Champion Hurdle and, in the circumstances, the scopey five-year-old ran a sound race in ninth. A ready 7l drubbing of the smart Copeland in a Class B event at Sandown rounded off his hurdling career on a high note.

Santenay's been well-schooled over birch since Christmas and jumped like an old pro on his eagerly-awaited chase bow at Warwick in May. Although he was unexpectedly turned over at cramped odds, connections were quick to blame the muddling pace that day. Granted more positive tactics, he should

soon open his chase account before going on to bigger and better things.

Established stars expected to shine this winter include **Azertyuiop**, mightily impressive winner of the Arkle Chase, and **Valley Henry**, who came of age when fourth in the Gold Cup.

The substantial financial backing behind *JONJO O'NEILL*, provided by the likes of JP McManus, already appears to be paying dividends, if last term's total win and placed prizemoney amassed of over £1.5m is any guide.

O'Neill's magnificent set-up at Jackdaws Castle houses a cornucopia of talent, epitomized by the awesome prospect **Rhinestone Cowboy**, who is fancied to take all before him on the road to Champion Hurdle glory in March.

This son of Be My Native lived up to his top-flight bumper form when stringing together a series of cheeky wins over timber. The manner with which he quickened in an instant to brush aside horses like Thisthatandtother prompted connections to go for gold in the Champion Hurdle and, for an inexperienced novice, third place was a major achievement.

Expect even better this time around.

A less exposed O'Neill representative to keep a look out for is **Lingo**, who left Lynda Ramsden's yard after a deal reportedly worth six figures. The exciting four-year-old grew into a tough and admirable middle-distance campaigner on the level, signing off with a strong-finishing Class B win (off a lofty rating of 94) at Epsom in April. With stamina and speed in plentiful supply, he's confidently expected to recoup his hefty price tag.

RHINESTONE COWBOY

Few have a brighter future than Triumph Hurdle hero **Spectroscope**, who was a model of consistency in hot Graded events as a juvenile. He showed resilience beyond his years when sticking his head out to beat Well Chief at the Festival, an attitude that will stand him in good stead when taking on his elders later in the year.

The top-class **Keen Leader** can readily be excused a poor show on unsuitably fast ground when favourite for the Royal & SunAlliance Chase. He's an awesome talent now that his early jumping frailties have been ironed out and, granted some juice in the ground, he should collect plenty of trophyware this term.

There are plentiful options open to **Iris's Gift**, one of the revelations of last season. Having split the mighty Baracouda and Limestone Lad in the Stayers' Hurdle, the grey youngster can be aimed at any number of valuable prizes, over fences or timber.

PHILIP HOBBS came in fourth in the prizemoney list last season, thanks partly to the remarkable exploits of the evergreen champion hurdler **Rooster Booster**.

A couple of highly promising hurdlers to take from his powerful Bilbrook camp are **Unleash** and **Andy Gin**. The former has thrived since winning a maiden hurdle in March and made light of ratings of 110 and 118 when landing a couple of Class B handicaps soon after.

The chestnut son of Benny The Dip showcased his versatility when plundering a decent renewal of the Northumberland Plate on a return to the level. The Cesarewitch is an ideal finale for the improving gelding on the Flat, before he resumes a thriving career over timber. He should keep RFO punters in pocket this winter.

French import Andy Gin has been described as "very tough" and looked the real deal when overcoming greenness to put daylight between himself and next-time-out winner Visibility in a 2m1f novice event on his hurdling bow at Exeter. At four, he's already amassed a wealth of Flat experience, having run no fewer than 16 times when trained across the Channel.

He lacked the hurdling experience to give his true running in the Triumph Hurdle, an effort that can be discounted.

Off his current mark, he'll hold his own in handicap company.

A positive word also goes to the exceptional prospect **Supreme Serenade**, who is held in very high regard and lived up to her billing when producing a smooth win on her sole bumper start, at Newton Abbot in April. She's immaculately bred for a jumping career and is destined for the top.

VENETIA WILLIAMS does well with her recruits from the Flat and the Kings Caple handler looks to have a decent prospect in **Chief Yeoman**, snapped up for a mere 21,000gns at Doncaster's August Sale.

Formerly with Sir Michael Stoute, this one managed to fill a place on more than one occasion off a rating of 87 on the level. The three-year-old hails from an excellent middle-distance family and shaped as though stamina was his main asset when last seen in August. A lucrative juvenile hurdling campaign is in the offing.

Williams's **Idole First** can rack up a sequence in novice company this season. Having won four of his 13 Flat starts when trained in France, it's easy to see why connections were keen to snap this one up.

He certainly kicked off his new hurdling career on the right note when, despite lacking fluency, he pulled clear of more experienced rivals to score over 2m3f at Stratford in July, providing sire Flemensfirth with his first National Hunt winner. He'll have learned plenty from that confidence-booster and, once finding fluency in his hurdling technique, will be a formidable opponent.

It's strongly advised that you follow the exploits of **Limerick Boy**. The five-year-old mixed it effectively in Group company on the Flat in Germany and confirmed the favourable impression of his sixth in the Supreme Novices Hurdle when running away from Man O'Mystery in a Grade 2 event at Aintree in April.

A subsequent second to Festival hero Back In Front at Punchestown highlights his progressive profile.

Ireland by Jerry M

IF ANYONE doubted the resurgent quality of Irish jump racing, they were emphatically set right last season, when we celebrated six Festival winners and a third Grand National success in five years.

JESSICA HARRINGTON alone bagged four major handicaps and the Champion Chase with her forays into England.

With the Istabraq reign behind us, the Champion Hurdle has gone to British-based horses in the last two years, but that could be about to end with the progression of *EDWARD O'GRADY*'s **Back In Front** from the novice ranks.

He was simply sensational in winning the Supreme Novices at the Festival last term, moving effortlessly through the pack before going on to win by a long-looking 10 lengths. The result got punters off to a dream start at what became a great meeting for them, and it certainly had his trainer dreaming too, of coming back in 2004 for the third race on the same card.

O'Grady took his star to Punchestown afterwards, to try for an ambitious double at the meeting. While the first leg came off comfortably, Jonjo O'Neill's Quazar scuppered the second.

In terms of Back In Front's Champion Hurdle aspirations, however, the Punchestown reverse is irrelevant. He more than put his marker down at Cheltenham, and clearly possesses all the attributes necessary to land the big race, with a potent mix of speed and stamina (he stays 2m4f) blended with some fluent hurdling.

He also seems to thrive on the undulations of Prestbury Park – in three course outings, he has won two and finished third in the other, which just happened to be the best bumper of recent years (Pizarro and Rhinestone Cowboy were first and second). Look no further for your Champion Hurdle bet.

JIMMY MANGAN's **Monty's Pass** continued Ireland's fantastic recent record in the Grand National but, while he will make a bold bid to repeat the dose, we have two other strong contenders who could easily beat him to it, namely Harrington's **Intelligent** and *TONY MULLINS*'s **Barrow Drive**.

CLEAR IN FRONT: not a rival in sight as Back In Front races up Cheltenham's famous hill

In an unforgettable week for the Harrington yard, Intelligent won the Midlands National after **Moscow Flyer** and **Spirit Leader** had gone in at Cheltenham.

In stamina-sapping conditions over 4m2f, Intelligent was given a patient ride, before going to the front in the home straight and staying on doggedly to beat Martin Pipe's Akarus. It was a further 28l back to Pipe's other runner, Jurancon II – who has since franked the form by winning the Summer National, again at Uttoxeter.

Harrington wisely put Intelligent away after that marathon, so he will start the season fresh and raring to go. He still has plenty of time to take in Aintree, as he will only be an eight-year-old by the time of the next National, but he is a mature type who jumps soundly, so the astute Harrington may well put him in the race this season and let him take his chance.

Barrow Drive completes the triumvirate, which gives the Irish formidable strength in depth for Aintree. Tony Mullins's doughty battler enjoyed a great novice campaign last season, culminating in a brave third behind One Knight and Jair Du Cochet in the Royal & SunAlliance Chase at the Festival.

He looked a big threat in that race, jumping well and racing prominently throughout, but could not quite match the turn of foot shown by the winner and the rallying

French horse up the hill.

On his final start, he went off a short-priced favourite to land a novice chase at the Punchestown Festival, but uncharacteristically fell six from home. That was a rare blemish, though, on a fine-looking CV and, as he doesn't look quite good enough to take on the best over 3m, expect this son of Gunner B to make his mark over further.

WILLIE MULLINS has been a prolific raider of big races in England, taking the King George VI Chase and Newbury's Hennessy Gold Cup in the last two seasons alone. Unfortunately, Be My Royal looks likely to be disqualified as the Hennessy winner because he subsequently tested positive for morphine.

It transpired that a batch of horse-feed had been accidentally contaminated – a number of winners from last autumn face disqualification as a result of having ingested feed from this batch, of whom Be My Royal is the highest profile.

Plainly, the horse's connections are blameless and Mullins reports that the matter is in the hands of their solicitors. There is still some hope that the horse will be allowed to keep the race, which would be fitting, since he injured himself so badly that day that he will be unable to race again.

Mullins has better news of stable stalwart **Alexander Banquet**, who missed all of last

A HORSE OF LEISURE: but Alexander Banquet will have to do some racing this season

season because of a suspensory ligament injury. The Irish Gold Cup winner of 2002, he now seems to have recovered and should be back in action at about Christmas-time, with the Cheltenham Gold Cup and the Grand National as his main objectives.

When Jerry M put it to Mullins that he had another Grand National type in **Macs Gildoran**, he said: "I thought so too, but the owners aren't keen on the race."

That's a pity because the horse took well to Aintree's big fences when running second in the Topham in April. Don't forget that Monty's Pass put up a similar performance to be second in the Topham the year before he landed the big race.

Let's hope Mullins can talk connections round to the idea – in the meantime, Macs Gildoran will be a strong candidate for some of the more valuable handicap chases.

English racegoers should get their first sight of **Nobody Told Me** this term. This five-year-old mare, who started her career in France before joining Mullins at the beginning of last season, made rapid progress under his care.

By midsummer, she'd won five times for the Carlow trainer, the pick of which was Auteuil's Grande Course de Haies, the French Champion Hurdle.

She'll be campaigned in quality staying races, with the Long Walk Hurdle at Ascot as an early-season target.

Another useful long-distance hurdler in Mullins' care is **Holy Orders**, who took the Grade 1 for stayers at Punchestown in May. He'll go to Australia for the Melbourne Cup in November, carrying high hopes of a second successive Irish win in the race after Dermot Weld's Media Puzzle last year, but the long-term plan is to return him to hurdles in time for a spring campaign.

His targets then would be Cheltenham's Stayers' Hurdle or the Martell Aintree Hurdle on Grand National day.

FRANCIS FLOOD has been bringing horses across to the mainland for years now, and he has some useful types to go to war with this season.

The mare **Newhall** has been a regular visitor to these shores, having finished second in both the 2001 Triumph Hurdle and last season's Imperial Cup.

The latter effort, behind Korelo, was a particularly good run, as Flood believes she is

Invincible Irish
Back In Front
Newhall
Nobody Told Me

much better on a sound surface (the race was run in a bog). She subsequently went to Aintree, where she ran well to finish sixth behind Risky Reef, but eventually ended the season winless.

That fate has befallen many a second-season hurdler, but she remains of interest in big handicaps, such as the Imperial Cup again, the County Hurdle (there is a big bonus for winning both) or anything at the spring Aintree meeting.

She deserves to win a big one, and could do so in a large field on a sound surface.

Two less exposed sorts from Flood's County Wicklow base to watch for are novice chasers **The Culdee** and **Aimees Mark**.

Aimees Mark enjoyed a great season last term, and had quickly rattled up a hat-trick in handicap hurdles by December. He was then prepared for a crack at the Coral Cup at Cheltenham, where he ran a super race to finish ninth of 27 behind Xenophon.

He subsequently tried fences for the first time at Gowran Park last May and disappointed, eventually being pulled up. But Flood explains that he was over the top after a long season and the run is probably best forgotten.

He remains one to watch.

The Culdee performed creditably last season without netting his head in front, and wasn't disgraced behind Inching Closer in the Pertemps Final at the Festival. Flood admits he isn't overbig, but he has schooled well and goes on testing ground – look out for him winning a few races in Ireland during the winter.

With *TONY MARTIN*'s **Xenophon** reportedly going over fences, too, this season (the Royal & SunAlliance is the probable target), Moscow Flyer going for his second Queen Mother and Spirit Leader a nicely-priced alternative to Back In Front for the Champion Hurdle, we're set for another solid year.

The North by Borderer

LAST WINTER was a frustrating one for *FERDY MURPHY*, his horses bursting into top gear only in the spring. In order to minimise the chances of a repeat, he's currently seeking planning permission for a new gallop to be laid out.

Just as the horses started winning in December, Middleham was hit by three feet of snow, adversely affecting the High Moor gallop which Murphy normally relies on.

Despite such difficulties, the stable took second place in the Gold Cup with **Truckers Tavern**, a result which went a long way to vindicating the trainer's faith in the horse (and ours – he was RFO's front-page tip, at 33-1). Murphy tells me: "I think he's going to get better because he is still very inexperienced compared with many.

"You wouldn't quite know how close he would have gone in the Gold Cup, had the ground been suitably soft. The days of soft ground at Cheltenham may have gone, with so much good drainage, but he'll win big races," the trainer asserts.

He starts in the Charlie Hall Chase at Wetherby in October before heading to Kempton for the King George. Murphy continues: "That wouldn't be his race but he will need the experience."

The Hennessy at Leopardstown is high on the agenda. The Pillar Chase is another obvious target and that would be an ideal springboard to another crack at racing's Blue Riband in March.

Ballinclay King confirmed he is no back-number when winning easily at Cheltenham in January. He also ran a great race behind another Cheltenham specialist, Lady Cricket, on his next start. Murphy reveals: "He goes for the Paddy Power Gold Cup and will probably keep returning to Cheltenham because there are so many suitable options on the course, at which he operates so well.

"He looks better than ever this year after

TRUCKERS TAVERN: pictured here taking the Peter Marsh Chase at Haydock in January

Sponsored by Stan James

> *"How the hell he didn't win last season, I'll never know. He's off an incredibly low mark and we'll have plenty of fun. He will run up a sequence"*
> *– Ferdy Murphy on Supreme Breeze*

his problems and I'm very happy with him."

Historg won at Cheltenham in December and has the Hennessy Gold Cup at Newbury as his main aim in the early part of the season. Murphy says: "He's a really good handicapper and a half-brother to Fadalko. He could be a similar type but wouldn't necessarily be a spring horse, unlike his sibling."

He ran well to finish sixth in the William Hill Handicap Chase at Cheltenham but would have finished closer under different tactics. The trainer explains: "Davy [Russell] took it up four out but you have to wait on him. We wanted him in front at the top of the hill but we've learned from that and he'll be ridden more patiently in future.

"He also put up one of his most creditable performances when sixth in the Racing Post Chase on unsuitably fast ground."

Green Ideal used to be trained by Nicky Henderson but Murphy expects him to enjoy a good campaign after a change of environment. He tells me: "He ran some good races on the Flat and I think he's a fair sort. Kieren Fallon rode him and absolutely loved him.

"He was winter favourite for the Triumph Hurdle at one stage and I was very keen to buy him at the Doncaster Sales. He'll go novice chasing and, as a five-year-old receiving all the allowances, I can't see why he won't run up a sequence."

Hot Weld finished second to a Murphy-trained winner in a bumper on his only start when trained by Tom Tate.

The Irishman tells me: "I think the world of the winner (**Riothamus**) but the runner-up got into a lot of traffic problems during the race, and would probably have beaten us with a clear run."

With an inside line on the strength of the form, Murphy was keen to buy the runner-up at Doncaster. He says: "I gave 49,000gns for him but he was in on the last day of the May sale and would have made a lot more if

others hadn't already spent."

Look out for him in 2m4f novice hurdles on soft ground. Murphy insists: "This is a star horse."

He says of the winner: "Riothamus is an absolutely gorgeous horse and really could be anything. He'll be campaigned in 2m4f novice hurdles on northern galloping tracks."

Garde Bien finished second in a point-to-point for the Bailey family and Murphy coughed up 36,000 guineas at Doncaster sales last year. He opines: "He was very big and weak and very backward, so we gave him loads of time but he looks fantastic. He'll go straight over fences and I think he's sharp enough for two miles.

"He did one particularly impressive piece of work but the owner is very patient and I'd like to think he might be an Arkle horse."

Tribal Venture was a good servant last year and should make his mark when he goes novice chasing. He won at Cheltenham and Ascot and put up a great effort when third in the Pertemps Final at the Festival.

The Middleham man says: "He was never a hurdler and will be so much better-suited by 3m over fences. I don't like the Royal & SunAlliance Chase because it takes a lot out of

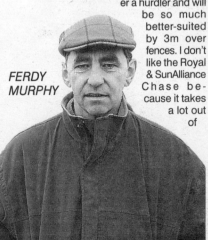

FERDY MURPHY

horses but I wouldn't worry about it with this fellow because he is so tough and would gallop all day."

Supreme Breeze was unlucky last year but should make amends at some stage of the new campaign. "How the hell he didn't win, I'll never know," says Murphy.

"He was four clear at the last at Catterick but fell, and next time the tactics were all wrong. He lost his confidence and we were chasing our tails with him but Davy will get the right tune out of him this year.

"He is off an incredibly low mark and we'll have plenty of fun with him. He will run up a sequence." You have been warned.

Man On The Hill is back in action after a long absence and will go for races like Haydock's Peter Marsh Chase. He won four races two years ago but missed the whole of last year with a minor tendon injury.

At a lower level, the Irishman reports: "We'll have a lot of bloody fun with **Tufty Hopper** when he goes over fences this year.

He won three races last season but jumps fences fantastically. He won't be going south but will win plenty of races and goes on any ground."

LEN LUNGO's horses suffered the effects of a bad virus in the middle of the season before hitting top form in the spring.

Full Irish isn't a big horse but has schooled well over fences. Lungo says: "We'll run him once or twice over hurdles but he's quite high in the handicap. If Tony (Dobbin) is happy with him, we'll go the fencing route."

The Bajan Bandit had a disappointing season but won his first two races over fences. The virus hit him particularly hard and he scoped dirty after being pulled up at Wetherby in February.

The trainer says: "We're hoping he's fresh and well this season but I thought he was jumping too carefully last term and you can't get away with that against good horses."

His breeding is causing his trainer to question his future handling of this horse. He tells me: "There have been many hundreds of winners by Commanche Run but not many over fences, so we might go back to hurdles for a while."

Armaguedon won his first two juvenile bumpers very impressively but the heavy ground was against him when he was third to Control Man in the championship bumper at Chepstow in December. He also pulled too hard when beaten at Aintree.

FINGERS CROSSED: Len Lungo (right) with his disappointing charge The Bajan Bandit

Sponsored by Stan James

ROYAL EMPEROR

Lungo states: "He'll go novice hurdling but he'll have to learn to settle and I'm hoping the flights of hurdles teach him to switch off. There's no doubt he could be very useful if relaxing in his races."

Brooklyn Breeze will go novice chasing, having won all three starts over hurdles impressively. Lungo says: "I hope he schools well because, although I'm usually very patient with my horses, he could be a suitable candidate for chasing a year early.

"He's a long-striding horse, so the undulations at Carlisle might not be ideal, but the fences at Newcastle have been remodelled and could be suitable."

Laouen is only small but did well to run up a sequence over hurdles. Lungo continues: "I'm not sure whether his ideal trip is 2m or 2m4f but he was exposed when beaten in the Swinton Hurdle at Haydock in the spring.

"I'm not ruling out the possibility of going over fences because he might be quick enough to contest the less competitive 2m chasing division."

Lungo becomes particularly animated when talking about **Paddy The Piper**. "He is an exciting horse!

"He was very weak and inexperienced as a youngster but was absolutely terrific last season. His win at Wetherby was very impressive because he settled well before cruising through to win comfortably."

The form was franked because the third (Random Native) didn't carry a penalty for winning but went on to slaughter a good field at Carlisle next time.

He adds: "Paddy The Piper is agile, with

lots of scope, and he schools well. He's a great prospect and I'm looking forward to running him in novice hurdles.

"He quickens well and will be one to follow over a stiff 2m, but I'm confident he'll stay 2m4f."

This time last year, Lungo named Armaguedon as the one horse to follow most closely from his yard. "I've picked out **L'Oiseau** for the readers this time," he says.

"He finished second in a bumper at Kelso on his only start but showed a real turn of foot. He was only beaten by greenness and wasn't knocked about, so he'll have learned a lot from that.

"He'll start in bumpers and, if he was very impressive, we might consider keeping him to win a decent bumper, but he has the novice hurdle option."

The name has already been written in Borderer's notebook.

SUE SMITH's **Ardent Scout** sustained an injury to a joint in the Red Square Vodka Gold Cup but he's had a successful operation and has been back in training since August.

Smith says: "He won the Becher Chase last season and that will be his ultimate objective this term.

"He then goes for the Grand National, after a couple of runs in major staying races. He has been a stuffy horse in the past but he has the right attitude and helps himself to get fit.

"He is very intelligent when jumping and goes exceptionally well around Aintree."

Royal Emperor emerged as a potential star as he progressed through the last campaign. He ran a terrific race when just touched off by Inching Closer in Cheltenham's Pertemps Final. He also ran creditably when second to Iris's Gift at Aintree.

Smith tells me: "Perhaps he was one per cent short at Aintree after his earlier exertions. I can't see why we won't go chasing with him this season and he has summered exceptionally well.

"We have high hopes for him, but we'll start him off small before aiming him at the Royal & SunAlliance Chase."

Simply Supreme will also contest long-distance races over fences but Smith insists: "We will have to keep them apart on the racecourse but if everything stays right and they enjoy the necessary luck, either one of them could play a big part in the Royal & SunAlliance at the Festival.

"Simply Supreme did nothing wrong apart from a disappointing run at Haydock but he wasn't right when we got him home. He was bought as a three-year-old and is related to The Last Fling on the dam's side.

"He will do particularly well with a bit of cut in the ground and I'm sure he will learn to settle better. He has grown tremendously over the summer and he is one horse we are really looking forward to."

Tipsy Mouse is another with a big future. He won a novice handicap chase at Hexham last backend and is a full-brother to Grand National winner Royal Athlete.

The timing of that success entitles him to retain his novice status and he "could quite easily run up a sequence", according to Smith. She says: "You wouldn't be frightened of going around Haydock with him and I might even target those sorts of meetings to exploit his superior fencing ability."

He also relishes a test of stamina because he stays all day. Smith adds: "Long distance chases will suit him perfectly and he could be a contender for the National with another year on his back."

Smith's main owner Trevor Hemmings was keen to win the Haydock race named in honour of his ill-fated star The Last Fling, and he achieved the feat last season with **Tonoco**. He will be aimed at the race again and his confidence and ability have increased with the fitting of a tube, which offset his breathing problems.

Smith explains: "Tonoco will jump the biggest fences in England and he is a strong possibility to go back to Aintree for the Topham Trophy again. I'm sure he'll be winning some good handicaps this season."

Mister McGoldrick was a smart performer over hurdles but goes novice chasing this year. Smith says: "That will definitely be his forte because he is an exceptional jumper. He really comes into his own when he gets soft ground and 2m will be ideal.

"He can run at the same speed on soft ground as he does on good ground and I really expect him to come to the fore over fences this season because he has so much talent and scope. This fellow is going to shine from now on."

Smiths Landing won his races over hurdles last season and is another exciting recruit to the novice chasing ranks. He likes good to soft ground.

The Kew Tour is also going to be a "cracking horse over fences", according to Smith. He recorded back-to-back successes over hurdles at Wetherby last term and Smith tells me: "He will be one to be reckoned with over fences because he is bred for the game and has lots of scope."

Newmarket by Aborigine

FROM HER small 19-box yard on the same Moulton Paddocks estate that houses the mighty Godolphin empire, former point-to-point rider *LUCY WADHAM* has rapidly established herself among the training ranks here at HQ.

This term, she's hoping her highly promising hurdler **Fantastic Champion** could live up to his name after a promising first season over jumps.

He looked useful from the time he started work on the Links and transferred that form to the racecourse with a couple of smart efforts. After a promising first run at Newbury, where he blew up, the smart ex-Flat performer finished second to Bal De Nuit in another hot novice hurdle at Kempton.

Three weeks later, he ran into a bit of a hot-pot when chasing home Bareme on good to soft ground at Kempton. He has thrived and strengthened during the summer break and, as his trainer puts it: "The great thing is that he's still a novice going into the new season, so we'll be looking for a nice race to make him a winner.

"Hopefully, if he then continues to go the right way, we could have a Cheltenham Festival horse on our hands."

Homeleigh Mooncoin was one of the most prolific Wadham winners last season, landing three hurdles races. Though he started at 50-1 when gaining his first win at Worcester, Team Wadham (Lucy's husband Justin does the entries) were harbouring no angels unawares, as they quietly fancied him!

This fine, strong gelding by 2,000 Guineas winner Entrepreneur went on to complete a hat-trick with a brace of fluent wins at Southwell, at the same time proving he has the stamina for 3m.

"He always went all right in his work at home and he could have a couple more runs over hurdles," says Wadham. "However, his future lies over fences and he has already schooled satisfactorily on the Links."

The Wadhams have followed a route taken by top Newmarket jumping trainers of the past like Tom Jones and the late David Morley, by shopping in the winner-producing French jumping market, and have found a couple of imports who are going to justify their purchase prices.

The appropriately-named **Euro Bleu** was put in at the deep end last season but ran a couple of encouraging races, with one particularly sound effort at Aintree. The plan is for him to go for handicap hurdles, though later in the season he could be allowed to tackle the larger obstacles, as that is where his future almost certainly lies.

Brigadier Du Bois, who started his racing career at uncelebrated Pau in the south of France, has settled in well and has done enough so far to suggest he will pay his way in decent company.

One of the Wadhams' favourites, the game mare **Tealby** has some pretty useful performances to her credit. Not only did she beat Intersky Falcon in winning a bumper a couple of seasons back, but last December she also gave Rhinestone Cowboy a fright when leading him over the last at Chel-

LUCY WADHAM: several jumps prospects

tenham and rallying when headed, going under by only a neck.

"She is on the delicate side, so we have to be careful with her," the trainer says, "but, granted the necessary luck, she could win a handicap or two off her current mark."

On the handicapping front, the five-year-old **Bound** ran some good races in decent handicaps, particularly when finishing third to Spectrometer at Cheltenham in December. He then appeared to go off the boil but it was eventually discovered he needed a wind operation.

As the indications are that that surgery has now done the trick, he could find his way back into the winners' enclosure off his current rating on the fast ground which he seems to relish.

A final mention must also be given to **The Dark Lord**, even though he did not win a race last season. His second to Immola at Sandown in March on bottomless ground indicates he has ability, though, and he has since won a modest 2m4f race at Worcester in the summer – he can get more wins at that trip and beyond.

JAMES FANSHAWE gave HQ our third Champion Hurdle winner in 12 years when scoring with Hors La Loi III in 2002. Paul and Jenny Green decided to retire their star this spring, after it become clear that he had lost his zest for racing, though I can't forget how brilliantly he schooled over

ETERNAL SPRING

fences during his build-up for his abortive bid to defend his crown this March.

Although it must be admitted that Fanshawe appears not to have any potential superstars waiting in the wings, the established hurdlers **Eternal Spring** and **Persian Waters** could provide the Pegasus Stables team with some winter action. Both are fully exposed but, if things go the right way, they could keep the winners rolling.

MARK TOMPKINS has greatly reduced the number of horses he sends jumping from his Flint Cottage Stables. Though one or two of the more stoutly-bred three-year-olds could go novice hurdling in due course, keep an eye open for previous Flat and hurdles winner **Niagara**, who will go novice chasing.

This one looks the type to take to fences, over which his lack of finishing pace will not be such a problem.

DON CANTILLON is one of Newmarket's characters but the hard-working Irishman can certainly spot and train a top jumper. A few years back, he ran up a flurry of chasing successes with Alpine Gale, a tough and hardy mare he owned himself.

He proudly reports: "She's had two foals, by Ascot Gold Cup winner Kayf Tara and Prince Of Wales's Stakes winner Bob Back, and is again in foal to Bob Back. They are lovely foals and I look forward to training them in due course.

"Nearer to hand, **Be Fair** should certainly be worth following this season."

It is easy to understand his enthusiasm for Be Fair, as the five-year-old won bumpers at Newton Abbot and Worcester before going to Cheltenham and Aintree. He did not get the best of rides at the Festival but ran a cracker at the Grand National meeting, finishing a well-backed 20-1 second to Classic Native.

Cantillon plans to run him over hurdles and, as his charge has looked like an old hand over the practice fences on the Links, will send him chasing in the fullness of time.

HUGH COLLINGRIDGE will also be putting his versatile performer **Forest Heath** over fences in the near future.

The grey had the speed to win a Goodwood maiden on the Flat and, even though he has not found the target over hurdles, he has put up some sound efforts. As Collingridge puts it:

146

"He looks a natural and, with a bit of luck, he could pay his way."

GILES BRAVERY has been accused of tilting at windmills with his game stayer **Lady Laureate**. However, his faith was justified by her third in the Grade 1 Challow Hurdle at Newbury, which greatly increased her prospective value as a jumping broodmare.

She lost her way towards the end of the last jumping campaign but having a couple of runs on the Flat has rekindled her interest and there are more races to be won with her on the fast ground she favours.

Not only does NICK LITTMODEN still rule as champion All-Weather trainer, but he also has one or two of his team lined up for duty over hurdles at his Southgate Stables, which saw the 1995 Champion Hurdle winner Alderbook start his jumping career under the care of the now-retired Julie Cecil.

Though Flat winners **Alessandro Severo** and **Mutared** might not reach such heights, they have already been schooled by former jump jockey Steve Smith-Eccles on the Links and their jumping indicates they can also win over hurdles.

NEIL GRAHAM has always held a high opinion of **King's Mill**, who has given him some notable wins on the Flat. When the horse went up for sale, Graham was happy to buy him back for some other owners in the yard, and he's convinced that they will have a lot of fun with him.

"The trouble is that he needs good to soft ground to produce his best form and the weather has been so unsettled over the last 18 months that it's difficult to plan ahead with him," said Graham.

Despite these downbeat words, I get the clear impression that Graham is delighted with him and, as the gelding still has his novice tag, he could win a novice hurdle to boost his confidence before going on to be as good a performer over timber as he was when racing on the level.

Hot off the Heath
Eternal Spring
Fantastic Champion
King's Mill

Midlands by John Bull

THE MIDLANDS area can often be over-looked by jumping enthusiasts, who naturally flock to the big names of Lambourn and the West Country for their winners.

But scratch the surface of our neglected heartland and you come up with many training talents who, between them, generate more than enough success to keep punters in clover during the long winter months.

HENRY DALY hasn't had an easy task at Downton Hall, since taking over from one of the most revered figures in the game – triple Grand National winner Captain Tim Forster. But Daly has handled the pressure with aplomb and, if his results at last season's Cheltenham Festival are anything to go by, he is a worthy successor.

He bagged two prizes at jump racing's biggest meeting, with stable stalwart **Young Spartacus** winning the Mildmay Of Flete and **Palarshan** taking the Grand Annual.

It was a tremendous feat by Daly to get the fragile Young Spartacus to win at the Fes-tival on his first start for 14 months but he'll find it devilishly difficult to place him now, as he has a high handicap rating and yet is slightly below the highest class.

He could run well at a fancy price in a King George (he's a previous winner of the Racing Post Chase at the same track) or a Gold Cup but Palarshan and **Haut Cercy** look more like the ones to follow from the yard.

The giant Palarshan took time to get the hang of things last season, but came good with a vengeance in the spring and decent ground might well be the key to him. He had disappointed on soft ground at Ascot, prior to hosing in at both Leicester and the Festival itself, on a much sounder surface.

The Cheltenham event was run at a furious pace throughout, but he jumped superbly under an astute ride from Mark Bradburne (who kept him wide throughout, giving him a good look at his fences). At the tender age of five, time is very much on his side, and it wouldn't be hard to see him em-

FAST AND FLUENT: Henry Daly's Haut Cercy has all the attributes of a National winner

ulating Edredon Bleu, who won the Grand Annual before graduating to the big league and scooping the Champion Chase.

There will be plenty of good races to be won with him before that, though, as long as the ground is suitable, and he is worth looking out for in a race such as the Victor Chandler at Ascot in January.

Haut Cercy, meanwhile, is a realistic contender to carry on the Grand National trend set by Daly's mentor Tim Forster. He improved throughout last season, winning at Chepstow and Wincanton, before narrowly going under to Youlneverwalkalone in a titanic battle for the Festival's William Hill National Hunt Handicap Chase.

He may have been unlucky, as he was only beaten three-quarters of a length after rooting the fourth-last, with Attheraces Gold Cup victor Ad Hoc nine lengths away in third.

He is the perfect age to launch a National bid (he'll be nine next year) and, as he normally jumps soundly, stays well and has a touch of class, It's easy to see him having a big impact at Aintree, particularly as he is certain to be in the handicap proper.

ROBIN DICKIN has proved a very capable trainer when given the right material, and he's particularly excited about his progressive stayer **Max Pride**, of whom he says: "I'd hope to win a National with him, although maybe not *the* National."

His charge has won over 3m6f at Bangor on soft ground, so obviously stays very well, and could defy further rises in the weights this season. Obvious targets would be the four-miler at Cheltenham on New Year's Day, and the Midlands National at Uttoxeter.

If winning either of those, he could even scrape into the Aintree field, and wouldn't disgrace himself.

On his final start last season, he finished second behind Simon Sherwood's Ballybrophy at Warwick, as did another of Dickin's inmates – **Channahrlie** – at Ascot.

Dickin has singled out this last-named as one to follow for the season, as the grey is well-handicapped and shouldn't prove too hard to place.

A series of seconds dogged him last season, but he isn't ungenuine, as he proved when winning at Southwell last March. His best distance is 3m (he tried further at Perth last season and didn't stay), while right-handed tracks will show him in his best light.

Midlands magic
Haditovski
Haut Cercy
Max Pride

TONY CARROLL produced a fine feat of training last season – he managed to get a win out of the infuriating **Moving Earth**.

Admittedly, it was only a claiming hurdle at Doncaster, but the horse then ran a tremendous race in the Atthraces Gold Cup, where Carroll believes he would have been placed if he hadn't have been running from out of the handicap.

He was bang there approaching the Pond Fence and, while he was eventually pulled-up, it was a great effort, and the same can be said of his subsequent second behind Ei Ei over 2m4f at Wetherby.

He definitely seems to have sweetened up for the move to a smaller yard and Carroll believes there are some good chases to be won with Moving Earth this season, culminating in a crack at the Grand National. He's a great jumper and the unique atmosphere of Aintree might well turn him on, plus he has plenty of ability.

Two others to look out for from the Carroll yard are **Baron's Pharaoh**, ready to return from injury having won his last two races, and **Mighty Glen**, a Roselier gelding who goes chasing and will need soft ground and three miles or further.

JOHN MACKIE had a rough time of things last season, but that could change, as two of his decent hurdlers, **Haditovski** and **Silk Trader**, are going over fences and both should win races.

Haditovski, a very useful hurdler on his day, has been crucified by the handicapper, so he's making a logical switch and, while he's not the biggest, he is very brave and hard to pass.

Mackie will start off low-key with him, and get a few confidence-boosters in first. Haditovski likes cut in the ground, as does Silk Trader, who won nicely at Sandown last season and is another who should make the grade over the larger obstacles.

The South
by Southerner

NICK GIFFORD, who has taken over the licence at The Downs near Findon from his legendary Grand National-winning father Josh, is understandably keen to make a rapid impact.

The Gifford stable strength has steadily declined in recent seasons and one of Nick's first priorities will be to reverse that trend. However, quality will not be sacrificed in an effort simply to fill boxes.

Of the horses Nick has inherited from his father, he has particularly great hopes for **Silver Streak**. The grey has had his share of injury problems but, if he stays sound, the Grand National will be his target this term.

His brace of novice wins in 2001-02 showed he had plenty of talent, but he's rarely had the chance to use it since.

Kopeck and **Telimar Prince** are two more expected to make their mark for the rookie handler this winter.

The last-named won a 2m3f handicap hurdle at Newbury in November on his reappearance last term. The following month, he just failed to hold off Spectrometer in a valuable 2m1f handicap hurdle at Cheltenham.

He was far from disgraced when third to subsequent Champion Hurdle winner Rooster Booster in the 2m110yds Agfa Hurdle at Sandown in February.

He signed off for the season with an excellent second to the smart Classified in a

SILVER STREAK: Grand National contender

2m4f Grade 2 hurdle at Fontwell two weeks later. The seven-year-old, who has very few miles on the clock for a horse of his age, should continue to progress and can enjoy a profitable campaign.

Kopeck made the perfect start to his jumping career when winning a 2m novices hurdle at Ascot in December last year. Although he started at the most rewarding odds of 33-1, the Gifford camp were far from surprised when he got the better of the odds-on Puntal at the Berkshire track.

The gelding had been giving every indication at home that he was of similar quality to his ill-fated brother Rouble, who was killed in action at the Cheltenham Festival nine months earlier.

Kopeck was last of the five finishers on his only other outing over timber, the 2m Grade 1 Tote Tolworth Hurdle in January at Wincanton. He struggled home a distance behind his old rival Puntal, who finished second to Thisthatandtother.

Kopeck had been coughing just a few days before that race and his performance should be overlooked – he remains a very exciting prospect.

LUKE DACE's training career continues to go from strength to strength. The former jockey did an excellent job with the modest material he had at his disposal when originally setting up in Lewes.

Now based in Findon, Dace has much better horses under his care, allowing him to make hay while the sun shone during the summer jumping season, when he registered a 33 per cent strike-rate from May to August.

Keltic Heritage has been Dace's flagship runner so far – the grey, who has never stopped improving, won three 3m1f chases last term. He jumps for fun and should continue to pay his way.

EMMA LAVELLE is another trainer very much on the up. Based in Hampshire, she really came to the notice of the general public when her **Self Defense** belied his SP of 100-1 to finish a highly creditable fourth to Rooster Booster in the Smurfit Champion

HAPPY DAYS: Tana River, jockey Barry Fenton, Emma Lavelle (left of Fenton) and friends

Hurdle at Cheltenham in March. The Warning entire was pulled up in the Martell Cognac Aintree Hurdle on his final start, but was found to be lame afterwards.

Tana River did Lavelle proud last season. After playing second fiddle to the highly-regarded Supreme Prince and Coolnagorna in 2m4f novice hurdles at Chepstow in October and November last year, the gelding won his three other starts last season.

He got off the mark over obstacles in a 2m3f novices hurdle at Exeter in December when beating Holland Park by a comfortable length and a half. He then easily accounted for Red Will Danagher in a 2m4f110yds novices hurdle run on heavy going at Leicester in January.

He confirmed his ability to handle testing conditions when coming from a long way back in the home straight to defy top weight in a 2m4f110yds Grade 3 novices handicap hurdle at Sandown in March.

Tana River showed tremendous courage at the Esher venue and is just the type to make up into a high class novice over fences this time around.

Lavelle's neighbour *BRENDAN POWELL* (once a top class jump jockey who partnered 1988 Grand National hero Rhyme 'N' Reason) has wasted no time in proving he also has what it takes to succeed as a trainer.

Powell believes that in **Glanamana** he has a horse in his care who may be capable of gaining him entry to the very exclusive club of those who have both ridden and trained winners of the Grand National. The gelding won a 3m110yds novices handicap chase at Sandown in February in testing conditions on his final start last term.

His jumping was a delight around the tricky Esher circuit and the way he powered up the final climb to the post convinced Powell that he is an ideal candidate for the famous Aintree marathon.

RICHARD ROWE's **Native New Yorker** has a very good strike-rate but remains something of an enigma. The eight-year-old either runs a blinder or a stinker.

He is, therefore, an ideal horse to follow, as, when he wins, he is likely to be returned at a good price.

Dorking trainer *ALBERT ENNIS* feels **Ibis Rochelais** was very unlucky last term. Although he won a 3m handicap chase at Sandown, he also finished second four times, notably to the very favourably handicapped La Landiere on a couple of occasions and when chasing home the revitalised Royal Predica at the Cheltenham Festival.

If the fates are on his side this time, the clean-jumping French-bred could easily pick up a decent prize or two.

GERRY ENRIGHT does well with his small string and the East Sussex trainer is looking forward to campaigning **High Point** in long-distance novice hurdles.

The five-year-old, who has plenty of good form in staying handicaps on the Flat, has shown plenty of aptitude for jumping in his schooling sessions.

Southern stars

Glanamana
Kopeck
Tana River

Stats for Jumpers

TRAINERS JUMP STATISTICS 2002-2003
£14.99 (+95p p&p)

An in-depth statistical analysis
of all winning British and Irish
Jumps Trainers in 2002-2003

ORDER FORM

Please send me..... copy(ies). I have enclosed the necessary remittance
– cheques made payable to Raceform Ltd. Or I wish to pay by
Visa/Mastercard Switch/Delta. My card number is

_ _ _ _   _ _ _ _   _ _ _ _   _ _ _ _   _ _ _ _   _ _ _ _

Card no.   Issue No.   Expiry date
                                   Switch only

Name:_ _

Address: _

_ _

_ _ _ _ _ _ _ _ _ _ _ _ _ _ _ _ Postcode: _ _ _ _ _ _ _ _ _

Email address:_ _

Tel No:_ _

Raceform Ltd, Compton, Newbury, Berkshire, RG20 6NL RPSEP03

WWW.RACEFORM.CO.UK
email:rfsubscription@mgn.co.uk

Raceform

CREDIT CARD HOTLINE:
01635 578080 (24 hours)

Races and Racecourses

Fixtures

October

1 Wednesday..Newcastle, Nottingham, Salisbury
2 Thursday...Brighton, **Hereford**, Newmarket
3 Friday...**Hexham**, Lingfield Park, Newmarket
4 Saturday..**Chepstow**, Epsom Downs, Newmarket,
....Redcar, **Uttoxeter**, *Wolverhampton*
5 Sunday...**Fontwell Park, Kelso, Market Rasen**
6 Monday...**Plumpton**, Pontefract, Windsor
7 Tuesday..Catterick Bridge, Southwell, **Stratford-On-Avon**
8 Wednesday...**Exeter**, Lingfield Park, **Towcester**
9 Thursday..**Ludlow, Wincanton**, York
10 Friday...**Carlisle, Huntingdon**, York
11 Saturday...........................Ascot, **Bangor-On-Dee, Hexham, Southwell**, York
12 Sunday..Bath, Goodwood, Newcastle
13 Monday..Ayr, Leicester, Windsor
14 Tuesday..Ayr, Leicester, **Sedgefield**
15 Wednesday...Lingfield Park, **Uttoxeter, Wetherby**
16 Thursday...Newmarket, Southwell, **Taunton**
17 Friday...Brighton, Newmarket, Redcar
18 Saturday.......................................Catterick Bridge, **Kelso, Market Rasen,**
....Newmarket, **Stratford-On-Avon**
20 Monday...**Plumpton**, Pontefract, Wolverhampton
21 Tuesday...**Exeter**, Southwell, Yarmouth
22 Wednesday..**Chepstow**, Newcastle, Nottingham
23 Thursday...Brighton, **Haydock Park, Ludlow**
24 Friday...Doncaster, **Fakenham**, Newbury
25 Saturday..............**Carlisle**, Doncaster, Musselburgh, **Kempton Park**, Newbury
26 Sunday..**Aintree, Towcester, Wincanton**
27 Monday..**Bangor-On-Dee**, Leicester, Lingfield Park
28 Tuesday...**Cheltenham**, Nottingham, Redcar
29 Wednesday..**Cheltenham, Sedgefield**, Yarmouth
30 Thursday......................................Lingfield Park, **Stratford-On-Avon, Taunton**
31 Friday...Brighton, Newmarket, **Wetherby**

November

1 Saturday.......................**Ascot, Kelso**, Newmarket, **Wetherby**, *Wolverhampton*
2 Sunday...**Carlisle, Huntingdon**, Lingfield Park
3 Monday...**Plumpton**, Redcar, **Warwick**
4 Tuesday...Catterick Bridge, **Exeter, Folkestone**
5 Wednesday...................................Musselburgh, **Kempton Park, Newton Abbot**
6 Thursday...**Haydock Park**, Nottingham, **Towcester**
7 Friday...Doncaster, **Hexham, Uttoxeter**
8 Saturday...........................**Chepstow**, Doncaster, **Sandown Park, Wincanton**
9 Sunday..**Southwell, Worcester**
10 Monday...**Carlisle, Fontwell Park**, Wolverhampton

11	Tuesday	**Huntingdon, Lingfield Park, Sedgefield**
12	Wednesday	**Kelso,** Lingfield Park, **Newbury**
13	Thursday	Lingfield Park, **Ludlow, Taunton**
14	Friday	**Cheltenham, Newcastle,** Wolverhampton
15	Saturday	**Ayr, Cheltenham, Uttoxeter, Wetherby,** *Wolverhampton*
16	Sunday	**Ayr, Cheltenham, Haydock Park**
17	Monday	**Folkestone, Leicester,** Wolverhampton
18	Tuesday	Lingfield Park, **Newton Abbot, Towcester**
19	Wednesday	**Hexham, Kempton Park,** Southwell
20	Thursday	**Hereford, Market Rasen, Wincanton**
21	Friday	**Ascot, Exeter,** Wolverhampton
22	Saturday	**Ascot, Catterick Bridge, Huntingdon,** Lingfield Park, **Aintree**
23	Sunday	**Fakenham, Aintree, Plumpton**
24	Monday	**Ludlow, Newcastle,** Southwell
25	Tuesday	**Sedgefield,** Southwell, **Warwick**
26	Wednesday	**Chepstow,** Lingfield Park, **Wetherby**
27	Thursday	**Carlisle, Taunton, Uttoxeter**
28	Friday	**Bangor-On-Dee, Musselburgh,** Wolverhampton
29	Saturday	**Haydock Park,** Lingfield Park, **Newbury, Newcastle, Towcester,** *Wolverhampton*
30	Sunday	**Doncaster, Newbury**

December

1	Monday	**Folkestone, Kelso,** Wolverhampton
2	Tuesday	**Hereford,** Lingfield Park, **Newton Abbot**
3	Wednesday	**Catterick Bridge, Plumpton,** Southwell
4	Thursday	**Leicester, Market Rasen, Wincanton**
5	Friday	**Exeter, Sandown Park, Southwell**
6	Saturday	**Chepstow,** Lingfield Park, **Sandown Park, Warwick, Wetherby,** *Wolverhampton*
8	Monday	**Ayr, Newcastle,** Wolverhampton
9	Tuesday	**Fontwell Park, Sedgefield,** Southwell
10	Wednesday	**Leicester,** Lingfield Park, **Newbury**
11	Thursday	**Huntingdon, Ludlow, Taunton**
12	Friday	**Cheltenham, Doncaster,** Wolverhampton
13	Saturday	**Cheltenham, Doncaster, Haydock Park, Lingfield Park,** Southwell, *Wolverhampton*
15	Monday	**Plumpton, Towcester,** Wolverhampton
16	Tuesday	**Musselburgh, Folkestone,** Southwell
17	Wednesday	**Bangor-On-Dee, Hexham,** Lingfield Park
18	Thursday	**Catterick Bridge, Exeter, Ludlow**
19	Friday	**Ascot, Uttoxeter,** Wolverhampton
20	Saturday	**Ascot, Hereford,** Lingfield Park, **Newcastle, Warwick**
22	Monday	**Fakenham, Fontwell Park,** Wolverhampton
26	Friday	**Ayr, Huntingdon, Kempton Park, Market Rasen, Sedgefield, Towcester, Uttoxeter, Wetherby, Wincanton,** Wolverhampton
27	Saturday	**Chepstow, Kempton Park, Leicester,** Southwell, **Wetherby**
29	Monday	**Haydock Park,** Lingfield Park, **Newbury, Taunton**
30	Tuesday	**Musselburgh,** Lingfield Park, **Southwell, Stratford-On-Avon**

January

1 Thursday.............................**Catterick Bridge, Cheltenham, Exeter,** Southwell
2 Friday..**Ayr, Folkestone,** Wolverhampton
3 Saturday ....Lingfield Park, **Newcastle, Sandown Park,** Wolverhampton
4 Sunday ....**Plumpton,** Southwell
5 Monday ....Southwell, Wolverhampton
6 Tuesday ....Lingfield Park, Southwell
7 Wednesday......................................**Musselburgh, Hereford,** Lingfield Park
8 Thursday..............................Southwell, **Wincanton,** Wolverhampton
9 Friday.....................................**Ludlow, Towcester,** Wolverhampton
10 Saturday................**Ascot, Haydock Park,** Lingfield Park, **Uttoxeter, Warwick**
12 Monday.............................**Fontwell Park,** Southwell, Wolverhampton
13 Tuesday ....**Leicester, Sedgefield,** Southwell
14 Wednesday..Lingfield Park, **Newbury,** Wolverhampton
15 Thursday ....**Catterick Bridge,** Lingfield Park, Southwell
16 Friday ....**Huntingdon, Kelso,** Wolverhampton
17 Saturday ....**Kempton Park,** Lingfield Park, **Wetherby, Wincanton**
19 Monday ....**Doncaster, Plumpton,** Wolverhampton
20 Tuesday..................................**Folkestone,** Southwell, **Towcester**
21 Wednesday.......................................**Fakenham,** Lingfield Park, **Newcastle**
22 Thursday..**Ludlow,** Southwell, **Taunton**
23 Friday ....**Chepstow, Musselburgh,** Wolverhampton
24 Saturday..........**Catterick Bridge, Cheltenham, Haydock Park,** Lingfield Park
26 Monday ....**Fontwell Park, Wetherby,** Wolverhampton
27 Tuesday ....**Leicester, Sedgefield,** Southwell
28 Wednesday ....**Hexham, Huntingdon,** Lingfield Park
29 Thursday ....**Plumpton,** Southwell, **Warwick**
30 Friday.....................................**Doncaster, Folkestone,** Wolverhampton
31 Saturday ....**Ascot, Ayr, Doncaster,** Lingfield Park, **Uttoxeter**

February

2 Monday...**Exeter, Kempton Park,** Wolverhampton
3 Tuesday...Lingfield Park, Southwell, **Taunton**
4 Wednesday ....**Leicester,** Lingfield Park, **Newcastle**
5 Thursday ....**Kelso,** Southwell, **Towcester**
6 Friday..............................**Catterick Bridge, Hereford,** Wolverhampton
7 Saturday ....**Chepstow,** Lingfield Park, **Sandown Park, Wetherby**
8 Sunday ....**Musselburgh,** Southwell
9 Monday.............................**Fontwell Park,** Southwell, Wolverhampton
10 Tuesday.................................**Market Rasen, Sedgefield,** Southwell
11 Wednesday......................................**Carlisle,** Lingfield Park, **Ludlow**
12 Thursday ....**Huntingdon,** Southwell, **Wincanton**
13 Friday......................................**Bangor-On-Dee, Kempton Park,** Wolverhampton
14 Saturday ....**Ayr, Haydock Park,** Lingfield Park, **Newbury,** *Wolverhampton*
15 Sunday ....**Hereford,** Southwell
16 Monday ....Lingfield Park, **Plumpton,** Wolverhampton
17 Tuesday.................................**Folkestone,** Southwell, Wolverhampton
18 Wednesday ....**Musselburgh, Leicester,** Lingfield Park
19 Thursday ....**Sandown Park,** Southwell, **Taunton**
20 Friday ....**Fakenham, Sandown Park,** Wolverhampton

21	Saturday	**Ascot,** Lingfield Park, **Newcastle, Wincanton**
22	Sunday	**Fontwell Park, Towcester**
23	Monday	**Carlisle,** Lingfield Park, Wolverhampton
24	Tuesday	Lingfield Park, **Sedgefield,** Southwell
25	Wednesday	**Doncaster,** Lingfield Park, **Ludlow**
26	Thursday	**Huntingdon,** Lingfield Park, Southwell
27	Friday	**Kempton Park, Warwick,** Wolverhampton
28	Saturday	**Chepstow, Haydock Park, Kempton Park,** Lingfield Park, **Warwick**
29	Sunday	**Musselburgh,** Southwell

March

1	Monday	**Newcastle, Plumpton,** Wolverhampton
2	Tuesday	**Catterick Bridge, Leicester,** Lingfield Park
3	Wednesday	**Folkestone,** Southwell, **Wetherby**
4	Thursday	Lingfield Park, **Ludlow, Taunton**
5	Friday	**Doncaster, Newbury,** Wolverhampton
6	Saturday	**Doncaster, Huntingdon, Kelso, Newbury**
7	Sunday	**Kempton Park, Market Rasen**
8	Monday	**Fontwell Park,** Lingfield Park, Wolverhampton
9	Tuesday	**Exeter, Hereford,** Lingfield Park
10	Wednesday	**Bangor-On-Dee, Catterick Bridge, Chepstow**
11	Thursday	**Carlisle, Towcester, Wincanton**
12	Friday	**Ayr, Leicester, Sandown Park**
13	Saturday	**Ayr, Newcastle, Sandown Park,** Wolverhampton
14	Sunday	Southwell, **Warwick**
15	Monday	**Plumpton, Stratford-On-Avon, Taunton**
16	Tuesday	**Cheltenham, Sedgefield,** Southwell
17	Wednesday	**Cheltenham, Huntingdon,** Wolverhampton
18	Thursday	**Cheltenham, Hexham,** Southwell
19	Friday	**Fakenham,** Lingfield Park, **Warwick**
20	Saturday	**Ascot,** Lingfield Park, **Newcastle, Uttoxeter**
21	Sunday	**Carlisle, Fontwell Park**
22	Monday	**Hereford, Wetherby,** Wolverhampton
23	Tuesday	**Exeter,** Lingfield Park, Southwell
24	Wednesday	**Chepstow,** Lingfield Park, **Towcester**
25	Thursday	Doncaster, **Ludlow, Wincanton**
26	Friday	Doncaster, Lingfield Park, **Newbury**
27	Saturday	**Bangor-On-Dee,** Doncaster, Kempton Park, **Newbury,** *Wolverhampton*
28	Sunday	**Kelso, Market Rasen**
29	Monday	Lingfield Park, Newcastle, Wolverhampton
30	Tuesday	Folkestone, **Sedgefield,** Southwell
31	Wednesday	Catterick Bridge, Lingfield Park, Nottingham

April

1	Thursday	Leicester, **Aintree, Taunton**
2	Friday	Lingfield Park, **Aintree,** Southwell
3	Saturday	**Hereford,** Lingfield Park, **Aintree,** Newcastle
4	Sunday	**Hexham, Lingfield Park, Wincanton**

5 Monday ....**Kelso,** Southwell, Windsor
6 Tuesday ....**Exeter,** Lingfield Park, Pontefract
7 Wednesday...Folkestone, **Fontwell Park,** Warwick
8 Thursday ....Bath, Musselburgh, **Ludlow**
10 Saturday ....**Carlisle,** Haydock Park, Kempton Park, **Newton Abbot**
11 Sunday ....Musselburgh, **Plumpton, Towcester**
12 Monday....................**Fakenham, Huntingdon,** Kempton Park, **Plumpton,**
....Redcar, **Sedgefield,** Warwick, Yarmouth
13 Tuesday ....**Chepstow, Exeter,** Newmarket
14 Wednesday ....Beverley, **Cheltenham,** Newmarket
15 Thursday...............**Cheltenham,** *Lingfield Park,* Newmarket, Ripon, *Southwell*
16 Friday ....**Ayr,** Newbury, *Southwell, Taunton,* Thirsk
17 Saturday **Ayr, Bangor-On-Dee,** Newbury, *Nottingham,* Thirsk, *Wolverhampton*
18 Sunday ....**Carlisle, Stratford-On-Avon, Wincanton**
19 Monday ....**Hexham,** Lingfield Park, Pontefract, *Windsor, Wolverhampton*
20 Tuesday...Folkestone, Newcastle, Southwell
21 Wednesday ....Catterick Bridge, Epsom Downs, *Lingfield Park,*
....**Perth,** *Worcester*
22 Thursday ....Beverley, **Fontwell Park, Perth,** *Salisbury, Wolverhampton*
23 Friday.................*Chepstow,* **Perth, Sandown Park,** *Warwick,* Wolverhampton
24 Saturday ....*Haydock Park,* Leicester, **Market Rasen,**
....Ripon, **Sandown Park,** *Wolverhampton*
25 Sunday..Brighton, **Ludlow, Wetherby**
26 Monday.........Hamilton Park, *Newcastle,* **Towcester,** *Windsor,* Wolverhampton
27 Tuesday ....Bath, *Lingfield Park,* **Newton Abbot,** *Southwell*
28 Wednesday.................................Ascot, **Cheltenham, Exeter, Kelso,** Pontefract
29 Thursday ....*Ayr,* **Hereford,** *Lingfield Park,* Redcar, Southwell
30 Friday ....**Bangor-On-Dee,** Musselburgh, Nottingham, **Sedgefield,** Worcester

May

1 Saturday...**Haydock Park, Hexham,** Newmarket,
....*Southwell,* Thirsk, **Uttoxeter**
2 Sunday..Hamilton Park, Newmarket, Salisbury
3 Monday..........Doncaster, **Fontwell Park,** Kempton Park, Newcastle, Warwick
4 Tuesday....................................Bath, Brighton, Carlisle, *Catterick Bridge,* **Exeter**
5 Wednesday................**Chepstow,** Chester, *Fakenham,* **Kelso,** *Wolverhampton*
6 Thursday ....Chester, Folkestone, **Ludlow,** Southwell, **Wetherby**
7 Friday.............Chester, *Hamilton Park,* Lingfield Park, Nottingham, **Wincanton**
8 Saturday ....Beverley, **Hexham,** Lingfield Park, *Thirsk,* **Warwick, Worcester**
9 Sunday ....**Market Rasen, Plumpton, Uttoxeter**
10 Monday ....Kempton Park, Redcar, **Towcester,** *Windsor,* Wolverhampton
11 Tuesday............**Hereford, Huntingdon,** *Newton Abbot, Wolverhampton,* York
12 Wednesday...Brighton, **Exeter,** Newcastle, **Perth,** York
13 Thursday ....*Lingfield Park,* **Ludlow, Perth,** Salisbury, York
14 Friday......................*Hamilton Park,* **Aintree,** Newbury, Nottingham, Yarmouth
15 Saturday...**Bangor-On-Dee,** Newbury, Nottingham,
....*Southwell,* Thirsk, **Uttoxeter**
16 Sunday ....**Fakenham,** Ripon, **Worcester**
17 Monday ....Bath, *Musselburgh,* **Newton Abbot,** *Windsor,* Wolverhampton
18 Tuesday............................Beverley, Goodwood, *Leicester,* Redcar, **Towcester**
158

19 Wednesday ....*Folkestone*, Goodwood, **Kelso**, *Sedgefield*, Southwell
20 Thursday.........................*Doncaster*, Goodwood, *Kelso*, Newcastle, **Wetherby**
21 Friday ....Ayr, *Bath*, Haydock Park, Newmarket, *Stratford-On-Avon*
22 Saturday...Ascot, Catterick Bridge, Haydock Park,
....*Kempton Park*, Newmarket, *Stratford-On-Avon*
23 Sunday ....Brighton, **Hereford**, **Southwell**
24 Monday...Beverley, Carlisle, Leicester, *Thirsk*, *Windsor*
25 Tuesday ....*Bangor-On-Dee*, Lingfield Park, Nottingham, Ripon, *Sedgefield*
26 Wednesday ....**Cartmel**, **Fontwell Park**, Lingfield Park, *Nottingham*, *Ripon*
27 Thursday............................Ayr, Bath, *Huntingdon*, **Newton Abbot**, *Wetherby*
28 Friday........Brighton, Catterick Bridge, *Pontefract*, *Towcester*, Wolverhampton
29 Saturday...**Cartmel**, Doncaster, Musselburgh,
....**Hexham**, Kempton Park, *Lingfield Park*
30 Sunday..**Fontwell Park**, Newmarket, **Uttoxeter**
31 Monday ....**Cartmel**, Chepstow, Leicester, Redcar, Sandown Park

June

1 Tuesday ....**Hexham**, Leicester, Redcar, *Sandown Park*
2 Wednesday ....*Beverley*, *Kempton Park*, Newcastle, Nottingham, Yarmouth
3 Thursday.Chepstow, Hamilton Park, Haydock Park, *Sandown Park*, **Uttoxeter**
4 Friday ....Catterick Bridge, Epsom Downs, *Goodwood*,
....*Haydock Park*, Wolverhampton
5 Saturday...Doncaster, Epsom Downs, Haydock Park,
....*Newmarket*, **Perth**, **Worcester**
6 Sunday...Brighton, **Perth**, **Stratford-On-Avon**
7 Monday ....Folkestone, **Newton Abbot**, *Pontefract*, *Windsor*
8 Tuesday ....*Chester*, **Huntingdon**, Redcar, Salisbury
9 Wednesday ....Beverley, *Hamilton Park*, **Hereford**, **Market Rasen**, *Newbury*
10 Thursday...........................*Brighton*, Newbury, Southwell, **Uttoxeter**, Yarmouth
11 Friday................*Chepstow*, *Goodwood*, Sandown Park, Wolverhampton, York
12 Saturday ....Bath, **Hexham**, *Leicester*, *Lingfield Park*, Sandown Park, York
13 Sunday ....Doncaster, Salisbury, **Stratford-On-Avon**
14 Monday ....Brighton, Carlisle, *Warwick*, *Windsor*
15 Tuesday ....Ascot, *Hereford*, *Newton Abbot*, Thirsk
16 Wednesday ....Ascot, Hamilton Park, *Ripon*, Southwell, **Worcester**
17 Thursday...Ascot, *Ayr*, *Beverley*, Ripon, Southwell
18 Friday ....Ascot, Ayr, *Goodwood*, *Newmarket*, Redcar
19 Saturday ....Ascot, Ayr, *Lingfield Park*, Newmarket, Redcar, *Warwick*
20 Sunday ....**Hexham**, Pontefract, Warwick
21 Monday.......................................*Chepstow*, Musselburgh, Nottingham, *Windsor*
22 Tuesday ....Beverley, Brighton, *Newbury*, **Newton Abbot**
23 Wednesday ....*Bath*, Carlisle, *Kempton Park*, Salisbury, **Worcester**
24 Thursday......................*Hamilton Park*, *Leicester*, Newcastle, Salisbury, Thirsk
25 Friday .....Folkestone, *Goodwood*, **Market Rasen**, *Newcastle*, Wolverhampton
26 Saturday...Chester, *Doncaster*, *Lingfield Park*,
....Newcastle, Newmarket, Windsor
27 Sunday ....Goodwood, **Uttoxeter**, Windsor
28 Monday ....*Musselburgh*, Pontefract, *Windsor*, Wolverhampton
29 Tuesday...Brighton, Hamilton Park, **Worcester**
30 Wednesday ...Catterick Bridge, *Kempton Park*, Lingfield Park, **Perth**, *Yarmouth*

Big-race dates

October

26 Sun Wincanton ....Desert Orchid South Western Pattern Chase (2m5f)

November

1 Sat Wetherby ....Peterhouse Group Charlie Hall Chase (3m1f)

Wetherby ....John Smith's West Yorkshire Hurdle (3m1f)

Wetherby....................................Stanley Racing Wensleydale Hurdle (2m)

4 Tue Exeter....williamhill.co.uk Haldon Gold Cup (Limited H'cap Chase) (2m1f110yds)

8 Sat Chepstow.......................Tote Silver Trophy Hurdle (H'cap) (2m4f110yds)

Chepstow..Courage Best Bitter Rising Star Novices Chase (2m3f110yds)

Chepstow ....Persian War Novices Hurdle (2m4f)

Wincanton.............................Badger Brewery H'cap Chase (3m1f110yds)

Wincanton ....Tanglefoot Elite Hurdle (Limited H'cap) (2m)

14 Fri Cheltenham.........................Sporting Index Cross Country Chase (3m7f)

Cheltenham...........................Gerrard Sharp Novices Hurdle (2m110yds)

15 Sat Cheltenham...........Paddy Power Gold Cup (H'cap Chase) (2m4f110yds)

16 Sun Haydock.............................Edward Hanmer Memorial H'cap Chase (3m)

21 Fri Ascot ....Pricewaterhousecoopers Ascot Hurdle (2m4f)

22 Sat Ascot ....First National Bank Gold Cup H'cap Chase (2m3f110yds)

Huntingdon ....Victor Chandler Peterborough Chase (2m4f110yds)

23 Sun Aintree ....Tote Becher Chase (3m3f)

29 Sat Newbury..........Hennessy Cognac Gold Cup H'cap Chase (3m2f110yds)

Newbury.................................Compaq Gerry Feilden Hurdle (2m110yds)

Newcastle...............................Pertempts Fighting Fifth H'cap Hurdle (2m)

December

5 Fri Sandown ....Bovis Lend Lease Winter Novices Hurdle (2m6f)

6 Sat Chepstow ....Rehearsal H'cap Chase (3m)

Sandown................Mitsubushi Shogun Tingle Creek Trophy Chase (2m)

Sandown..William Hill H'cap Hurdle (2m110yds)

Sandown...................................Extraman Henry VIII Novices Chase (2rn)

13 Sat Cheltenham..Bonusprint Bula Hurdle (2m1f)

Cheltenham ....Tripleprint Gold Cup H'cap Chase (2m5f)

Cheltenham ....Tripleprint Bristol Novices Hurdle (3m110yds)

Haydock ....Tommy Whittle Chase (3m)

20 Fri Ascot..........................Cantor Fitzgerald Long Walk Hurdle (3m1f110yds)

Ascot...Gerrard Kennel Gate Hurdle (2m110yds)

20 Sat Ascot ....Tote Silver Cup H'cap Chase (3m110yds)

26 Fri Kempton ....Pertemps King George VI Chase (3m)

Kempton..Pertemps Christmas Hurdle (2m)

Kempton...........................Network Design Feltham Novices Chase (3m)

Wetherby..Castleford Chase (2m)

27 Sat Chepstow....................Coral Welsh National H'cap Chase (3m5f110yds)

Wetherby .... Rowland Meyrick H'cap Chase (3m110yds)
29 Mon Newbury .... Challow Hurdle (2m5f)

January

 1 Thu Cheltenham .... Unicoin H'cap Chase (2m5f)
 3 Sat Sandown .... Gerrard Tolworth Novices Hurdle (2m110yds)
       Sandown .... Anthony Mildmay Peter Cazalet H'cap Chase (3m5f110yds)
       Newcastle .... Cantor Index Dipper Novices Chase (2m4f)
10 Sat Ascot .... Victor Chandler H'cap Chase (2m)
       Ascot .... Lightning Novices Chase (2m)
       Warwick .... Tote Scoop6 Warwick National H'cap Chase (3m5f)
17 Sat Kempton .... Tote Lanzarote H'cap Hurdle (2m)
24 Sat Cheltenham .... Byrne Brothers Cleeve Hurdle (2m5f110yds)
       Cheltenham .... Pillar Property Chase (3m1f110yds)
       Cheltenham .. Wragge & Co Finesse Four-year-old Novices Hurdle (2m1f)
31 Sat Doncaster .... Pertemps Great Yorkshire H'cap Chase (3m)
       Doncaster .... River Don Novices Hurdle (2m4f)
       Uttoxeter .... Singer & Friedlander National Trial H'cap Chase (4m2f)

February

 7 Sat Sandown .... Tote Scoop6 Sandown H'cap Hurdle (2m6f)
       Sandown .... Weatherbys Scilly Isles Novices Chase (2m4f110yds)
       Sandown .... Agfa Diamond H'cap Chase (3m110yds)
       Wetherby .... Gerrard Rossington Main Novices Hurdle (2m)
14 Sat Newbury .... Tote Gold Trophy H'cap Hurdle (2m110yds)
       Newbury .... Sodexho Prestige Game Spirit Chase (2m1f)
       Newbury .... Aon Chase (3m)
21 Sat Ascot .... Ritz Club Ascot Chase (2m3f110yds)
       Ascot .... Gerrard Reynoldstown Novices Chase (3m110yds)
       Newcastle .... Tote Eider National H'cap Chase (4m1f)
       Wincanton .... Axminster Kingwell Hurdle (2m)
       Wincanton .... Jim Ford Challenge Cup (3m1f110yds)
22 Sun Fontwell .... Collins Stuart National Spirit Hurdle (2m4f)
27 Fri Warwick .... Michael Page International Kingmaker Novices Chase (2m)
       Kempton .. Extraman Recruitment Rendlesham H'cap Hurdle (3m110yds)
       Kempton .... Dovecote Novices Hurdle (2m)
28 Sat Kempton .... Racing Post H'cap Chase (3m)

March

 6 Sat Kelso .... Tote Exacta Premier Kelso Novices Hurdle (2m2f)
13 Sat Sandown .... Sunderlands Imperial Cup H'cap Hurdle (2m110yds)
16 Tue Cheltenham .... Irish Independent Arkle Novices Chase (2m)
       Cheltenham ..... Smurfit Champion Hurdle Challenge Trophy (2m110yds)
       Cheltenham .... Gerrard Supreme Novices Hurdle (2m110yds)
       Cheltenham .... Fulke Walwyn Kim Muir H'cap Chase (3m1f)
       Cheltenham .... William Hill National Hunt H'cap Chase (3m110yds)
       Cheltenham .... Pertemps Final H'cap Hurdle (3m1f110yds)

17	Wed	Cheltenham.............................Royal & SunAlliance Novices Chase (3m1f)
		Cheltenham.....................................Queen Mother Champion Chase (2m)
		Cheltenham ....Royal & SunAlliance Novices Hurdle (2m5f)
		Cheltenham.......................National Hunt Challenge Cup (Amateurs) (4m)
		Cheltenham...............................Coral Eurobet Cup (H'cap Hurdle) (2m5f)
		Cheltenham.........................Mildmay of Flete H'cap Chase (2m4f110yds)
		Cheltenham ....Weatherbys Champion Bumper (2m110yds)
18	Thu	Cheltenham..............................Tote Cheltenham Gold Cup Chase (3m2f)
		Cheltenham..Bonusprint Stayers' Hurdle (3m)
		Cheltenham ....JCB Triumph Novices Hurdle (2m1f)
		Cheltenham ....County H'cap Hurdle (2m1f)
		Cheltenham ....Cathcart Chase (2m5f)
		Cheltenham ....Grand Annual Chase (H'cap) (2m110yds)
		Cheltenham............................Christie's Foxhunter Chase (3m2f110yds)
20	Sat	Uttoxeter .....John Smith's Midlands Grand National H'cap Chase (4m2f)
		Uttoxeter........EBF Tattersalls Mares Final Novices Chase (H'cap) (2m5f)
27	Sat	Newbury........Crandon Park Stud EBF Mares' NH Final (Novices) (2m5f)
28	Sun	Kelso..Ashleybank Investments Scottish Border National H'cap Chase (4m)

April

1	Thu	Aintree...Martell Cup Chase (3m1f)
		Aintree...................Martell XO Anniversary Novices Hurdle (2m2f100yds)
		Aintree ....Martell Red Rum H'cap Chase (2m)
		Aintree ....Martell Cognac Fox Hunters' Chase (2m5f110yds)
		Aintree ....Martell Mersey Novices Hurdle (2m4f)
2	Fri	Aintree...Martell Mildmay Novices Chase (3m1f)
		Aintree ....Martell Top Novices Hurdle (2m110yds)
		Aintree ....Martell Cognac H'cap Chase (3m1f)
		Aintree ....John Hughes Trophy (H'cap Chase) (2m6f)
		Aintree....................................Martell Sefton Novices Hurdle (3m110yds)
		Aintree..Martell Melling Chase (2m4f)
		Aintree ....Martell Mersey Novices Hurdle (2m4f)
3	Sat	Aintree...Martell Grand National Chase (4m4f)
		Aintree..Martell Aintree Hurdle (2m4f)
		Aintree ....Martell Maghull Novices Chase (2m)
		Aintree...............................Cordon Bleu Handicap Hurdle (2m110yds)
		Aintree ....Martell Champion Bumper (2m110yds)
13	Tue	Cheptow..............................Welsh Champion Hurdle (2m110yds)
		Cheltenham.....................Faucets For Mira Showers Silver Trophy (2m5f)
17	Sat	Ayr ..Gala Casinos Daily Record Scottish Grand National H'cap Chase (4m1f)
		Ayr ....Samsung Electronics Scottish Champion H'cap Hurdle (2m)
		Ayr .....Ashleybank Investments Future Champion Novices Chase (2m4f)
24	Sat	Sandown.......................Attheraces Gold Cup H'cap Chase (3m5f110yds)

May

| 1 | Sat | Haydock............................Merewood Homes Swinton H'cap Hurdle (2m) |
| 29 | Sat | Stratford....Intrum Justitia Horse And Hound Cup (Hunter Chase) (3m4f) |

Sponsored by Stan James

Big-race Records

Year	Form	Winner	Age-weight	Trainer	Jockey	SP	Ran

Charlie Hall Chase (3m110yds) Wetherby

Year	Form	Winner	Age-weight	Trainer	Jockey	SP	Ran
1993	-	Barton Bank	7-11-2	D Nicholson	A Maguire	12-1	7
1994	-	Young Hustler	7-11-10	N Twiston-Davies	C Llewellyn	8-1	7
1995	-	Barton Bank	9-11-2	D Nicholson	A Maguire	8-15f	3
1996	-	One Man	8-11-10	G Richards	R Dunwoody	8-11f	4
1997	-	One Man	9-11-10	G Richards	R Dunwoody	4-7f	4
1998	-5	Strath Royal	12-11-3	O Brennan	M Brennan	14-1	5
1999	-	See More Business	9-11-12b	P Nicholls	M Fitzgerald	11-4j	6
2000	-	See More Business	10-11-12b	P Nicholls	M Fitzgerald	1-3f	4
2001	-13	Sackville	8-11-5	F Crowley	D Casey	5-1	9
2002	-	Marlborough	10-11-0	N Henderson	M Fitzgerald	7-2	8

Traditionally a race for small fields (resulting in four odds-on winners in the last eight years), the last two renewals of this, the race that marks the start of the jumps season proper, have been more competitive. Even so, a good proportion of the runners have been some way short of peak fitness, and it must pay to look for trainers who can be relied on to have their horse ready, or horses who've already had a run.

Paddy Power Gold Cup (2m4f110yds) Cheltenham

Year	Form	Winner	Age-weight	Trainer	Jockey	SP	Ran
1993	-1	Bradbury Star	8-11-8	J Gifford	D Murphy	13-2	15
1994	-2	Bradbury Star	9-12-0	J Gifford	P Hide	5-1	14
1995	-	Dublin Flyer	9-11-8	T Forster	B Powell	4-1j	12
1996	-	Challenger Du Luc	6-10-2b	M Pipe	R Dunwoody	7-1	12
1997	-F2	Senor El Betrutti	8-10-0	S Nock	J Osborne	33-1	9
1998	-	Cyfor Malta	5-11-3	M Pipe	A McCoy	3-1f	12
1999	-1	The Outback Way	9-10-0	V Williams	N Williamson	9-1	14
2000	-	Lady Cricket	6-10-13b	M Pipe	A McCoy	5-1f	15
2001	-1	Shooting Light	8-11-3v	M Pipe	A McCoy	9-4f	14
2002	-	Cyfor Malta	9-11-9	M Pipe	B Geraghty	16-1	15

AKA 'The Thomas Pink', 'The Murphys','The Mackeson'. As with all valuable chases at Cheltenham, winning form at the track counts for a lot – of the past ten winners, only Senor El Betrutti had not previously won over fences here. In over 40 renewals of this race, just three winners have been aged ten or over, so side with up-and-coming talent.

First National Gold Cup H'cap Chase (2m3f110yds) Ascot

Year	Form	Winner	Age-weight	Trainer	Jockey	SP	Ran
1993		*Abandoned*					
1994	-	Raymylette	7-11-10	N Henderson	M Fitzgerald	10-1	11
1995	-1	Sound Man	7-12-0	E O'Grady	R Dunwoody	4-5f	5
1996	-2112	Strong Promise	5-10-5	G Hubbard	K Gaule	6-4f	8
1997	-1	Simply Dashing	6-11-10	T Easterby	R Dunwoody	4-1	11
1998	-11	Red Marauder	8-10-11	N Mason	R Guest	5-1	11
1999	-	Nordance Prince	8-10-9	V Williams	R Johnson	8-1	11
2000	-2	Upgrade	6-11-8	M Pipe	A McCoy	7-4j	4
2001	-	Wahiba Sands	8-10-4	M Pipe	A McCoy	4-1	4
2002		*Abandoned*					

Confined to chasers who are either novices or just out of their novice season, this race demands an unusual mix of stamina and speed.

Hennessy Cognac Gold Cup H'cap Chase (3m2f) Newbury

1993	-2	**Cogent**	9-10-1	A Turnell	D Fortt	10-1	9
1994	-1	**One Man**	6-10-0	G Richards	R Dunwoody	4-1	16
1995	-1	**Couldnt Be Better**	8-10-8	C Brooks	G Bradley	15-2	11
1996	-11	**Coome Hill**	7-10-0	W Dennis	J Osborne	11-2	11
1997	-1	**Suny Bay**	8-11-8	C Brooks	G Bradley	9-4f	14
1998	-1	**Teeton Mill**	9-10-5	V Williams	N Williamson	5-1	16
1999	-1	**Ever Blessed**	7-10-0	M Pitman	T Murphy	9-2f	13
2000	-2	**King's Road**	7-10-7	N Twiston-Davies	J Goldstein	7-1	17
2001	-	**What's Up Boys**	7-10-12	P Hobbs	P Flynn	14-1	14
2002	-1311	**Be My Royal**	8-10-0	W Mullins	D Casey	33-1	25

This often goes to improving second-season chasers, a description which applied to the last four winnners (though Be My Royal may yet be disqualified, as one of a number of victims of morphine-contaminated feed last autumn). Only a top class horse can win if carrying a lot of weight; Burrough Hill Lad, Mill House and Arkle all won with more than 11st10lb. Suny Bay was the first outright favourite to go in since Burrough Hill Lad in 1985.

Fighting Fifth Hurdle (2m) Newcastle

1993		*Abandoned*					
1994	-4	**Batabanoo**	5-11-0	M Reveley	P Niven	6-4f	4
1995*	-118	**Padre Mio**	7-10-10	C Brooks	Richard Guest	5-1	7
1996*	-122121	**Space Trucker**	5-10-4	J Harrington	J Shortt	5-2	8
1997*	-15	**Star Rage**	7-11-2	M Johnston	D Gallagher	6-1	8
1998	-	**Dato Star**	7-11-8	J M Jefferson	L Wyer	13-8f	6
1999	-	**Dato Star**	8-11-8	J M Jefferson	L Wyer	4-9f	9
2000	-	**Barton**	7-11-0	T Easterby	A Dobbin	8-13f	6
2001	-	**Landing Light**	6-11-8	N Henderson	M Fitzgerald	4-5f	5
2002	-11	**Intersky Falcon**	5-11-8	J O'Neill	L Cooper	11-10f	6

run as a limited handicap

A race whose influence has been in decline for at least 15 years. The experiment of turning it into a handicap didn't work and since then the field has usually consisted of a Champion Hurdle contender and a bunch of no-marks, with the favourite winning every time.

Tingle Creek Trophy Chase (2m) Sandown

1993*	-	**Sybillin**	7-11-9	J Fitzgerald	P Niven	6-1	7
1994	-	**Viking Flagship**	7-11-7	D Nicholson	A Maguire	9-2	6
1995	-11	**Sound Man**	7-11-7	E O'Grady	R Dunwoody	5-6f	5
1996	-121	**Sound Man**	8-11-7	E O'Grady	R Dunwoody	10-11f	4
1997	-P	**Ask Tom**	8-11-7	T Tate	R Garritty	6-1	7
1998	-2	**Direct Route**	7-11-7	J H Johnson	N Williamson	7-1	10
1999	-1	**Flagship Uberalles**	5-11-7	P Nicholls	J Tizzard	100-30	6
2000**	-	**Flagship Uberalles**	6-11-7	N Chance	R Johnson	3-1f	7
2001	-	**Flagship Uberalles**	7-11-7	P Hobbs	R Widger	7-2	6
2002	-	**Cenkos**	8-11-7	P Nicholls	R Walsh	6-1	6

run as a handicap

**run at Cheltenham*

Changed from a handicap to a conditions event ahead of the 1994 renewal. In 30 runnings of the race, no horse older than nine has won and only three nine-year-olds have done so. Outsiders hardly ever get a look-in.

William Hill H'cap Hurdle (2m) Sandown

1993	-014	**Land Afar**	6-11-2	J Webber	W Marston	13-2	12
1994	-11	**Relkeel**	5-10-2	D Nicholson	A Maguire	4-5f	7
1995	-U91	**Chief's Song**	5-10-10	S Dow	R Dunwoody	15-2	22
1996	-111125	**Make A Stand**	5-10-5	M Pipe	G Tormey (3)	9-1	15
1997	-0545	**Major Jamie**	6-10-0	A Moore	R Walsh	25-1	21
1998	-22253	**Polar Prospect**	5-10-0	P Hobbs	G Tormey	16-1	13
1999	-21	**Copeland**	4-10-5b	M Pipe	D Casey	7-1	12
2000		*Abandoned*					
2001	-1431	**Rob Leach**	4-9-12b	G L Moore	F Keniry (3)	14-1	11
2002	-	**Spirit Leader**	6-10-0	J Harrington	N Williamson	9-2	12

Often run on dead ground or going with some give, exaggerating the effect of weight carried, so that topweights have not done well. Martin Pipe can usually be expected to have a contender, though note that Copeland beat a more fancied stablemate. The race often features Irish raiders, who've won twice in the last five renewals.

Tripleprint Gold Cup H'cap Chase (2m5f) Cheltenham

1993	-	**Fragrant Dawn**	9-10-2	M Pipe	D Murphy	14-1	11
1994	-1	**Dublin Flyer**	8-10-2	T Forster	B Powell	10-3	11
1995		*Abandoned*					
1996	-3	**Addington Boy**	8-11-10	G Richards	A Dobbin	7-4f	10
1997	-F21	**Senor El Betrutti**	8-11-3	S Nock	G Bradley	9-1	9
1998	-3	**Northern Starlight**	7-10-1	M Pipe	A McCoy	15-2	13
1999	-P11	**Legal Right**	6-10-13	J O'Neill	R Johnson	6-1	9
2000	-2	**Go Roger Go**	8-11-0	E O'Grady	N Williamson	7-1	12
2001		*Abandoned*					
2002	-3	**Fondmort**	6-10-5	N Henderson	M Fitzgerald	5-1	9

AKA 'The Massey-Ferguson'. The Paddy Power Gold Cup, held here four weeks earlier, is a useful guide and three of the last 11 winners of this have come from that race. Senor El Betrutti did the double, whilst Addington Boy and Another Coral stepped up on placed efforts. To underline the trend, Challenger du Luc followed home Senor El Betrutti in a reproduction of their Paddy Power one-two. The last seven winners had had at least one prep-run.

Bula Hurdle (2m1f) Cheltenham

1993	-1	**Staunch Friend**	5-11-8	M Tompkins	D Murphy	6-1	7
1994	-21	**Large Action**	6-11-4	O Sherwood	J Osborne	8-11f	8
1995		*Abandoned*					
1996	-111	**Large Action**	8-11-8	O Sherwood	J Osborne	5-4f	7
1997	-	**Relkeel**	8-11-0	D Nicholson	R Johnson	8-1	8
1998	-	**Relkeel**	9-11-8	D Nicholson	A Maguire	8-1	5
1999	-	**Relkeel**	10-11-8	A King	R Johnson	13-2	7
2000	-3	**Geos**	5-11-4	N Henderson	M Fitzgerald	14-1	8
2001		*Abandoned*					
2002	-11	**Rooster Booster**	8-11-4	P Hobbs	R Johnson	11-8f	9

Ought to be an ideal trial for the Champion Hurdle but serious contenders have not been much in evidence in recent seasons – though it's possible that Rooster Booster's success may make it more fashionable. Again, Cheltenham specialists are usually to the fore.

Long Walk Hurdle (3m1f110yds) Ascot

1993	-222	**Sweet Duke**	6-11-7	N Twiston-Davies	C Llewellyn	7-2	9
1994	-21	**Hebridean**	7-11-7	D Nicholson	A Maguire	10-3	8
1995	-3	**Silver Wedge**	4-11-7	O Sherwood	J Osborne	7-1	11

1996	-12	**Ocean Hawk**	4-11-7	N Twiston-Davies	C Llewellyn	7-1	6
1997	-5	**Paddy's Return**	5-11-7	F Murphy	N Williamson	8-1	7
1998	-1	**Princeful**	7-11-7	J Pitman	R Dunwoody	11-4f	11
1999	-3	**Anzum**	8-11-7	A King	R Johnson	4-1	6
2000	-	**Baracouda**	5-11-7	F Doumen	T Doumen	11-4	9
2001	-1	**Baracouda**	6-11-7	F Doumen	T Doumen	2-5f	5
2002	-23	**Deano's Beeno**	10-11-7	M Pipe	A McCoy	14-1	5

Silver Wedge was the first four-year-old to win and was also untypical in that he was un-proven over the trip. The two key races have been Chepstow's Tote Silver Trophy and Newbury's Long Distance Hurdle, which Princeful bagged en route to this race in 1998 and in which Anzum finished third in 1999. Only appalling riding by Thierry Doumen pre-vented Baracouda from taking this for the third time last season.

Silver Cup H'cap Chase (3m110yds) Ascot

1993	-2	**Young Hustler**	6-10-1	N Twiston-Davies	C Llewellyn	11-8f	8
1994	-1	**Raymylette**	7-10-9	N Henderson	M Fitzgerald	3-1j	8
1995	-12	**Unguided Missile**	7-10-8	G Richards	R Dunwoody	7-2c	9
1996	-412	**Go Ballistic**	7-10-0	J O'Shea	A McCoy	4-1f	9
1997	-71	**Cool Dawn**	9-10-5	R Alner	A Thornton	5-2f	6
1998	-12	**Torduff Express**	7-10-0	P Nicholls	N Williamson	9-2	7
1999	-4F	**Tresor de Mai**	5-11-1b	M Pipe	A McCoy	10-1	9
2000	-	**Legal Right**	7-12-0	J O'Neill	N Williamson	7-1	7
2001	-11	**Shooting Light**	8-11-6v	M Pipe	A McCoy	5-2f	9
2002	-6	**Behrajan**	7-11-12	H Daly	R Johnson	7-1	7

AKA 'The SGB', 'The Betterware Gold Cup'. Some indication of how small the gap is be-tween races like the Cheltenham Gold Cup and a competitive handicap such as this is illustrated by Go Ballistic, who won with bottom weight and went on to finish fourth, beat-en 15l by Mr Mulligan at Cheltenham. Cool Dawn went three better in the '98 Blue Riband, but the last renewal lost a lot of quality when subsequent Gold Cup runner-up Truckers Tavern fell at the first.

King George VI Chase (3m) Kempton

1993	-11	**Barton Bank**	7-11-10	D Nicholson	A Maguire	9-2	10
1994	-	**Algan**	6-11-10	F Doumen	P Chevallier	16-1	9
1995*	-11	**One Man**	8-11-10	G Richards	R Dunwoody	11-4f	11
1996	-1	**One Man**	8-11-10	G Richards	R Dunwoody	8-13f	5
1997	-31	**See More Business**	7-11-10	P Nicholls	A Thornton	10-1	8
1998	-11	**Teeton Mill**	9-11-10	V Williams	N Williamson	7-2	9
1999	-1	**See More Business**	9-11-10b	P Nicholls	M Fitzgerald	5-2	9
2000	-1	**First Gold**	7-11-10	F Doumen	T Doumen	5-2	9
2001	-31	**Florida Pearl**	9-11-10	W Mullins	A Maguire	8-1	8
2002	-1	**Best Mate**	7-11-10	H Knight	A McCoy	11-8f	10

run at Sandown in January 1996

A race which the best performers often manage to win several times. Francois Doumen has won this race five times with four different horses. Runners with course form do well, while stamina doubts count for less over this quick 3m than at other top-flight tracks.

Christmas Hurdle (2m) Kempton

1993	-03	**Muse**	6-11-7	D Elsworth	M Richards	3-1	5
1994	-12213	**Absalom's Lady**	6-11-2	D Elsworth	P Holley	9-2	6
1995		*Abandoned*					
1996		*Abandoned*					

166

1997	-230	**Kerawi**	4-11-7	N Twiston-Davies	C Llewellyn	4-1	5
1998	-P2	**French Holly**	7-11-7	F Murphy	A Thornton	5-2	5
1999	-1	**Dato Star**	8-11-7	J M Jefferson	L Wyer	11-8	4
2000	-31	**Geos**	5-11-7	N Henderson	M Fitzgerald	9-4	7
2001	-1	**Landing Light**	6-11-7	N Henderson	M Fitzgerald	5-4f	5
2002	-11	**Intersky Falcon**	5-11-7b	J O'Neill	C Swan	Evensf	6

A small but competitive field is the order of the day, which makes it pretty unappetising fare for punters. The winner has often come from just below Champion Hurdle standard in recent seasons.

Welsh National H'cap Chase (3m5f110yds) Chepstow

1993	-2	**Riverside Boy**	10-10-0	M Pipe	R Dunwoody	6-4f	8
1994*	-1	**Master Oats**	8-11-6	K Bailey	N Williamson	5-2f	8
1995		*Abandoned*					
1996		*Abandoned*					
1997	-55	**Earth Summit**	9-10-13b	N Twiston-Davies	T Jenks	25-1	14
1998	-2	**Kendal Cavalier**	8-10-0	N Hawke	B Fenton	14-1	14
1999	-11	**Edmond**	7-10-0	H Daly	R Johnson	4-1	16
2000	-42	**Jocks Cross**	9-10-4	V Williams	B Crowley	14-1	19
2001	-14	**Supreme Glory**	8-10-0	P Murphy	L Aspell	10-1	13
2002	-4	**Mini Sensation**	9-10-4	J O'Neill	A Dobbin	8-1	16

*run at Newbury

As with most staying handicap chases that are often run in the mud, horses outside the handicap have a better chance of winning and a much better chance of making the frame than their odds generally suggest; Kendal Cavalier was 13lb 'wrong', Supreme Glory 3lb. Dom Samourai, from 5lb out of the handicap, would have won in 1997, given a few more strides. This was a Martin Pipe benefit between 1988 and 1993 – his stable won five out of the six runnings. In over 50 runnings, only three winners have carried 11st10lb or more.

Rowland Meyrick Chase (3m1f) Wetherby

1993	-2346	**General Pershing**	7-10-13	G Richards	N Doughty	3-1	5
1994	-F4	**Cogent**	10-10-8	J Glover	Mr C Bonner (5)	7-2	3
1995		*Abandoned*					
1996		*Abandoned*					
1997	-2111	**Strath Royal**	11-10-10	O Brennan	M Brennan	3-1	4
1998	-U14121	**Random Harvest**	9-9-11	M Reveley	A Dempsey (3)	9-4	4
1999		*Abandoned*					
2000		*Abandoned*					
2001	-332	**Behrajan**	6-11-10	H Daly	M Bradburne	5-2f	12
2002		*Abandoned*					

A race that has often been disrupted by small fields and abandonments, so it's hard to be bullish about any particular trends, but there are usually some quality runners when it's actually staged, so it's always worth watching for clues to the future.

Mildmay, Cazalet Memorial H'cap Chase (3m5f110yds) Sandown

1994		*Abandoned*					
1995	-00	**Deep Bramble**	8-11-3	P Nicholls	C Maude	11-2	10
1996	-33	**Superior Finish**	10-10-9	J Pitman	A Maguire	8-1	16
1997		*Abandoned*					
1998	-111	**Him Of Praise**	8-10-10	O Sherwood	J McCarthy	3-1f	14
1999	-24	**Eudipe**	7-12-0	M Pipe	A McCoy	6-1	9
2000	-12	**Lancastrian Jet**	9-10-10	H Daly	A Thornton	4-1	8

2001		Abandoned
2002		Abandoned
2003		Abandoned

Eight-year-olds have taken almost half of the runnings. Superior Finish was only the fifth winner aged over nine. Good recent form is a bonus, as is proven stamina over at least 3m2f. Most of the winners had run in the Hennessy and/or the Welsh National. You wouldn't want your house on this race taking place, though.

Pierse H'cap Hurdle (2m) Leopardstown

1994	-123	Atone	7-10-8	J Cox	K O'Brien	10-1	25
1995	-121114	Anusha	5-10-2	M Hourigan	J Broderick	25-1	17
1996	-231131	Dance Beat	5-9-12	J Harrington	A Powell	12-1	22
1997	-02	Master Tribe	7-10-4	J Pitman	N Williamson	16-1	23
1998	-	Graphic Equaliser	6-10-0	A Moore	C O'Dwyer	5-1f	20
1999	-005	Archive Footage	7-11-8b	P Mullins	D Evans	25-1	25
2000	-215	Mantles Prince	6-9-12	P Hughes	F Berry	12-1	14
2001	-2	Grinkov	6-10-7	P Hughes	C Swan	11-2	24
2002	-54	Adamant Approach	8-11-1	W Mullins	R Walsh	8-1	26
2003	-2	Xenophon	7-10-11	A Martin	M Fitzgerald	12-1	28

AKA 'The Ladbroke'. Master Tribe was Britain's only winner since 1987 – there were 49 British-trained losers between the two success stories and there have been plenty more since. Arthur Moore has a fantastic record, winning this five times between 1979 and 1988 and again in 1998. Most winners are aged five, six or seven. Adamant Approach was only the third older winner and no four-year-old has won since 1977. Favourites have a dismal record.

Tote Gold Trophy H'cap Hurdle (2m110yds) Newbury

1994	-2111	Large Action	6-10-8	O Sherwood	J Osborne	9-2	11
1995	-01	Mysilv	5-10-8	C Egerton	J Osborne	9-4f	8
1996	-1404	Squire Silk	7-10-12	A Turnell	P Carberry	13-2	18
1997	-25111	Make A Stand	6-11-7	M Pipe	A McCoy	6-1	18
1998	-26	Sharpical	6-11-1b	N Henderson	M Fitzgerald	10-1	14
1999	-242	Decoupage	7-11-0	C Egerton	J McCarthy	6-1	18
2000	-132	Geos	5-11-3	N Henderson	M Fitzgerald	15-2	17
2001	-31	Landing Light	6-10-2	N Henderson	M Fitzgerald	4-1f	20
2002	-21	Copeland	7-11-7v	M Pipe	A McCoy	13-2	16
2003	-2315	Spirit Leader	7-10-0	J Harrington	N Williamson	14-1	27

AKA 'The Schweppes'. Copeland was only the eighth winner since 1970 to have defied more than 11st. On the usual soggy going, lightweights have a pronounced advantage in what is invariably a strongly-run race. January's Lanzarote Hurdle at Kempton often supplies a fancied contender but only Grey Salute has completed the double; Copeland was only beaten a length in the Kempton race in 2002, while Lanzarote winner Non So was just edged out by Spirit Leader.

Eider National H'cap Chase (4m1f) Newcastle

1994		Abandoned					
1995	-1D14121	Willsford	12-10-6	J Pitman	P Niven	4-1	10
1996	-557321	Killeshin	10-10-0	H Manners	S Curran	9-1	15
1997	-511	Seven Towers	8-11-8	M Reveley	P Niven	2-1f	12
1998	-1P14	Domaine de Pron	7-10-0	L Taylor	R Supple	9-2	11
1999	-003201P	Hollybank Buck	9-10-11t	A Martin	F Flood	10-1	15
2000	-23P21	Scotton Green	9-10-2	T Easterby	L Wyer	8-1	16

2001	-121	**Narrow Water**	8-11-5*t*	F Murphy	A Maguire	6-1	12
2002	-301	**This Is Serious**	8-11-2	C Swan	A Dobbin	4-1f	15
2003		*Abandoned*					

AKA 'The Northern National'. Though regarded as a Grand National pointer, this is a race for dour stayers who lack the pace and class for Aintree. Five winners have been veterans aged 12 or over, though some progressive young horses have won recently.

Racing Post H'cap Chase (3m) Kempton

1994	-522U14	**Antonin**	6-10-9	S Bramall	J Burke	7-1	16
1995	-211	**Val D'Alene**	8-11-2	F Doumen	A Kondrat	11-2	9
1996	-F22F	**Rough Quest**	10-10-8	T Casey	R Dunwoody	3-1j	9
1997	-42	**Mudahim**	11-10-2	J Pitman	R Farrant	14-1	9
1998	-113U2	**Super Tactics**	10-10-10	R Alner	A Thornton	4-1	7
1999	-63411	**Dr Leunt**	8-11-5	P Hobbs	R Dunwoody	3-1f	8
2000	-131	**Gloria Victis**	6-11-10	M Pipe	R Johnson	100-30f	13
2001	-321	**Young Spartacus**	4-11-0	H Daly	R Johnson	9-1	15
2002	-2221	**Gunther McBride**	7-10-3	P Hobbs	R Johnson	5-1	14
2003	-211111	**La Landiere**	8-11-7	R Phillips	W Marston	5-1j	14

With 1998's substandard renewal apart, this is a race for class horses, but it has also proved a fine pointer to both the Aintree and Irish Grand Nationals. Of the 50 winners of this race, 28 carried 11st or more, with 12 defying 11st10lb or more. Richard Johnson's agent seems to have developed a good nose for the sort of horse that does well here, though he turned down the winning ride last season in favour of staying loyal to runner-up Gunther McBride.

Red Square Vodka Gold Cup H'cap Chase (3m4f) Haydock

1994*	-1121	**Master Oats**	8-10-2	K Bailey	N Williamson	11-4j	12
1995	-12223	**Nuaffe**	10-11-0	P Fahy	S O'Donovan	4-1	10
1996	-12	**Lo Stregone**	10-10-0	T Tate	C Swan	7-2	11
1997	-5	**Suny Bay**	10-10-8	C Brooks	J Osborne	7-2	5
1998	-121242	**Dom Samourai**	7-10-0	M Pipe	C Maude	10-1	15
1999	-22412U	**Young Kenny**	8-10-0	P Beaumont	B Powell	9-1	13
2000	-1421	**The Last Fling**	10-11-1	S Smith	S Durack	5-1	7
2001	-U21	**Frantic Tan**	9-10-4	N Twiston-Davies	C Llewellyn	7-2f	18
2002		*Abandoned*					
2003	-	**Shotgun Willy**	9-11-12	P Nicholls	R Walsh	10-1	17

*run at Kempton

AKA 'The Greenalls', 'The De Vere Gold Cup'. This race is usually run on soft and can prove a real test of stamina. It's also a decent trial for the Grand National, with Earth Summit finishing fifth before his moment of glory; the consensus is that Haydock's drop fences are a good preparation for Aintree. Shotgun Willy was sent off as National favourite after winning this, but was weighted out of it on the big day.

Imperial Cup H'cap Hurdle (2m) Sandown

1994	-4F	**Precious Boy**	8-11-7	M Meagher	L Wyer	33-1	13
1995	-44	**Collier Bay**	5-10-2	J Old	T Grantham	6-1	10
1996	-0002	**Amancio**	5-10-8	G Harwood	M Fitzgerald	5-1	11
1997	-4141	**Carlito Brigante**	5-10-0	P Webber	J Osborne	10-1	18
1998	-403	**Blowing Wind**	5-11-10	M Pipe	A McCoy	5-1f	15
1999	-00	**Regency Rake**	7-10-7	A Moore	A Maguire	7-1	9
2000	-P	**Magic Combination**	7-10-0	B Curley	D Casey	11-1	18
2001	-213	**Ibal**	5-9-9	N Smith	B Hitchcott	16-1	23

| 2002 | -2221 | **Polar Red** | 5-11-1*v* | M Pipe | A McCoy | 6-4f | 16 |
| 2003 | -25053141 | **Korelo** | 5-11-6 | M Pipe | A McCoy | 9-4f | 17 |

This falls on the eve of Cheltenham and, with the sponsors putting up a bonus for horses winning here as well as at Cheltenham, a strong field is usually assured. Look for a young horse with just a handful of runs that season and, ideally, a weight of around 10st. Martin Pipe loves to win this and doesn't seem to have lost the knack of getting one to Esher on a fair mark.

Supreme Novices' Hurdle (2m110yds) Cheltenham

1994	-16143	**Arctic Kinsman**	6-11-8	N Twiston-Davies	C Llewellyn	50-1	18
1995	-2134	**Tourist Attraction**	7-11-3	W Mullins	Mark Dwyer	25-1	20
1996	-311	**Indefence**	5-11-8	J Pitman	W Marston	25-1	27
1997	-11	**Shadow Leader**	6-11-8	C Egerton	J Osborne	5-1	16
1998	-31	**French Ballerina**	5-11-3	P Flynn	G Bradley	10-1	30
1999	-111	**Hors La Loi III**	4-11-0	M Pipe	A McCoy	9-2	20
2000	-11	**Sausalito Bay**	6-11-8	N Meade	P Carberry	14-1	15
2001		*Abandoned*					
2002	-1111	**Like-A-Butterfly**	8-11-3	C Roche	C Swan	7-4f	28
2003	-211	**Back In Front**	6-11-8	E O'Grady	N Williamson	3-1f	19

Like-A-Butterfly was the first winning favourite for over a decade. A happy hunting ground for the Irish, with five of the last eight winners, though only two of those started as the most fancied raider. Not all horses cope well with big fields; eight of the last ten winners had already won in fields of 15 or more.

Arkle Chase (2m) Cheltenham

1994	-11	**Nakir**	6-11-8	S Christian	J Osborne	9-1	10
1995	-F1211	**Klairon Davis**	6-11-8	A Moore	F Woods	7-2f	20
1996	-112F2	**Ventana Canyon**	7-11-8	E O'Grady	R Dunwoody	7-1	16
1997	-112	**Or Royal**	6-11-8*b*	M Pipe	A McCoy	11-2	9
1998	-11311	**Champleve**	5-11-0	M Pipe	A McCoy	13-2	16
1999	-221211	**Flagship Uberalles**	5-11-0	P Nicholls	J Tizzard	11-1	14
2000	-111	**Tiutchev**	7-11-8	N Henderson	M Fitzgerald	8-1	12
2001		*Abandoned*					
2002	-111F	**Moscow Flyer**	8-11-8	J Harrington	B Geraghty	11-2	12
2003	-111	**Azertyuiop**	6-11-8	P Nicholls	R Walsh	5-4f	9

A typical Arkle winner tends to have plenty of winning experience over fences but that doesn't mean they always start favourite – Sybillin (5-6), Mulligan (11-10), Baydon Star (5-2), Seebald (5-2) and Deep Sensation (3-1) were heavily-backed beaten favourites. Moscow Flyer was the third winner in the last ten years to have previously come a cropper, but none of the last ten winners was ever outside the first two in their previous completed starts over fences.

Champion Hurdle (2m110yds) Cheltenham

1994	-43421131	**Flakey Dove**	8-11-9	R Price	Mark Dwyer	9-1	15
1995	-1	**Alderbrook**	6-12-0	K Bailey	N Williamson	11-2	14
1996	-11	**Collier Bay**	6-12-0	J Old	G Bradley	9-1	16
1997	-1251111	**Make A Stand**	6-12-0	M Pipe	A McCoy	7-1	17
1998	-1111	**Istabraq**	6-12-0	A O'Brien	C Swan	3-1f	18
1999	-1111	**Istabraq**	7-12-0	A O'Brien	C Swan	4-9f	14
2000	-1211	**Istabraq**	8-12-0	A O'Brien	C Swan	8-15f	12
2001		*Abandoned*					
2002	-2331	**Hors La Loi III**	7-12-0*t*	J Fanshawe	D Gallagher	10-1	15
2003	-1111	**Rooster Booster**	9-12-0	P Hobbs	R Johnson	9-2	17

Sponsored by Stan James

More competitive than the short winning SPs would suggest – Hors La Loi was the fifth winner from the last ten to feature outside the front three in the betting. Group-class Flat racers Royal Gait and Alderbrook encouraged several to follow the same path, while Istabraq was a classy handicapper on the Flat. A big-priced runner often makes the frame, with Martin Pipe supplying two such placed outsiders (Pridwell and Westender, both 33-1) in the last seven runnings.

William Hill National Hunt H'cap Chase (3m110yds) Cheltenham

1994	-522U141	Antonin	6-11-5	S Bramall	J Burke (5)	4-1f	11
1995	-332	Rough Quest	9-10-3	T Casey	M Fitzgerald	16-1	16
1996	-U121	Maamur	8-10-0	T Forster	A Thornton	13-2	10
1997	-P1P	Flyer's Nap	11-11-2	R Alner	D Bridgwater	20-1	14
1998	-642F4	Unguided Missile	10-11-10	G Richards	P Carberry	10-1	13
1999	-16	Betty's Boy	10-10-2	K Bailey	N Williamson	25-1	18
2000	-PU12	Marlborough	8-10-3	N Henderson	M Fitzgerald	11-2	12
2001		*Abandoned*					
2002	-133	Frenchman's Creek	8-10-5	H Morrison	P Carberry	8-1	23
2003	-131	Youlneverwalkalone	9-10-11	C Roche	B Geraghty	7-1	18

AKA 'The Ritz Club'. Not a strong 'trends' race, with winners spread evenly across weights and ages. Only two of the last ten winners lacked previous winning form at 3m or further, and both had previously been placed over that trip on soft ground.

Fulke Walwyn Kim Muir H'cap Chase (3m110yds) Cheltenham

1994	-23316	Fighting Words	8-10-0	J Gifford	Mr T McCarthy (7)	9-2f	15
1995	-11102	Flyer's Nap	9-9-10	R Alner	Mr P Henley (7)	11-1	16
1996	1FF22212	Stop The Waller	7-9-11	F Murphy	Mr K Whelan (5)	16-1	22
1997	-3322	King Lucifer	8-11-5	D Nicholson	Mr R Thornton (5)	7-2	11
1998	-23242225	In Truth	10-9-9	S Gollings	Mr S Durack (5)	20-1	14
1999	-1	Celtic Giant	9-10-0	L Lungo	Mr B Gibson (3)	20-1	22
2000	-212341	Honey Mount	9-9-12	R Alner	Mr R Walford (5)	8-1	23
2001		*Abandoned*					
2002	-1	The Bushkeeper	8-11-2	N Henderson	Mr D Crosse	9-2f	23
2003	-	Royal Predica	9-10-13	M Pipe	Mr S McHugh (7)	33-1	23

Weight counts for plenty, with six of the last nine winners carrying 10st or less. Though favourites have a moderate record, this has usually been one of the more predictable handicaps at the Festival. An impressive proportion of the succesful jockeys have gone on to professional careers.

Pertemps Final H'cap Hurdle (3m1f110yds) Cheltenham

1994	-453	Tindari	6-10-9	J M Jefferson	P Williams (3)	20-1	32
1995	-111	Miracle Man	7-10-11	C Weedon	Peter Hobbs	9-2f	23
1996	-5211	Great Easeby	6-10-1	W Storey	R McGrath (7)	7-1	24
1997	-31F1	Pharanear	7-11-9	D Nicholson	R Thornton (5)	14-1	24
1998	-111	Unsinkable Boxer	9-10-12	M Pipe	A McCoy	5-2f	24
1999	-250	Generosa	6-10-1	J L Hassett	N Williamson	12-1	24
2000	-341551	Rubhahunish	9-11-2	N Twiston-Davies	C Llewellyn	8-1	24
2001		*Abandoned*					
2002	-341	Freetown	6-11-2	L Lungo	A Dobbin	20-1	24
2003	-	Inching Closer	6-11-2	J O'Neill	B Geraghty	6-1f	24

AKA 'The Ladbroke Casinos' and many other names due to rapid change of sponsors. Winners have usually had recent winning form and not figured too close to the bottom of the handicap. Martin Pipe has had one in the frame in each of the last six renewals, including Danjing (third at 33-1 in 1997) and Montreal (third at 25-1 in 2002).

Royal & SunAlliance Novices' Hurdle (2m5f) Cheltenham

1994	-11321	Danoli	6-11-7	T Foley	C Swan	7-4f	23
1995	-11411	Putty Road	5-11-7	D Nicholson	N Williamson	7-1	21
1996	-2212	Urubande	6-11-7	A O'Brien	C Swan	8-1	24
1997	-2111	Istabraq	5-11-7	A O'Brien	C Swan	6-5f	17
1998	-1111	French Holly	7-11-7	F Murphy	A Thornton	2-1f	18
1999	-11111	Barton	6-11-7	T Easterby	L Wyer	2-1f	18
2000	-11111	Monsignor	6-11-7	M Pitman	N Williamson	5-4f	14
2001		Abandoned					
2002	-1	Galileo	6-11-7	T George	J Maguire	12-1	14
2003	-51112	Hardy Eustace	6-11-7	D Hughes	K Kelly	6-1	19

Has proved a spectacularly good race for favourites, though all five who scored in the last decade were returned at very short prices, particularly when one considers the size of the field that usually lines up; this is often a race in which punters can't see past a single horse. Over the last seven runnings, two of the three beaten favourites were also by far the weakest, at 5-1 and 11-2, though Pizarro was turned over at 2-1 last season. Four of the last five winners have entered the race unbeaten that season.

Royal & SunAlliance Novices' Chase (3m1f) Cheltenham

1994	-2F42111	Monsieur Le Cure	8-11-4	J Edwards	P Niven	15-2	18
1995	-231	Brief Gale	8-10-13	J Gifford	P Hide	13-2	13
1996	-12112	Nahthen Lad	7-11-4	J Pitman	W Marston	7-1	12
1997	-1U31	Hanakham	8-11-4	R Hodges	R Dunwoody	13-2	14
1998	-11	Florida Pearl	6-11-4	W Mullins	R Dunwoody	11-8f	10
1999	-U2511	Looks Like Trouble	7-11-4	N Chance	P Carberry	16-1	14
2000	-212	Lord Noelie	7-11-4	H Knight	J Culloty	9-2	9
2001		Abandoned					
2002	-21F2	Hussard Collonges	7-11-4	P Beaumont	R Garritty	33-1	19
2003	-1311	One Knight	7-11-4	P Hobbs	R Johnson	15-2	9

Ascot's Reynoldstown Chase is the obvious race from which to follow on but, in recent years, it has provided some high-profile failures such as Lord Of The River, Mr Mulligan, Sweet Duke and One Man. The Irish ended a long drought thanks to Florida Pearl in 1998 but have continued to find this a difficult race to win since. All 19 runners aged nine or over have been beaten since Miinnehoma won in 1992.

Queen Mother Champion Chase (2m) Cheltenham

1994	-2211	Viking Flagship	7-12-0	D Nicholson	A Maguire	4-1	8
1995	-110F2	Viking Flagship	8-12-0	D Nicholson	C Swan	5-2f	10
1996	-1FU2	Klairon Davis	7-12-0	A Moore	F Woods	9-1	7
1997	-	Martha's Son	10-12-0	T Forster	R Farrant	9-1	6
1998	-1151	One Man	10-12-0	G Richards	B Harding	7-2	8
1999	-1	Call Equiname	9-12-0	P Nicholls	M Fitzgerald	7-2	13
2000	-5133	Edredon Bleu	8-12-0t	H Knight	A McCoy	7-2	9
2001		Abandoned					
2002	-1	Flagship Uberalles	8-12-0	P Hobbs	R Johnson	7-4f	12
2003	-1U11	Moscow Flyer	9-12-0	J Harrington	B Geraghty	7-4f	11

In over 40 runnings there have been only three winners at double-figure prices, though winning favourites have been surprisingly scarce. This generally features small fields, so that few horses start at big odds, but it's reliably competitive and a tricky call – Moscow Flyer wouldn't have had it so easy last time if it hadn't been for the simultaneous falls of

Sponsored by Stan James

two challengers at the penultimate fence.

Coral Cup (2m5f) Cheltenham

1994	-3571	Time For A Run	7-11-8	E O'Grady	C Swan	11-1	30
1995	-73	Chance Coffey	10-10-0	P O'Donnell	G O'Neill	11-1	30
1996	-11	Trainglot	9-10-3	J Fitzgerald	M Dwyer	11-2	20
1997	-121	Big Strand	8-10-0	M Pipe	Jamie Evans	16-1	28
1998	-585	Top Cees	8-10-0	L Ramsden	B Fenton	11-1	21
1999	-6	Khayrawani	7-11-3	C Roche	F Berry	16-1	30
2000	-11P3	What's Up Boys	6-10-3	P Hobbs	P Flynn (3)	33-1	26
2001		*Abandoned*					
2002	-54U	Ilnamar	6-10-5	M Pipe	R Greene	25-1	27
2003	-21	Xenophon	7-11-0	A Martin	M Fitzgerald	4-1f	27

As tough a handicap as there is at the Festival, though the lightly-raced Xenophon turned out, as punters expected, to be well ahead of the handicapper in the latest renewal. Irish raiders have dominated to an impressive extent – in addition to Xenophon, they accounted for the first five home in 1999, the first three in 1995, four of the first five in 1998 and two of the first three in 1994. If What's Up Boys hadn't finished so strongly in 2000, they'd have had the first three then, too.

National Hunt Chase Challenge Cup (4m) Cheltenham

1994	-34B12	Christmas Gorse	8-12-4	N Gaselee	Mr M Armytage	14-1	19
1995	-213431	Front Line	8-12-7*b*	J O'Neill	Mr J Berry	7-1	25
1996	-3433F17	Loving Around	8-11-13	E O'Grady	Mr P Fenton	10-1	22
1997	-P221314	Flimsy Truth	11-12-7	M Weston	Mr M Harris	33-1	23
1998	-11	Wandering Light	9-12-7	T Forster	Mr R Wakley	10-1	24
1999	-514314	Deejaydee	7-12-0	M Hourigan	Mr A Martin	13-2	21
2000	-F24U2	Relaxation	8-12-0	H Daly	Mr M Bradburne	8-1	21
2001		*Abandoned*					
2002	-32232212	Rith Dubh	10-11-11*b*	J O'Neill	Mr JT McNamara	10-1	26
2003	-FF342	Sudden Shock	8-11-7	J O'Neill	Mr D Cullen	25-1	24

A staying novice chase for amateur riders, this is a strange race to have anywhere, never mind the Festival, and it's by no means a safe vehicle for heroic gambling, as was underlined when hot favourite Stormez got turned over last March. Six of the last nine winners were aged seven or eight.

Mildmay Of Flete H'cap Chase (2m4f110yds) Cheltenham

1994	-224	Elfast	11-11-4	J Webber	G McCourt	8-1	18
1995	-2332112	Kadi	6-10-4	D Nicholson	N Williamson	11-2	12
1996	-2F1	Old Bridge	8-9-7	A Turnell	G Crone (7)	14-1	13
1997	-6P492	Terao	11-10-7	M Pipe	T Murphy	20-1	13
1998	-33111	Super Coin	10-10-10	R Lee	N Williamson	7-1	14
1999	-111	Majadou	5-11-0	M Pipe	A McCoy	7-4f	18
2000	-24P1	Dark Stranger	9-10-3*b*	M Pipe	R Johnson	14-1	18
2001		*Abandoned*					
2002	-P5	Blowing Wind	9-10-9	M Pipe	R Walsh	25-1	21
2003	-	Young Spartacus	10-10-9	H Daly	R Johnson	16-1	19

A great race for followers of Martin Pipe, trainer of the only winning favourite in the last ten years. But be careful – Pipe's other three winners hadn't seemed to be the stable's first string, judged on jockey bookings, which explains their healthy SPs (all three paid even better on the Tote).

Sponsored by Stan James

Weatherbys Champion Bumper (2m110yds) Cheltenham

1994	-351	Mucklemeg	6-11-5	E O'Grady	C Swan	7-2f	25
1995	-11	Dato Star	4-10-12	J M Jefferson	M Dwyer	7-2	21
1996	-1	Wither Or Which	5-11-6	W Mullins	Mr W Mullins	11-4	24
1997	-1	Florida Pearl	5-11-6	W Mullins	R Dunwoody	6-1	25
1998	-1	Alexander Banquet	5-11-6	W Mullins	R Walsh	9-1	25
1999	-134	Monsignor	5-11-6	M Pitman	B Powell	50-1	25
2000	-1	Joe Cullen	5-11-6	W Mullins	C Swan	14-1	17
2001		*Abandoned*					
2002	-1	Pizarro	5-11-6	E O'Grady	J Spencer	14-1	23
2003	-12	Liberman	5-11-6	M Pipe	A McCoy	2-1f	25

Bonanza time for the Irish, winners of eight of the 11 runnings. Willie Mullins has led the way in jaw-dropping style, with four of the last seven winners and a 100 per cent record with his three runners from 1996 to 1998 (though he ran four, all unplaced, last time).

Triumph Hurdle (2m1f) Cheltenham

1994	-11111	Mysilv	4-10-9	D Nicholson	A Maguire	2-1f	28
1995	-311	Kissair	4-11-0	M Pipe	J Lower	16-1	26
1996	-1122	Paddy's Return	4-11-0b	F Murphy	R Dunwoody	10-1	29
1997	-111	Commanche Court	4-11-0	T Walsh	N Williamson	9-1	28
1998	-P151	Upgrade	4-11-0	N Twiston-Davies	C Llewellyn	14-1	25
1999	-111	Katarino	4-11-0	N Henderson	M Fitzgerald	11-4f	23
2000	-41	Snow Drop	4-10-9	F Doumen	T Doumen	7-1f	28
2001		*Abandoned*					
2002	-1	Scolardy	4-11-0	W Mullins	C Swan	16-1	28
2003	-01141B41	Spectroscope	4-11-0	J O'Neill	B Geraghty	20-1	27

A nightmare race for punters, though there's a pronounced recent trend against home-breds. We flagged this up in the *Outlook* ahead of the 2002 running, in which all nine home-breds missed the frame, while French and Irish-breds filled nine of the first ten places. Last time, the first eight home were either bred in Ireland (5), France (2) or Germany (1). Only four home-breds even showed up, though they included 13-2 shot Red Wine (ninth).

Stayers' Hurdle (3m1f) Cheltenham

1994	-41	Balasani	8-11-10	M Pipe	M Perrett	9-2j	14
1995	-1221	Dorans Pride	6-11-10	M Hourigan	J Broderick	11-4f	11
1996	-	Cyborgo	6-11-10	M Pipe	D Bridgwater	8-1	19
1997	-0213	Karshi	7-11-10	H Knight	J Osborne	20-1	17
1998	-24124	Princeful	7-11-10	J Pitman	R Farrant	16-1	9
1999	-752	Anzum	8-11-10	D Nicholson	R Johnson	40-1	12
2000	-12	Bacchanal	6-11-10	N Henderson	M Fitzgerald	11-2	10
2001		*Abandoned*					
2002	-111	Baracouda	7-11-10	F Doumen	T Doumen	13-8f	16
2003	-12	Baracouda	8-11-10	F Doumen	T Doumen	9-4j	11

There seems a slim career-window in which a horse can win this; six or seven-year-olds are ideal. None of the 32 five-year-olds to take part in the race have so far won, though two were second and three third. Of the three eight-year-olds to score, one was awarded the race in the Stewards' Room, while 61 others aged eight or over have tried and failed in the last 11 runnings; Baracouda, however, seems a true champion, regardless of his age. The Irish have won five of the last 16 runnings, all of their winners having previously run first or second in the Boyne Hurdle at Navan; Bannow Bay, beaten a neck by Baracouda in 2002, would have made it six.

174

Cheltenham Gold Cup (3m2f110yds) Cheltenham

1994	-3333	**The Fellow**	9-12-0*b*	F Doumen	A Kondrat	7-1	15
1995	-111	**Master Oats**	9-12-0	K Bailey	N Williamson	10-3f	15
1996	-1F11	**Imperial Call**	7-12-0	F Sutherland	C O'Dwyer	9-2	10
1997	-4F	**Mr Mulligan**	9-12-0	N Chance	A McCoy	20-1	14
1998	-0111P	**Cool Dawn**	10-12-0	R Alner	A Thornton	25-1	17
1999	-4103	**See More Business**	9-12-0*b*	P Nicholls	M Fitzgerald	16-1	12
2000	-31P1	**Looks Like Trouble**	8-12-0	N Chance	R Johnson	9-2	12
2001		*Abandoned*					
2002	-122	**Best Mate**	7-12-0	H Knight	J Culloty	7-1	18
2003	-11	**Best Mate**	8-12-0	H Knight	J Culloty	13-8f	15

Best Mate was the first dual winner since L'Escargot in 1971, and will join the immortals of steeplechasing if he becomes the first triple winner since Arkle (1964-66). Outsiders have a fine record of winning and reaching the frame, bolstered by the placed performances of Truckers Tavern (33-1) and Harbour Pilot (40-1) in the latest running. From the previous ten renewals, four winners were returned at double-figure prices (Cool Ground was 25-1 in 1992), while the placed horses included runners-up Go Ballistic (66-1), Barton Bank (33-1) and Commanche Court (25-1), as well as third-placed Royal Athlete (66-1), See More Business (40-1), Strong Promise (20-1), Dubacilla (20-1) and Young Hustler (20-1). The 1996 race was the first time since 1986 when none of the first three returned at 20-1 or over. Short-priced favourites who have bitten the dust in recent years include Florida Pearl (5-2), See More Business (9-4), One Man (11-8), Jodami (6-4), The Fellow (5-4) and Carvills Hill (Evens). Any runner older than ten can be counted out as a possible winner – from 23 attempts in ten runnings, they've made the frame only twice and didn't get within 9l of the winner either time. There have been just two attempts by six-year-olds in the last 12 runnings – The Fellow was beaten a short-head in 1991, while the ill-fated Gloria Victis was still in the front rank when falling two out in 2000; both were French-breds and therefore precocious. An Irish raider has made the frame in each year since Imperial Call's win last took the prize across the Irish Sea. Martin Pipe has run 17 without success in the last nine renewals but Henrietta Knight has done rather better – Best Mate was only her second runner in the race in 2002.

Christie's Foxhunter Chase (3m2f110yds) Cheltenham

1994	-111	**Double Silk**	10-12-0	R Wilkins	Mr R Treloggen	2-5f	5
1995	-	**Fantus**	8-12-0	R Barber	Miss P Curling	8-1	13
1996	-1	**Elegant Lord**	8-12-0	E Bolger	Mr E Bolger	3-1f	17
1997	-	**Fantus**	10-12-0	R Barber	Mr T Mitchell	10-1	18
1998	-1111	**Earthmover**	7-12-0	R Barber	Mr J Tizzard	3-1	11
1999	-1	**Castle Mane**	7-12-0	Caroline Bailey	Mr B Pollock	9-2	24
2000	-21	**Cavalero**	11-12-0	H Manners	Mr A Charles-Jones	16-1	24
2001		*Abandoned*					
2002	-3	**Last Option**	10-12-0	R Tate	Mrs F Needham	20-1	20
2003	-1	**Kingscliff**	6-12-0	S Alner	Mr R Young	11-4f	24

Noy usually very competitive, with six of the last nine winners having won a hunter chase last time out. Fantus, trained by Foxhunter's specialist Richard Barber, has been the only winner in the last decade not to have been prepped in hunter chases.

Grand Annual H'cap Chase (2m110yds) Cheltenham

1994	-43342	**Snitton Lane**	8-10-0	W Clay	D Bridgwater	33-1	17
1995	-1111P	**Sound Reveille**	7-10-10	C Brooks	G Bradley	7-1	8
1996	-1142	**Kibreet**	9-10-12	P Hobbs	A McCoy	7-1	13
1997	-434	**Uncle Ernie**	12-11-4	J Fitzgerald	G Bradley	20-1	16

1998	-4111	**Edredon Bleu**	6-11-6	H Knight	A McCoy	7-2f	17
1999	-F3	**Space Trucker**	8-10-1	J Harrington	J Barry	7-2f	15
2000	-111	**Samakaan**	7-10-11	V Williams	N Williamson	9-2f	16
2001		*Abandoned*					
2002	-321	**Fadoudal Du Cochet**	9-10-0	A Moore	D Casey	6-1	18
2003	-2231	**Palarshan**	5-10-0	H Daly	M Bradburne	8-1	21

Palarshan maintained a fine record for young horses, and was the third novice to win in the last decade, following Sound Reveille and Samakaan. He was also the second to score from out of the handicap, after Snitton Lane, an amazing 12lb wrong in 1994; such horses have also had a good record in making the places.

Cathcart Chase (2m5f) Cheltenham

1994	-11	**Raymylette**	7-11-0	N Henderson	M Fitzgerald	7-4	4
1995	-11P32	**Coulton**	8-11-7	O Sherwood	J Osborne	11-2	11
1996	-21213	**Challenger Du Luc**	6-11-3b	M Pipe	D Bridgwater	10-1	11
1997	-1111	**Sparky Gayle**	7-11-3	C Parker	B Storey	3-1f	10
1998	-321112	**Cyfor Malta**	5-10-8	M Pipe	A McCoy	9-4f	8
1999	-1331	**Stormyfairweather**	7-11-3	N Henderson	M Fitzgerald	9-1	10
2000	-P	**Stormyfairweather**	8-11-12	N Henderson	M Fitzgerald	11-2	8
2001		*Abandoned*					
2002	-F11	**Royal Auclair**	5-10-11	M Pipe	A McCoy	2-1f	11
2003	-2111111	**La Landiere**	8-10-12	R Phillips	R Johnson	5-4f	9

Three winners each for Messrs Pipe and Henderson, including the only two priced higher than 11-2. La Landiere was the seventh winning novice in ten renewals. The race was opened to five-year-olds in 1998, and the only two to turn up so far (both French-breds trained by Pipe) have won.

County H'cap Hurdle (2m1f) Cheltenham

1994	-06222	**Dizzy**	6-10-0	P Monteith	A Dobbin	12-1	24
1995	-051223	**Home Counties**	6-10-12	D Moffatt	D J Moffatt (3)	14-1	23
1996	-3112341	**Star Rage**	6-10-0	J Harris	D Gallagher	14-1	28
1997	-43364	**Barna Boy**	9-10-12	N Henderson	R Dunwoody	14-1	20
1998	-724831	**Blowing Wind**	5-11-8	M Pipe	A McCoy	15-8f	27
1999	-152	**Sir Talbot**	5-10-0	J Old	T Murphy	10-1	28
2000	-04811	**Master Tern**	5-10-3	J O'Neill	A Dobbin	9-2f	21
2001		*Abandoned*					
2002	-55422	**Rooster Booster**	8-11-1	P Hobbs	R Johnson	8-1	21
2003	-23151	**Spirit Leader**	7-11-7	J Harrington	B Geraghty	10-1	28

Had been a rotten race for the Irish until Spirit Leader. Martin Pipe has had just one winner (at a lowly SP of 15-8) from over 30 runners in the last 11 renewals. One of the more predictable of the Festival handicaps, particularly over the last five runnings.

Martell Cup Chase (3m1f) Aintree

1994	-3726	**Docklands Express**	12-11-5	K Bailey	R Dunwoody	5-2	4
1995	-431F124	**Merry Gale**	7-11-9	T Dreaper	G Bradley	5-2	6
1996	-21111P	**Scotton Banks**	7-11-5	T Easterby	L Wyer	9-2	6
1997	-25322	**Barton Bank**	11-11-5	D Nicholson	D Walsh	100-30	5
1998	-12112	**Escartefigue**	6-11-13	D Nicholson	R Johnson	11-2	8
1999	-12644	**Macgeorge**	9-11-5	R Lee	A Maguire	11-1	5
2000	-1114	**See More Business**	10-12-0b	P Nicholls	M Fitzgerald	5-4f	4
2001	-3211112	**First Gold**	8-12-0	F Doumen	T Doumen	7-4f	7
2002	-31140	**Florida Pearl**	10-11-12	W Mullins	B Geraghty	5-2	6

176   *Sponsored by Stan James*

| 2003 | -373P | **First Gold** | 10-11-2*b* | F Doumen | T Doumen | 14-1 | 7 |

A dramatic uplift in prizemoney has improved the quality of this race, Florida Pearl getting almost twice as much for his win as Macgeorge did. Aintree's Mildmay course is flat and sharp, similar to Kempton except for being left-handed; horses who run well at the Sunbury track are likely to do similarly well here. The last four to succeed were all previous King George winners (as was Barton Bank), while dual winner Docklands Express was also a dual winner of Kempton's Racing Post Chase.

Grand National H'cap Chase (4m4f) Aintree

1994	-10	**Minnehoma**	11-10-8	M Pipe	R Dunwoody	16-1	36
1995	-3020	**Royal Athlete**	12-10-6	J Pitman	J Titley	40-1	35
1996	-F22F12	**Rough Quest**	10-10-7	T Casey	M Fitzgerald	7-1f	27
1997	-23112	**Lord Gyllene**	9-10-0	S Brookshaw	A Dobbin	14-1	36
1998	-55165	**Earth Summit**	10-10-5*b*	N Twiston-Davies	C Llewellyn	7-1f	37
1999	-580541	**Bobbyjo**	9-10-0	T Carberry	P Carberry	10-1	32
2000	-875493	**Papillon**	9-10-12	T Walsh	R Walsh	10-1	40
2001	-14552F	**Red Marauder**	11-10-11	N Mason	R Guest	33-1	40
2002	-753367	**Bindaree**	8-10-4	N Twiston-Davies	J Culloty	20-1	40
2003	3P631364	**Monty's Pass**	10-10-7	J Mangan	B Geraghty	16-1	40

It's usually been advisable to rule out all horses more than a few pounds out of the handicap, but more and more have been getting into the handicap in recent years (only three carried more weight than they were allotted last time). Forget the old adage about class horses with winning form over 2m4f; even with the modified fences, this race is a severe test of stamina and proven ability to last home over 3m or further is essential. Look for horses who've run with credit in other major staying handicaps – Earth Summit had won the Welsh and Scottish Nationals, while Bobbyjo and Papillon had been first and second (9l clear) in the '98 Irish National. At a more prosaic level, Monty's Pass was a Kerry National winner before becoming the third Irish victor at Aintree in five years. Be careful with Hennessy form – Suny Bay and What's Up Boys, both Newbury winners, were rewarded with hefty loads when they then attempted the National and, though best at the weights, were beaten by the handicapper. By contrast, Bindaree and Red Marauder were both down the field in the Hennessy before carrying more reasonable burdens to Liverpool glory, while Rough Quest was a 14l second in the '95 Hennessy. Only Papillon and Red Marauder (a fluke winner) have shouldered more than 10st8lb to victory since 1988, so knock out anything carrying more than that – the effect of weight is exaggerated by such marathon conditions. Don't back at starting price but take the best available odds 'with a run' in the days before the race, and don't be put off backing more than one – this is a race in which bad luck can easily strike down a single, carefully-chosen selection.

Scottish Grand National H'cap Chase (4m120yds) Ayr

1994	162112P7	**Earth Summit**	6-10-0*b*	N Twiston-Davies	D Bridgwater	16-1	22
1995	1412118	**Willsford**	12-10-12	J Pitman	R Farrant	16-1	22
1996	-P403	**Moorcroft Boy**	11-10-0	D Nicholson	Mark Dwyer	14-1	20
1997	-102	**Belmont King**	9-11-10	P Nicholls	A McCoy	16-1	17
1998	-34F15	**Baronet**	8-10-0	D Nicholson	A Maguire	7-1	18
1999	-22412U11	**Young Kenny**	8-11-10	P Beaumont	B Powell	5-2f	15
2000	-12111	**Paris Pike**	8-11-0	F Murphy	A Maguire	5-1j	18
2001	-2P4	**Gingembre**	7-11-2	L Taylor	A Thornton	12-1	30
2002	-36P4P5	**Take Control**	8-10-6	M Pipe	R Walsh	20-1	18
2003	-31223	**Ryalux**	10-10-5	A Crook	R McGrath	15-2	19

The first rule is to avoid runners who had a hard race in the Grand National – Shotgun Willy, a distant fifth behind Ryalux after pulling up at Aintree, was just the latest example of a horse too tired by recent exertions to produce his best form here. These fences are not nearly as severe as Aintree's, so novices, usually in-form horses at the right end of the handicap, have an excellent record. Nigel Twiston-Davies has won this twice with a novice, the first being Captain Dibble in 1992, while Paris Pike was one of the most improved chasers in 1999 and Young Kenny was firmly on the upgrade at the time of his win. It goes without saying that proven stamina is a major plus and lightweights have an excellent record. Six of the last 15 winners carried the minimum of 10st, ranging up to 17lb out of the handicap. The ground can be on the fast side for this, Gingembre's year being a notable example, so soft-ground midwinter form may prove redundant – focus instead on those with form at Ayr and/or on fast going.

Irish Grand National H'cap Chase (3m5f) Fairyhouse

1994	-31033	Son Of War	7-10-10	P McCreery	F Woods	12-1	18
1995	-331F	Flashing Steel	10-12-0	J Mulhern	J Osborne	9-1	18
1996	-1U2	Feathered Gale	9-10-0	A Moore	F Woods	8-1	17
1997	-42161	Mudahim	11-10-5	J Pitman	J Titley	13-2	20
1998	-102	Bobbyjo	8-11-3	T Carberry	P Carberry	8-1	22
1999	-8493F30	Glebe Lad	7-10-0	M O'Brien	T Rudd	8-1c	18
2000	-332B	Commanche Court	7-11-4	T Walsh	R Walsh	14-1	24
2001	-7119F61	Davids Lad	7-10-0t	A Martin	T Murphy	10-1	19
2002	-5312F1	The Bunny Boiler	8-9-9	N Meade	R Geraghty	12-1	17
2003	-P24	Timbera	9-10-12t	D Hughes	J Culloty	11-1	21

Flashing Steel, Commanche Court and, going further back, Desert Orchid have demonstrated that classy types can win this despite hefty burdens – indeed, 11 winners since the war have carried 11st10lb and above to victory – but lightweights predominate just the same. The three winners before Timbera were all young chasers whose recent form had shown them to be firmly on the upgrade. It took until 1985 for a British-trained horse to win this race and the record has barely been improved since.

Attheraces Gold Cup H'cap Chase (3m5f) Sandown

1994	-1F2P6U	Ushers Island	8-10-0	J H Johnson	C Swan	25-1	12
1995	U231321	Cache Fleur	9-10-0v	M Pipe	R Dunwoody	10-1	14
1996	-1111P7	Life Of A Lord	10-11-10	A O'Brien	C Swan	12-1	17
1997	-P12	Harwell Lad	8-10-0	R Alner	Mr R Nuttall	14-1	9
1998	-3224F3	Call It A Day	8-10-10	D Nicholson	A Maguire	8-1	19
1999	-20	Eulogy	9-10-0	R Rowe	B Fenton	14-1	19
2000	-2412112	Beau	7-10-9	N Twiston-Davies	C Llewellyn	6-1c	20
2001	-FFP52	Ad Hoc	7-10-4	P Nicholls	R Walsh	14-1	25
2002	32143356	Bounce Back	6-10-9	M Pipe	A McCoy	14-1	20
2003	-51233U	Ad Hoc	9-10-10	P Nicholls	R Walsh	7-1	16

AKA 'The Whitbread'. As in so many staying chases, lightweights are favoured – ten of the last 15 winners have carried 10st6lb or less. This is despite the fast ground that usually prevails at such a late stage of the season and which might be thought to play into the hands of quality horses with more to carry. Five of the last 14 winners had run in the Grand National, but Mr Frisk remains the only horse ever to win both races – he did it in the same season.

178

Outlook

By The Numbers by
Chris Cook

Play the numbers game

BY THE NUMBERS is a new feature in *Racing & Football Outlook*. Having made its debut last December, providing in-depth analysis of the biggest handicaps, the concept has already proved its worth.

As we go to press, the record for runners tipped in this feature is five wins from 24 bets for a PROFIT of 23 points (96% of total stakes). Those winners have included County Hurdle winner Spirit Leader (10-1) and Lanzarote Hurdle hero Non So (9-1).

But it's not just about tipping – we hope the format provides you with plenty of raw data that you'll find helpful in sorting out some of the year's trickiest races. We don't necessarily have space for By The Numbers every week in the RFO but we've made space here so that you have some time to ponder our stats.

Over the next ten pages, we've produced statistical breakdowns of ten of the biggest betting races of the jumps season.

The idea here is to provide you with as much information as we think will be relevant to analysis of the big race and let you get on with it.

The following ten races are some of the highlights of any punter's jump racing season. We'll be covering these races in the RFO, space permitting, in the week each one takes place.

When we do so, we'll also give you a rundown on the leading contenders, showing you how their profile compares to those that have won the race over the previous decade and giving our top three picks, in order.

You'll find additional stats in the feature when it appears in the RFO. In the paper, we look at the historical record of the first three in the betting, and break down all runners over the last ten years according to their experience over fences or hurdles.

For the purposes of this guide, however, each race is analysed under five headings; age of the runners, the weight they carried, the Official Ratings they were assigned at the time of running, their SPs and their sex.

Under each heading, all the runners in the race over the last ten years are sorted into their appropriate categories. In each case, we tell you how many times horses from that category won the race in the last ten years, how many runners there were in total from that category, their strike-rate, the outcome if you had backed them all to a £1 stake and the percentage return on your total stakes which that outcome represents.

For example, let's take nine-year-olds in the Paddy Power Gold Cup (formerly the Thomas Pink, the Murphy's or the Mackeson, depending how far you go back). You'll see that nine-year-olds have won four times from 24 runners over the last decade.

That's a strike-rate of 17 per cent. If you'd had a quid on all 24, you'd have made a net profit of £14. To put that in context, it's a 58 per cent return on your money (£24 in total stakes).

In the bottom half of each page, we also analyse the place statistics. Those sections that have produced more placed runners than average are shaded.

Here's hoping our data will lead you to profitable conclusions.

Win stats

	Age	Wins/runs	%	£+-	% of stakes
Age	5	1/8	13	-£4.00	-50
	6	2/10	20	+£4.00	+40
	7	0/26	0	-£26.00	-100
	8	3/42	7	+£2.75	+7
	9	4/24	17	+£14.00	+58
	10	0/13	0	-£13.00	-100
	11	0/8	0	-£8.00	-100
	12+	0/1	0	-£1.00	-100

	OR	Wins/runs	%	£+-	% of stakes
Official Ratings	Under 130	0/8	0	-£8.00	-100
	130-139	3/38	8	-£18.75	-49
	140-149	1/43	2	-£35.00	-81
	150+	6/43	14	+£30.50	+71

	SP	Wins/runs	%	£+-	% of stakes
Starting Prices	Under 5-1	3/12	25	+£0.25	+2
	5-1 to 7-1	4/19	21	+£8.50	+45
	15-2 to 9-1	1/16	6	-£6.00	-38
	10-1 to 12-1	0/22	0	-£22.00	-100
	14-1 to 18-1	1/22	5	-£5.00	-23
	20-1 to 25-1	0/19	0	-£19.00	-100
	28-1 to 33-1	1/16	6	+£18.00	+113
	40-1+	0/6	0	-£6.00	-100

	Weight	Wins/runs	%	£+-	% of stakes
Weight	Under 10st	0/5	0	-£5.00	-100
	10st-10st6lb	3/64	5	-£12.00	-19
	10st7lb-10st13lb	1/24	4	-£18.00	-75
	11st-11st4lb	2/10	20	-£2.75	-28
	11st5lb-11st9lb	3/16	19	+£13.50	+84
	11st10lb+	1/13	8	-£7.00	-54

	Sex	Wins/runs	%	£+-	% of stakes
Sex	Mare	1/3	33	+£3.00	+100

Place stats

	Age	Wins/runs	%
Age	5	4/8	50
	6	3/10	30
	7	8/26	31
	8	8/42	19
	9	7/24	29
	10	0/13	0
	11	0/8	0
	12+	0/1	0

	Weight	Wins/runs	%
Weight	Under 10st	1/5	20
	10st-10st6lb	13/64	20
	10st7lb-10st13lb	8/24	33
	11st-11st4lb	2/10	20
	11st5lb-11st9lb	4/16	25
	11st10lb+	2/13	15

	OR	Wins/runs	%
Official Ratings	Under 130	2/8	25
	130-139	8/38	21
	140-149	8/43	19
	150+	12/43	28

	Sex	Wins/runs	%
Sex	Mare	1/3	33

	SP	Wins/runs	%
Starting Prices	Under 5-1	4/12	33
	5-1 to 7-1	9/19	47
	15-2 to 9-1	6/16	38
	10-1 to 12-1	4/22	18
	14-1 to 18-1	4/22	18
	20-1 to 25-1	1/19	5
	28-1 to 33-1	2/16	13
	40-1+	0/6	0

Win stats

Age	Wins/runs	%	£+-	% of stakes
5	0/3	0	-£3.00	-100
6	1/15	7	-£10.00	-67
7	4/30	13	+£5.00	+17
8	3/36	8	+£9.75	+27
9	2/32	6	-£15.00	-47
10	0/22	0	-£22.00	-100
11	0/7	0	-£7.00	-100
12+	0/1	0	-£1.00	-100

OR	Wins/runs	%	£+-	% of stakes
Under 140	5/43	12	+£15.50	+36
140-149	4/66	6	-£25.00	-38
150-159	0/27	0	-£27.00	-100
160+	1/10	10	-£6.75	-68

SP	Wins/runs	%	£+-	% of stakes
Under 5-1	3/12	25	+£1.75	+15
5-1 to 7-1	3/23	13	-£2.50	-11
15-2 to 9-1	1/16	6	-£7.50	-47
10-1 to 12-1	1/21	5	-£10.00	-48
14-1 to 18-1	1/21	5	-£6.00	-29
20-1 to 25-1	0/21	0	-£21.00	-100
28-1 to 33-1	1/13	8	+£21.00	+162
40-1+	0/19	0	-£19.00	-100

Weight	Wins/runs	%	£+-	% of stakes
Under 10st	0/4	0	-£4.00	-100
10st-10st6lb	6/64	9	+£4.00	+6
10st7lb-10st13lb	3/42	7	-£10.50	-25
11st-11st4lb	0/14	0	-£14.00	-100
11st5lb-11st9lb	1/11	9	-£7.75	-70
11st10lb+	0/11	0	-£11.00	-100

Sex	Wins/runs	%	£+-	% of stakes
Mare	0/7	0	-£7.00	-100

Place stats

Age	Wins/runs	%
5	1/3	33
6	7/15	47
7	9/30	30
8	8/36	22
9	6/32	19
10	2/22	10
11	1/7	14
12+	0/1	0

Weight	Wins/runs	%
Under 10st	0/4	0
10st-10st6lb	13/64	20
10st7lb-10st13lb	13/42	31
11st-11st4lb	4/14	29
11st5lb-11st9lb	3/11	27
11st10lb+	1/11	9

OR	Wins/runs	%
Under 140	9/43	21
140-149	17/66	26
150-159	6/27	22
160+	2/10	20

Sex	Wins/runs	%
Mare	3/7	43

SP	Wins/runs	%
Under 5-1	6/12	50
5-1 to 7-1	7/23	30
15-2 to 9-1	7/16	44
10-1 to 12-1	5/21	24
14-1 to 18-1	5/21	24
20-1 to 25-1	2/21	10
28-1 to 33-1	2/13	15
40-1+	0/19	0

Win stats

Age	Wins/runs	%	£+-	% of stakes
5	2/47	4	-£35.25	-75
6	4/49	8	-£20.50	-42
7	4/42	10	-£5.00	-12
8	0/16	0	-£16.00	-100
9	0/9	0	-£9.00	-100
10+	0/4	0	-£4.00	-100

OR	Wins/runs	%	£+-	% of stakes
Under 130	0/13	0	-£13.00	-100
130-139	5/93	5	-£46.50	-50
140-149	5/55	9	-£24.25	-44
150+	0/6	0	-£6.00	-100

SP	Wins/runs	%	£+-	% of stakes
Under 5-1	3/13	23	+£0.75	+6
5-1 to 7-1	4/18	22	+£11.00	+61
15-2 to 9-1	1/15	7	-£6.50	-43
10-1 to 12-1	1/19	5	-£8.00	-42
14-1 to 18-1	1/23	4	-£8.00	-35
20-1 to 25-1	0/29	0	-£29.00	-100
28-1 to 33-1	0/18	0	-£18.00	-100
40-1+	0/32	0	-£32.00	-100

Weight	Wins/runs	%	£+-	% of stakes
Under 10st	0/17	0	-£17.00	-100
10st-10st6lb	2/45	4	-£25.00	-56
10st7lb-10st13lb	3/53	6	-£36.75	-69
11st-11st4lb	3/18	17	+£8.50	+47
11st5lb-11st9lb	2/15	13	-£0.50	-3
11st10lb+	0/19	0	-£19.00	-100

Sex	Wins/runs	%	£+-	% of stakes
Mare	2/15	13	+£3.25	+22
Entire	0/6	0	-£6.00	-100

Place stats

Weight	Wins/runs	%
Under 10st	4/17	24
10st-10st6lb	11/45	24
10st7lb-10st13lb	10/53	19
11st-11st4lb	6/18	33
11st5lb-11st9lb	3/15	20
11st10lb+	3/19	16

Sex	Wins/runs	%
Mare	5/15	33
Entire	0/6	0

SP	Wins/runs	%
Under 5-1	6/13	46
5-1 to 7-1	10/18	56
15-2 to 9-1	4/15	27
10-1 to 12-1	2/19	11
14-1 to 18-1	6/23	26
20-1 to 25-1	5/29	17
28-1 to 33-1	1/18	6
40-1+	3/32	9

Age	Wins/runs	%
5	17/47	36
6	10/49	20
7	8/42	19
8	2/16	13
9	0/9	0
10+	0/4	0

OR	Wins/runs	%
Under 130	3/13	23
130-139	20/93	22
140-149	13/55	24
150+	1/6	17

Win stats

Age	Wins/runs	%	£+-	% of stakes
6	2/4	50	+£8.33	+208
7	1/15	7	-£9.00	-60
8	4/26	15	+£0.50	+2
9	0/20	0	-£20.00	-100
10	2/24	8	-£15.00	-63
11	1/16	6	-£1.00	-6
12+	0/9	0	-£9.00	-100

OR	Wins/runs	%	£+-	% of stakes
Under 130	1/13	8	-£7.00	-54
130-139	1/39	3	-£24.00	-62
140-149	5/42	12	-£9.00	-21
150+	3/20	15	-£5.17	-26

SP	Wins/runs	%	£+-	% of stakes
Under 5-1	4/14	29	+£3.33	+24
5-1 to 7-1	4/23	17	+£3.50	+15
15-2 to 9-1	1/13	8	-£3.00	-23
10-1 to 12-1	0/13	0	-£13.00	-100
14-1 to 18-1	1/18	6	-£3.00	-17
20-1 to 25-1	0/20	0	-£20.00	-100
28-1 to 33-1	0/6	0	-£6.00	-100
40-1+	0/7	0	-£7.00	-100

Weight	Wins/runs	%	£+-	% of stakes
Under 10st	0/6	0	-£6.00	-100
10st-0st6lb	3/35	9	-£6.00	-17
10st7lb-10st13lb	2/34	6	-£25.00	-74
11st-11st4lb	2/20	10	-£3.50	-18
11st5lb-11st9lb	2/8	25	+£2.00	+25
11st10lb+	1/11	9	-£6.67	-61

Sex	Wins/runs	%	£+-	% of stakes
Mare	1/1	100	+£5.00	+100

Place stats

Weight	Wins/runs	%
Under 10st	0/6	0
10st-10st6lb	8/35	23
10st7lb-10st13lb	10/34	29
11st-11st4lb	5/20	25
11st5lb-11st9lb	3/8	38
11st10lb+	5/11	45

Sex	Wins/runs	%
Mare	1/1	100

Age	Wins/runs	%
6	2/4	50
7	4/15	27
8	10/26	38
9	3/20	15
10	7/24	29
11	4/16	25
12+	1/9	11

OR	Wins/runs	%
Under 130	1/13	8
130-139	9/39	23
140-149	12/42	29
150+	9/20	45

SP	Wins/runs	%
Under 5-1	7/14	50
5-1 to 7-1	11/23	48
15-2 to 9-1	2/13	15
10-1 to 12-1	1/13	8
14-1 to 18-1	4/18	22
20-1 to 25-1	5/20	25
28-1 to 33-1	0/6	0
40-1+	1/7	14

Win stats

	Age	Wins/runs	%	£+-	% of stakes
Age	4	0/2	0	-£2.00	-100
	5	7/42	17	+£10.75	+26
	6	0/43	0	-£43.00	-100
	7	2/41	5	-£21.00	-51
	8	1/13	8	+£21.00	+162
	9+	0/9	0	-£9.00	-100

	OR	Wins/runs	%	£+-	% of stakes
Official Ratings	Under 120	3/29	10	+£11.00	+38
	120-129	4/62	7	-£37.75	-61
	130-139	2/49	4	-£40.50	-83
	140+	1/10	10	+£24.00	+240

	SP	Wins/runs	%	£+-	% of stakes
Starting Prices	Under 5-1	2/11	18	-£5.25	-48
	5-1 to 7-1	4/17	24	+£10.00	+59
	15-2 to 9-1	0/10	0	-£10.00	-100
	10-1 to 12-1	2/24	8	-£1.00	-4
	14-1 to 18-1	1/31	3	-£14.00	-45
	20-1 to 25-1	0/26	0	-£26.00	-100
	28-1 to 33-1	1/17	6	+£17.00	+100
	40-1+	0/14	0	-£14.00	-100

	Weight	Wins/runs	%	£+-	% of stakes
Weight	Under 10st	1/14	7	+£3.00	+21
	10st-10st6lb	3/43	7	-£13.00	-30
	10st7lb-10st13lb	2/39	5	-£25.00	-64
	11st-11st4lb	1/30	3	-£27.50	-92
	11st5lb-11st9lb	2/14	14	+£23.25	+166
	11st10lb+	1/10	10	-£4.00	-40

	Sex	Wins/runs	%	£+-	% of stakes
Sex	Mare	0/10	0	-£10.00	-100
	Entire	0/4	0	-£4.00	-100

Place stats

	Age	Wins/runs	%
Age	4	0/2	0
	5	12/42	29
	6	9/43	21
	7	9/41	22
	8	3/13	23
	9+	2/9	22

	Weight	Wins/runs	%
Weight	Under 10st	4/14	29
	10st-10st6lb	8/43	19
	10st7lb-10st13lb	10/39	26
	11st-11st4lb	5/30	17
	11st5lb-11st9lb	4/14	29
	11st10lb+	4/10	40

	OR	Wins/runs	%
Official Ratings	Under 120	6/29	21
	120-129	17/62	27
	130-139	8/49	16
	140+	4/10	40

	SP	Wins/runs	%
Starting Prices	Under 5-1	4/11	36
	5-1 to 7-1	7/17	41
	15-2 to 9-1	2/10	20
	10-1 to 12-1	7/24	29
	14-1 to 18-1	9/31	29
	20-1 to 25-1	3/26	12
	28-1 to 33-1	3/17	18
	40-1+	0/14	0

	Sex	Wins/runs	%
Sex	Mare	2/10	20
	Entire	1/4	25

Sponsored by Stan James

Win stats

Age	Wins/runs	%	£+-	% of stakes
5	0/47	0	-£47.00	-100
6	3/76	4	-£11.00	-14
7	3/69	4	-£35.00	-51
8	2/33	6	-£4.00	-12
9	1/20	5	-£13.50	-68
10+	1/15	7	-£3.00	-20

Weight	Wins/runs	%	£+-	% of stakes
Under 10st	0/29	0	-£29.00	-100
10st-10st6lb	7/135	5	-£22.50	-17
10st7lb-10st13lb	0/47	0	-£47.00	-100
11st-11st4lb	2/26	8	-£4.00	-15
11st5lb-11st9lb	1/16	6	-£4.00	-25
11st10lb+	0/7	0	-£7.00	-100

Sex	Wins/runs	%	£+-	% of stakes
Mare	0/26	0	-£26.00	-100
Entire	0/7	0	-£7.00	-100

OR	Wins/runs	%	£+-	% of stakes
Under 120	0/6	0	-£6.00	-100
120-129	4/81	5	-£35.00	-43
130-139	4/136	3	-£59.00	-43
140-149	2/32	6	-£8.50	-27
150+	0/5	0	-£5.00	-100

SP	Wins/runs	%	£+-	% of stakes
Under 5-1	2/5	40	+£5.00	+100
5-1 to 7-1	1/11	9	-£4.50	-41
15-2 to 9-1	0/9	0	-£9.00	-100
10-1 to 12-1	3/34	9	+£2.00	+6
14-1 to 18-1	2/39	5	-£5.00	-13
20-1 to 25-1	1/55	2	-£29.00	-53
28-1 to 33-1	1/53	2	-£19.00	-36
40-1 to 66-1	0/46	0	-£46.00	-100
80-1+	0/8	0	-£8.00	-100

Place stats

Weight	Wins/runs	%
Under 10st	1/29	3
10st-10st6lb	25/135	19
10st7lb-10st13lb	5/47	11
11st-11st4lb	4/26	15
11st5lb-11st9lb	3/16	19
11st10lb+	2/7	29

OR	Wins/runs	%
Under 120	2/6	33
120-129	12/81	15
130-139	18/136	13
140-149	6/32	19
150+	2/5	40

Age	Wins/runs	%
5	5/47	11
6	12/76	16
7	11/69	16
8	7/33	21
9	3/20	15
10+	2/15	13

Sex	Wins/runs	%
Mare	1/26	4
Entire	0/7	0

SP	Wins/runs	%
Under 5-1	3/5	60
5-1 to 7-1	5/11	45
15-2 to 9-1	4/9	44
10-1 to 12-1	12/34	35
14-1 to 18-1	5/39	13
20-1 to 25-1	8/55	15
28-1 to 33-1	3/53	6
40-1 to 66-1	0/46	0
80-1+	0/8	0

Win stats

	Age	Wins/runs	%	£+-	% of stakes
	5	3/67	4	-£47.62	-71
	6	3/73	4	-£30.00	-41
Age	7	2/55	4	-£27.00	-49
	8	1/32	3	-£23.00	-72
	9	1/10	10	+£5.00	+50
	10+	0/4	0	-£4.00	-100

	OR	Wins/runs	%	£+-	% of stakes
	Under 120	1/17	6	-£2.00	-12
Official Ratings	120-129	2/90	2	-£60.00	-67
	130-139	4/94	4	-£47.50	-51
	140+	3/40	8	-£17.12	-43

	Weight	Wins/runs	%	£+-	% of stakes
	Under 10st	0/28	0	-£28.00	-100
	10st-10st6lb	5/114	4	-£52.50	-46
Weight	10st7lb-10st13lb	2/47	4	-£17.00	-36
	11st-11st4lb	1/22	5	-£13.00	-59
	11st5lb-11st9lb	2/21	10	-£7.12	-34
	11st10lb+	0/9	0	-£9.00	-100

	SP	Wins/runs	%	£+-	% of stakes
	Under 5-1	2/7	29	+£1.38	+20
	5-1 to 7-1	0/12	0	-£12.00	-100
	15-2 to 9-1	1/17	6	-£8.00	-47
Starting Prices	10-1 to 12-1	3/28	11	+£7.00	+25
	14-1 to 18-1	4/45	9	+£17.00	+38
	20-1 to 25-1	0/45	0	-£45.00	-100
	28-1 to 33-1	0/33	0	-£33.00	-100
	40-1 to 66-1	0/40	0	-£40.00	-100
	80-1+	0/14	0	-£14.00	-100

	Sex	Wins/runs	%	£+-	% of stakes
Sex	Mare	2/19	11	+£5.00	+26
	Entire	0/6	0	-£6.00	-100

Place stats

	Age	Wins/runs	%
	5	12/67	18
	6	11/73	15
Age	7	6/55	11
	8	7/32	22
	9	3/10	30
	10+	1/4	25

	Weight	Wins/runs	%
	Under 10st	2/28	7
	10st-10st6lb	19/114	17
Weight	10st7lb-10st13lb	9/47	19
	11st-11st4lb	2/22	9
	11st5lb-11st9lb	8/21	38
	11st10lb+	0/9	0

	OR	Wins/runs	%
	Under 120	3/17	18
Official Ratings	120-129	14/90	16
	130-139	15/94	16
	140+	8/40	20

	SP	Wins/runs	%
	Under 5-1	4/7	57
	5-1 to 7-1	2/12	17
	15-2 to 9-1	5/17	29
	10-1 to 12-1	10/28	36
Starting Prices	14-1 to 18-1	7/45	16
	20-1 to 25-1	7/45	16
	28-1 to 33-1	2/33	6
	40-1 to 66-1	2/40	5
	80-1+	1/14	7

	Sex	Wins/runs	%
Sex	Mare	4/19	21
	Entire	0/6	0

Win stats

Age	Wins/runs	%	£+-	% of stakes
6	0/6	0	-£6.00	-100
7	0/11	0	-£11.00	-100
8	1/45	2	-£24.00	-53
9	3/99	3	-£62.00	-63
10	3/88	3	-£55.00	-63
11	2/66	3	-£15.00	-23
12	1/35	3	+£6.00	+17
13+	0/13	0	-£13.00	-100

Weight	Wins/runs	%	£+-	% of stakes
Under 10st	No runners			
10st-10st6lb	5/260	2	-£164.00	-63
10st7lb-10st13lb	5/54	9	+£33.00	+61
11st-11st4lb	0/22	0	-£22.00	-100
11st5lb-11st9lb	0/16	0	-£16.00	-100
11st10lb+	0/11	0	-£11.00	-100

OR	Wins/runs	%	£+-	% of stakes
Under 130	0/24	0	-£24.00	-100
130-139	3/82	4	-£33.00	-40
140-149	4/187	2	-£119.00	-64
150+	3/70	4	-£4.00	-6

SP	Wins/runs	%	£+-	% of stakes
Under 5-1	No runners			
5-1 to 7-1	2/10	20	+£6.00	+60
15-2 to 9-1	0/14	0	-£14.00	-100
10-1 to 12-1	2/35	6	-£13.00	-37
14-1 to 18-1	3/39	8	+£10.00	+26
20-1 to 25-1	1/44	2	-£23.00	-52
28-1 to 33-1	1/36	3	-£2.00	-6
40-1 to 66-1	1/106	1	-£65.00	-61
75-1+	0/79	0	-£79.00	-100

Sex	Wins/runs	%	£+-	% of stakes
Mare	0/7	0	-£7.00	-100

Place stats

Age	Wins/runs	%
6	0/6	0
7	0/11	0
8	5/45	11
9	17/99	17
10	7/88	8
11	9/66	14
12	2/35	6
13+	0/13	0

Sex	Wins/runs	%
Mare	2/7	29

Weight	Wins/runs	%
Under 10st	No runners	
10st-10st6lb	27/260	10
10st7lb-10st13lb	8/54	15
11st-11st4lb	1/22	5
11st5lb-11st9lb	3/16	19
11st10lb+	1/11	9

OR	Wins/runs	%
Under 130	3/24	13
130-139	8/82	10
140-149	19/187	10
150+	10/70	14

SP	Wins/runs	%
Under 5-1	No runners	
5-1 to 7-1	4/10	40
15-2 to 9-1	5/14	36
10-1 to 12-1	5/35	14
14-1 to 18-1	10/39	26
20-1 to 25-1	7/44	16
28-1 to 33-1	3/36	8
40-1 to 66-1	4/106	4
75-1+	2/79	3

Win stats

Age

Age	Wins/runs	%	£+-	% of stakes
6	1/5	20	+£12.00	+240
7	1/23	4	-£10.00	-43
8	4/44	9	-£5.50	-13
9	1/42	2	-£25.00	-60
10	1/36	3	-£27.50	-76
11	1/32	3	-£11.00	-34
12	1/11	9	+£6.00	+55
13+	0/5	0	-£5.00	-100

Weight

Weight	Wins/runs	%	£+-	% of stakes
Under 10st	0/21	0	-£21.00	-100
10st-10st6lb	5/122	4	-£46.50	-38
10st7lb-10st13lb	1/27	4	-£10.00	-37
11st-11st4lb	2/11	18	+£8.00	+73
11st5lb-11st9lb	0/9	0	-£9.00	-100
11st10lb+	2/8	25	+£12.50	+156

Official Ratings

OR	Wins/runs	%	£+-	% of stakes
Under 120	0/10	0	-£10.00	-100
120-129	1/68	1	-£51.00	-75
130-139	2/64	3	-£43.00	-67
140-149	6/45	13	+£32.00	+71
150+	1/11	9	+£6.00	+55

Starting Prices

SP	Wins/runs	%	£+-	% of stakes
Under 5-1	1/7	14	-£3.50	-50
5-1 to 7-1	2/20	10	-£6.00	-30
15-2 to 9-1	1/15	7	-£6.50	-43
10-1 to 12-1	1/25	4	-£12.00	-48
14-1 to 18-1	3/37	8	+£14.00	+38
20-1 to 25-1	2/25	8	+£17.00	+68
28-1 to 33-1	0/22	0	-£22.00	-100
40-1+	0/47	0	-£47.00	-100

Sex

Sex	Wins/runs	%	£+-	% of stakes
Mare	0/6	0	-£6.00	-100

Place stats

Age

Age	Wins/runs	%
6	3/5	60
7	6/23	26
8	14/44	32
9	8/42	19
10	3/36	8
11	3/32	9
12	1/11	9
13+	1/5	20

Weight

Weight	Wins/runs	%
Under 10st	2/21	10
10st-10st6lb	17/122	14
10st7lb-10st13lb	9/27	33
11st-11st4lb	5/11	45
11st5lb-11st9lb	2/9	22
11st10lb+	4/8	50

Official Ratings

OR	Wins/runs	%
Under 120	1/10	10
120-129	9/68	13
130-139	8/64	13
140-149	16/45	36
150+	5/11	45

Starting Prices

SP	Wins/runs	%
Under 5-1	3/7	43
5-1 to 7-1	8/20	40
15-2 to 9-1	4/15	27
10-1 to 12-1	8/25	32
14-1 to 18-1	10/37	27
20-1 to 25-1	4/25	16
28-1 to 33-1	0/22	0
40-1+	2/47	4

Sex

Sex	Wins/runs	%
Mare	0/6	0

Win stats

Age	Wins/runs	%	£+-	% of stakes
6	1/8	13	+£7.00	+88
7	2/17	12	+£5.00	+29
8	3/32	9	+£18.00	+56
9	3/46	7	-£12.00	-26
10	1/38	3	-£25.00	-66
11	0/17	0	-£17.00	-100
12+	0/13	0	-£13.00	-100

OR	Wins/runs	%	£+-	% of stakes
Under 130	0/6	0	-£6.00	-100
130-139	3/72	4	-£27.00	-38
140-149	6/65	9	+£11.00	+17
150+	1/28	4	-£15.00	-54

SP	Wins/runs	%	£+-	% of stakes
Under 5-1	0/10	0	-£10.00	-100
5-1 to 7-1	2/21	10	-£6.00	-29
15-2 to 9-1	1/13	8	-£4.00	-31
10-1 to 12-1	2/21	10	+£3.00	+14
14-1 to 18-1	4/28	14	+£32.00	+114
20-1 to 25-1	1/25	4	+£1.00	+4
28-1 to 33-1	0/13	0	-£13.00	-100
40-1+	0/40	0	-£40.00	-100

Weight	Wins/runs	%	£+-	% of stakes
Under 10st	0/11	0	-£11.00	-100
10st-10st6lb	5/92	5	-£10.00	-11
10st7lb-10st13lb	4/34	12	+£5.00	+15
11st-11st4lb	0/11	0	-£11.00	-100
11st5lb-11st9lb	0/14	0	-£14.00	-100
11st10lb+	1/9	11	+£4.00	+44

Sex	Wins/runs	%	£+-	% of stakes
Mare	0/2	0	-£2.00	-100

Place stats

Age	Wins/runs	%
6	4/8	50
7	4/17	24
8	10/32	31
9	6/46	13
10	8/38	21
11	4/17	24
12+	1/13	8

Weight	Wins/runs	%
Under 10st	1/11	9
10st-10st6lb	20/92	22
10st7lb-10st13lb	11/34	32
11st-11st4lb	2/11	18
11st5lb-11st9lb	1/14	7
11st10lb+	2/9	22

SP	Wins/runs	%
Under 5-1	4/10	40
5-1 to 7-1	10/21	48
15-2 to 9-1	4/13	31
10-1 to 12-1	6/21	29
14-1 to 18-1	6/28	21
20-1 to 25-1	3/25	12
28-1 to 33-1	1/13	8
40-1+	3/40	8

OR	Wins/runs	%
Under 130	1/6	17
130-139	17/72	24
140-149	15/65	23
150+	4/28	14

Sex	Wins/runs	%
Mare	1/2	50

Track Facts

YOU WANT course statistics? Look no further – this section contains all the numbers you'll need, for every jumps track in the country.

Course by course, we've set out four-year trainer and jockey statistics, favourites records, winning pointers and three-dimensional racecourse maps, plus details of how to get there and every fixture date for the new season.

Following that (page 236), we've got details of course record times, plus standard times for each track – by comparing the time of any race this season with the relevant standard time, you should get an indication of the quality of that race. Note that we have been unable to produce standard times in a very small number of cases, as there have not been enough recent races over the trip at the track in question.

See also our five-year statistical assessment of Britain's top 20 trainers (page 27).

AINTREE

Ormskirk Rd, Liverpool, L9 5AS. Tel. 0151 523 2600

How to get there - Road: M6, M62, M57, M58. Rail: Liverpool Lime St + taxi
Features: The LH 2m2f giant triangular Grand National course is perfectly flat. Inside it, the sharp LH Mildmay course is 1m4f in circumference
2003-04 Fixtures: Oct 26, Nov 22, 23, **Apr 1, 2, 3**, May 14
Winning Pointers: The trainer to follow remains Jonjo O Neill, who's enjoyed four winners at the Grand National meeting in each of the last two seasons. Philip Hobbs and Tim Easterby also have records of note, but Martin Pipe's runners haven't generally excelled.

Trainers	Wins-Runs	%	Hurdles	Chases	£1 level stks
Jonjo O'Neill	13-45	28.9	4-25	8-16	+95.71
F Doumen	3-14	21.4	1-7	2-7	+6.50
T Easterby	5-25	20.0	4-11	1-13	+24.50
L Lungo	4-21	19.0	2-14	0-3	+12.13
P Hobbs	9-54	16.7	4-26	5-26	+26.00
N Mason	4-26	15.4	0-7	4-17	+19.75
J Howard Johnson	4-28	14.3	1-7	3-21	-5.63
Miss H Knight	4-32	12.5	2-14	2-16	-9.14
F Murphy	4-34	11.8	1-8	3-25	+0.10
P Nicholls	7-64	10.9	1-12	6-51	-4.40
Mrs M Reveley	3-29	10.3	2-17	1-10	-1.00
Miss V Williams	6-63	9.5	3-25	3-35	-26.67
M Pipe	12-157	7.6	8-81	3-74	-69.72

Jockeys	Wins-Rides	%	£1 level stks	Best Trainer	W-R
R Walsh	8-29	27.6	+76.75	P Nicholls	3-10
T Doumen	3-13	23.1	+7.50	F Doumen	3-13
R Guest	4-19	21.1	+26.75	N Mason	4-13
B J Geraghty	4-23	17.4	+12.41	Miss F Crowley	1-1
A Dobbin	11-69	15.9	+25.38	L Lungo	3-10
L Cooper	3-19	15.8	+9.00	Jonjo O'Neill	3-17
R Garritty	5-32	15.6	+19.75	T Easterby	3-13
A McCoy	15-98	15.3	-34.89	M Pipe	9-71
B J Crowley	3-22	13.6	-6.67	Miss V Williams	3-20
M Fitzgerald	7-54	13.0	-12.87	N Henderson	4-39
R McGrath	4-32	12.5	+16.80	Jonjo O'Neill	2-2
J Culloty	4-34	11.8	+7.36	Miss H Knight	3-22
R Johnson	7-60	11.7	-2.00	P Hobbs	6-27
N Williamson	6-56	10.7	-18.38	Miss V Williams	2-25
G Lee	3-35	8.6	-8.00	J Howard Johnson	2-6

Mildmay hurdles

Favourites

Chases	26.1%	-£11.43
Hurdles	26.0%	-£29.12
Overall	26.1%	-£40.55

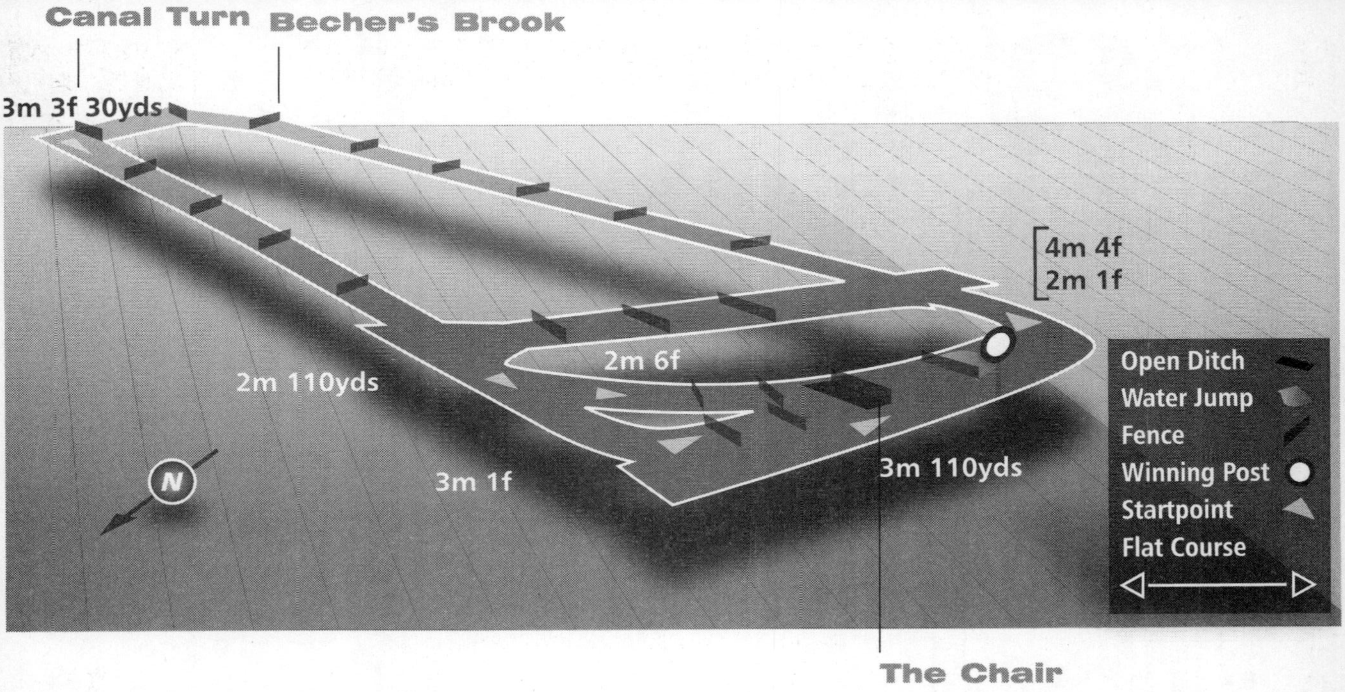

Grand National and Mildmay chase courses

Legend:
- Open Ditch
- Water Jump
- Fence
- Winning Post
- Startpoint
- Flat Course

4m 4f
2m 1f

Canal Turn Becher's Brook

3m 3f 30yds

2m 110yds

3m 1f

2m 6f

3m 110yds

The Chair

N

ASCOT

How to get there – Road: M4 Jct 6, M3 Jct 6, M25 Jct 13. Rail: Ascot from London Waterloo

Features: Galloping RH 1m6f triangular circuit, uphill finish

2003-04 Fixtures: Nov 1, 21, 22, Dec 19, 20, Jan 10, 31, Feb 21, Mar 20

Winning Pointers: Pipe and McCoy are out in front, with both enjoying huge level-stakes profits. Hughie Morrison has an eye-catching record; he doesn't run many (only five in five years) but, of those, three have hit the target. Francois Doumen's raiders have a 50 per cent strike-rate, but Nicky Henderson hasn't fared as well, showing a level stakes deficit.

Chases

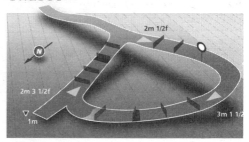

Hurdles

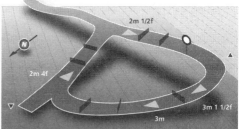

Favourites

Chases	36.2%	-£1.46
Hurdles	24.2%	-£48.64
Overall	29.7%	-£50.10

Trainers

Trainers	Wins-Runs	%	Hurdles	Chases	£1 level stks
H Morrison	3-5	60.0	2-4	1-1	+12.13
F Doumen	7-14	50.0	6-11	1-3	+11.90
J Akehurst	5-12	41.7	5-11	0-1	+21.50
N Chance	5-15	33.3	3-7	0-0	+18.25
M Pipe	42-132	31.8	23-80	19-49	+102.25
H Daly	4-16	25.0	3-10	1-5	+18.83
C Egerton	3-14	21.4	2-10	1-2	+10.00
M Pitman	9-42	21.4	6-25	3-14	+26.03
P Nicholls	8-38	21.1	1-8	7-29	-12.29
G L Moore	5-28	17.9	5-25	0-1	+13.50
Jonjo O'Neill	5-30	16.7	0-14	3-11	-13.90
N Henderson	14-96	14.6	7-54	6-38	-38.40

Jockeys

Jockeys	Wins-Rides	%	£1 level stks	Best Trainer	W-R
T Doumen	7-15	46.7	+10.90	F Doumen	7-14
R Walsh	4-10	40.0	+18.73	P Nicholls	2-5
A McCoy	48-132	36.4	+101.27	M Pipe	36-84
S Durack	4-16	25.0	+8.00	N Chance	2-2
N Williamson	13-64	20.3	+1.26	H Morrison	2-2
L Aspell	5-26	19.2	+51.13	J Gifford	2-3
R Johnson	12-83	14.5	-10.75	P Hobbs	4-25
T Scudamore	3-21	14.3	+5.00	M Pipe	3-10
F Keniry	3-22	13.6	+1.50	M Ryan	1-2
M Fitzgerald	15-112	13.4	-52.91	N Henderson	10-72
J Culloty	6-45	13.3	-4.42	Miss H Knight	2-21
N Fehily	4-36	11.1	-16.92	C Mann	2-22

Whitletts Road Ayr KA8 0JE
Tel: 01292 264179

AYR

How to get there – Road: south
from Glasgow on A77 or A75,
A70, A76. Rail: Ayr
Features: LH 1m4f oval, easy
turns, slight uphill finish
2003-04 Fixtures: Nov 15, 16,
Dec 8, 26, Jan 2, 31, Feb 14,
Mar 12, 13, Apr 16, 17
Winning Pointers: The combination of Paul Nicholls and Ruby
Walsh should be noted. Both
are showing healthy level-stakes
profits, with Walsh having won
10 races from 24 rides, six of
which were provided by
Nicholls. Lavinia Taylor has won
three from just seven raiders, so
her runners are worth considering, particularly at the Scottish
National meeting.

Chases

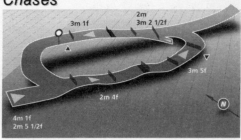

Hurdles

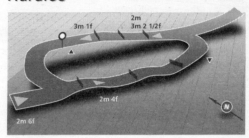

Favourites

Chases	36.6%	-£13.81
Hurdles	41.1%	-£13.85
Overall	39.0%	-£27.66

Trainers	Wins-Runs	%	Hurdles	Chases	£1 level stks
Miss P Robson	3-4	75.0	0-0	3-4	+7.77
Mrs L Taylor	3-7	42.9	0-2	3-5	+26.00
R Phillips	4-11	36.4	2-4	2-6	-3.47
T Tate	3-10	30.0	2-6	0-1	+7.00
N Richards	18-62	29.0	8-35	7-19	-2.13
Miss V Williams	3-11	27.3	3-4	0-7	+0.50
P Hobbs	6-22	27.3	3-6	2-15	+5.50
P Nicholls	9-34	26.5	2-8	6-25	+3.32
L Lungo	42-165	25.5	21-92	15-47	-57.87
N Twiston-Davies	3-12	25.0	1-1	0-8	+9.25
N Henderson	4-16	25.0	3-9	1-5	-9.88
I Williams	4-16	25.0	0-6	4-9	+16.75

Jockeys	Wins-Rides	%	£1 level stks	Best Trainer	W-R
W L Morgan	3-4	75.0	+6.77	Miss P Robson	2-2
W Marston	3-4	75.0	+9.70	R Phillips	2-3
R Walsh	10-24	41.7	+66.67	P Nicholls	6-17
M Fitzgerald	6-15	40.0	+4.88	N Henderson	3-10
A Dobbin	44-131	33.6	+0.83	L Lungo	26-54
P Robson	5-20	25.0	+23.63	A Whillans	3-5
R Johnson	10-45	22.2	-6.67	P Hobbs	4-12
F King	3-16	18.8	-8.17	Mrs M Reveley	3-11
D N Russell	3-16	18.8	+2.00	F Murphy	3-15
I Jardine	6-37	16.2	+10.00	A Whillans	6-22
A Thornton	4-26	15.4	+2.80	Mrs L Taylor	2-4
A McCoy	6-41	14.6	-24.34	M Pipe	2-24

BANGOR

Bangor-on-Dee, Nr Wrexham, Clwyd. Tel 01948 860438

How to get there – Road: A525.
Rail: Wrexham
Features: 1m4f LH, quite sharp.
Last fence gets plenty of fallers
2003-04 Fixtures: Oct 11, 27,
Nov 28, Dec 17, Feb 13, Mar 10,
27, Apr 17, 30, May 15, 25
Winning Pointers: Alan King
and Malcolm Jefferson both
have solid records. Of the jockeys, Robert Widger has done
well when riding Philip Hobbs's
horses (presumably when
Richard Johnson is elsewhere)
and has ridden some juicily-
priced winners.

Chases

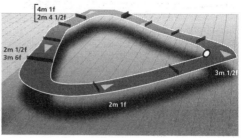

Hurdles

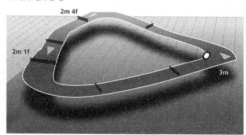

Favourites

Chases	38.6%	-£17.48
Hurdles	35.6%	-£28.90
Overall	36.9%	-£46.38

Trainers	Wins-Runs	%	Hurdles	Chases	£1 level stks
Miss H Knight	7-15	46.7	3-6	4-6	+5.03
Mrs E Crow	4-9	44.4	0-0	4-9	+1.78
P Nicholls	5-13	38.5	1-3	4-8	+2.55
M D Hammond	3-9	33.3	1-3	2-6	+10.50
M J Evans	4-13	30.8	0-1	4-12	+63.00
Jonjo O'Neill	22-81	27.2	16-49	6-29	+17.17
Mrs H Dalton	8-30	26.7	2-12	6-12	+9.60
M Pipe	20-77	26.0	17-61	3-15	-18.81
O Sherwood	3-12	25.0	2-4	1-5	-3.27
A King	5-20	25.0	3-10	1-9	+23.00
J Jefferson	5-22	22.7	2-13	3-6	+23.88
N Henderson	6-27	22.2	3-17	1-5	-13.15

Jockeys	Wins-Rides	%	£1 level stks	Best Trainer	W-R
A H Crow	3-6	50.0	-0.72	Mrs E Crow	3-6
R Burton	6-15	40.0	+4.10	Mrs H Dalton	2-4
P Robson	3-8	37.5	+19.00	R Phillips	1-1
A McCoy	25-80	31.3	-17.83	M Pipe	15-33
F Keniry	3-12	25.0	+45.62	Mrs S Williams	1-1
R Widger	7-28	25.0	+49.83	P Hobbs	4-9
L Cooper	8-36	22.2	+3.10	Jonjo O'Neill	8-33
A S Smith	5-23	21.7	+47.63	J Jefferson	2-3
J Culloty	6-28	21.4	-9.77	Miss H Knight	6-9
J Tizzard	4-19	21.1	-9.20	P Nicholls	3-9
R Johnson	19-90	21.1	+2.91	H Daly	4-19
R Garrity	6-29	20.7	+21.08	P R Webber	2-4

Sponsored by Stan James

Blackwell, Carlisle, Cumbria, CA2 4TS.
Tel: 01228 522973.

CARLISLE

How to get there – Road: M6 Jctn 42. Rail: 2m from Citadel Station, Carlisle

Features: Pear-shaped, 1m5f circuit, RH, undulating, tough uphill home stretch

2003-04 Fixtures: Oct 10, 25, Nov 2, 10, 27, Feb 11, 23, Mar 11, 21, Apr 10, 18

Winning Pointers: Tom George has done well but with very few runners (three from five). Among the jocks, Graham Lee's track record is excellent, with his 15 winners returning a level-stakes profit of £119.02. Also, watch Tony McCoy's rides for Jonjo O'Neill.

Chases

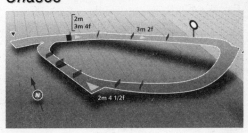

Hurdles

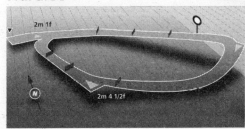

Favourites

Chases	27.9%	-£33.79
Hurdles	37.7%	-£10.20
Overall	33.3%	-£43.99

Trainers	Wins-Runs	%	Hurdles	Chases	£1 level stks
T George	3-5	60.0	0-0	1-3	+20.50
R C Guest	3-7	42.9	1-1	2-4	+4.66
Mrs S Bramall	3-8	37.5	1-4	2-4	+14.00
Mrs D Sayer	4-14	28.6	2-7	2-3	+7.50
Mrs A M Naughton	3-11	27.3	2-8	1-3	+7.75
L Lungo	26-113	23.0	13-66	9-32	-14.81
A Parker	9-42	21.4	2-15	6-18	+16.83
R Fahey	3-15	20.0	0-10	3-4	+2.50
J Howard Johnson	8-40	20.0	4-17	4-21	+7.28
Jonjo O'Neill	18-96	18.8	9-48	5-40	+8.87
Mrs M Reveley	11-59	18.6	7-29	4-21	+0.44
Mrs S J Smith	15-83	18.1	7-31	8-42	-9.95

Jockeys	Wins-Rides	%	£1 level stks	Best Trainer	W-R
A McCoy	5-10	50.0	+5.55	Jonjo O'Neill	4-6
K Renwick	7-20	35.0	+31.21	C Parker	3-6
P Ryan	7-27	25.9	+30.75	N Mason	4-12
W Marston	7-32	21.9	-11.10	Mrs S J Smith	5-14
A Dempsey	7-34	20.6	+1.60	Mrs M Reveley	6-24
C Llewellyn	3-18	16.7	-5.75	N Twiston-Davies	2-14
A Dobbin	20-124	16.1	-77.44	L Lungo	11-32
G Lee	17-107	15.9	+119.02	J Jefferson	8-35
P Robson	4-26	15.4	+9.00	T J FitzGerald	1-1
D Elsworth	6-39	15.4	-7.75	Mrs S J Smith	6-24
L Cooper	7-50	14.0	+7.25	Jonjo O'Neill	6-23
B Gibson	6-45	13.3	-20.28	L Lungo	6-36

CARTMEL

Cartmel, Grange-over-Sands,
Penrith, Cumbria, CA10 2HG.
Tel 015935 36340

How to get there – Road: M6 Jctn 36, A591. Rail: Cark-in-Cartmel or Grange-over-Sands
Features: Tight LH, only 1m round, undulating, half-mile run-in from last (longest in country)
2003-04 Fixtures: May 26, 29, 31

Winning Pointers: Not much to go on, due to the relative lack of meetings here. Anything trained by Brian Ellison and ridden by Vinnie Keane could be worth a second look.

Chases

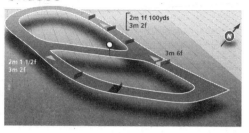

Hurdles

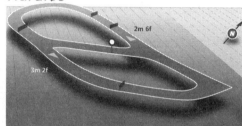

Favourites

Chases	23.9%	-£16.49
Hurdles	24.0%	-£24.13
Overall	24.0%	-£40.62

Trainers

Trainers	Wins-Runs	%	Hurdles	Chases	£1 level stks
M Pipe	6-16	37.5	5-11	1-5	+0.59
Mrs M Reveley	4-13	30.8	3-10	1-3	+9.25
N Richards	5-18	27.8	2-11	3-7	+6.25
B Ellison	3-11	27.3	2-7	1-4	+6.87
P Monteith	4-15	26.7	3-8	1-7	+2.50
F Murphy	3-17	17.6	2-9	1-8	-2.12
Mrs S J Smith	6-34	17.6	1-15	5-19	+3.50
D Moffatt	3-20	15.0	3-20	0-0	-1.50
M Chapman	6-42	14.3	5-28	1-14	+2.00
M Todhunter	4-39	10.3	1-22	3-17	-17.75
N Mason	3-33	9.1	2-18	1-15	-11.25
D McCain	3-33	9.1	2-22	1-11	-5.50

Jockeys

Jockeys	Wins-Rides	%	£1 level stks	Best Trainer	W-R
V T Keane	3-7	42.9	+12.88	B Ellison	2-6
A McCoy	7-25	28.0	-6.42	M Pipe	4-12
W Marston	3-11	27.3	+3.75	P Bowen	1-1
G Lake	3-12	25.0	+24.50	Mrs D Sayer	1-1
P Ryan	3-13	23.1	-2.50	B Ellison	1-1
K Renwick	4-18	22.2	-2.50	P Monteith	3-6
J Crowley	3-14	21.4	+11.50	M Todhunter	2-4
A Dobbin	5-32	15.6	-3.25	W Storey	1-1
D Moffatt	3-20	15.0	-1.50	D Moffatt	3-18
W M Worthington	5-42	11.9	-6.00	M Chapman	5-35
B Harding	3-26	11.5	-12.75	M D Hammond	2-6
G Lee	3-26	11.5	-9.75	E W Tuer	2-2
R McGrath	3-27	11.1	+11.33	C Wilson	1-1

Sponsored by Stan James

Catterick Bridge, Richmond,
N.Yorkshire, DL10 7PE.
Tel: 01748 811478

CATTERICK

How to get there – Road: A1.
Rail: Darlington
Features: LH 1m2f oval,
undulating, sharp turns,
favouring small, handy horses
2003-04 Fixtures: Nov 22,
Dec 3, 18, Jan 1, 15, 24, Feb 6,
Mar 2, 10
Winning Pointers: The Richard
Fahey/Padge Whelan combination has proved rewarding, and
they should be noted when
teaming up. Tony Dobbin has
ticks in all the right boxes.

Chases

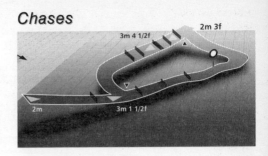

Hurdles

Favourites

Chases	38.2%	+£5.90
Hurdles	31.5%	-£18.49
Overall	34.0%	-£12.59

Trainers	Wins-Runs	%	Hurdles	Chases	£1 level stks
R Fahey	6-23	26.1	4-14	1-3	+14.65
T Easterby	10-47	21.3	8-30	2-13	-1.03
Jonjo O'Neill	6-30	20.0	2-20	3-8	-4.00
L Lungo	6-31	19.4	3-19	1-8	-4.88
F Kirby	3-16	18.8	0-6	3-9	-4.25
Mrs M Reveley	24-129	18.6	13-74	9-45	-25.12
M W Easterby	11-72	15.3	4-37	5-24	-1.54
J Howard Johnson	10-67	14.9	6-39	4-25	-10.73
M D Hammond	10-73	13.7	5-37	4-32	-28.68
Mrs V Ward	3-22	13.6	3-17	0-5	+15.00
M Todhunter	3-28	10.7	3-13	0-13	-8.00
W Storey	3-29	10.3	2-24	1-4	-3.00

Jockeys	Wins-Rides	%	£1 level stks	Best Trainer	W-R
R Guest	9-31	29.0	+27.75	N Mason	4-15
A Dobbin	15-59	25.4	+34.21	J Howard Johnson	4-7
G Carenza	3-14	21.4	+6.67	M W Easterby	2-12
P Aspell	5-27	18.5	-3.92	Mrs M Reveley	3-15
A Ross	7-39	17.9	-5.86	Mrs M Reveley	4-16
D Byrne	3-18	16.7	-1.10	R Fahey	2-3
R Garritty	12-73	16.4	+6.44	T Easterby	6-26
P Whelan	5-31	16.1	+13.87	R Fahey	3-7
A Dempsey	8-65	12.3	-25.53	Mrs M Reveley	8-40
J P McNamara	6-49	12.2	-16.88	F Murphy	2-13
L Cooper	4-33	12.1	-14.00	Jonjo O'Neill	3-10
B Storey	4-35	11.4	+11.00	J Walton	2-4

CHELTENHAM

Prestbury Park,
Cheltenham,
Glos GL50 4SH.
Tel. 01242 513014.

How to get there - Road: A435, 5 miles north of M5 Jcts 9, 10, 11.
Rail: Cheltenham

Features: There are two LH courses; the Old Course is 1m4f around, the slightly longer New Course is similar. Both end with a testing uphill finish, making Cheltenham a stiff track.

2003-04 Fixtures: Oct 28, 29, Nov 14, 15, 16, Dec 12, 13, Jan 1, 24, **Mar 16**, **17**, **18**, Apr 14, 15, 28

Winning Pointers: Martin Pipe has had plenty of winners but, if you'd backed his horses blindly, you would be facing a deficit of £31.05. Henry Daly doesn't waste any ammunition when sending horses to HQ. He enjoyed a great Festival last season, with Young Spartacus and Palarshan both winning, and Haut Cercy going very close. Davy Russell has done well with limited rides, while Barry Geraghty, Tony Dobbin and Richard Johnson have also returned profits.

Favourites: Chases 30.3% -£5.26   Hurdles 34.4% +£10.27   Overall 32.3% +£5.01

New Course

Chases

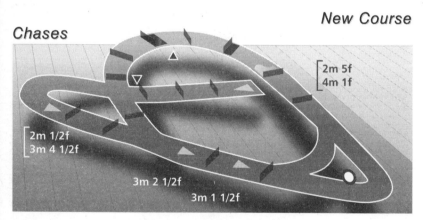

Hurdles

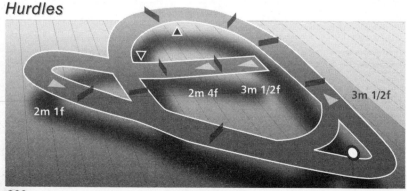

Trainers	Wins-Runs	%	Hurdles	Chases	£1 level stks
Mrs J Harrington	3-10	30.0	1-5	2-5	+10.25
N Chance	5-19	26.3	2-6	3-8	+3.16
H Daly	9-38	23.7	2-12	7-25	+37.75
K Bishop	3-13	23.1	2-5	1-6	+18.50
A J Martin	6-26	23.1	4-15	2-10	+6.50
H Morrison	3-15	20.0	0-6	3-8	+4.50
C Tizzard	3-15	20.0	0-1	3-14	+28.00
E O'Grady	4-21	19.0	1-9	1-8	+10.33
Jonjo O'Neill	18-95	18.9	10-61	7-28	+43.59
R Alner	5-28	17.9	1-9	4-18	+8.83
F Doumen	3-18	16.7	3-12	0-6	-4.12
Miss V Williams	15-99	15.2	5-36	9-59	-8.17
N Henderson	22-145	15.2	8-77	12-55	-13.81
P Hobbs	23-151	15.2	14-86	7-57	-13.34
M Pipe	55-380	14.5	28-226	26-150	-31.05
P Nicholls	23-165	13.9	9-40	13-120	-73.26
Miss H Knight	14-103	13.6	0-27	12-64	-15.80
R Phillips	3-23	13.0	1-12	2-11	+10.75
R Rowe	3-26	11.5	1-12	2-13	-4.50

Old Course

Chases

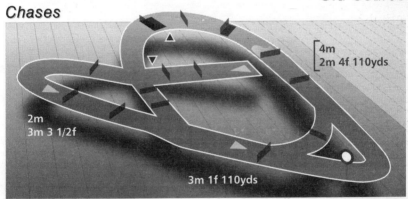

4m
2m 4f 110yds

2m
3m 3 1/2f

3m 1f 110yds

Hurdles

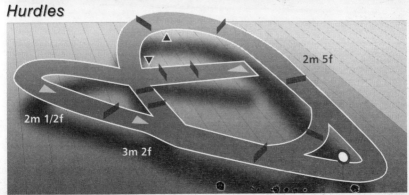

2m 5f

2m 1/2f

3m 2f

CHELTENHAM ctd

Jockeys	Wins-Rides	%	£1 level stks	Best Trainer	W-R
R Walford	3-6	50.0	+22.33	R Alner	3-5
A Charles-Jones	3-11	27.3	+30.75	H Manners	2-4
D N Russell	4-15	26.7	+11.50	F Murphy	4-11
A McCoy	56-240	23.3	-19.63	M Pipe	45-187
M Fitzgerald	28-150	18.7	-3.81	N Henderson	18-89
B J Geraghty	9-49	18.4	+41.25	Mrs J Harrington	3-5
T Doumen	3-17	17.6	-3.12	F Doumen	3-16
R Johnson	29-173	16.8	+23.95	P Hobbs	11-57
R Walsh	14-89	15.7	-10.65	P Nicholls	9-41
N Williamson	23-150	15.3	-10.66	Miss V Williams	11-39
Paul Carberry	5-33	15.2	+5.00	H Morrison	1-2
J Tizzard	10-73	13.7	+14.00	P Nicholls	5-44
J Culloty	14-102	13.7	+6.70	Miss H Knight	13-75
A Dobbin	7-55	12.7	+19.50	Jonjo O'Neill	2-6
J M Maguire	3-24	12.5	+3.00	T George	2-16
S Durack	5-44	11.4	-1.67	I Williams	2-10
M Foley	3-28	10.7	-5.25	K Bishop	1-1
L Cooper	3-36	8.3	-24.75	Jonjo O'Neill	3-31

THE TOUGHEST TEST: the undulating track at Prestbury Park is daunting at racing speed

Chepstow, Gwent, NP6 5YH.
Tel: 01291 622260.

CHEPSTOW

How to get there – Road: three mins west of Severn Bridge (M4). Rail: Chepstow
Features: LH undulating oval, nearly 2m round, suits long-striding front-runners
2003-04 Fixtures: Oct 4, 22, Nov 8, 26, Dec 6, 27, Jan 23, Feb 7, 28, Mar 10, 24, Apr 13, May 5
Winning Pointers: Paul Nicholls scores heavily, with a pleasing percentage of winners. Norman Williamson has done well, although his visits are less frequent these days, as have Timmy Murphy and Richard Johnson. The latter has been particularly successful when combining with Philip Hobbs.

Chases

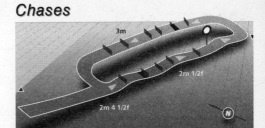

Hurdles

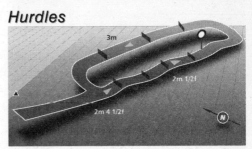

Favourites

Chases	31.5%	-£23.19
Hurdles	37.4%	-£16.43
Overall	35.0%	-£39.62

Trainers	Wins-Runs	%	Hurdles	Chases	£1 level stks
S Gollings	3-5	60.0	3-5	0-0	+27.00
G Macaire	3-10	30.0	2-7	1-3	+8.00
P Nicholls	44-151	29.1	15-64	25-76	+9.80
P Rich	3-11	27.3	3-11	0-0	+3.75
J Portman	3-11	27.3	2-8	1-1	+13.00
R J Smith	3-12	25.0	2-9	0-0	0.00
P Hobbs	9-119	24.4	15-62	12-49	+12.86
A Carroll	4-19	21.1	2-14	2-4	+11.50
M Pipe	38-181	21.0	25-123	9-50	-22.19
Miss V Williams	12-60	20.0	7-25	5-29	+15.27
R Lee	4-22	18.2	3-8	1-14	+2.58
R Hodges	3-17	17.6	2-9	1-4	+11.00

Jockeys	Wins-Rides	%	£1 level stks	Best Trainer	W-R
R Walsh	10-25	40.0	-2.47	P Nicholls	9-23
C Williams	4-13	30.8	-1.29	P Nicholls	3-4
J Huet	3-10	30.0	+25.50	G Fierro	1-1
T J Murphy	26-100	26.0	+23.80	P Nicholls	15-40
T Scudamore	7-28	25.0	-6.45	M Pipe	4-16
W Hutchinson	3-13	23.1	+33.50	R J Price	1-1
A McCoy	34-155	21.9	-36.78	M Pipe	26-110
R Johnson	26-119	21.8	+10.24	P Hobbs	15-49
B J Crowley	8-39	20.5	+6.78	Miss V Williams	8-35
M Bradburne	5-25	20.0	+8.25	H Daly	4-10
N Williamson	7-36	19.4	+16.91	Miss V Williams	2-12
J M Maguire	3-17	17.6	+5.00	T George	3-12

DONCASTER

Grand Stand, Leger Way,
Doncaster, DN2 6BB.
Tel: 01302 320066/7.

How to get there – Road: M18 Jctn 3, A638, A18 to Hull. Rail: Doncaster Central

Features: LH, flat, 2m, run-in of just over a furlong, rarely heavy, speed horses are generally favoured.

2003-04 Fixtures: Nov 30, Dec 12, 13, Jan 19, 30, 31, Feb 25, Mar 5, 6

Winning Pointers: No outstanding pointers, although Tim Easterby's level-stakes profit is impressive. Just over one in three of Martin Pipe's horses win, while Jim Culloty, Russ Garrity and the unheralded Eugene Husband have led the way in the riding stakes.

Chases

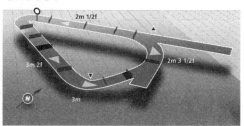

Hurdles

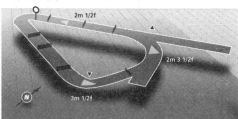

Favourites

Chases	28.1%	-£24.43
Hurdles	32.6%	-£17.41
Overall	30.7%	-£41.85

Trainers	Wins-Runs	%	Hurdles	Chases	£1 level stks
T Tate	5-14	35.7	2-3	2-7	+9.76
M Pipe	11-31	35.5	6-15	5-14	+14.54
N Henderson	8-25	32.0	3-15	5-8	-5.83
T George	3-11	27.3	2-7	1-4	+20.75
R Fahey	4-15	26.7	3-11	1-4	+24.00
Jonjo O'Neill	11-44	25.0	10-31	1-11	+6.74
N Mason	6-25	24.0	2-14	4-10	+8.38
P Nicholls	3-13	23.1	0-3	3-10	+2.00
T Easterby	9-41	22.0	3-19	3-17	+49.45
K Bailey	4-22	18.2	0-9	4-13	+8.50
M W Easterby	8-47	17.0	4-25	2-15	-16.16
M Pitman	3-19	15.8	1-9	2-8	-3.50

Jockeys	Wins-Rides	%	£1 level stks	Best Trainer	W-R
A McCoy	6-17	35.3	+3.88	M Pipe	6-9
L Cooper	8-24	33.3	+23.08	Jonjo O'Neill	6-19
M Foley	4-14	28.6	+2.61	N Henderson	3-5
A Garrity	3-11	27.3	+39.00	Mrs M Reveley	3-11
R Guest	7-29	24.1	+8.38	N Mason	6-12
E Husband	4-17	23.5	+38.50	G McCourt	2-5
M Fitzgerald	5-22	22.7	-11.14	N Henderson	3-9
J Culloty	8-37	21.6	+42.11	Miss H Knight	5-22
J Kavanagh	4-19	21.1	+36.48	Mrs M Reveley	1-1
J P McNamara	8-39	20.5	+38.48	R Fahey	2-2
D O'Meara	4-20	20.0	+21.50	T Easterby	3-7
J M Maguire	4-20	20.0	+11.88	T Tate	2-3

Kennford, nr Exeter, Devon EX6 7XS.
Tel 01392 832599

How to get there – Road: 5m south of M5, A38. Rail: Exeter
Features: RH, 2m, hilly, the half-mile home straight is all uphill, with a 300yds run-in
2003-04 Fixtures: Oct 8, 21, Nov 4, 21, Dec 5, 18, Jan 1, Feb 2, Mar 9, 23, Apr 6, 13, 28, May 4, 12,
Winning Pointers: Sara Williams (not to be confused with Venetia) has an impressive level-stakes profit, albeit from relatively few runners. Robert Walford has done well when partnering Robert Alner's horses but Richard Johnson's many winners belie the fact that they're mostly at short odds.

Chases

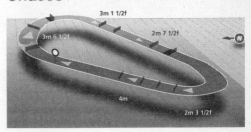

Hurdles

Favourites

Chases	36.1%	-£21.03
Hurdles	34.8%	-£25.62
Overall	35.3%	-£46.65

Trainers	Wins-Runs	%	Hurdles	Chases	£1 level stks
M Bradstock	7-14	50.0	2-5	5-8	+32.75
Miss V Williams	8-28	28.6	4-13	3-14	+3.76
Mrs A Thorpe	3-12	25.0	3-7	0-4	+22.50
P Hobbs	46-214	21.5	23-121	20-84	-32.79
J C Fox	3-15	20.0	3-14	0-1	+9.62
I Williams	5-26	19.2	3-18	2-8	-6.60
M Pipe	46-246	18.7	30-175	14-59	-25.54
P Nicholls	23-125	18.4	11-44	12-72	-30.54
J R Payne	3-17	17.6	3-14	0-3	+40.00
Mrs S Williams	6-34	17.6	5-24	1-10	+72.20
A King	4-24	16.7	2-19	2-5	+7.25
Miss H Knight	11-66	16.7	4-32	7-31	-15.47

Jockeys	Wins-Rides	%	£1 level stks	Best Trainer	W-R
A McCoy	43-160	26.9	-0.45	M Pipe	30-124
M Foley	4-15	26.7	+7.75	K Bishop	3-4
R Walford	5-19	26.3	+19.50	R Alner	4-12
D O'Meara	3-12	25.0	-0.09	P Hobbs	3-8
R Walsh	6-25	24.0	-0.39	P Nicholls	6-24
R Johnson	35-151	23.2	-36.55	P Hobbs	25-88
J Huet	5-23	21.7	+7.44	M Pipe	5-22
J M Maguire	3-16	18.8	-2.50	M Muggeridge	2-3
S Fox	3-17	17.6	+7.62	J C Fox	3-12
T Scudamore	5-29	17.2	-9.70	N Twiston-Davies	3-8
D R Dennis	4-26	15.4	-2.50	W Dennis	2-3
B Fenton	8-53	15.1	+0.46	I Balding	2-2

FAKENHAM

The Racecourse, Fakenham, Norfolk, NR21 7NY. Tel 01328 862 388

How to get there – Road: A1065 from Swaffham, A148 Kings Lynn, A1067 from Norwich. Rail: Kings Lynn, Norwich

Features: LH, 1m round, undulating, a run-in of little more than a furlong, unsuitable for long-striding horses

2003-04 Fixtures: Oct 24, Nov 23, Dec 22, Jan 21, Feb 20, Mar 19, Apr 12, May 5, 16

Winning Pointers: Nicky Henderson leads the way in terms of winners-to-runners but, for a decent profit, look to Lucy Wadham, whose horses are more likely to go off at reasonable prices. As a result, Leighton Aspell has also done well.

Chases

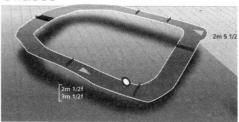

Hurdles

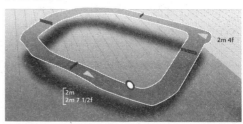

Favourites

Chases	36.7%	-£16.36
Hurdles	31.2%	-£16.23
Overall	33.6%	-£32.59

Trainers

Trainers	Wins-Runs	%	Hurdles	Chases	£1 level stks
D Cantillon	3-5	60.0	2-4	1-1	+21.60
P Nicholls	5-12	41.7	0-3	5-9	+3.12
N Henderson	11-27	40.7	5-16	2-4	-6.64
C M Kinane	4-12	33.3	2-3	2-8	+7.25
Miss V Williams	9-27	33.3	5-14	3-11	+3.98
N Mason	8-26	30.8	4-13	4-12	+3.73
P S McEntee	3-10	30.0	3-10	0-0	+8.00
N Chance	3-10	30.0	1-7	1-2	+3.00
S Dow	3-10	30.0	2-6	1-4	+4.76
I Williams	6-22	27.3	2-9	4-13	-1.10
Mrs L Wadham	4-16	25.0	3-14	1-2	+15.91
O Brennan	6-24	25.0	1-8	5-12	+10.50

Jockeys

Jockeys	Wins-Rides	%	£1 level stks	Best Trainer	W-R
R Guest	4-10	40.0	+3.98	N Mason	4-8
M Fitzgerald	15-42	35.7	-8.85	N Henderson	9-19
L McGrath	3-9	33.3	+1.67	R C Guest	1-2
A S Smith	3-9	33.3	+8.17	K Morgan	1-2
N Williamson	8-27	29.6	-4.20	Miss V Williams	6-13
A McCoy	7-24	29.2	+2.83	I Williams	2-3
T Doyle	4-15	26.7	+3.75	N Chance	2-3
L Aspell	6-23	26.1	+26.50	Mrs L Wadham	2-6
T J Phelan	3-12	25.0	+5.87	Jonjo O'Neill	1-1
D R Dennis	3-12	25.0	+1.75	I Williams	2-6
J A McCarthy	6-29	20.7	-0.18	P S McEntee	3-3
B J Crowley	3-15	20.0	-0.38	Miss V Williams	3-10

How to get there – Road: M20 Jctn 11, A20 nr Westenhanger. Rail: Westenhanger

Features: RH, easy-turning, undulating, about 1m3f round

2003-04 Fixtures: Nov 4, 17, Dec 1, 16, Jan 2, 20, 30, Feb 17, Mar 3, May 19

Winning Pointers: Ferdy Murphy has solid statistics. He has a 36 per cent strike-rate and a level-stakes profit of £10.35. Guillaume Macaire often introduces good horses here, and they usually win (three from four). but they don't go off at big prices. J P McNamara emerges with credit from the jockeys list.

Chases

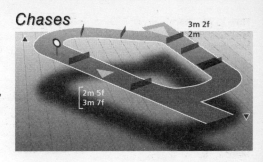

Hurdles

Favourites

Chases	38.2%	-£8.29
Hurdles	40.2%	-£2.15
Overall	39.3%	-£10.44

Trainers

Trainers	Wins-Runs	%	Hurdles	Chases	£1 level stks
G Macaire	3-4	75.0	0-1	3-3	-0.90
N Gifford	3-5	60.0	0-0	3-5	+12.75
M Pipe	14-26	53.8	12-21	1-3	+0.78
M Hogan	3-6	50.0	3-4	0-2	+9.75
S Sherwood	3-7	42.9	2-3	1-1	+21.60
N Henderson	11-29	37.9	5-16	5-8	-1.54
F Murphy	4-11	36.4	0-4	2-5	+10.35
P Hobbs	5-14	35.7	4-9	1-4	-0.20
P Nicholls	9-26	34.6	3-10	6-15	-5.72
Miss V Williams	11-34	32.4	6-13	2-17	+6.58
Miss E Lavelle	4-13	30.8	4-9	0-4	+3.25
D L Williams	4-16	25.0	1-5	3-11	+1.50

Jockeys

Jockeys	Wins-Rides	%	£1 level stks	Best Trainer	W-R
J Ricou	3-4	75.0	-0.90	G Macaire	3-4
P Bull	3-7	42.9	+4.50	Miss A M N-Smit	2-2
C Williams	3-9	33.3	-2.63	D L Williams	2-3
D J Casey	3-9	33.3	+1.80	O Sherwood	2-6
A McCoy	26-78	33.3	-13.01	M Pipe	14-22
M Fitzgerald	16-49	32.7	+2.96	N Henderson	10-21
B J Crowley	7-26	26.9	+0.33	Miss V Williams	7-19
R Johnson	9-37	24.3	+8.63	P Hobbs	3-4
J P McNamara	4-19	21.1	+15.60	F Murphy	3-9
T J Murphy	11-57	19.3	-20.80	M Pitman	5-19
P York	3-16	18.8	+2.65	R York	2-8
B Hitchcott	6-32	18.8	+19.50	D Grissell	4-14

FONTWELL

How to get there – Road: A29 to Bognor Regis. Rail: Barnham
Features: 1m4f LH, quite sharp. Last fence gets plenty of fallers
2003-04 Fixtures: Oct 5, Nov 10, Dec 9, 22, Jan 12, 26, Feb 9, 22, Mar 8, 21, Apr 7, 22, May 3, 26, 30,
Winning Pointers: Sam Stronge and Timmy Murphy have good strike-rates when riding for Paul Nicholls. Mick Fitzgerald has also done well when riding for his guv'nor Nicky Henderson.

Chases

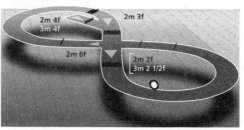

Hurdles

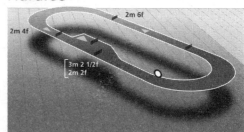

Favourites

Chases	33.5%	-£39.76
Hurdles	29.4%	-£75.55
Overall	31.1%	-£115.30

Trainers

Trainers	Wins-Runs	%	Hurdles	Chases	£1 level stks
C Egerton	4-11	36.4	2-5	0-1	+2.46
G Wareham	3-9	33.3	0-6	3-3	+11.10
A Hobbs	3-9	33.3	1-6	2-3	+29.73
P Nicholls	37-113	32.7	12-39	24-66	+21.82
V Dartnall	4-16	25.0	1-4	2-6	-1.38
M Pipe	34-138	24.6	27-103	4-25	-30.23
Lady Herries	3-13	23.1	3-9	0-3	+6.36
Miss V Williams	11-51	21.6	4-17	7-28	-7.22
P Hobbs	17-84	20.2	9-50	8-28	-15.42
C Mann	11-57	19.3	9-46	2-10	+27.04
P Bowen	5-26	19.2	1-13	4-10	+15.00
G L Moore	21-111	18.9	14-81	7-29	+20.54

Jockeys

Jockeys	Wins-Rides	%	£1 level stks	Best Trainer	W-R
R P McNally	5-15	33.3	+1.00	P Nicholls	5-9
R Walsh	5-16	31.3	-2.02	P Nicholls	5-14
T J Phelan	4-13	30.8	+17.26	Jonjo O'Neill	1-1
N Williamson	11-42	26.2	-2.99	Miss V Williams	7-22
A McCoy	38-148	25.7	-35.04	M Pipe	22-80
T J Murphy	18-81	22.2	+22.14	P Nicholls	6-14
M Fitzgerald	21-99	21.2	+23.87	N Henderson	9-38
S Stronge	11-57	19.3	+24.50	P Nicholls	4-8
J Tizzard	19-102	18.6	-19.93	P Nicholls	13-47
R Flavin	3-17	17.6	+5.00	D Elsworth	1-2
D R Dennis	3-17	17.6	-5.65	G McCourt	1-1
N Fehily	9-53	17.0	+1.33	C Mann	5-31

Newton-Le-Willows, Lancashire,
WA12 0HQ. Tel: 01942 725963.

How to get there – Road: M6
Jctn 23 on A49 to Wigan. Rail:
Wigan or Warrington Bank Quay
(main line)
Features: 1m5f round, flat, with
a quarter-mile run-in, chase
course suits galloping-types,
hurdles track is sharper
2003-04 Fixtures: Oct 23,
Nov 6, 16, 29, Dec 13, 29,
Jan 10, 24, Feb 14, 28, May 1
Winning Pointers: Martin Todhunter does well, although the
statistics are somewhat skewed
by the successes of his course
specialist Kingsmark. Sue Smith
often runs her best horses at
this track, while the combination
of Ollie McPhail and Alan King is
worth looking at.

HAYDOCK

Chases

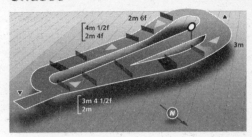

Hurdles

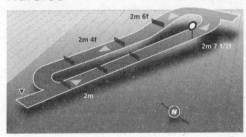

Favourites

Chases	31.2%	-£26.26
Hurdles	42.0%	+£23.55
Overall	37.8%	-£2.72

Trainers	Wins-Runs	%	Hurdles	Chases	£1 level stks
N Richards	7-25	28.0	4-17	2-5	+12.41
M Todhunter	5-18	27.8	2-7	3-9	+24.46
Miss V Williams	18-65	27.7	8-34	10-29	-3.75
R Lee	3-12	25.0	1-6	2-6	+13.00
R Alner	3-13	23.1	2-8	1-4	+12.75
Jonjo O'Neill	19-85	22.4	16-59	2-21	-16.65
P R Webber	4-18	22.2	1-7	2-8	+11.55
Mrs S J Smith	16-72	22.2	9-39	6-27	+83.10
T George	5-26	19.2	3-13	2-12	+12.50
R Phillips	3-16	18.8	1-11	1-4	+4.50
A King	6-33	18.2	3-20	2-6	+33.50
Mrs M Reveley	14-88	15.9	13-73	1-11	-0.46

Jockeys	Wins-Rides	%	£1 level stks	Best Trainer	W-R
J E Moore	3-4	75.0	+9.41	M Pipe	3-3
P Flynn	5-16	31.3	+1.05	Miss V Williams	2-2
A Thornton	12-43	27.9	+22.01	Miss V Williams	2-3
A McCoy	17-63	27.0	-14.29	M Pipe	10-45
J Crowley	4-16	25.0	+4.61	G A Swinbank	1-2
J Mogford	4-16	25.0	+24.50	R Alner	1-2
O McPhail	5-21	23.8	+60.00	A King	3-7
L Cooper	9-39	23.1	-1.25	Jonjo O'Neill	9-36
J Kavanagh	4-18	22.2	-2.15	Jonjo O'Neill	2-3
R Johnson	8-39	20.5	-8.08	P Hobbs	4-9
D J Casey	3-15	20.0	+12.00	I Williams	1-1
A Dobbin	14-72	19.4	-3.21	N Richards	7-15

HEREFORD

Roman Road, Holmer, Hereford
HR4 9QU. Tel 01981 250 436

How to get there – Road: A49 1m north of Hereford. Rail: Hereford

Features: RH, 1m4f round, fences trickier than those at most minor tracks

2003-04 Fixtures: Oct 2, Nov 20, Dec 2, 20, Jan 7, Feb 6, 15, Mar 9, 22, Apr 3, 29, May 11, 23, June 9, 15

Winning Pointers: Henrietta Knight often runs her better novices here and has a good-looking strike-rate and level-stakes profit to show for it. Robert Biddlecombe has been the beneficiary, picking up rides when Jim Culloty isn't available. Liam Cummins has a 100 per cent record for Emma Lavelle.

Chases

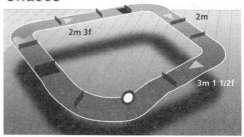

Hurdles

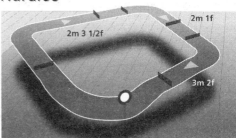

Favourites

Chases	29.6%	-£55.18
Hurdles	40.4%	+£17.49
Overall	36.0%	-£37.69

Trainers	Wins-Runs	%	Hurdles	Chases	£1 level stks
K Goldsworthy	3-6	50.0	0-0	3-6	+11.58
J Frost	3-9	33.3	3-5	0-2	+10.75
N Henderson	13-39	33.3	7-20	3-10	+28.58
Miss H Knight	17-53	32.1	10-29	5-16	+81.78
M Pipe	28-90	31.1	19-67	8-20	-11.06
B Ryall	4-14	28.6	0-2	4-12	+71.00
Miss E Lavelle	3-12	25.0	0-5	2-6	+5.50
P Rich	3-12	25.0	3-9	0-0	+20.00
C Egerton	4-17	23.5	2-8	0-3	-0.94
A King	10-46	21.7	8-32	2-10	+10.41
Miss S Wilton	4-19	21.1	4-17	0-2	+18.25
C Mann	5-24	20.8	3-21	2-3	+33.00

Jockeys	Wins-Rides	%	£1 level stks	Best Trainer	W-R
R Young	3-8	37.5	+22.00	C J Gray	1-1
R Biddlecombe	4-12	33.3	+21.75	Miss H Knight	2-4
A McCoy	31-97	32.0	-11.52	M Pipe	20-42
P J Brennan	4-13	30.8	+1.54	P Nicholls	2-2
R Guest	3-10	30.0	+1.36	N Mason	2-6
R Biddlecombe	4-16	25.0	+4.58	K Goldsworthy	2-2
L Cummins	12-51	23.5	+28.18	Miss E Lavelle	2-2
M Fitzgerald	13-62	21.0	-17.02	N Henderson	11-28
B J Crowley	7-34	20.6	-7.20	Miss V Williams	6-23
D Crosse	3-15	20.0	+22.50	C Mann	2-2
W M Worthington	4-20	20.0	+16.50	B Leavy	2-8
B Fenton	8-40	20.0	-2.84	S Brookshaw	1-1

Sponsored by Stan James

High Yarridge, Hexham, Northumberland NE46 2JP.
Tel 01434 606 881

How to get there – Road: A69.
Rail: Hexham

Features: LH, 1m4f round, very stiff, back straight runs downhill most of the way and is followed by a steep uphill run from the bottom turn

2003-04 Fixtures: Oct 3, 11, Nov 7, 19, Dec 17, Jan 28, Mar 18, Apr 4, 19, May 1, 8, 29, June 1, 12, 20

Winning Pointers: The stats say that Tony Dobbin does well when riding for Len Lungo. Tony McCoy is a rare visitor to the track, but doesn't make the journey for nothing, and has won five times from nine rides. Padge Whelan has an unblemished record riding for Richard Fahey.

Chases

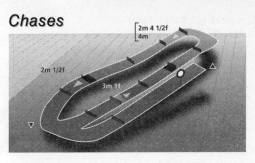

Hurdles

Favourites

Chases	29.3%	-£26.03
Hurdles	40.2%	-£9.16
Overall	35.6%	-£35.19

Trainers

Trainers	Wins-Runs	%	Hurdles	Chases	£1 level stks
N Twiston-Davies	4-9	44.4	2-5	2-4	-0.53
N Richards	11-28	39.3	5-13	6-14	+14.50
Mrs H Graham	5-14	35.7	3-6	2-6	+37.50
Mrs K Walton	3-10	30.0	3-8	0-1	+16.00
T Walford	3-12	25.0	0-2	3-10	+5.87
R Fahey	3-13	23.1	1-8	1-3	-4.75
R Barr	3-14	21.4	3-7	0-6	+0.13
Jonjo O'Neill	6-30	20.0	3-19	2-9	-5.88
L Lungo	14-71	19.7	11-52	1-13	-16.31
F Murphy	16-86	18.6	11-49	4-31	-20.33
M D Hammond	6-34	17.6	2-15	3-16	-7.83
J Jefferson	7-40	17.5	5-22	2-10	-3.92

Jockeys

Jockeys	Wins-Rides	%	£1 level stks	Best Trainer	W-R
A McCoy	5-9	55.6	+8.88	C Kellett	1-1
L Hislop	3-9	33.3	+16.50	Mrs H Graham	3-6
P Whelan	7-23	30.4	+7.50	R Fahey	2-2
A Dobbin	30-110	27.3	+21.08	L Lungo	7-21
A Thornton	3-12	25.0	+1.50	T Etherington	1-1
W Marston	3-14	21.4	-1.00	R Phillips	1-2
R Garritty	9-60	15.0	-28.70	G M Moore	4-36
J Crowley	13-91	14.3	+0.95	Mrs S J Smith	4-9
N Hannity	6-43	14.0	-8.75	J R Norton	2-5
N Horrocks	4-29	13.8	-0.25	M D Hammond	2-7
G Thomas	3-22	13.6	+17.00	F Murtagh	2-3
P Ryan	3-22	13.6	-3.50	N Mason	2-3

HUNTINGDON

Brampton, Huntingdon, Cambs
PE18 8NN. Tel 01480 453373

How to get there – Road: Off A14 Cambridge to Kettering road. Rail: Huntingdon

Features: RH, flat track, short 200yds run-in gets plenty horses beaten for toe

2003-04 Fixtures: Oct 10, Nov 2, 11, 22, Dec 11, 26, Jan 16, 28, Feb 12, 26, Mar 6, 17, Apr 12, May 11, 27, June 8

Winning Pointers: Nicky Henderson's horses win, on average, once every four starts, but at unremarkable odds. Don Cantillon does well with few runners, while Richard Johnson is consistent in the jockeys list, with 16 winners from 73 rides.

Chases

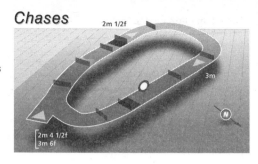

Hurdles

Favourites

Chases	36.9%	-£25.70
Hurdles	32.2%	-£12.09
Overall	34.3%	-£37.79

Trainers

Trainers	Wins-Runs	%	Hurdles	Chases	£1 level stks
S Dow	3-5	60.0	1-2	2-3	+13.00
D Cantillon	6-11	54.5	3-4	2-3	+43.10
D Cosgrove	4-9	44.4	4-9	0-0	+4.16
J Jefferson	3-11	27.3	1-5	1-4	+31.00
A P Jones	3-11	27.3	0-0	3-11	+6.20
C Mann	11-42	26.2	7-31	3-9	+4.55
Jonjo O'Neill	10-40	25.0	4-18	6-12	-3.59
N Henderson	18-72	25.0	10-41	5-18	-8.90
Miss V Williams	8-34	23.5	5-12	2-17	+7.57
Miss H Knight	20-89	22.5	3-21	14-50	-2.45
O Brennan	4-18	22.2	2-10	2-3	+4.00
T George	7-32	21.9	2-12	4-17	+30.63

Jockeys

Jockeys	Wins-Rides	%	£1 level stks	Best Trainer	W-R
A McCoy	21-76	27.6	-2.94	Jonjo O'Neill	6-11
L Cooper	3-11	27.3	+3.00	Jonjo O'Neill	3-9
A Dempsey	8-30	26.7	+11.71	Mrs M Reveley	7-24
C Rafter	5-20	25.0	+28.80	C Mann	2-3
J M Maguire	7-28	25.0	+22.13	T George	6-13
R Johnson	16-73	21.9	+39.04	H Daly	4-16
W Hutchinson	7-33	21.2	+43.25	J Hetherton	2-2
N Williamson	14-70	20.0	-4.09	K Bailey	3-14
M Fitzgerald	18-91	19.8	-18.76	N Henderson	13-47
J Culloty	21-108	19.4	-5.87	Miss H Knight	17-60
B Fenton	13-71	18.3	+17.27	Miss E Lavelle	4-14
N Fehily	11-64	17.2	+10.50	C Mann	8-23

Kelso, Roxburghshire.
Tel 01668 281 611

KELSO

How to get there – Road: 1m north of Kelso on B6461 to Ednam. Rail: Berwick on Tweed
Features: Tight, LH, hurdles course is 1m2f round, chase course 1m3f, quarter-mile run-in
2003-04 Fixtures: Oct 5, 18, Nov 1, 12, Dec 1, Jan 16, Feb 5, Mar 6, 28, Apr 5, 28, May 5, 19, 20
Winning Pointers: Len Lungo, Mary Reveley and Tony Dobbin are the names to remember in terms of numbers, but sadly you wouldn't be able to give up the day job by following them.

Chases

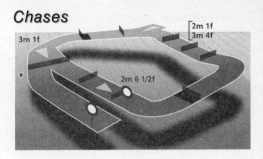

Hurdles

Favourites

Chases	30.3%	-£33.13
Hurdles	36.6%	-£10.71
Overall	33.8%	-£43.84

Trainers	Wins-Runs	%	Hurdles	Chases	£1 level stks
A Bailey	3-4	75.0	3-4	0-0	+14.75
K Ryan	3-5	60.0	3-4	0-1	+17.25
Mrs J Hollands	3-7	42.9	0-0	3-7	+11.50
E Elliott	3-8	37.5	1-4	2-4	+14.75
T Easterby	6-16	37.5	5-10	1-6	+2.00
M W Easterby	4-14	28.6	1-9	3-5	-3.75
L Lungo	27-113	23.9	20-93	7-20	+14.98
E W Tuer	3-13	23.1	2-11	1-2	+20.00
Mrs M Reveley	23-108	21.3	15-66	8-42	+0.88
N Richards	8-38	21.1	3-25	5-13	-10.02
M Todhunter	6-30	20.0	4-17	2-13	+3.13
J Jefferson	8-41	19.5	5-28	3-13	-12.94

Jockeys	Wins-Rides	%	£1 level stks	Best Trainer	W-R
B Powell	3-12	25.0	+19.37	P Beaumont	1-1
S Durack	6-25	24.0	+5.62	Jonjo O'Neill	2-2
D Jewett	4-19	21.1	+14.38	R Kyle	1-1
A Dobbin	24-116	20.7	-15.18	L Lungo	11-29
D Elsworth	4-21	19.0	-4.83	Mrs S J Smith	2-10
P Aspell	4-23	17.4	-7.50	M Todhunter	2-2
A Dempsey	11-64	17.2	-3.10	Mrs M Reveley	11-44
K Renwick	3-18	16.7	+6.00	Mrs J Hollands	2-2
R Garritty	4-26	15.4	-16.13	P Beaumont	2-6
G Lee	18-121	14.9	-30.94	J Jefferson	7-28
P Ryan	4-28	14.3	-9.50	J Charlton	2-5
B Gibson	9-71	12.7	+3.00	L Lungo	8-40

KEMPTON

Sunbury-On-Thames, Middlesex, TW16 5AQ. Tel: 01932 782292.

How to get there – Road: M3 Jctn 1. Rail: Kempton Park
Features: RH, flat, 1m5f round, suits a horse with a turn of foot
2003-04 Fixtures: Oct 25, Nov 5, 19, Dec 26, 27, Jan 17, Feb 2, 13, 27, 28, Mar 7
Winning Pointers: French pair Francois Doumen and Guillaume Macaire won't let you down, and nor will Nicky Henderson. All three are particularly predatory at the Christmas fixture. Tony McCoy comes out best of the jocks, although Thierry Doumen has a respectable record.

Chases

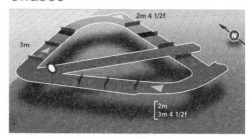

Hurdles

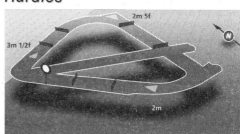

Favourites

Chases	32.8%	-£2.78
Hurdles	31.1%	-£23.25
Overall	31.9%	-£26.03

Trainers	Wins-Runs	%	Hurdles	Chases	£1 level stks
G Macaire	5-11	45.5	2-6	3-5	+2.88
V Dartnall	4-11	36.4	3-8	1-2	+11.30
F Doumen	6-21	28.6	5-12	1-6	+2.83
N Henderson	33-150	22.0	14-85	14-51	+21.66
P R Webber	8-38	21.1	3-20	4-16	+13.75
P Nicholls	15-76	19.7	4-21	11-54	+1.12
R Phillips	4-21	19.0	2-12	2-6	+2.00
A King	10-54	18.5	7-35	3-17	-8.71
D Gandolfo	4-22	18.2	0-9	3-11	+20.41
Miss V Williams	9-51	17.6	3-20	6-29	-3.80
Miss H Knight	14-83	16.9	5-26	8-50	-20.43
T George	4-24	16.7	2-14	2-8	+22.00

Jockeys	Wins-Rides	%	£1 level stks	Best Trainer	W-R
B Gicquel	3-6	50.0	-0.12	G Macaire	3-6
T Doumen	7-23	30.4	+8.83	F Doumen	6-21
A McCoy	26-100	26.0	+25.18	M Pipe	10-54
M Fitzgerald	27-129	20.9	-29.46	N Henderson	23-95
J Tizzard	8-41	19.5	+6.75	P Nicholls	7-23
M Foley	5-26	19.2	+1.43	N Henderson	4-15
J Culloty	14-82	17.1	-18.32	Miss H Knight	9-57
R Walsh	4-25	16.0	-0.13	P Nicholls	3-15
B Hitchcott	4-25	16.0	-4.37	D C Robinson	2-4
J M Maguire	3-19	15.8	+33.00	T George	2-8
N Williamson	11-71	15.5	-14.58	Miss V Williams	5-19
R Johnson	14-92	15.2	-25.92	A King	4-14

How to get there – Road: On A6, 2m south of city centre, 5m from M1 Jctn 21. Rail: Leicester
Features: RH, 1m6f round, stiffish uphill run-in
2003-04 Fixtures: Nov 17, Dec 4, 10, 27, Jan 13, 27, Feb 4, 18, Mar 2, 12
Winning Pointers: No meaningful trends amongst trainers, but that man McCoy is the jockey to follow, with a reassuringly high winning percentage of rides and level-stakes profit, particularly for his guv'nor.

Chases

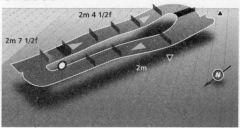

Hurdles

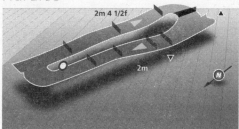

Favourites

Chases	30.6%	-£29.54
Hurdles	33.6%	-£12.88
Overall	32.0%	-£42.42

Trainers

Trainers	Wins-Runs	%	Hurdles	Chases	£1 level stks
Miss E Lavelle	3-4	75.0	2-3	1-1	+21.29
W G M Turner	4-9	44.4	4-9	0-0	+9.83
Mrs C Bailey	3-7	42.9	0-0	3-7	+0.30
C Mann	4-10	40.0	4-6	0-4	+23.75
S Sherwood	3-8	37.5	1-4	2-4	0.00
K Morgan	4-11	36.4	4-11	0-0	+0.88
M Pipe	17-53	32.1	13-41	4-12	-2.51
J Mackie	6-21	28.6	6-21	0-0	+45.50
N Henderson	8-28	28.6	2-5	6-23	-3.89
P Nicholls	3-11	27.3	1-3	2-8	-2.17
G M Moore	3-11	27.3	0-8	3-3	-1.64
R Phillips	3-11	27.3	2-7	1-4	+0.20

Jockeys

Jockeys	Wins-Rides	%	£1 level stks	Best Trainer	W-R
R Garritty	4-9	44.4	+2.56	G M Moore	3-5
J Crowley	4-9	44.4	+15.96	T Watson	1-1
A McCoy	23-56	41.1	+20.18	M Pipe	14-34
J Tizzard	5-13	38.5	+6.83	P Nicholls	3-9
R Guest	4-13	30.8	+7.63	N Mason	3-9
N Williamson	12-40	30.0	+2.74	Miss V Williams	4-12
C Rafter	4-15	26.7	+22.50	C Mann	2-2
M Foley	6-29	20.7	+49.91	S T Lewis	3-7
T J Murphy	6-29	20.7	+18.75	S Sherwood	2-2
M Fitzgerald	6-30	20.0	-13.62	N Henderson	4-20
P Flynn	5-28	17.9	-3.63	P R Webber	2-2
W Marston	8-46	17.4	-4.02	Mrs P Sly	2-9

LINGFIELD

Lingfield, Surrey, RH7 6PQ.
Tel: 01342 834800

How to get there – Road: M25 Jctn 6, south on A22.
Rail: Lingfield (from London Bridge and Victoria)
Features: LH, hilly, 1m4f round
2003-04 Fixtures: Nov 11, Dec 13, Apr 4
Winning Pointers: There are too few meetings here these days for any reliable pointers to be derived from the results.

Chases

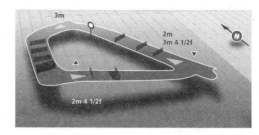

Hurdles

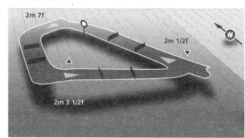

Favourites

Chases	31.6%	+£1.65
Hurdles	35.7%	+£1.87
Overall	33.3%	+£3.52

Trainers	Wins-Runs	%	Hurdles	Chases	£1 level stks
M Pipe	3-10	30.0	0-6	3-4	+0.82

Jockeys	Wins-Rides	%	£1 level stks	Best Trainer	W-R
A McCoy	3-6	50.0	+6.19	M Pipe	2-5

THE REASON WHY: this is what the Lingfield execs prefer to jumps racing in the winter

Sponsored by Stan James

Bromfield, Ludlow, Shrewsbury, Shropshire. Tel 01981 250 052

LUDLOW

How to get there – Road: 2m north of Ludlow on A49.
Rail: Ludlow

Features: Flat, RH, sharp corners and a testing run-in of 450yds.

2003-04 Fixtures: Oct 9, 23, Nov 13, 24, Dec 11, 18, Jan 9, 22, Feb 11, 25, Mar 4, 25, Apr 8, 25, May 6, 13

Winning Pointers: Jonjo O'Neill has done well and should be followed. Richard Johnson and Tony McCoy far outstrip their rivals in terms of winners, but Johnson's have provided a much better return, £31.72 to level-stakes.

Chases

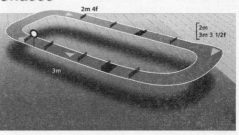

Hurdles

Favourites

Chases	29.9%	-£35.75
Hurdles	38.2%	-£19.21
Overall	34.8%	-£54.96

Trainers	Wins-Runs	%	Hurdles	Chases	£1 level stks
G Brown	3-5	60.0	1-3	2-2	+30.00
M Jackson	3-5	60.0	0-0	3-5	-0.73
R Frost	3-6	50.0	3-5	0-1	+10.75
B De Haan	3-8	37.5	1-3	2-5	+17.50
C Egerton	3-8	37.5	1-3	0-1	+0.11
N Henderson	16-48	33.3	5-21	6-13	+3.81
Jonjo O'Neill	10-32	31.3	5-15	4-16	+35.24
M Pipe	23-86	26.7	19-67	3-14	-31.15
P Hobbs	25-95	26.3	11-45	12-37	-17.13
O Sherwood	8-33	24.2	3-15	3-11	+6.87
Miss H Knight	15-67	22.4	7-28	6-28	+4.71
K Bailey	14-70	20.0	5-29	9-33	+16.67

Jockeys	Wins-Rides	%	£1 level stks	Best Trainer	W-R
W A Worthington	3-8	37.5	+5.58	I Williams	3-4
P Hide	3-9	33.3	+27.50	A P Jones	1-1
A McCoy	35-108	32.4	-7.31	M Pipe	20-46
P J Brennan	4-13	30.8	+49.00	W G M Turner	2-6
N Williamson	18-67	26.9	+41.41	Miss V Williams	6-25
R Burton	4-15	26.7	-7.05	M Jackson	2-2
R Johnson	29-112	25.9	+31.72	P Hobbs	13-35
D Flavin	4-16	25.0	+6.33	K Bailey	4-14
M Fitzgerald	13-59	22.0	-14.99	N Henderson	11-34
P Flynn	12-56	21.4	-11.61	P Hobbs	9-28
J Culloty	14-71	19.7	+8.11	Miss H Knight	11-38
B Fenton	6-31	19.4	+39.00	C Hemsley	2-2

MARKET RASEN

Legsby Rd, Mkt Rasen,
Lincolnshire LN8 3EA.
Tel 01673 843434

Chases

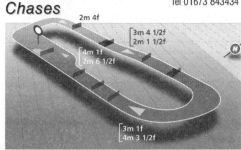

How to get there – Road: A46
to Market Rasen, course on
A631. Rail: Market Rasen (1m)
Features: RH, easy fences, run-
in of 250yds
2003-04 Fixtures: Oct 5, 18,
Nov 20, Dec 4, 26, Feb 10,
Mar 7, 28, Apr 24, May 9,
June 9, 25
Winning Pointers: Martin Pipe
rules, but Micky Hammond has-
n't done too badly, easily clear-
ing the benchmark 25 per cent
strike-rate. Predictably, Richard
Johnson and Tony McCoy get
their share of winners, but at no
great reward.

Hurdles

Favourites

Chases	34.3%	-£34.27
Hurdles	33.8%	-£23.22
Overall	34.0%	-£57.49

Trainers	Wins-Runs	%	Hurdles	Chases	£1 level stks
R C Guest	4-6	66.7	1-1	3-4	+15.75
A King	3-6	50.0	2-3	1-1	+7.62
N Richards	3-7	42.9	1-4	2-2	-1.20
Mrs L Wadham	9-22	40.9	8-19	0-0	+24.46
M Bradstock	3-9	33.3	2-7	0-0	-1.39
M Pipe	26-80	32.5	18-55	8-24	+4.09
M D Hammond	12-39	30.8	2-13	10-23	+18.78
Miss V Williams	8-27	29.6	4-14	3-12	-1.25
C Egerton	6-21	28.6	3-13	3-7	-9.44
Miss H Knight	3-11	27.3	0-2	3-8	-4.55
P Nicholls	4-15	26.7	1-3	3-11	+5.17
C Mann	1	2-53	22.6	7-33	5-20

Jockeys	Wins-Rides	%	£1 level stks	Best Trainer	W-R
A McCoy	35-101	34.7	-7.15	M Pipe	21-47
G Tormey	3-10	30.0	0.00	I Williams	3-3
M Nicolls	3-11	27.3	+1.75	M W Easterby	3-6
D Crosse	4-15	26.7	+40.75	C Mann	2-5
G Carenza	4-15	26.7	-0.38	M W Easterby	3-7
B J Crowley	5-19	26.3	+5.86	Miss V Williams	4-12
L Aspell	9-35	25.7	+13.63	Mrs L Wadham	7-12
N Fehily	12-55	21.8	+28.50	C Mann	7-31
R Guest	6-29	20.7	-0.55	N Mason	5-23
H Oliver	8-42	19.0	+17.60	J Spearing	3-7
T J Murphy	5-27	18.5	+15.25	P Nicholls	2-4
R Johnson	17-96	17.7	-26.85	D L Williams	4-11

Musselburgh Racecourse,
East Lothian. Tel: 01316 652859.

MUSSELBURGH

Chases

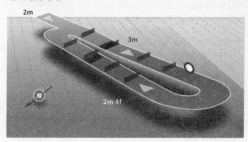

How to get there – Road: A1 east out of Edinburgh.
Rail: Musselburgh from Edinburgh
Features: RH, 1m2f round, almost perfectly flat, sharp bends favour handily-placed runners and pace-setters
2003-04 Fixtures: Nov 28, Dec 16, 30, Jan 7, 23, Feb 8, 18, 29
Winning Pointers: Len Lungo and Mary Reveley are the trainers to concentrate on. Among the jockeys it may be worth looking at 22-year-old Dale Jewett; he's had few rides, but is competent and could reward followers with some decent-priced winners.

Hurdles

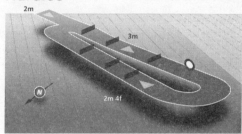

Favourites

Chases	29.9%	-£24.71
Hurdles	41.1%	+£3.27
Overall	37.2%	-£21.44

Trainers	Wins-Runs	%	Hurdles	Chases	£1 level stks
G A Swinbank	4-9	44.4	3-7	0-0	+0.80
R Fahey	5-16	31.3	3-9	0-2	+2.25
Mrs M Reveley	22-72	30.6	13-43	5-16	+41.84
L Lungo	20-66	30.3	13-38	5-14	+10.54
E W Tuer	4-17	23.5	2-11	2-5	+1.17
R Ford	4-17	23.5	3-11	1-5	+2.87
N Richards	7-33	21.2	5-17	1-10	-6.84
B Ellison	6-30	20.0	2-20	4-8	-17.27
Jonjo O'Neill	5-27	18.5	2-19	3-4	+3.25
N Mason	4-26	15.4	1-14	3-12	-12.27
F Murphy	9-67	13.4	5-37	4-26	-19.38
J Howard Johnson	8-73	11.0	6-49	2-20	-23.27

Jockeys	Wins-Rides	%	£1 level stks	Best Trainer	W-R
F King	3-6	50.0	+2.90	Mrs M Reveley	3-5
D Jewett	3-8	37.5	+23.50	Mrs D Sayer	2-2
A Dobbin	21-94	22.3	-12.19	L Lungo	9-22
R Guest	4-19	21.1	-8.27	N Mason	3-12
B Gibson	6-34	17.6	-14.94	L Lungo	6-18
V T Keane	7-42	16.7	-20.27	B Ellison	5-24
A Dempsey	8-48	16.7	+9.05	Mrs M Reveley	6-25
L Cooper	4-27	14.8	+5.75	Jonjo O'Neill	3-14
J Crowley	4-40	10.0	-13.96	G A Swinbank	2-4
A S Smith	7-70	10.0	-14.00	J Howard Johnson	2-22
G Lee	9-94	9.6	-36.50	J Barclay	2-4
M Bradburne	4-49	8.2	-26.00	Mrs S Bradburne	4-38

NEWBURY

Newbury, Berkshire, RG14 7NZ.
Tel: 01635 40015 or 41485.

How to get there – Road: Signposted from M4 and A34.
Rail: Newbury racecourse
Features: LH, flat, 1m6f round, suits galloping sorts with stamina, tough fences
2003-04 Fixtures: Nov 12, 29, 30, Dec 10, 29, Jan 14, Feb 14, Mar 5, 6, 26, 27
Winning Pointers: At the lesser meetings, local trainer Robert Stronge warrants noting, as he's showing a level-stakes profit of £30. At the bigger meets, Nicky Henderson is the man. Marcus Foley and Norman Williamson ride the track very well.

Chases

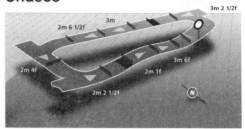

Hurdles

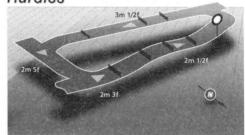

Favourites

Chases	28.2%	-£26.04
Hurdles	32.5%	-£24.01
Overall	30.7%	-£50.06

Trainers

Trainers	Wins-Runs	%	Hurdles	Chases	£1 level stks
V Dartnall	3-9	33.3	2-4	0-4	+0.12
J Mackie	3-13	23.1	3-13	0-0	+6.00
M Pipe	32-147	21.8	20-93	9-44	-42.49
N Henderson	36-167	21.6	27-117	7-35	+27.97
R Stronge	3-15	20.0	1-9	2-6	+30.00
T George	4-25	16.0	1-13	3-9	+13.00
Miss V Williams	8-51	15.7	3-29	5-17	-15.19
M Pitman	7-45	15.6	3-24	2-9	-2.25
P Nicholls	11-72	15.3	1-20	9-49	-26.40
J Mullins	4-27	14.8	3-16	0-8	+0.25
D Gandolfo	3-21	14.3	2-11	1-9	+30.00
Jonjo O'Neill	7-50	14.0	4-31	2-14	-19.16

Jockeys

Jockeys	Wins-Rides	%	£1 level stks	Best Trainer	W-R
J Diment	3-6	50.0	+9.50	M Hazell	2-3
B J Geraghty	3-8	37.5	+2.13	P Nicholls	1-1
A McCoy	35-138	25.4	-26.99	M Pipe	28-95
M Foley	5-20	25.0	+20.00	N Henderson	5-15
M Fitzgerald	29-141	20.6	-19.82	N Henderson	23-97
N Williamson	15-73	20.5	+15.45	Miss V Williams	6-18
J M Maguire	3-15	20.0	+16.00	T George	2-11
J Goldstein	4-23	17.4	-2.25	N Twiston-Davies	2-6
P Aspell	3-19	15.8	-3.25	Mrs M Reveley	3-15
T Scudamore	3-19	15.8	-9.26	M Pipe	2-8
R Johnson	16-106	15.1	-24.42	P Hobbs	7-35
C Llewellyn	12-98	12.2	-10.85	N Twiston-Davies	9-55

High Gosforth Park, Newcastle-
Upon-Tyne, NE3 5HP.
Tel: 01912 362020.

How to get there – Road:
Signposted from A1.
Rail: Necastle Central (4m)
Features: LH, 1m6f round, half-
mile straight is all uphill, fences
are stiff
2003-04 Fixtures: Nov 14, 24,
29, Dec 8, 20, Jan 3, 21, Feb 4,
21, Mar 1, 13, 20
Winning Pointers: The best
idea for making profits at this
track is to look at whatever Tony
Dobbin or Richard Johnson is
riding. Dobbin has ridden almost twice as many winners as
anyone else in the table.

NEWCASTLE

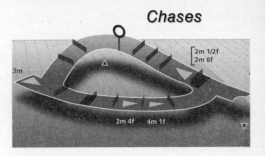

Chases

Hurdles

Favourites

Chases	37.0%	-£8.33
Hurdles	32.2%	-£26.53
Overall	34.3%	-£34.86

Trainers	Wins-Runs	%	Hurdles	Chases	£1 level stks
R Phillips	3-6	50.0	3-5	0-1	+6.50
R C Guest	3-8	37.5	1-4	2-4	+9.00
R Ford	4-13	30.8	1-9	3-4	+23.00
P Haslam	4-14	28.6	2-9	2-5	+12.67
N Mason	15-60	25.0	5-29	10-29	+102.00
Mrs K Walton	5-21	23.8	1-9	4-11	+31.50
M W Easterby	21-100	21.0	13-55	6-35	+4.05
P Monteith	7-35	20.0	5-25	1-8	+57.50
T Easterby	11-55	20.0	5-33	6-16	-9.83
Mrs M Reveley	32-176	18.2	17-108	12-44	-25.30
L Lungo	22-122	18.0	14-90	4-20	-25.62
A Scott	3-18	16.7	3-14	0-1	-4.63

Jockeys	Wins-Rides	%	£1 level stks	Best Trainer	W-R
R Guest	5-11	45.5	+14.12	N Mason	3-6
R Johnson	8-19	42.1	+45.25	R Phillips	2-2
F Keniry	3-10	30.0	+21.00	Miss K Milligan	2-5
A Dobbin	32-125	25.6	+20.76	L Lungo	11-30
A McCoy	3-12	25.0	-5.00	L Lungo	2-2
G Carenza	4-16	25.0	+7.00	M W Easterby	4-13
S Durack	8-41	19.5	-8.51	A Scott	2-4
R Wakley	3-16	18.8	+30.00	P Monteith	1-1
P Aspell	5-28	17.9	+2.23	Mrs M Reveley	2-12
A Dempsey	18-102	17.6	-18.81	Mrs M Reveley	16-66
R Guest	7-41	17.1	+9.83	N Mason	6-19
L McGrath	3-18	16.7	+4.50	R C Guest	2-2

NEWTON ABBOT

How to get there – Road: On A380 Newton Abbot to Torquay road. Rail: Newton Abbot

Features: LH, tight, 1m1f round

2003-04 Fixtures: Nov 5, 18, Dec 2, Apr 10, 27, May 11, 17, 27, June 7, 15, 22

Winning Pointers: At one of their local tracks, it's no shock to see that Pipe and McCoy dominate. That doesn't convert into profits, however, with so many short-priced favourites obliging. Paul Nicholls could provide a better route to long-term profits, and he could be set to challenge Pipe's dominance of the track in seasons to come. Ruby Walsh's stats are also likely to improve.

Chases

Hurdles

Favourites

Chases	35.7%	-£39.47
Hurdles	36.8%	-£60.38
Overall	36.4%	-£99.85

Trainers

Trainers	Wins-Runs	%	Hurdles	Chases	£1 level stks
Lady Herries	3-4	75.0	1-2	0-0	+7.23
G Chambers	3-5	60.0	0-0	3-5	+14.25
M Pipe	93-306	30.4	57-206	33-90	-21.84
C Egerton	3-10	30.0	2-6	1-3	+7.00
P Nicholls	25-90	27.8	9-28	15-54	+16.18
A King	3-13	23.1	2-4	0-6	+2.44
P Hobbs	42-185	22.7	24-105	16-73	-31.35
P Ritchens	4-18	22.2	1-5	3-13	-3.75
Jonjo O'Neill	3-14	21.4	2-8	0-4	+4.94
N Henderson	3-14	21.4	1-7	2-2	-4.06
I Williams	7-33	21.2	4-21	3-12	-7.62
K Bailey	3-15	20.0	0-4	3-9	-8.72

Jockeys

Jockeys	Wins-Rides	%	£1 level stks	Best Trainer	W-R
R Walsh	4-10	40.0	+1.75	P Nicholls	4-10
R P McNally	5-15	33.3	+7.61	P Nicholls	5-11
N Williamson	16-48	33.3	+13.58	K Bailey	3-5
A McCoy	83-257	32.3	-48.98	M Pipe	72-193
R Johnson	39-181	21.5	-20.59	P Hobbs	23-70
M Fitzgerald	6-33	18.2	-1.56	N Henderson	3-11
N Fehily	5-28	17.9	-0.10	C Mann	5-18
S Durack	8-48	16.7	+74.88	Mrs A Thorpe	3-7
R Widger	9-56	16.1	-16.58	P Hobbs	4-23
A Thornton	16-102	15.7	+4.56	P Ritchens	4-7
R Greene	16-110	14.5	+15.54	M Pipe	8-35
P Flynn	11-79	13.9	+2.96	R Baker	4-15

Scone Palace Park, Perth PH2 6BB.
Tel 01683 220 131

How to get there – Road: Off A93. Rail: Perth, free bus service
Features: RH, flat, 1m2f round
2003-04 Fixtures: Apr 21, 22, 23, May 12, 13, June 5, 6, 30
Winning Pointers: Nigel Twiston-Davies horses deserve the closest scrutiny, particularly the staying chasers. In line with that, the best jockey stats belong to weighing room veteran Carl Llewellyn.

Chases

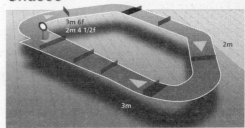

Hurdles

Favourites

Chases	34.0%	-£14.67
Hurdles	34.1%	-£20.72
Overall	34.1%	-£35.40

Trainers	Wins-Runs	%	Hurdles	Chases	£1 level stks
Mrs A Hamilton	3-7	42.9	1-2	2-5	+2.30
R Fahey	3-7	42.9	2-3	0-1	+3.50
P Nicholls	6-18	33.3	0-2	5-15	+6.80
N Twiston-Davies	12-38	31.6	6-21	6-17	+37.28
E W Tuer	5-16	31.3	5-15	0-1	+28.33
Jonjo O'Neill	21-68	30.9	10-37	8-26	+19.67
Mrs S J Smith	4-13	30.8	0-5	4-7	+34.00
D Whillans	3-10	30.0	1-5	2-4	+4.75
R Ford	8-29	27.6	3-14	5-15	+13.10
A J Martin	6-22	27.3	3-16	3-6	-2.65
G M Moore	4-15	26.7	4-12	0-3	+16.00
P Hobbs	8-31	25.8	6-16	2-15	-8.11

Jockeys	Wins-Rides	%	£1 level stks	Best Trainer	W-R
M Fitzgerald	4-10	40.0	+0.64	T Walsh	1-1
A McCoy	12-35	34.3	+4.24	Jonjo O'Neill	4-6
C Llewellyn	10-32	31.3	+44.53	N Twiston-Davies	9-27
A Dobbin	30-119	25.2	-10.76	L Lungo	9-30
J P McNamara	4-18	22.2	+12.50	F Murphy	2-6
R Garritty	7-33	21.2	+17.67	P Beaumont	4-17
W Marston	3-16	18.8	+13.50	Mrs S J Smith	2-6
A Thornton	3-17	17.6	+1.50	P Nicholls	1-1
R Johnson	18-106	17.0	-17.08	Miss L Russell	4-38
R McGrath	17-104	16.3	+12.22	R Ford	6-14
B Harding	12-78	15.4	+17.70	N Richards	5-16
B Gibson	4-27	14.8	-11.00	L Lungo	4-13

PLUMPTON

How to get there – Road: A274 or A275, off B2116.
Rail: Plumpton
Features: LH, 1m1f round, emphatic undulations, straight is uphill, track is so quirky that it has many course specialists who are quick, handy jumpers
2003-04 Fixtures: Oct 6, 20, Nov 3, 23, Dec 3, 15, Jan 4, 19, 29, Feb 16, Mar 1, 15, Apr 11, 12, May 9
Winning Pointers: Pipe and Mc-Coy to the fore once more. Noel Chance also merits respect, with an impressive wins-to-runs ratio. Robbie McNally has benefited from riding some of Paul Nicholls's lesser lights and is likely to get more opportunities.

Chases

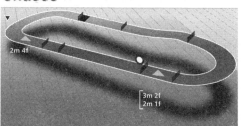

Hurdles

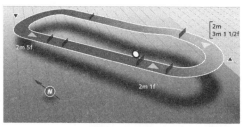

Favourites

Chases	36.5%	-£13.09
Hurdles	34.2%	-£50.53
Overall	35.2%	-£63.62

Trainers

Trainers	Wins-Runs	%	Hurdles	Chases	£1 level stks
Mrs M Reveley	3-4	75.0	2-3	1-1	+6.00
V Dartnall	3-5	60.0	2-4	1-1	+8.57
N Hawke	4-9	44.4	2-3	2-6	+63.50
N Chance	10-24	41.7	6-17	3-5	+61.69
P Nicholls	19-48	39.6	4-13	14-33	-1.92
Mrs N Smith	8-22	36.4	6-10	2-11	+45.30
N Henderson	9-26	34.6	5-20	4-6	+13.46
C Drewe	3-9	33.3	0-0	3-9	+45.00
I Williams	6-18	33.3	3-11	3-7	+16.50
M Pipe	37-122	30.3	27-98	9-22	-11.47
C Egerton	3-10	30.0	2-7	1-3	+0.88
M Usher	3-11	27.3	2-8	1-3	+7.50

Jockeys

Jockeys	Wins-Rides	%	£1 level stks	Best Trainer	W-R
R Walsh	3-7	42.9	+0.79	P Nicholls	3-6
R P McNally	3-7	42.9	+4.36	P Nicholls	2-4
A Honeyball	3-8	37.5	+3.37	M Usher	1-1
A McCoy	40-132	30.3	-42.18	M Pipe	27-75
J P Byrne	3-10	30.0	+6.75	C Kellett	1-1
M Fitzgerald	16-60	26.7	+3.01	N Henderson	8-17
R Young	4-17	23.5	+12.00	N Mitchell	1-2
W Hutchinson	3-13	23.1	+7.00	M Usher	2-5
N Williamson	9-40	22.5	-14.21	Miss V Williams	5-16
P Hide	17-82	20.7	+17.87	J Gifford	7-17
P Flynn	6-35	17.1	-1.50	P Hobbs	2-4
T J Murphy	13-76	17.1	-0.67	M Pitman	4-17

Esher, Surrey, KT10 9AJ.
Tel: 01372 463072 or 464348.

How to get there – Road: From north and south-west M25 Jctn 10 and A3, from south-east M25 Jctn 9 and A224. Rail: Esher (from Waterloo)
Features: RH, 1m5f round, tough fences of which three are close together down the back, steep uphill finish puts a premium on stamina
2003-04 Fixtures: Nov 8, Dec 5, 6, Jan 3, Feb 7, 19, 20, Mar 12, 13, Apr 23, 24
Winning Pointers: Martin Pipe has a one-in-four hit-rate, and his runners are always worth the closest inspection in the Imperial Cup and the Whitbread. Tony McCoy, Ruby Walsh and Ben Hitchcott should be respected.

Chases

Hurdles

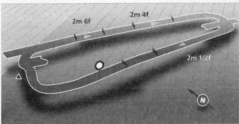

Favourites

Chases	34.7%	+£4.06
Hurdles	33.9%	-£11.01
Overall	34.3%	-£6.95

Trainers

Trainers	Wins-Runs	%	Hurdles	Chases	£1 level stks
V Dartnall	3-7	42.9	2-5	0-0	+14.50
P Chamings	4-10	40.0	0-1	4-8	+43.50
N Henderson	23-86	26.7	9-46	11-32	+33.11
R Phillips	3-12	25.0	2-6	1-4	+4.88
M Pipe	25-100	25.0	17-61	8-39	+11.49
P Nicholls	18-77	23.4	1-10	17-67	+25.25
C Egerton	3-13	23.1	1-8	2-5	+1.50
O Sherwood	3-13	23.1	0-1	3-10	-3.40
N Twiston-Davies	7-35	20.0	4-14	3-17	+10.25
D Grissell	3-18	16.7	0-5	3-12	+1.43
Miss H Knight	9-56	16.1	2-17	6-33	-18.62
M Pitman	4-26	15.4	1-9	2-11	-10.75

Jockeys

Jockeys	Wins-Rides	%	£1 level stks	Best Trainer	W-R
Lt Col O Ellwood	3-9	33.3	+4.10	N Henderson	1-1
R Walsh	7-22	31.8	+31.17	P Nicholls	7-18
B Hitchcott	3-10	30.0	+13.43	D Grissell	2-6
A McCoy	25-89	28.1	+18.53	M Pipe	18-50
B J Geraghty	3-11	27.3	+9.62	P Nicholls	2-6
R Wakley	3-13	23.1	+22.50	J Portman	1-1
N Williamson	18-82	22.0	+20.90	Miss V Williams	3-20
D J Casey	3-15	20.0	+7.50	B Curley	1-1
M Fitzgerald	19-95	20.0	-27.69	N Henderson	17-52
A Dobbin	4-21	19.0	-1.00	A Ennis	1-1
R Thornton	6-38	15.8	+9.25	P Nicholls	2-6
J Tizzard	6-42	14.3	-7.05	P Nicholls	5-23

SEDGEFIELD

How to get there – Road: A689, 2 mins from A1. Rail: Stockton, Darlington

Features: LH, 1m2f round, no water jump, undulating and sharp, suits handy types

2003-04 Fixtures: Oct 14, 29, Nov 11, 25, Dec 9, 26, Jan 13, 27, Feb 10, 24, Mar 16, 30, Apr 12, 30, May 19, 25

Winning Pointers: Anything Richard Phillips sends up requires a second look, otherwise it's the Lungo/Dobbin combination that dominate.

Chases

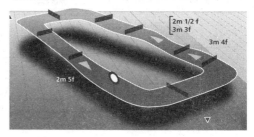

Hurdles

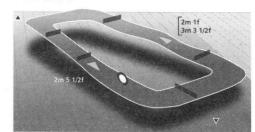

Favourites

Chases	39.5%	-£10.59
Hurdles	31.1%	-£47.28
Overall	34.5%	-£57.87

Trainers	Wins-Runs	%	Hurdles	Chases	£1 level stks
G Tuer	4-5	80.0	0-0	4-5	+6.60
R Phillips	3-7	42.9	2-5	1-2	+3.13
Mrs A Hamilton	3-7	42.9	2-3	1-4	+2.25
M Pipe	7-17	41.2	4-10	3-6	+11.34
G A Swinbank	6-17	35.3	6-16	0-1	+16.55
L Lungo	14-50	28.0	6-32	6-12	+26.31
Miss S Forster	6-22	27.3	2-11	4-11	+29.42
I Williams	6-22	27.3	3-12	3-10	-3.59
N Richards	10-39	25.6	3-21	6-14	-12.16
Mrs E Slack	9-36	25.0	5-23	4-13	+20.25
D M Forster	5-21	23.8	2-6	3-15	+27.63
R Fahey	3-13	23.1	1-8	1-4	-2.00

Jockeys	Wins-Rides	%	£1 level stks	Best Trainer	W-R
G Tuer	4-7	57.1	+4.60	G Tuer	4-4
T Hogg	4-9	44.4	+12.29	G M Moore	4-8
P Whelan	3-7	42.9	+4.00	R Fahey	3-5
F King	4-16	25.0	-13.00	Mrs M Reveley	3-6
N Williamson	4-16	25.0	-2.69	C Egerton	2-5
A McCoy	13-53	24.5	-11.33	M Pipe	6-13
C Storey	6-25	24.0	+30.42	Miss S Forster	5-14
R Johnson	12-56	21.4	+7.45	J G O'Shea	2-3
A Dobbin	36-179	20.1	+31.27	L Lungo	10-16
M Fitzgerald	3-15	20.0	-3.50	R O'Leary	1-1
H Oliver	4-21	19.0	+15.00	I Williams	1-1
R Garritty	19-100	19.0	+19.38	G M Moore	9-46

Rolleston, Nr. Newark, Notts,
NG25 0TS. Tel: 01636 814481.

SOUTHWELL

How to get there – Road: A1 to
Newark, A617 to Southwell or
M1 to A52 to Nottingham then
A612 to Southwell.
Rail: Rolleston
Features: LH, 1m2f round, flat
2003-04 Fixtures: Oct 11,
Nov 9, Dec 5, 30, May 1, 23
Winning Pointers: Anything
Liam Cooper rides for his boss
Jonjo O'Neill warrants attention.
This isn't a happy hunting
ground for Mick Fitzgerald and
he is best given a wide berth.

Chases

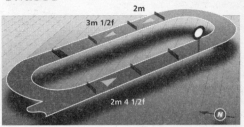

Hurdles

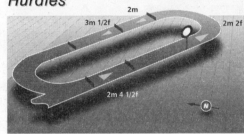

Favourites

Chases	32.1%	-£20.65
Hurdles	36.1%	-£14.95
Overall	34.4%	-£35.61

Trainers	Wins-Runs	%	Hurdles	Chases	£1 level stks
D Wintle	5-11	45.5	2-7	3-4	+10.73
Miss V Williams	10-23	43.5	4-11	3-8	+6.50
Mrs L Wadham	3-7	42.9	3-6	0-0	+0.37
P Hobbs	4-10	40.0	4-7	0-3	+8.30
P Nicholls	4-11	36.4	2-4	2-7	+6.53
N Twiston-Davies	5-16	31.3	3-6	2-7	+17.07
W G M Turner	3-10	30.0	3-9	0-1	+6.30
M D Hammond	3-10	30.0	1-4	2-6	+17.50
H Daly	6-21	28.6	4-12	2-9	+16.19
R Buckler	6-22	27.3	3-8	3-13	+42.75
A Streeter	3-12	25.0	1-8	1-3	+2.25
Jonjo O'Neill	9-36	25.0	6-23	2-9	+2.67

Jockeys	Wins-Rides	%	£1 level stks	Best Trainer	W-R
B Hitchcott	7-23	30.4	+1.57	R Dickin	3-7
L Cooper	7-24	29.2	+13.23	Jonjo O'Neill	6-20
A McCoy	24-84	28.6	-15.84	M Pipe	10-42
B J Crowley	6-23	26.1	-7.32	Miss V Williams	6-12
R Johnson	17-69	24.6	+10.43	J G O'Shea	3-5
M Bradburne	4-18	22.2	+1.44	H Daly	3-6
S Durack	10-48	20.8	-9.63	Mrs S J Smith	6-21
N Williamson	3-15	20.0	-5.18	C Egerton	1-1
R Forristal	3-16	18.8	-0.25	H Daly	1-2
C Llewellyn	4-22	18.2	+4.81	N Twiston-Davies	3-10
J Crowley	6-33	18.2	+3.53	Mrs S J Smith	5-12
M Fitzgerald	3-17	17.6	-6.50	K R Pearce	1-1

STRATFORD

Luddington Road, Stratford, Warwickshire CV37 9SE. Tel 01789 267 949

Chases

How to get there – Road: M40 Jctn 15, A3400, B439, A46. Rail: Stratford-upon-Avon
Features: Sharp, LH, 1m2f round
2003-04 Fixtures: Oct 7, 18, 30, Dec 30, Mar 15, Apr 18, May 21, 22, June 6, 13
Winning Pointers: Richard Johnson and Philip Hobbs regularly click, as do Jim Crowley and Sue Smith. Crowley has a 50 per cent record on Smith's horses, so that could be the partnership to follow.

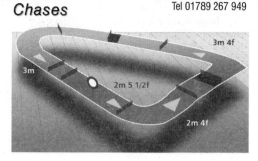

Hurdles

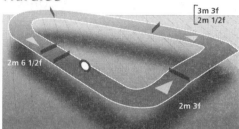

Favourites

Chases	29.9%	-£31.93
Hurdles	40.5%	-£2.66
Overall	35.6%	-£34.58

Trainers	Wins-Runs	%	Hurdles	Chases	£1 level stks
J Adam	3-7	42.9	0-2	3-5	+12.50
Nick Williams	4-10	40.0	3-7	1-3	+18.50
W G M Turner	3-8	37.5	3-8	0-0	+25.50
P Hobbs	34-109	31.2	17-58	16-48	+19.97
M Pipe	32-122	26.2	24-81	8-41	-20.64
Jonjo O'Neill	13-50	26.0	8-34	5-16	+16.65
Miss V Williams	9-35	25.7	4-16	4-17	-5.43
K R Burke	3-12	25.0	1-3	2-9	+3.41
Mrs P Dutfield	4-18	22.2	2-8	2-10	-1.87
P Nicholls	9-41	22.0	4-7	5-34	+8.86
S Sherwood	3-15	20.0	1-7	2-8	+1.22
Mrs S J Smith	5-25	20.0	2-12	3-13	-1.25

Jockeys	Wins-Rides	%	£1 level stks	Best Trainer	W-R
P Scouller	3-6	50.0	+3.38	M Pipe	2-5
D H Dunsdon	3-8	37.5	+10.50	N Gifford	2-4
A McCoy	41-140	29.3	-28.36	M Pipe	24-77
N Williamson	14-48	29.2	+42.81	Miss V Williams	7-15
R Johnson	44-157	28.0	-0.81	P Hobbs	18-43
J M Pritchard	3-11	27.3	+9.75	M Jackson	1-1
J Crowley	5-19	26.3	+39.63	Mrs S J Smith	3-6
P Holley	4-17	23.5	-0.87	Mrs P Dutfield	4-10
M Foley	3-16	18.8	+7.00	J Adam	2-3
B Hitchcott	6-35	17.1	+38.38	Jonjo O'Neill	2-4
D R Dennis	9-53	17.0	+12.75	I Williams	4-24
L Aspell	10-66	15.2	-10.09	Miss S Edwards	2-5

Sponsored by Stan James

TAUNTON

How to get there – Road: M5
Jctn 25. Rail: Taunton
Features: RH, 1m2f round
2003-04 Fixtures: Oct 16, 30,
Nov 13, 27, Dec 11, 29, Jan 22,
Feb 3, 19, Mar 4, 15, Apr 1, 16
Winning Pointers: Martin Pipe
leads the way numerically but,
not for the first time, the Paul
Nicholls stable outstrips him
profit-wise. Timmy Murphy
excels, while Jamie Moore is
likely to come to the fore with
Martin Pipe's support.

Chases

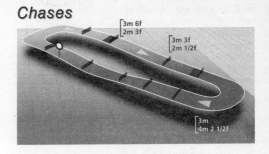

Hurdles

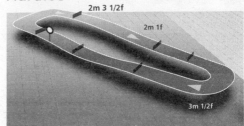

Favourites

Chases	27.7%	-£24.41
Hurdles	35.5%	-£39.75
Overall	32.9%	-£64.16

Trainers

Trainers	Wins-Runs	%	Hurdles	Chases	£1 level stks
S Young	3-10	30.0	0-1	3-9	+20.00
P Nicholls	35-126	27.8	15-61	18-56	+14.14
Miss H Knight	9-35	25.7	2-13	6-20	-6.23
H Daly	4-16	25.0	3-8	1-7	+5.75
Miss V Williams	12-50	24.0	5-27	6-20	+6.50
R Phillips	4-17	23.5	3-14	1-3	+29.00
J G O'Shea	3-13	23.1	3-11	0-1	+17.25
G L Moore	3-14	21.4	2-11	1-3	-2.50
M Pipe	58-278	20.9	50-240	7-32	-22.33
P Hobbs	30-156	19.2	18-96	10-54	-25.41
A King	4-21	19.0	2-15	1-3	2.88
K Bishop	9-50	18.0	5-31	4-18	+9.66

Jockeys

Jockeys	Wins-Rides	%	£1 level stks	Best Trainer	W-R
J E Moore	4-10	40.0	+16.83	M Pipe	3-5
C Williams	3-9	33.3	-1.33	Mrs K Sanderson	2-2
A McCoy	52-168	31.0	-7.37	M Pipe	39-117
S Young	3-10	30.0	+20.00	S Young	3-10
R Walsh	5-17	29.4	-5.56	P Nicholls	4-15
T J Murphy	20-83	24.1	+45.18	P Nicholls	6-13
R P McNally	6-26	23.1	+11.75	P Nicholls	4-13
B J Crowley	6-28	21.4	+6.50	Miss V Williams	6-24
R Johnson	24-112	21.4	+7.96	P Hobbs	13-57
X Aizpuru	4-21	19.0	+18.50	M E Hill	2-6
J A McCarthy	4-21	19.0	+9.00	Mrs P Robeson	1-3
D R Dennis	3-16	18.8	-2.62	I Williams	2-6

TOWCESTER

Easton Newston, Towcester, Northants
NN12 7HS. Tel 01327 353 414

How to get there – Road: M1 Jctn 15a, A43 west, south from Towcester. Rail: Northampton (8m) and bus service

Features: RH, 1m6f round, demanding uphill run from back straight

2003-04 Fixtures: Oct 8, 26, Nov 6, 18, 29, Dec 15, 26, Jan 9, 20, Feb 5, 22, Mar 11, 24, Apr 11, 26, May 10, 18, 28

Winning Pointers: No recent racing to draw on. This is a very stiff track that suits stayers, so Henry Daly and Ferdy Murphy ought to be worth watching, along with Brian Crowley when teaming up with Venetia Williams.

Chases

Hurdles

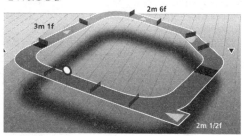

Favourites

Chases	27.1%	-£39.19
Hurdles	35.2%	-£13.50
Overall	31.4%	-£52.69

Trainers	Wins-Runs	%	Hurdles	Chases	£1 level stks
N Callaghan	3-5	60.0	2-3	1-2	+9.91
Mrs L Wadham	4-9	44.4	3-5	1-4	+12.50
J Mackie	3-7	42.9	3-7	0-0	+7.83
M Pipe	11-31	35.5	8-20	0-7	-1.70
C Egerton	4-12	33.3	3-8	0-3	-0.20
Miss V Williams	12-41	29.3	2-14	10-24	+12.75
M Pitman	4-15	26.7	3-8	1-4	+1.08
C Popham	3-12	25.0	0-3	3-9	+6.00
N Henderson	6-24	25.0	3-12	1-6	+1.62
R Buckler	5-22	22.7	1-13	4-7	+23.75
F Murphy	4-19	21.1	1-10	2-6	+7.25
H Daly	11-57	19.3	2-23	9-30	-17.89

Jockeys	Wins-Rides	%	£1 level stks	Best Trainer	W-R
L Jefford	3-6	50.0	+18.75	Mrs V Graham	1-1
B J Crowley	9-26	34.6	+51.19	Miss V Williams	7-16
A McCoy	15-48	31.3	-8.69	M Pipe	9-22
J Diment	6-20	30.0	+33.75	M Bosley	2-3
D Crosse	5-21	23.8	+7.58	J Mackie	2-2
N Williamson	13-58	22.4	-1.42	Miss V Williams	4-15
P Flynn	4-19	21.1	+1.75	C Popham	3-6
T J Murphy	7-39	17.9	+7.50	J Old	3-12
Gary Lyons	3-17	17.6	+52.00	A Streeter	1-1
J Goldstein	6-34	17.6	+19.50	N Twiston-Davies	4-17
X Aizpuru	3-18	16.7	-1.18	N Dunger	1-1
J Kavanagh	5-30	16.7	-6.49	N Henderson	2-3

Wood Lane, Uttoxeter, Staffs ST14 8BD.
Tel 01889 562 561

UTTOXETER

Chases

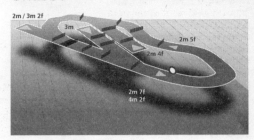

How to get there – Road: M6 Jctn 14, M1 Jctns 22-25, A38, A5151. Rail: Uttoxeter

Features: LH, 1m2f round, undulating, sweeping curves, suitable for gallopers

2003-04 Fixtures: Oct 4, 15, Nov 7, 15, 27, Dec 19, 26, Jan 10, 31, Mar 20, May 1, 9, 15, 30, June 3, 10, 27

Winning Pointers: Ferdy Murphy does particularly well and his runners merit close attention, particularly in long-distance chases. Note anything ridden by Barry Geraghty for Jonjo O'Neill.

Hurdles

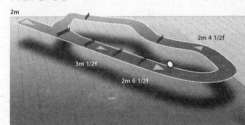

Favourites

Chases	39.5%	-£5.79
Hurdles	38.6%	-£21.75
Overall	39.0%	-£27.54

Trainers	Wins-Runs	%	Hurdles	Chases	£1 level stks
D Cantillon	4-7	57.1	0-1	4-6	+2.40
N Richards	5-11	45.5	1-4	3-6	+8.00
A Turnell	3-7	42.9	2-6	1-1	+26.00
G Hubbard	3-8	37.5	1-5	2-3	+12.50
N Gaselee	4-11	36.4	1-4	3-7	+14.33
F Murphy	8-26	30.8	3-10	5-16	+24.88
P Nicholls	18-67	26.9	7-16	10-49	+4.82
R Phillips	3-12	25.0	3-10	0-2	-5.24
R Stronge	6-24	25.0	2-13	4-11	+14.73
M Pipe	33-136	24.3	26-106	7-30	-42.91
P Hobbs	18-75	24.0	10-40	8-35	+19.94
J Jefferson	4-17	23.5	4-11	0-5	-5.53

Jockeys	Wins-Rides	%	£1 level stks	Best Trainer	W-R
R H Fowler	4-6	66.7	+3.40	D Cantillon	4-5
R Biddlecombe	3-5	60.0	+1.68	Mrs L Williamson	1-1
R Walford	3-5	60.0	+13.75	T Walford	1-1
B J Geraghty	3-9	33.3	-0.92	Jonjo O'Neill	2-4
A McCoy	44-139	31.7	-16.00	M Pipe	28-74
J Tizzard	12-38	31.6	-5.48	P Nicholls	9-27
B Grattan	5-17	29.4	+34.13	J Upson	4-12
B Hitchcott	6-22	27.3	+14.03	Jonjo O'Neill	2-3
B Fenton	3-12	25.0	+8.50	D Gandolfo	1-1
L Cooper	11-46	23.9	-4.99	Jonjo O'Neill	10-35
D Flavin	3-13	23.1	+9.58	K Bailey	3-12
R Widger	5-24	20.8	+36.43	P Hobbs	3-9

WARWICK

How to get there – Road: M40 Jctn 15, A429, follow signs to town centre. Rail: Warwick
Features: LH, 1m6f round, full of undulations
2003-04 Fixtures: Nov 3, 25, Dec 6, 20, Jan 10, 29, Feb 27, 28, Mar 14, 19, May 8
Winning Pointers: Charlie Mann and Noel Fehily are the winning team, while Mick Fitzgerald wouldn't count this as one of his favourite tracks. Paul Flynn does well when getting the chance on Philip Hobbs horses.

Chases

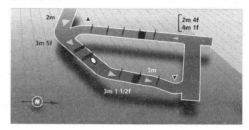

Hurdles

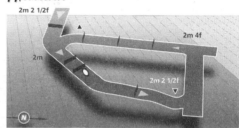

Favourites

Chases	36.4%	-£13.91
Hurdles	31.8%	-£8.43
Overall	33.8%	-£22.34

Trainers

Trainers	Wins-Runs	%	Hurdles	Chases	£1 level stks
C Von Der Recke	3-4	75.0	3-4	0-0	+14.75
P Winkworth	3-6	50.0	3-5	0-0	+17.00
N Chance	7-19	36.8	3-10	2-4	+4.54
P Nicholls	13-45	28.9	1-15	12-30	-0.65
C Mann	6-23	26.1	2-14	2-5	+33.88
Jonjo O'Neill	11-50	22.0	6-30	2-13	+2.20
M Pipe	29-132	22.0	14-85	13-40	-22.25
M Pitman	7-34	20.6	3-17	3-12	+6.32
R Phillips	4-20	20.0	2-17	0-1	+3.75
J Spearing	4-21	19.0	4-17	0-2	+29.50
P Hobbs	12-66	18.2	7-28	4-30	-10.68
N Henderson	6-35	17.1	4-20	2-11	-14.02

Jockeys

Jockeys	Wins-Rides	%	£1 level stks	Best Trainer	W-R
F Windsor Clive	3-6	50.0	+18.00	Miss V Williams	2-4
N Williamson	14-38	36.8	+17.66	Jonjo O'Neill	3-3
A McCoy	27-77	35.1	+5.46	M Pipe	17-54
J Tizzard	7-26	26.9	-4.55	P Nicholls	4-14
T Scudamore	3-15	20.0	-0.75	M Pipe	2-4
T J Murphy	12-65	18.5	-5.46	M Pitman	2-10
N Fehily	6-33	18.2	+53.88	C Mann	5-14
M Fitzgerald	5-30	16.7	-18.35	H Daly	2-2
R Wakley	7-42	16.7	-0.25	I Williams	3-15
B Hitchcott	5-33	15.2	+4.20	R Dickin	4-14
L Cooper	3-20	15.0	+0.75	Jonjo O'Neill	3-19
P Flynn	6-40	15.0	+14.07	P Hobbs	3-13

How to get there – Road: A1, from Leeds A58, from York B1224. Rail: Leeds, Harrogate, York

Features: Long, LH, chases 1m4f round, hurdles 1m2f, long-striding gallopers do well

2003-04 Fixtures: Oct 15, 31, Nov 1, 15, 26, Dec 6, 26, 27, Jan 17, 26, Feb 7, Mar 3, 22, Apr 25, May 6, 20, 27

Winning Pointers: Jonjo O'Neill sends many of his top-notchers to this track, and both Rhinestone Cowboy and Keen Leader won here last season. He is definitely the man to follow but blind faith in Tony Dobbin and Len Lungo would result in losses.

Chases

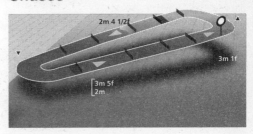

Hurdles

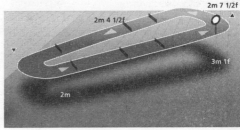

Favourites

Chases	34.9%	-£32.78
Hurdles	41.3%	+£6.12
Overall	38.4%	-£26.66

Trainers	Wins-Runs	%	Hurdles	Chases	£1 level stks
M Morris	3-5	60.0	2-4	1-1	+14.25
R Tate	4-10	40.0	0-2	4-8	+19.08
J Eyre	3-11	27.3	3-9	0-1	+8.33
Jonjo O'Neill	22-81	27.2	15-56	6-21	+22.68
N Henderson	5-19	26.3	3-12	2-5	-6.15
P Nicholls	7-27	25.9	2-10	5-17	-12.83
N Richards	4-16	25.0	2-10	2-6	+5.75
Miss V Williams	5-23	21.7	2-9	3-14	-4.74
Mrs M Reveley	51-251	20.3	27-158	18-77	+8.21
A King	3-15	20.0	1-8	2-7	+1.33
L Lungo	11-55	20.0	8-42	1-9	10.45
P R Webber	7-36	19.4	1-10	6-25	+3.96

Jockeys	Wins-Rides	%	£1 level stks	Best Trainer	W-R
D J Casey	5-8	62.5	+23.00	M Morris	2-3
T Greenall	3-6	50.0	+1.15	M W Easterby	2-3
B Murphy	3-6	50.0	+5.01	Mrs M Reveley	3-6
T Eaves	3-8	37.5	+2.50	Mrs M Reveley	3-8
G Berridge	3-9	33.3	+9.25	L Lungo	2-6
R Johnson	9-34	26.5	+4.69	A King	2-4
T J Phelan	3-12	25.0	+26.63	Jonjo O'Neill	3-7
J P Byrne	3-12	25.0	+4.25	O Brennan	3-6
J Tizzard	3-13	23.1	-0.25	P Nicholls	2-4
R Wakley	3-13	23.1	+7.50	A Dickman	1-1
N Williamson	9-39	23.1	+12.66	Mrs H Dalton	2-2
A Dobbin	29-133	21.8	-16.09	L Lungo	5-15

WINCANTON

Wincanton, Somerset BA9 8BJ.
Tel 01963 323 44

How to get there – Road: A303 to Wincanton, track on B3081, 1m from town centre.
Rail: Gillingham
Features: RH, fast-drying, 1m4f round
2003-04 Fixtures: Oct 9, 26, Nov 8, 20, Dec 4, 26, Jan 8, 17, Feb 12, 21, Mar 11, 25, Apr 4, 18, May 7
Winning Pointers: Paul Nicholls often uses this track for some of his leading lights and has an excellent 28.6 per cent strike-rate. Martin Pipe's chasers don't have a great record, although his hurdlers have fared better.

Chases

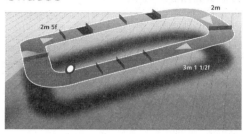

Hurdles

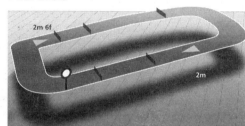

Favourites

Chases	40.9%	+£9.09
Hurdles	31.8%	-£35.25
Overall	35.8%	-£26.16

Trainers

	Wins-Runs	%	Hurdles	Chases	£1 level stks
Dr J Naylor	4-13	30.8	0-7	4-6	+21.00
N Chance	4-13	30.8	2-6	1-4	+17.00
P Nicholls	64-224	28.6	26-98	36-118	+31.81
N Henderson	13-48	27.1	5-28	5-12	+1.36
P Hobbs	31-139	22.3	20-78	7-49	+12.74
Miss H Knight	15-74	20.3	7-42	8-23	-29.09
M Pipe	26-143	18.2	21-101	4-34	-8.33
Miss V Williams	8-48	16.7	3-18	4-26	-17.02
D Gandolfo	4-25	16.0	1-10	3-9	+5.50
A King	7-47	14.9	2-27	5-17	+4.00
P R Webber	4-29	13.8	3-14	1-13	+28.00
K Bishop	3-22	13.6	3-22	0-0	+11.00

Jockeys

	Wins-Rides	%	£1 level stks	Best Trainer	W-R
B J Geraghty	4-8	50.0	+15.00	P Nicholls	2-3
R Walsh	5-17	29.4	-2.34	P Nicholls	4-16
A McCoy	24-88	27.3	+8.27	M Pipe	16-58
R P McNally	4-15	26.7	-6.32	P Nicholls	4-9
P J Brennan	7-27	25.9	-1.53	P Nicholls	5-13
A Bateman	4-17	23.5	+3.20	P Hobbs	4-10
J Culloty	14-69	20.3	-20.82	Miss H Knight	12-46
R Young	3-15	20.0	-1.25	Mrs S Alner	1-1
S Durack	4-20	20.0	+7.00	N Chance	2-2
M Fitzgerald	15-78	19.2	-11.90	N Henderson	6-24
T J Murphy	23-122	18.9	-0.90	P Nicholls	16-51
M Foley	3-16	18.8	+1.53	N Henderson	3-7

Sponsored by Stan James

Pitchcroft, Worcester WR1 3EJ.
Tel 01905 253 64

WORCESTER

How to get there – Road: From north M5 Jctn 6, from south Jctn 7 or A38. Rail: Worcester (Forgate St)
Features: LH, 1m5f round, subject to flooding from the nearby Severn
2003-04 Fixtures: Nov 9, 21, 30, May 8, 16, June 5, 16, 23, 29
Winning Pointers: Paul Nicholls again comes out favourably from the statistics, with both his hurdlers and chasers faring well. Joe Tizzard has been the grateful recipient, recording a £23.75 profit to level-stakes.

Chases

Hurdles

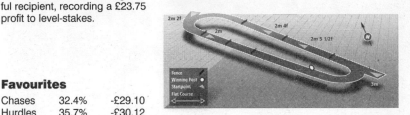

Favourites

Chases	32.4%	-£29.10
Hurdles	35.7%	-£30.12
Overall	34.6%	-£59.23

Trainers	Wins-Runs	%	Hurdles	Chases	£1 level stks
B McMahon	3-4	75.0	0-1	0-0	+22.50
Lady Herries	3-6	50.0	0-2	0-0	+7.13
C Egerton	4-9	44.4	2-6	1-2	+7.83
P Nicholls	10-34	29.4	3-10	7-22	+16.90
Miss V Williams	7-24	29.2	5-13	0-4	+21.95
R Ford	4-14	28.6	4-11	0-1	+11.83
S Sherwood	5-18	27.8	1-5	3-7	+9.75
M Pipe	45-166	27.1	29-121	14-42	-23.48
D Nicholson	4-15	26.7	0-5	4-9	-1.22
R O'Sullivan	3-12	25.0	1-7	2-4	+13.63
R Phillips	4-16	25.0	3-9	1-5	-3.89
Mrs H Dalton	8-32	25.0	2-11	6-16	+7.25

Jockeys	Wins-Rides	%	£1 level stks	Best Trainer	W-R
P Robson	3-4	75.0	-0.75	Mrs H Dalton	1-1
A McCoy	46-172	26.7	-23.29	M Pipe	38-107
N Williamson	14-58	24.1	+20.44	Miss V Williams	3-6
A Dobbin	3-14	21.4	+9.00	Mrs H Dalton	1-1
R Johnson	44-220	20.0	-2.04	P Hobbs	14-62
J Tizzard	8-41	19.5	+23.75	P Nicholls	3-13
C Llewellyn	22-129	17.1	+2.07	N Twiston-Davies	15-65
T Scudamore	3-19	15.8	-7.13	P Bowen	2-7
M Fitzgerald	17-111	15.3	-15.68	N Henderson	10-35
J M Maguire	3-20	15.0	+3.50	T Tate	1-1
P Flynn	7-50	14.0	+3.88	T Watson	2-5
S Fox	5-37	13.5	+52.00	M Gingell	4-21

Record times, standard times

Course

Distance (number of obstacles)	Record holder (date set)	record time	standard time
Aintree, Mildmay course			
2m Ch (12)	Nohalmdun (7 Apr 1990)	3m45.30s	3m48s
2m110yds Hdl (9)	Spinning (3 Apr 1993)	3m44.80s	3m50s
2m1f110yds Ch (14)	Pats Minstrel (17 Nov 1995)	4m21.90s	/
2m4f Ch (16)	Wind Force (2 Apr 1993)	4m46.60s	4m48s
2m4f Hdl (11)	Gallateen (2 Apr 1993)	4m37.10s	4m40s
3m110yds Hdl (13)	Andrew's First (1 Apr 1993)	5m50.70s	5m51s
3m1f Ch (19)	Cab On Target (2 Apr 1993)	6m3.40s	6m6s

Aintree, Grand National course

Distance (number of obstacles)	Record holder (date set)	record time	standard time
2m5f110yds Ch (18)	Its Time For A Win (5 Apr 2002)	5m25.60s	5m21s
2m6f Ch (18)	Sirrah Jay (1 Apr 1993)	5m26.50s	5m29s
3m3f Ch (22)	Young Hustler (18 Nov 1995)	6m54.50s	6m49s
4m4f Ch (30)	Mr Frisk (7 Apr 1990)	8m47.80s	9m5s

Ascot

Distance (number of obstacles)	Record holder (date set)	record time	standard time
2m Ch (12)	With Gods Help (1 May 1990)	3m45.80s	3m48s
2m110yds Hdl (9)	Fred The Tread (13 Apr 1988)	3m43.40s	3m46s
2m3f110yds Ch (16)	Wise King (7 Apr 1999)	4m38.20s	4m41s
2m4f Hdl (11)	Babil (31 Mar 1990)	4m38.50s	4m40s
3m Hdl (13)	Shah's Choice (13 Apr 1988)	5m25.20s	5m39s
3m110yds Ch (20)	Lord Seamus (3 Apr 2002)	6m2.10s	6m3s
3m1f110yds Hdl (14)	Floyd (15 Dec 1990)	6m6.40s	6m0s
3m5f Ch (22)	Kilburn (17 Feb 1966)	7m54.50s	7m15s

Ayr

Distance (number of obstacles)	Record holder (date set)	record time	standard time
2m Ch (12)	Clay County (12 Oct 1991)	3m38.60s	3m43s
2m Hdl (9)	Secret Ballot (19 Apr 1980)	3m27.40s	3m37s
2m4f Ch (17)	Chandigar (15 May 1972)	4m44.10s	4m44s
2m4f Hdl (11)	Moss Royal (19 Apr 1974)	4m35.00s	4m36s
2m5f110yds Ch (18)	Star To The North (9 May 2001)	5m10.20s	5m6s
2m6f Hdl (12)	Any Second (19 Apr 1980)	5m6.80s	5m7s
3m110yds Hdl (12)	Nautical Lad (6 Apr 1964)	5m42.00s	5m43s
3m1f Ch (19)	Top 'N' Tale (12 May 1982)	5m57.70s	5m59s
3m2f110yds Hdl (14)	Meditator (18 Apr 1997)	6m26.90s	6m14s
3m3f110yds Ch (21)	Straight Vulgan (18 Nov 1974)	6m51.40s	6m39s
3m5f Ch (24)	Prime Example (7 Dec 1998)	8m24.30s	7ms2s
4m1f Ch (27)	Young Ash Leaf (17 Apr 1971)	8m0.40s	8m4s

Bangor

Distance (number of obstacles)	Record holder (date set)	record time	standard time
2m1f Hdl (9)	Andy Rew (24 Apr 1982)	3m44.50s	3m50s

2m1f110yds Ch (12)	Bunrannoch House (16 Aug 1986)	4m7.70s	4m9s
2m4f Hdl (11)	Smithy's Choice (25 Apr 1987)	4m34.10s	4m34s
2m4f110yds Ch (15)	Alqairawaan (17 Aug 1996)	4m55.30s	4m57s
2m7f110yds Hdl (12)	Desperate (12 Apr 1993)	5m41.00s	5m25s
3m Hdl (12)	General Pershing (20 Apr 1991)	5m34.00s	5m32s
3m110yds Ch (18)	Tartan Trademark (15 Sep 1990)	5m57.70s	5m58s
3m6f Ch (21)	Kaki Crazy (23 May 2001)	7m34.10s	7m24s
4m1f Ch (24)	Nazzaro (13 Dec 1995)	8m50.60s	8m14s

Carlisle

2m Ch (12)	Cape Felix (20 Apr 1981)	3m55.80s	3m58s
2m1f Hdl (9)	Supertop (25 Oct 1997)	4m2.60s	4m5s
2m4f Ch (16)	Flying Dancer (29 Sep 1990)	5m3.90s	4m58s
2m4f Hdl (11)	Gods Law (29 Sep 1990)	4m50.60s	4m47s
2m4f110yds Ch (16)	Pentlands Flyer (25 Oct 1997)	5m1.80s	/
2m4f110yds Hdl (11)	Sujud (21 Sep 1996)	4m45.40s	/
3m Ch (18)	The Blue Boy (21 Sep 1996)	5m59.90s	6m33s
3m110yds Hdl (12)	Kinda Groovy (25 Oct 1997)	5m46.50s	5m53s
3m2f Ch (19)	Lady Of Gortmerron (6 Oct 2000)	6m40.40s	/
3m4f Ch (21)	Cedar Green (15 Jan 2002)	7m55.20s	7m4s

Cartmel

2m1f110yds Ch (12)	Clever Folly (27 May 1992)	4m7.50s	4m10s
2m1f110yds Hdl (8)	Sayeh (28 Aug 1999)	3m57.90s	3m59s
	Indian Jockey (24 May 1997)	3m57.90s	
	Kalshan (26 May 1990)	3m57.90s	
2m5f110yds Ch (14)	Corrarder (30 May 1994)	5m6.50s	5m9s
2m6f Hdl (11)	Woodstock Wanderer (23 May 1998)	5m14.50s	5m6s
3m2f Ch (18)	Better Times Ahead (28 Aug 1999)	6m13.40s	6m16s
3m2f Hdl (12)	Portonia (30 May 1994)	5m58.00s	6m4s
3m6f Ch (20)	I'm The Man (27 May 2000)	7m29.30s	7m16s

Catterick

2m Ch (12)	Preston Deal (18 Dec 1971)	3m44.60s	3m47s
2m Hdl (8)	Lunar Wind (22 Apr 1982)	3m36.50s	3m39s
2m3f Ch (15)	Fear Siuil (24 Nov 2001)	4m41.90s	4m37s
2m3f Hdl (10)	Bo Dancer (1 Dec 1999)	4m34.80s	4m23s
3m1f110yds Ch (19)	Clever General (7 Nov 1981)	6m14.00s	6m15s
3m1f110yds Hdl (12)	Seamus O'Flynn (8 Nov 1986)	6m3.80s	6m4s
3m4f110yds Ch (21)	The Wilk (19 Jan 1990)	7m15.30s	7m3s
3m6f Ch (23)	Russian Castle (14 Feb 1998)	7m51.00s	7m26s

Cheltenham, New course

2m110yds Ch (14)	Samakaan (16 Mar 2000)	3m52.40s	3m55s
2m1f Hdl (8)	Moody Man (15 Mar 1990)	3m51.20s	3m55s
2m4f110yds Hdl (9)	Sir Dante (15 Apr 1997)	4m45.00s	4m40s
2m5f Ch (17)	Barnbrook Again (18 Apr 1990)	5m1.60s	5m4s

2m5f110yds Hdl (10)	Fashion House (19 Sep 1968)	4m53.60s	5m1s
3m Hdl (12)	Bacchanal (16 Mar 2000)	5m36.60s	5m39s
3m1f110yds Ch (21)	Bigsun (15 Mar 1990)	6m13.40s	6m18s
3m2f110yds Ch (22)	Looks Like Trouble (16 Mar 2000)	6m30.30s	6m34s
3m4f110yds Ch (24)	*not known*		7m4s
4m1f Ch (27)	Rusty Bridge (30 Apr 1997)	8m37.50s	8m17s

Cheltenham, Old course

2m Ch (12)	Edredon Bleu (15 Mar 2000)	3m44.70s	3m50s
2m110yds Hdl (8)	Istabraq (14 Mar 2000)	3m48.10s	3m51s
2m4f110yds Ch (15)	Dark Stranger (15 Mar 2000)	4m49.60s	5m0s
2m5f Hdl (10)	Monsignor (15 Mar 2000)	4m52.00s	4m59s
3m110yds Ch (19)	Marlborough (14 Mar 2000)	5m59.70s	6m6s
3m1f110yds Hdl (13)	Rubhahunish (14 Mar 2000)	6m3.40s	6m10s
3m2f Ch (19)	The Pooka (26 Sep 1973)	6m20.60s	6m30s
3m3f110yds Ch (21)	Run And Skip (12 Nov 1988)	7m3.90s	6m54s
4m Ch (24)	Relaxation (15 Mar 2000)	8m0.60s	8m4s

Cheltenham, Park course

2m110yds Ch (13)	Clever Folly (3 Oct 1991)	3m56.00s	3m59s
2m110yds Hdl (8)	Cloghans Bay (29 Sep 1993)	3m54.40s	3m55s
2m4f110yds Hdl (9)	Gospel (20 Apr 1994)	4m45.00s	/
2m5f Ch (16)	Tri Folene (29 Sep 1993)	5m5.90s	5m8s
	Lusty Light (29 Sep 1994)	5m5.90s	
2m5f110yds Hdl (10)	Fuzzy Logic (20 Oct 1993)	5m11.20s	5m8s
2m7f110yds Hdl (12)	Bankroll (29 Sep 1993)	5m29.90s	5m37s
3m1f110yds Ch (19)	Whatagale (29 Sep 1994)	6m15.80s	6m18s

Cheltenham, cross-country course

3m1f Ch (25)	Linden's Lotto (1 Jan 1999)	6m59.30s	/
3m7f Ch (32)	Linden's Lotto (13 Nov 1998)	8m22.70s	/

Chepstow

2m110yds Ch (12)	Panto Prince (9 Apr 1989)	3m54.10s	3m58s
2m110yds Hdl (8)	Tingle Bell (4 Oct 1986)	3m43.20s	3m45s
2m3f110yds Ch (16)	Armala (14 May 1996)	4m45.00s	4m47s
2m4f Hdl (11)	Court Appeal (8 May 1990)	4m38.80s	4m32s
2m4f110yds Hdl (11)	Aileen's Cacador (23 Apr 1957)	4m36.20s	/
3m Ch (18)	Broadheath (4 Oct 1986)	5m47.90s	5m51s
3m Hdl (12)	Chucklestone (11 May 1993)	5m33.60s	5m35s
3m2f110yds Ch (22)	Jaunty Jane (26 May 1975)	6m39.40s	6m33s
3m5f110yds Ch (22)	Creeola (27 Apr 1957)	7m24.00s	7m25s

Doncaster

2m110yds Ch (12)	Itsgottabealright (28 Jan 1989)	3m51.90s	3m57s
2m110yds Hdl (8)	Good For A Loan (24 Feb 1993)	3m46.60s	3m49s
2m3f Ch (15)	Ulusaba (28 Feb 2003)	4m49.80s	4m38s

Sponsored by Stan James

2m3f110yds Ch (15)	Powder Horn (25 Feb 1985)	4m45.40s	/
2m3f110yds Hdl (10)	Moving Earth (28 Feb 2003)	4m42.00s	4m32s
2m4f Hdl (10)	Magic Court (21 Nov 1964)	4m34.60s	/
3m Ch (18)	Dalkey Sound (26 Jan 1991)	5m52.40s	5m54s
3m110yds Hdl (11)	Pondolfi (4 Nov 1972)	5m45.30s	5m47s
3m2f Ch (19)	Saggarts Choice (25 Mar 1970)	6m18.40s	6m24s
3m4f Ch (21)	Shraden Leader (5 Mar 1994)	7m4.80s	6m56s
4m Ch (24)	Drops O'Brandy (10 Mar 1994)	8m11.70s	8m2s

Exeter

2m1f Ch (12)	Niknaks Nephew (28 Aug 1998)	4m6.80s	/
2m1f Hdl (8)	Present Bleu (2 Oct 2001)	3m53.10s	3m54s
2m1f110yds Ch (12)	Some Jinks (23 Aug 1984)	4m6.80s	4m7s
2m1f110yds Hdl (8)	Athar (4 Aug 1993)	3m57.20s	/
2m2f Ch (12)	Travado (2 Nov 1993)	4m13.80s	/
2m2f Hdl (8)	Major Dundee (15 Apr 1997)	4m3.10s	/
2m3f Ch (15)	James Pigg (25 Aug 1995)	4m31.50s	/
2m3f Hdl (9)	Il Capitano (9 Oct 2002)	4m16.50s	4m20s
2m3f110yds Ch (15)	Gay Edition (2 Oct 1990)	4m34.80s	4m36s
2m3f110yds Hdl (9)	Northern Starlight (15 Apr 1997)	4m23.70s	/
2m6f Hdl (11)	Owenius (21 Aug 1980)	4m59.90s	/
2m6f110yds Ch (17)	James Pigg (6 Sep 1995)	5m22.70s	5m23s
2m6f110yds Hdl (11)	Dandonell (16 May 2001)	5m20.00s	5m13s
	Sammy Samba (9 Oct 2002)	5m20.00s	
2m7f Hdl (11)	Fly-Away Gunner (21 Mar 2000)	5m29.00s	/
2m7f110yds Ch (17)	Noyan (23 Apr 2002)	5m31.80s	5m36s
3m110yds Hdl (12)	Il Capitano (1 Oct 2002)	5m42.30s	5m42s
3m1f Ch (19)	Hand Woven (17 May 2000)	6m7.30s	/
3m1f110yds Ch (19)	Ballysicyos (16 May 2001)	6m9.00s	6m8s
3m2f Ch (19)	The Leggett (24 Mar 1993)	6m30.70s	6m7s
3m6f Ch (21)	Samlee (7 Mar 2000)	8m9.40s	7m19s
3m6f110yds Ch (21)	Mister One (5 Mar 2002)	7m48.60s	7m27s
4m Ch (21)	Lancastrian Jet (7 Dec 2001)	8m17.90s	7m52s

Fakenham

2m Hdl (9)	Cobbet (CZE) (9 May 2001)	3m45.70s	3m42s
2m110yds Ch (12)	Cheekie Ora (23 Apr 1984)	3m44.90s	3m56s
2m110yds Hdl (9)	Tom Clapton (25 May 1992)	3m47.80s	3m50s
2m4f Hdl (11)	Ayem (16 May 1999)	4m41.20s	4m42s
2m5f Hdl (11)	Lobric (21 Apr 1992)	4m51.80s	4m57s
2m5f110yds Ch (16)	Skipping Tim (25 May 1992)	5m10.30s	5m12s
2m7f110yds Hdl (13)	Laughing Gas (20 May 1995)	5m37.10s	5m34s
3m Ch (18)	Saldatore (23 Apr 1984)	5m55.70s	5m50s
3m110yds Ch (18)	Specialize (16 May 1999)	5m56.90s	5m58s
3m5f110yds Ch (22)	Ibin St James (24 Nov 2002)	8m11.30s	7m18s

Folkestone

2m Ch (12)	High Gale (30 Apr 1999)	3m48.80s	3m50s
2m1f110yds Hdl (9)	Super Tek (14 Nov 1983)	3m56.20s	4m5s
2m4f110yds Hdl (10)	Circus Colours (2 Apr 1996)	4m57.00s	4m50s
2m5f Ch (15)	Silver Buck (14 Nov 1983)	5m6.40s	5m7s
2m6f110yds Hdl (11)	Royalty Miss (30 Apr 1985)	5m18.20s	5m20s
3m1f Ch (18)	Highland (23 May 2001)	6m11.40s	6m10s
3m2f Ch (19)	Bolt Hole (26 Apr 1988)	6m23.00s	6m26s
3m4f Hdl (13)	North West (25 Nov 1985)	6m43.20s	6m46s

Fontwell

2m2f Ch (13)	A Thousand Dreams (3 Jun 2002)	4m14.50s	4m18s
2m2f Hdl (9)	Fighting Days (14 Aug 1990)	4m5.90s	/
2m2f110yds Hdl (9)	Hyperion Du Moulin II (3 Jun 2002)	4m6.80s	4m11s
2m3f Ch (14)	Connaught Cracker (3 May 1999)	4m32.00s	4m33s
2m4f Ch (15)	Chalcedony (3 Jun 2002)	4m38.10s	4m46s
2m4f Hdl (10)	Hillswick (27 Aug 1999)	4m30.50s	4m33s
2m6f Ch (16)	Contes (3 Jun 2002)	5m13.90s	5m17s
2m6f Hdl (11)	Doualago (29 May 1995)	5m3.00s	/
2m6f110yds Hdl (11)	Mister Pickwick (3 Jun 2002)	5m6.70s	5m9s
3m2f110yds Ch (19)	Il Capitano (6 May 2002)	6m24.30s	6m25s
3m2f110yds Hdl (13)	Punch's Hotel (27 Apr 1995)	6m14.80s	/
3m3f Hdl (13)	Lord of The Track (18 Aug 2003)	6m21.60s	6m19s
3m4f Ch (21)	Ice Cool Lad (17 Mar 2003)	7m34.30s	6m48s

Haydock

2m Ch (12)	Teddy Bear II (5 Mar 1976)	3m55.40s	3m55s
2m Hdl (8)	She's Our Mare (1 May 1999)	3m32.30s	3m40s
2m4f Ch (15)	Hallo Dandy (12 Dec 1984)	4m56.50s	4m57s
2m4f Hdl (10)	Moving Out (6 May 1995)	4m35.30s	4m41s
2m6f Ch (17)	Arlequin de Sou (24 Oct 2002)	5m27.70s	5m29s
2m6f Hdl (12)	Peter the Butchers (3 May 1982)	5m12.70s	5m13s
2m7f110yds Hdl (12)	Boscean Chieftain (3 May 1993)	5m32.30s	5m37s
3m Ch (18)	Eau de Cologne (29 Mar 2003)	6m1.60s	6m3s
3m4f110yds Ch (22)	Rubstic (15 Oct 1975)	7m17.90s	7m19s
4m110yds Ch (25)	Jer (29 Nov 1979)	8m37.40s	8m23s

Hereford

2m Ch (12)	Smolensk (21 Mar 1998)	3m46.10s	3m48s
2m1f Hdl (8)	Tasty Son (11 Sep 1973)	3m42.20s	3m45s
2m3f Ch (14)	Kings Wild (28 Sep 1990)	4m30.00s	4m31s
2m3f110yds Hdl (10)	Polden Pride (6 May 1995)	4m22.20s	4m23s
3m1f110yds Ch (19)	Gilston Lass (8 Apr 1995)	6m10.60s	6m11s
3m2f Hdl (13)	Clifton Set (8 Apr 1995)	6m5.60s	6m6s

Hexham

2m Hdl (8)	In Good Faith (17 Jun 2000)	3m46.20s	/
2m110yds Ch (12)	Adamatic (17 Jun 2000)	3m53.60s	3m56s
2m110yds Hdl (8)	Covent Garden (15 Sep 2002)	3m58.40s	3m53s
2m4f110yds Ch (15)	Saskia's Hero (17 Jun 2000)	4m56.20s	4m57s
2m4f110yds Hdl (10)	Pappa Charlie (27 May 1997)	4m31.50s	4m50s
3m Hdl (12)	Fingers Crossed (29 Apr 1991)	5m45.50s	5m46s
3m1f Ch (19)	Silent Snipe (1 Jun 2002)	6m7.60s	6m6s
4m Ch (25)	Rubika (15 Mar 1990)	8m37.60s	8m0s

Huntingdon

2m110yds Ch (12)	Who's To Say (19 Sep 1998)	3m54.40s	3m55s
2m110yds Hdl (8)	Wakeel (19 Sep 1998)	3m35.00s	3m38s
2m4f110yds Ch (16)	Glemot (9 Nov 1999)	4m50.50s	4m52s
2m4f110yds Hdl (10)	Richies Delight (30 Aug 1999)	4m32.90s	4m36s
2m5f110yds Hdl (10)	Sound of Laughter (14 Apr 1984)	4m45.80s	4m50s
3m Ch (19)	Ozzie Jones (18 Sep 1998)	5m44.40s	5m48s
3m2f Hdl (12)	Weather Wise (18 Sep 1998)	5m54.60s	5m59s
3m6f110yds Ch (25)	Kinnahalla (24 Nov 2001)	8m2.70s	7m33s

Kelso

2m110yds Hdl (8)	The Premier Expres (2 May 1995)	3m39.60s	3m42s
2m1f Ch (12)	Mr Coggy (2 May 1984)	4m2.40s	4m4s
2m2f Hdl (10)	All Welcome (15 Oct 1994)	4m11.40s	4m7s
2m6f110yds Ch (17)	Bas De Laine (13 Nov 1996)	5m29.60s	5m26s
2m6f110yds Hdl (11)	Hit The Canvas (30 Sep 1995)	5m12.20s	5m13s
3m1f Ch (19)	McGregor The Third (19 Sep 1999)	6m1.20s	6m3s
3m3f Hdl (13)	Dook's Delight (19 May 1995)	6m10.10s	6m15s
3m4f Ch (21)	Seven Towers (2 Dec 1996)	7m2.30s	6m53s
4m Ch (24)	Seven Towers (17 Jan 1997)	8m7.50s	7m58s

Kempton

2m Ch (13)	Young Pokey (27 Dec 1991)	3m42.90s	3m47s
2m Hdl (8)	Freight Forwarder (20 Oct 1979)	3m37.00s	3m40s
2m4f110yds Ch (17)	Mr Entertainer (27 Dec 1991)	4m55.80s	4m56s
2m5f Hdl (10)	Grand Canyon (15 Oct 1977)	4m51.60s	4m53s
3m Ch (19)	One Man (26 Dec 1996)	5m45.30s	5m50s
3m110yds Hdl (12)	Esmenella (17 Oct 1964)	5m45.60s	5m47s
3m4f110yds Ch (23)	Master Oats (26 Feb 1994)	7m52.70s	7m0s

Leicester

2m Ch (12)	Bow Strada (18 Nov 2002)	3m58.80s	3m57s
2m Hdl (9)	Ryde Again (20 Nov 1989)	3m39.60s	3m41s
2m1f Ch (12)	Noon (2 Nov 1971)	4m10.20s	4m12s
2m4f110yds Ch (15)	Sire Nantais (5 Dec 1989)	5m4.40s	5m6s
2m4f110yds Hdl (12)	Prince of Rheims (5 Dec 1989)	4m45.50s	4m47s
2m7f110yds Ch (18)	MacGeorge (17 Feb 1998)	5m51.10s	5m51s

3m Ch (18)	Sorbus (24 Apr 1967)	5m55.40s	/
3m Hdl (13)	King Tarquin (1 Apr 1967)	5m48.00s	5m44s

Lingfield

2m Ch (12)	Cotapaxi (19 Jan 1992)	3m51.90s	3m54s
2m110yds Hdl (8)	Va Utu (19 Mar 1993)	3m48.00s	3m51s
2m3f110yds Hdl (10)	Bellezza (20 Mar 1993)	4m37.30s	4m39s
2m4f110yds Ch (14)	Kisu Kali (20 Mar 1993)	5m9.10s	5m3s
2m7f Hdl (12)	Navarone (18 Mar 2000)	5m39.40s	5m30s
3m Ch (18)	Mighty Frolic (19 Mar 1993)	5m58.40s	5m57s
3m4f110yds Ch (21)	Tylo Steamer (16 Mar 2001)	8m37.50s	7m6s

Ludlow

2m Ch (13)	Pridewood Picker (21 Oct 1999)	3m57.30s	3m52s
2m Hdl (9)	Desert Fighter (11 Oct 2001)	3m36.40s	3m36s
2m4f Ch (17)	Mulkev Prince (19 Mar 2003)	4m55.00s	4m49s
2m5f Hdl (11)	Willy Willy (11 Oct 2001)	4m54.70s	4m49s
3m Ch (19)	Major Adventure (6 May 2002)	5m54.50s	5m49s
3m Hdl (12)	Go-Onmyson (11 Oct 2001)	5m37.30s	5m34s
3m2f110y Hdl (13)	Gysart (9 Oct 1997)	6m7.50s	6m10s
3m3f110y Ch (22)	Act In Time (13 Dec 2001)	6m58.50s	6m40s
3m7f Ch (26)	Storm Of Gold (28 Feb 2002)	8m51.80s	7m37s

Market Rasen

2m1f110yds Ch (13)	Cape Felix (14 Aug 1982)	4m11.90s	4m14s
2m1f110yds Hdl (8)	Border River (30 Jul 1977)	3m54.40s	4m0s
2m3f110yds Hdl (10)	Coble Lane (29 May 1999)	4m30.70s	4m32s
2m4f Ch (15)	Fleeting Mandate (24 Jul 1999)	4m42.80s	4m51s
2m5f110yds Hdl (10)	Pandolfi (3 Oct 1970)	5m3.80s	5m3s
2m6f110yds Ch (15)	Annas Prince (19 Oct 1979)	5m24.20s	5m27s
3m Hdl (12)	Trustful (21 May 1977)	5m38.80s	5m40s
3m1f Ch (19)	Allerlea (1 May 1985)	6m1.00s	6m6s
3m4f110yds Ch (21)	Grate Deel (1 Oct 2000)	7m32.70s	7m1s
4m1f Ch (23)	Barkin (23 Nov 1991)	8m51.20s	8m12s

Musselburgh

2m Ch (12)	Sonsie Mo (6 Dec 1993)	3m48.10s	3m49s
2m Hdl (9)	Joe Bumpas (11 Dec 1989)	3m35.90s	3m38s
2m1f Hdl (9)	Bodfari Signet (3 Apr 2001)	4m4.60s	3m54s
2m4f Ch (16)	Sir Peter Lely (20 Dec 1993)	4m53.00s	4m53s
2m4f Hdl (12)	Old Feathers (3 Apr 2001)	4m40.70s	4m41s
3m Ch (18)	Charming Gale (9 Dec 1996)	5m50.70s	5m52s
3m Hdl (13)	Supertop (17 Dec 1996)	5m39.10s	5m42s

Sponsored by Stan James

Newbury

2m110yds Hdl (8)	Dhofar (25 Oct 1985)	3m45.20s	3m49s
2m1f Ch (13)	Barnbrook Again (25 Nov 1989)	3m58.20s	4m1s
2m2f110yds Ch (15)	Coral Island (21 Mar 2003)	4m33.00s	4m24s
2m3f Hdl (11)	Quiet Water (21 Mar 2003)	4m33.30s	4m27s
2m4f Ch (16)	Espy (25 Oct 1991)	4m47.90s	4m49s
2m5f Hdl (12)	Flagship Therese (27 Mar 1999)	4m54.90s	4m57s
2m6f110yds Ch (17)	Cape Stormer (21 Mar 2003)	5m36.80s	5m27s
3m Ch (18)	The Toiseach (27 Mar 1999)	5m47.00s	5m49s
3m110yds Hdl (13)	Landsdowne (25 Oct 1996)	5m45.40s	5m48s
3m2f110yds Ch (21)	Topsham Bay (26 Mar 1993)	6m27.10s	6m29s

Newcastle

2m Hdl (9)	Padre Mio (25 Nov 1995)	3m40.70s	3m42s
2m110yds Ch (14)	Greenheart (7 May 1990)	3m56.70s	3m58s
2m110yds Hdl (8)	Mr Woodcock (23 Oct 1991)	3m49.40s	/
2m4f Ch (17)	Snow Blessed (19 May 1984)	4m46.70s	4m51s
2m4f Hdl (11)	Mils Mij (13 May 1989)	4m42.00s	4m42s
3m Ch (20)	Even Swell (30 Oct 1975)	5m48.10s	5m51s
3m Hdl (13)	Withy Bank (29 Nov 1986)	5m40.10s	5m42s
3m6f Ch (25)	Charlie Potheen (28 Apr 1973)	7m30.00s	7m30s
4m1f Ch (27)	Domaine Du Pron (21 Feb 1998)	8m30.40s	8m20s

Newton Abbot

2m110yds Ch (13)	Noble Comic (24 Jun 2000)	3m53.20s	3m51s
2m1f Hdl (8)	Windbound Lass (1 Aug 1988)	3m45.00s	3m48s
2m5f Ch (15)	Rahiib (13 Aug 1987)	4m56.40s	/
2m5f110yds Ch (16)	Karadin (13 Aug 2002)	5m6.30s	5m4s
2m6f Hdl (10)	Virbian (30 Jun 1983)	4m55.40s	4m58s
3m2f110yds Ch (20)	Just In Business (14 May 2001)	6m21.50s	6m19s
3m3f Hdl (12)	La Carotte (31 Jul 1989)	6m17.60s	6m18s

Perth

2m Ch (12)	Beldine (22 Aug 1992)	3m47.50s	3m50s
2m110yds Hdl (8)	Molly Fay (23 Sep 1971)	3m40.40s	3m44s
2m4f110yds Ch (15)	General Chandos (17 Aug 1990)	4m56.30s	4m57s
	Fiveleigh Builds (15 May 1996)	4m56.30s	
2m4f110yds Hdl (10)	Valiant Dash (19 May 1994)	4m41.20s	4m43s
3m Ch (18)	Mac's Supreme (25 Jun 2000)	5m54.20s	5m56s
3m110yds Hdl (12)	Mystic Memory (20 Aug 1994)	5m43.10s	5m45s
3m2f110yds Ch (20)	Creon (25 Apr 2002)	6m46.50s	6m37s
3m3f Hdl (14)	Pontius (25 Apr 2003)	6m48.50s	6m24s
3m7f Ch (23)	General Wolfe (25 Apr 2002)	7m58.90s	7m48s

Plumpton

2m Ch (13)	Brinkwater (10 Aug 1991)	3m47.10s	3m49s
2m Hdl (9)	Royal Derbi (19 Sep 1988)	3m31.00s	3m40s

2m1f Ch (12)	Janiture (19 Apr 2003)	4m5.90s	4m4s
2m1f Hdl (10)	Striding Edge (7 Aug 1992)	3m58.60s	3m54s
2m2f Ch (14)	Pats Minstrel (15 Apr 1995)	4m24.10s	4m19s
2m4f Ch (14)	Chalcedony (7 Oct 2002)	4m50.70s	4m49s
2m4f Hdl (12)	Director's Choice (30 Apr 1994)	4m37.60s	4m38s
2m5f Ch (16)	Preenka Girl (4 Aug 1995)	5m4.20s	/
2m5f Hdl (12)	Majestic (18 Oct 1999)	4m50.10s	4m52s
3m1f110yds Ch (20)	Betton Gorse (29 Apr 1982)	6m9.20s	6m14s
3m1f110yds Hdl (14)	Bali Strong (18 Oct 1999)	6m0.10s	6m1s
3m2f Ch (18)	Sunday Habits (19 Apr 2003)	6m23.50s	6m21s
3m5f Ch (21)	Ecuyer Du Roi (15 Apr 02)	7m19.80s	7m8s

Sandown

2m Ch (13)	News King (23 Apr 1982)	3m44.30s	3m49s
2m110yds Hdl (8)	Olympian (13 Mar 1993)	3m42.00s	3m47s
2m4f110yds Ch (17)	Coulton (29 Apr 1995)	4m57.10s	4m58s
2m4f110yds Hdl (9)	Errand Boy (11 Mar 2000)	4m51.50s	4m46s
2m6f Hdl (11)	Kintbury (5 Nov 1983)	5m5.60s	5m8s
3m Hdl (12)	Rostropovich (27 Apr 2002)	5m39.10s	5m38s
3m110yds Ch (22)	Arkle (6 Nov 1965)	5m59.00s	6m0s
3m5f110yds Ch (24)	Cache Fleur (29 Apr 1995)	7m9.10s	7m15s

Sedgefield

2m110yds Ch (13)	Suas Leat (16 Sep 1997)	3m53.60s	3m54s
2m1f Ch (13)	Stay Awake (18 May 1994)	4m0.40s	/
2m1f Hdl (8)	Country Orchid (5 Sep 1997)	3m45.70s	3m48s
2m1f110yds Hdl (8)	Byzantine (4 Sep 1992)	3m51.50s	/
2m5f Ch (16)	Pennybridge (30 Sep 1997)	4m59.20s	5m0s
2m5f110yds Hdl (10)	Palm House (4 Sep 1992)	4m46.30s	4m50s
3m3f Ch (21)	The Gallopin' Major (14 Sep 1996)	6m29.30s	6m31s
3m3f110yds Hdl (13)	Tsanga (10 Jul 1999)	6m21.90s	6m21s
3m4f Ch (22)	Mister Muddypaws (5 May 2000)	6m46.50s	6m46s

Southwell

2m Ch (13)	Stay Awake (11 May 1994)	3m51.30s	3m52s
2m Hdl (9)	Merlins Wish (2 May 1994)	3m36.60s	3m40s
2m1f Ch (14)	Versicium (19 Jul 2002)	4m4.80s	4m6s
2m1f Hdl (10)	Jack Dawson (13 Sep 2002)	3m52.10s	3m54s
2m2f Hdl (10)	Here's The Deal (8 May 1995)	4m19.60s	4m12s
2m4f110yds Ch (16)	Bally Parson (8 May 1995)	5m2.90s	5m4s
2m4f110yds Hdl (11)	Man of The Grange (2 May 1994)	4m47.90s	4m49s
2m5f110yds Ch (17)	Castle Folly (13 Sep 2002)	5m16.60s	5m18s
2m5f110yds Hdl (12)	Glacial Missile (12 Aug 2002)	5m3.70s	5m3s
3m110yds Ch (19)	Soloman Springs (6 May 1999)	6m1.90s	6m6s
3m110yds Hdl (13)	Soloman Springs (8 May 1995)	5m47.10s	5m48s
3m2f Ch (21)	Son Of Light (12 Aug 2002)	6m25.90s	6m28s
3m2f Hdl (15)	Navarre Samson (12 Aug 2002)	6m15.10s	6m10s

Sponsored by Stan James

Stratford

2m110yds Hdl (9)	Chusan (7 May 1956)	3m40.40s	3m44s
2m1f110yds Ch (13)	Money In (5 Sep 1981)	4m0.20s	4m2s
2m3f Hdl (10)	Mister Ermyn (29 Jul 2000)	4m19.70s	4m20s
2m4f Ch (15)	Stately Home (11 Jul 1999)	4m42.00s	4m42s
2m5f110yds Ch (16)	Father Rector (16 Oct 1999)	5m3.00s	5m3s
2m6f110yds Hdl (12)	Broken Wing (31 May 1986)	5m6.80s	5m11s
3m Ch (18)	Horus (28 Jun 2002)	5m43.60s	5m44s
3m3f Hdl (14)	Space Kate (3 Jun 1989)	6m21.30s	6m19s
3m4f Ch (21)	Gold Castle (1 Jun 1985)	6m44.80s	6m47s
4m Ch (24)	Stewarts Pride (1 Jul 2001)	7m53.90s	7m50s

Taunton

2m110yds Ch (12)	I Have Him (28 Apr 1995)	3m49.50s	3m51s
2m1f Hdl (9)	Indian Jockey (3 Oct 1996)	3m39.40s	3m44s
2m3f Ch (14)	Harik (24 Mar 2003)	4m30.70s	4m31s
2m3f110yds Hdl (10)	Nova Run (14 Nov 1996)	4m21.70s	4m23s
3m Ch (17)	Art Prince (14 Oct 1999)	5m38.30s	5m46s
3m110yds Hdl (12)	On My Toes (15 Oct 1998)	5m30.20s	5m33s
3m3f Ch (19)	En Gounasi Theon (12 Apr 1990)	6m52.90s	6m30s
3m6f Ch (21)	Torside (26 Mar 1987)	7m50.50s	7m20s
4m2f110yds Ch (24)	Woodlands Genhire (16 Jan 1997)	9m1.50s	8m33s

Towcester

2m Hdl (8)	Nascracker (22 May 1987)	3m39.50s	3m45s
2m110yds Ch (12)	Silver Knight (25 May 1974)	3m59.00s	4m1s
2m4f Ch (13)	Millersford (24 May 2002)	5m13.90s	4m53s
2m5f Hdl (11)	Mailcom (3 May 1993)	5m0.90s	5m1s
2m6f Ch (16)	Whiskey Eyes (10 May 1988)	5m30.00s	5m24s
3m Hdl (12)	Dropshot (25 May 1984)	5m44.00s	5m46s
3m1f Ch (18)	Veleso (22 May 1987)	6m12.30s	6m13s

Uttoxeter

2m Ch (12)	Tapageur (8 Aug 1991)	3m41.50s	3m49s
2m Hdl (10)	Mill De Lease (21 Sep 1989)	3m28.20s	3m38s
2m4f Ch (15)	Bertone (5 Oct 1996)	4m42.60s	4m47s
2m4f110yds Hdl (12)	Chicago's Best (11 Jun 1995)	4m39.10s	4m43s
2m5f Ch (16)	McKenzie (27 Apr 1974)	4m54.20s	5m2s
2m6f110yds Hdl (12)	Springfield Scally (18 Mar 2000)	5m14.90s	5m12s
2m7f Ch (16)	Certain Angle (9 Jun 1996)	5m26.80s	5m34s
3m Ch (18)	Jimmy O'Dea (19 May 1999)	6m1.50s	5m49s
3m110yds Hdl (14)	Volcanic Dancer (19 Sep 1991)	5m35.30s	5m40s
3m2f Ch (20)	McGregor The Third (5 Oct 1996)	6m23.60s	6m20s
3m4f Ch (21)	Ottowa (7 Feb 1998)	7m33.90s	6m52s
4m110yds (24)	Stormez (30 Jun 2002)	8m8.10s	8m10s
4m2f Ch (24)	Seven Towers (15 Mar 1997)	8m33.70s	8m34s

Warwick

2m Ch (12)	Super Sharp (2 Nov 1996)	3m49.10s	/
2m Hdl (8)	High Knowl (17 Sep 1988)	3m30.80s	3m37s
2m110yds Ch (12)	Cenkos (12 May 2001)	3m48.10s	3m51s
2m2f110yds Hdl (9)	Itsonlyme (2 Nov 1999)	4m22.60s	/
2m3f Hdl (10)	Runaway Pete (2 Nov 1996)	4m15.00s	4m20s
2m4f Ch (17)	Dictum (2 Nov 1999)	4m56.20s	/
2m4f110yds Ch (17)	Dudie (16 May 1987)	4m53.30s	4m54s
2m4f110yds Hdl (11)	Carrymore (19 Sep 1970)	4m43.00s	/
2m5f Hdl (11)	Three Eagles (11 May 2002)	4m43.60s	4m48s
3m110yds Ch (18)	Shepherds Rest (2 Apr 2002)	6m3.90s	5m56s
3m1f Hdl (11)	City Poser (2 Apr 2002)	5m53.50s	5m50s
3m1f110yds Ch (20)	Brush With Fame (2 Nov 1999)	6m30.00s	/
3m2f Ch (20)	Castle Warden (6 May 1989)	6m16.10s	6m19s
3m5f Ch (22)	Purple Haze (18 Sep 1982)	7m13.20s	7m9s
4m1f110yds Ch (27)	Jolly's Clump (24 Jan 1976)	8m36.40s	8m20s

Wetherby

2m Ch (12)	Cumbrian Challenge (22 Oct 1995)	3m47.20s	3m48s
2m Hdl (9)	Red Guard (13 Oct 1999)	3m39.00s	3m41s
2m4f110yds Ch (15)	Toogood To Be True (11 Oct 1995)	4m52.00s	4m55s
2m4f110yds Hdl (10)	Master Sandy (8 May 1996)	4m45.30s	4m46s
2m5f Ch (14)	Don't Forget (9 May 1984)	5m1.40s	5m3s
2m7f Hdl (12)	Frankie Anson (21 Apr 2003)	5m40.20s	5m24s
2m7f110yds Ch (18)	Joint Account (23 Apr 2002)	5m43.70s	5m40s
3m110yds Ch (16)	Barton Bank (28 Oct 1995)	6m0.60s	/
3m1f Ch (18)	See More Business (30 Oct 1999)	6m3.50s	6m5s
3m1f Hdl (12)	Trainglot (2 Nov 1996)	5m58.00s	5m53s

Wincanton

2m Ch (13)	Kescast (11 May 1988)	3m44.40s	3m46s
2m Hdl (8)	Mulciber (6 May 1994)	3m28.30s	3m34s
2m5f Ch (17)	Coulton (22 Oct 1995)	4m59.70s	5m2s
2m6f Hdl (11)	St Mellion Green (9 May 1995)	5m1.80s	5m4s
3m1f110yds Ch (21)	Doulago (6 May 1997)	6m10.00s	6m14s

Worcester

2m Ch (12)	Full Strength (30 Aug 1990)	3m45.50s	3m49s
2m Hdl (8)	Santopadre (11 May 1988)	3m35.30s	3m40s
2m2f Hdl (9)	Lady For Life (5 Aug 2000)	4m2.50s	4m6s
2m4f Hdl (10)	Wottashambles (13 Sep 1996)	4m34.50s	4m35s
2m4f110yds Ch (15)	Gladiateur IV (11 May 2002)	4m55.70s	4m57s
2m5f110yds Hdl (10)	Elite Reg (19 May 1993)	4m48.50s	4m56s
2m7f Ch (18)	Tanora (2 May 1981)	5m37.60s	/
2m7f110yds Ch (18)	Arlas (22 Jul 1998)	5m43.00s	5m43s
3m Hdl (12)	Polar Champ (5 Aug 2000)	5m29.80s	5m32s

BETTING CHART

ON	ODDS	AGAINST
50	Evens	50
52.4	11-10	47.6
54.5	6-5	45.5
55.6	5-4	44.4
58	11-8	42
60	6-4	40
62	13-8	38
63.6	7-4	36.4
65.3	15-8	34.7
66.7	2-1	33.3
68	85-40	32
69.2	9-4	30.8
71.4	5-2	28.6
73.4	11-4	26.6
75	3-1	25
76.9	100-30	23.1
77.8	7-2	22.2
80	4-1	20
82	9-2	18
83.3	5-1	16.7
84.6	11-2	15.4
85.7	6-1	14.3
86.7	13-2	13.3
87.5	7-1	12.5
88.2	15-2	11.8
89	8-1	11
89.35	100-12	10.65
89.4	17-2	10.6
90	9-1	10
91	10-1	9
91.8	11-1	8.2
92.6	12-1	7.4
93.5	14-1	6.5
94.4	16-1	5.6
94.7	18-1	5.3
95.2	20-1	4.8
95.7	22-1	4.3
96.2	25-1	3.8
97.2	33-1	2.8
97.6	40-1	2.4
98.1	50-1	1.9
98.5	66-1	1.3
99.0	100-1	0.99

The table above (often known as the 'Field Money Table') shows both bookmakers' margins and how much a backer needs to invest to win £100. To calculate a bookmaker's margin, simply add up the percentages of all the odds on offer. The sum by which the total exceeds 100% gives the 'over-round' on the book. To determine what stake is required to win £100 (includes returned stake) at a particular price, just look at the relevant row, either odds-against or odds-on.

RULE 4 DEDUCTIONS

When a horse is withdrawn before coming under starter's orders, but after a market has been formed, bookmakers are entitled to make the following deductions from win and place returns (excluding stakes) in accordance with Tattersalls' Rule 4(c).

	Odds of withdrawn horse	Deduction from winnings
(1)	3-10 or shorter	75p in the £
(2)	2-5 to 1-3	70p in the £
(3)	8-15 to 4-9	65p in the £
(4)	8-13 to 4-7	60p in the £
(5)	4-5 to 4-6	55p in the £
(6)	20-21 to 5-6	50p in the £
(7)	Evens to 6-5	45p in the £
(8)	5-4 to 6-4	40p in the £
(9)	13-8 to 7-4	35p in the £
(10)	15-8 to 9-4	30p in the £
(11)	5-2 to 3-1	25p in the £
(12)	100-30 to 4-1	20p in the £
(13)	9-2 to 11-2	15p in the £
(14)	6-1 to 9-1	10p in the £
(15)	10-1 to 14-1	5p in the £
(16)	longer than 14-1	no deductions

(17) ....When more than one horse is withdrawn without coming under starter's orders, total deductions shall not exceed 75p in the £.

Starting-price bets are affected only when there was insufficient time to form a new market.

Feedback!

If you have any comments or critiscism about this book, or suggestions for future editions, please tell us.

Write
Chris Cook,
2003-2004 Jumps Annual
Racing & Football Outlook
Floor 23,
1 Canada Square,
London E14 5AP

email
c.cook@mgn.co.uk

Fax
FAO Chris Cook, 0207 510 6457

WIN!

. . . . a free subscription to Chaseform!

THIS YEAR'S QUIZ could hardly be more simple, and the prize should prove invaluable to our lucky winner. We're offering a free subscription to Chaseform, the BHB's official form book – every week from November to April, you could be getting the previous week's results in full, together with note-book comments highlighting future winners, adjusted Official Ratings and Raceform's *Performance* ratings. The winner will also get a copy of last year's complete form book.

All you have to do is identify the ***three mystery horses*** pictured on the following pages. Each of them is a Cheltenham Festival winner, one from each of the last three Festivals.

Send your answers along with your details on the entry form below, to:

**Jumps Annual Competition, Racing & Football Outlook,
Floor 23, 1 Canada Square, London, E14 5AP.**

Entries must reach us no later than first post on Monday November 10. The winner and the right answers will be printed in the RFO's November 18 edition. Six runners-up will receive a copy of last year's complete form book.

1	
2	
3	

Name

Address

Town

Postcode

In the event of more than one correct entry, the winner will be drawn at random from the correct entries. The Editor's decision is final and no correspondence will be entered into.

Sponsored by Stan James

See quiz, p249

mystery horse no. 1

See quiz, p249

mystery horse no. 2

See quiz, p249

mystery horse no. 3

Horse index

All horses discussed, with page numbers, except for references in the 'Big Race Results' section, for which there is a seperate index on pages 100-103